The School that Escaped the Nazis

The True Story of the Schoolteacher Who Defied Hitler

Deborah Cadbury

PUBLICAFFAIRS

New York

PublicAffairs
Hachette Book Group
1290 Avenue of the Americas, New York, NY 10104
www.publicaffairsbooks.com
@Public_Affairs

Printed in the United States of America
Originally published in Great Britain in 2022 by Two Roads
An imprint of John Murray Press
An Hachette UK company

First US Edition: June 2022

Published by PublicAffairs, an imprint of Perseus Books, LLC,
a subsidiary of Hachette Book Group, Inc. The PublicAffairs name and
logo is a trademark of the Hachette Book Group.

The Hachette Speakers Bureau provides a wide range of authors for speaking events.
To find out more, go to www.hachettespeakersbureau.com or call (866) 376-6591.

The publisher is not responsible for websites (or their content)
that are not owned by the publisher.

Typeset in Janson by Palimpsest Book Production Limited, Falkirk, Stirlingshire

Library of Congress Control Number: 2021952858

ISBNs: 9781541751194 (hardcover), 9781541751200 (ebook)

LSC-C

Printing 1, 2022

Contents

'It was all about giving. The whole school was about giving. The teachers had very little at their disposal but they gave what they could and it was a lot.'

Anna John, former British pupil

'All the violence I had experienced before felt like a bad dream. It was paradise. I think most of the children felt it was paradise.'

Leslie Brent, former German pupil

'Some have called Bunce Court a second home. It is more than that. It is a way of life, a state of mind ... Tante Anna has made a great achievement.'

Megan Ryan, wife of former pupil

Prologue

Well before dawn on 14 August 1942, twelve-year-old Sam Oliner woke to the sound of gunshots. There was screaming outside, so close at hand it could have been in the room. He crept out into the dark alleyway and saw a crush of people rushing this way and that, clearly terrified. This was no ordinary harassment. Nazi soldiers had arrived in force. Sam could hear their vicious commands: '*Alle Juden raus . . . raus!*': 'All Jews out!'[1]

The several hundred Jews of Bobowa Ghetto in southern Poland were brutalised with clubs and rifle butts as they were rounded up and driven like animals towards the town's market square. Unknown to Sam and his family, for almost three years the Nazis had been herding Poland's three and a half million Jews into over a thousand similar ghettos scattered across Poland. Now plans were in place to liquidate them all. Sam was living through 'the final solution'.

Outside in the darkness of Bobowa ghetto there was terrible confusion as people were chased out of their homes by fright and fear. Sam managed to make his way back to their room. His father had vanished. His stepmother, Ester, ordered him to run and hide.[2]

'Where?' he cried.

She stared as though she hardly recognised him, as though their plight was beyond all comprehension.

'Anywhere,' she cried. 'Hide. Hide. *Hide*. They're killing us all. I am sure of it now . . .'[3]

I

His stepmother's eyes were large dark circles. Fear transformed her into something hardly human. Something terrible was going to happen. It was written in her face. This was the end.

Sam fled. He clambered onto a roof and curled up under its rotting fabric. From his vantage point less than three hundred yards from the central square, if he dared tilt his head slightly he could see what was happening. Hundreds were being made to lie down before it was their turn to be beaten and herded onto military trucks. Anyone who resisted was shot. Sam couldn't make sense of what he was seeing. 'Was I awake or alive or dead? Was this a nightmare?'[4]

For the rest of the night and most of the following day the sounds of terror continued against the background roar of military trucks. The stench of the rubbish and the tar of the roof made Sam feel ill. Flies buzzed around him. Would they give him away? It was late afternoon before the gunshots became more sporadic and eventually silence descended on the ghetto.

As Sam crept alone through the now deserted dwellings he was overcome by a powerful new feeling of intense loneliness. The empty ghetto felt so unreal he thought he must have already died. Then he heard German voices. Suddenly he was on full alert. Despite his blond hair, Sam was still wearing his pyjamas, which marked him out at once as a Jewish inhabitant of the ghetto. There was the sound of movement outside, the clicking of boot heels. He peered through a crack. Nazi soldiers had returned and were searching the houses with meticulous care, the attics, the roofs, the basements . . . There were screams as they came across a woman and her baby. A gunshot rang out. He almost choked with fear. Sam ran like a wild creature until he reached the barbed wire perimeter. That was when he remembered the picture.

The picture of his mother was the only thing left of value and it was back in the ghetto. In his dazed state, the picture was all Sam could think of. It was sacred. Even at the risk of losing his life, he must get the picture of his mother.

Suppressing his feelings of panic, he made his way back, creeping through undergrowth, edging his way along the walls towards the room where they had been living. But there was nothing there. Thieves had already ransacked the place for scraps. Sam fell to the floor, scrabbling for the precious picture. He was sobbing, silently; he did not dare make a sound. He could not see for tears. He had lost everything.

Sam was quite alone now. There was no one to whom he could turn. His family had disappeared. Nothing remained of them – not even a picture. Fear immobilised him, but he had to move. He would have to live off his wits. As he tried to retrace his path to the perimeter fence, a Polish boy caught sight of him. '*Jude. Jude!*' the hateful cry rang out. For Sam, 'it was like the devil taunting me.'[5] He fled for cover again. Was escape possible? Even if he could get out of the ghetto alive, as a Jewish boy in Nazi-occupied Poland he would be a target. He would be hunted. He could trust no one. His fellow Poles were just as likely to turn him in for the money as the Nazis were to hunt him down.

Sam had thought there was nothing left to lose but, as he embarked on his life on the run, he understood that there was worse. He would have to do bad things to survive. The fight for survival would strip Sam of his humanity; it would turn him into 'a savage' living 'in a state of darkness, of uncertainty, of primitivity, in a state which was a complete void.' He would come to know 'only misery, killings and bad experiences . . .'[6]

In the months that followed, hiding in plain sight, Sam tried to sustain himself by dreaming of his old life. He half believed he would return to his childhood when the war was over. His family had vanished so fast it was incomprehensible. A local farmer told him what had happened that night in Bobowa Ghetto, not realising that blond-haired Sam was himself a Jewish boy on the run.

The trucks had been driven to a nearby wood where a mass grave had already been dug. The Jews were stripped naked, lined up in front of the grave, and shot.

Sam was desperate not to give himself away but when he heard himself speak his voice was unrecognisable, incredulous. '*Everyone* was shot?' he asked.

'The Germans organised the whole thing,' the farmer explained, as though the Nazis had done the Polish people a favour. For eighteen hours the trucks had gone back and forth, bringing people from the ghetto to the woods. The farmer had heard that some of the Jews from the ghetto were still alive when they fell onto the pile of bodies, and that one managed to get away. The man who escaped from the pit appeared to have lost his mind. 'He looked totally insane as if his brain had snapped.'[7]

Even knowing all this, Sam clung stubbornly to the hope that his family was somewhere safe in England or America. He sustained himself by dreaming of a time when Hitler was gone, when he would see all those he loved and there would be a school, a wonderful school. There would be peace . . . It was possible to conjure up this vision so vividly in his mind he could almost make that all-pervasive, gut-wrenching fear that owned him now disappear. He could almost make his dream real.

Introduction

In March 1933, within days of Hitler coming to power, Anna Essinger, the headmistress at Landschulheim Herrlingen in southern Germany, was ordered to fly a swastika over her school. Outraged at the prospect of the despised symbol of fascism being hoisted above her progressive academy, 'Tante Anna', as she was known to her pupils, staged a one-woman protest. She hastily organised a three-day camping trip for her pupils and only when no one was left in the school did she raise the Nazi flag, which fluttered over the deserted buildings.[1]

Everything that Hitler stood for clashed with Tante Anna's radical educational ideals. Ever since reading his autobiography, *Mein Kampf,* she believed that under him Germany would plunge into an abyss, where there was no place for freedom of thought or expression – or perhaps even for survival itself. Hitler cast history as a struggle between races and in his early impassioned speeches he had vilified the 'parasitic' Jew as 'the enemy within' and the embodiment of evil. For Anna, this was pure poison. It was hard to understand how such a man had come to power in her country. Germany's half a million Jews were integrated at every level of society and acclaimed for their contribution to science, arts, literature and theatre. If the views Hitler had expressed were put into action all this was in danger.

In 1933 many around her thought she was overreacting. 'Stop worrying,' friends advised. 'It will all blow over.' Anna saw things differently. Nazi Germany was no place for her school. The violence, hatred and blame openly promoted by the Nazi Party stood in opposition to everything she was trying to achieve. It was hard to see how humanity could progress in the kind of society Hitler was making. But there was a traitor at the school, the husband of one of the staff. He denounced Tante Anna to the authorities, recommending that a Nazi inspector was appointed immediately. It was not just Tante Anna's unwillingness to embrace the swastika that provoked his anger but the entire educational direction of her enterprise. His letter of denouncement not only threatened the school, which could be forced to close, but also put all those involved in danger. Anna did not wait. She had already resolved to move her entire establishment, lock, stock and barrel, out of Germany, right under the noses of the Nazi authorities. She felt certain the Gestapo would never permit the mass emigration of an entire school, so she started work on a secret plan to outsmart them, a feat that no other teacher managed to pull off.[2]

This is the story of the school created by Anna Essinger in Kent, the garden of England. Although Anna and the first seventy children escaped Nazi Germany in 1933, many of the pupils who came to her 'home-school' at Bunce Court, near Otterden, fled much later and had first-hand experience of the ever-escalating catastrophe. The refuge that Tante Anna tried to create grew in parallel to the horrors unleashed by the Nazis on Jewish children across the continent. In time she would accept waves of increasingly traumatised children from Germany, Austria, Czechoslovakia and then Poland as the crisis spread, and the task she had set herself would call on all her reserves and exact a heavy toll.

By 1938 confused and bewildered children had started to arrive in Britain on Kindertransports. Children such as thirteen-year-old Leslie Brent, who arrived from Berlin on the very first Kindertransport from Germany subdued and restrained. His self-control was remarkable for a child who had been through so much Nazi persecution – but would it be lost when the reality of what had happened to him set in?[3] By contrast, the unruly thirteen-year-old, Gerard Hoffnung, was an uncontainable force who seemed to seek out conflict with Tante Anna. There were others, such as fourteen-year-old Ruth Boronow from Breslau in eastern Germany, who felt harmed by all that Hitler had done to change her life. 'I spat on Germany as I left . . .' she says, trying to express her revulsion at Nazi ideology.[4] Most of the children who arrived in Britain from Germany before the war had been damaged in some way by five years of escalating deprivations that had seen their families impoverished and abused, parents imprisoned or even killed, but for Jewish schoolchildren arriving from Austria after the *Anschluss*, the horror that had been inflicted on German Jews over time happened in a few short weeks.

Later came children who had experienced hell; these were the children who survived the Holocaust in concentration camps or labour camps and those who survived by living underground. By their own admission they had become little more than wild animals. Sam Oliner found that while he was living in disguise on the run, the boundaries of his world shrank. The Nazis had always claimed the Jews were 'subhuman', and he felt 'inferior as an uninformed person'. Sam had 'a longing for more knowledge because my world was so narrow.'[5] He describes himself as among 'two thousand "savages" who survived the Hitler period.' Sam had lost all bearings on what it was to be human. Acts of kindness meant nothing. 'It took a great deal of love and determination to help us,' he wrote later.[6]

Fourteen-year-old Sidney Finkel from Poland was also among this group of concentration camp survivors sent to Anna's school after the war. He had endured the destruction of his family, the 'liquidation' of his ghetto, slave labour camps, concentration camps and typhus. He had lost all concept of normal living. Even simple things were full of threat, such as the pyjamas neatly laid out for him on his bed; Sidney was too frightened to undress, fearing that he must always be ready in case bombs fell or there was some sort of roll call from which people did not return. Dinner time was also fraught. Sidney was no longer accustomed to eating with a knife and fork, and he refused vegetables because they reminded him of the grass that he had had to eat to survive. Tante Anna sat with him during mealtimes and taught him how to eat and to stop bolting his food. Still if Sidney encountered any sort of caring thoughtfulness at Anna's school, at first he thought such people were weak. The only thing he understood was how to survive: this was part of him now, in his bones, in his clothes, in his life. He would gaze in wonder at the food or fine clothes in shops. Why had no one broken the glass and taken them? His first outing to a British tea shop was equally baffling. Served tea and cakes in elegant surroundings, he was unable to understand why no one grabbed at the cakes. He tried to copy the other customers when all his instincts urged otherwise. Inside he was in turmoil. He felt anger, barely controllable, at any mention of Hitler and the Germany he had created. It took Sidney a little while to grasp that the very behaviours that had helped him survive were now holding him back.[7]

Anna sought to create a home where children, traumatised by war, could not only recover but be inspired. These children were not just damaged; they were lost souls. The fundamental protective warmth given by loving parents was gone. These were innocents who had fought against all odds for a chance to live. And she would make their lives count. She wanted to inspire those who had experienced the worst of humanity with the very best; children like Sam and Sidney who had been stripped of all hope and seen things no child should witness.

Tante Anna aimed to transform children's lives through her school. Education was a precious gift, she thought, always nourished against a background of love. She encouraged questioning and freedom of thought. There was always music, too, recalls Sidney. 'Music was the soul of this school.' The grand piano was in the hallway at the bottom of the wide staircase; there were concerts and recitals. Music haunted the school like an atmosphere, enveloping all those troubled minds, resounding through gracious rooms, drifting from open windows. It was part of daily life.

And most of all, Anna's pupils were expected to help each other. 'Children, you must love one another and if that is not possible, at least respect each other,' she would say to them.[8] Tante Anna applied herself with single-minded determination. Even when war threatened her school, she would ensure her pupils had a place of safety. She drew around her a dedicated team attracted to her idealism, and in their desire to inspire troubled youngsters they created something unique. Years later, pupils would refer to the 'Bunce Court spirit' that infused all their efforts and pervaded the atmosphere. For them the school seemed to stand apart, an oasis in a world that was overwhelmed by the forces of Nazi evil. 'I treasure those years . . . they were full of high points. It was transformative,' observed one orphan, Anna Rose.[9]

This is the story of the school that got away from the Nazis and the staff and the children who made it. Their story stands for all children caught up in war and revolution.

Part One

———

1933–September 1939

I

'I could no longer raise children in honesty and freedom'

Tante Anna, Germany, 1933

Anna Essinger, the accomplished headmistress of a progres-sive boarding school in southern Germany, was not a woman prone to alarm or overreaction. Self-contained, capable, respected both by her staff and the educational authorities in the state of Württemberg, she rarely expressed any excess of emotion. But as Anna followed the political upheaval in her country in late 1932 it was hard not to feel a lurching sense of unease, as though the ground was slipping from beneath her feet. What was happening in Germany was unthinkable. The far-right Nazi Party, which only a few years before had been seen as the lunatic fringe – its leader, Adolf Hitler, in prison for high treason – was rapidly gaining the political upper hand. Anna was beginning to feel like a stranger in her own country.

Shortly before the elections of November 1932, Adolf Hitler came to campaign in Anna's home town of Ulm, not far from the school she had created in the peaceful backwater of Herrlingen. In the days leading up to the event, posters sprung up promoting the Nazi rally in Münsterplatz, the church square, and by the day of the rally the glaring red, white and black of giant swastikas festooned the town's streets. A huge crowd gathered for the event.

That day Anna's younger sister, Paula, happened to be picking up pupils from Ulm station for the new school term. 'We stood in front of the Russischer Hof,' wrote one boy, Max Kantorovitz, to his mother – everyone knew Hitler was staying in this hotel. 'After twenty minutes he really came outside, just like I imagined him . . .' Hitler seemed insignificant, a man of medium height with an unsmiling, almost hangdog expression, remarkable only in his ordinariness. But when he spoke there was a transformation, as though he came to life. The rapturous crowd went wild, in thrall to Hitler's extreme nationalism and assurances of 'Bread and Work'. To his supporters he was the saviour of the nation, a true patriot with a glorious vision that would make Germany great again. When Max finally arrived at school, he chattered about his eventful day to Tante Anna as she took him to his room.[1]

Tante Anna, of course, did not share the excitement of the crowd. For her, the Nazi Party appealed to the worst in human nature, to greed and fear. This was the party that had bullied its path to power through its large paramilitary arm, the notorious brown-shirted *Sturmabteilung*, or SA. Numbering two million men by early 1933, armed with knives or guns, SA troops openly attacked Hitler's political opponents. To win over the middle classes Hitler had recently forsworn violence and promised to recognise the authority of the state, but Anna had seen newspaper reports that showed this was not true; the violence continued. The Nazi Party also peddled lies and hatred, falsely identifying scapegoats for Germany's misfortunes, such as the Jews. Hitler and other leading Nazis described Jews as '*Untermenschen*' or 'subhuman', racially inferior to the supposedly tall, blond, blue-eyed German or 'Aryan' types who they deemed the master race.[2] If during the Great War, twelve or fifteen thousand Jews 'had been held under poison gas,' Hitler had written in *Mein Kampf,* 'the sacrifice of millions at the front would not have been in vain.' Would such murderous claims be dispensed with if Hitler came to power, Anna wondered? How was it possible that such a man was being taken seriously? Max wrote home that, in Anna's school, 'the mood is generally very against Hitler'.[3]

Anna found that many of her older pupils, like Max, who wrote for the school's newspaper, were politically astute beyond their years, asking questions as events came swiftly to a head. On 30 January 1933, in the absence of a parliamentary majority the ageing president, Paul von Hindenburg, appointed Hitler as chancellor. What happened next was almost inconceivable. Germany's fledgling democracy was dismantled with lightning speed. An election was planned for early March, but on 27 February the parliament building, the *Reichstag,* went up in flames. Anna wondered whether the fires might have been started by the Nazis, though Hitler blamed his key political opponents, the communists, and under this pretext began to arrest his political enemies en masse. The next day, 28 February 1933, Hitler assumed emergency powers. As the political opposition to Nazism was violently crushed, the party continued to gain support and in the general election of 5 March, the Nazi Party won forty-five per cent of the vote in Anna's home town of Ulm.[4] The 'Enabling Act' of 23 March gave Hitler the right to make laws without consulting the *Reichstag,* transforming him into Germany's all-powerful dictator.

Anna knew she must act immediately. Germany under Hitler was no longer a suitable home for her school and the swastika banner that had been unfurled over Herrlingen was like a terrible warning. Anna had to have the freedom to teach what she saw as the truth; that was the underlying treasure, the firm foundation of her school. It came down to one core issue: freedom. Freedom to think, to question, to challenge, to live without fear; freedom of spirit – this was her life's work. In Hitler's Germany, lies were being turned into the truth; black was being turned into white. How could she teach the next generation if she couldn't speak the truth without fear? This was no time for prevarication. Somehow, she had to smuggle her school out of Germany.[5]

Anna confided in her younger sisters, Klara – who ran a children's home and sent many pupils to Anna's school – and Paula, the school nurse. At night, Anna, Klara and Paula discussed their plans for escape. 'Obviously mass emigration was prohibited,' observed Paula in her memoirs. 'We had to avoid all suspicion.' If the Nazis learned that Anna was planning to remove an entire school from Germany they could have put insuperable obstacles in her path or imposed punitive financial sanctions. If the press got hold of the story it could cause a sensation. 'No one should find out about it,' wrote Paula, otherwise she feared 'our school would be requisitioned and used by the Hitler Youth'.[6] Yet to move her pupils abroad, Anna had to involve parents and staff, which risked exposing her, the staff and even the parents to danger. To add to her difficulties, within weeks of Hitler coming to power, Anna was denounced to the Nazi authorities.

'I found the spirit of Landschulheim Herrlingen so little to my liking,' wrote the informant, Helman Speer, to the Minister of Culture in Württemberg on 10 May 1933, 'that in the light of today's politico-cultural requirements, feel reluctant to conceal my serious doubts about the situation there.' His wife worked at the school and confirmed his grave concerns about Anna Essinger's 'rather airy-fairy humanism', which he claimed was 'altogether uncongenial' to National Socialism. His wife, he explained, had accepted a teaching position at the school in 'the belief she would be able to bring about the necessary changes'. Another teacher at the school, a Mr von Reuttern, shared his wife's views, claimed Speer, and had joined the Nazi Party. Since many of the teachers at Anna's school at Herrlingen were 'Aryan', he had hoped they could join forces 'and endow the school with a spirit different from that of the present director. This hope of ours is now endangered by the director herself!' The informant concluded his report by requesting that a Nazi spy be placed at the school, 'a commissar . . . who would be prepared to come to an understanding with those members willing to cooperate.'[7]

It is unlikely that Anna Essinger was aware she was denounced, but she certainly knew of the dangers of crossing the Nazi authorities. Within weeks of him becoming chancellor, Hitler's government openly established a new kind of prison, where people could be held without trial: the concentration camp. On 22 March 1933, Dachau was set up in an old munitions works outside Munich. That same week, closer to home, the Heuberg army barracks thirteen miles south of Ulm were converted into one of the very first concentration camps. Up to two thousand of Hitler's political opponents, the communists and social democrats, were imprisoned at Heuberg, including one local MP, Kurt Schumacher, and three priests. Schumacher had been vocal in his opposition to the Nazis, condemning them for 'appealing to the inner swine in human beings'. Now he woke up in prison under so-called 'protective custody' to discover that the legal system, as well as democracy, in Germany had effectively disappeared. The prisoners were held indefinitely and, even when they were beaten up, there was no one to whom they could appeal.[8]

The Nazi Party did not conceal the mass arrests of the opposition. The names of the prisoners at Heuberg were publicised in the local paper. This was intended as a warning to show people like Anna what could happen if they did not express sufficient support for the National Socialists. When prisoners were released they were forced to sign a declaration not to speak about their treatment in prison, but word got out. Anna soon learned of the inhumane beatings of the inmates at Heuberg.[9] As early as March 1933 she almost certainly knew of the arrest of one famous German educator, Kurt Hahn, founder of the acclaimed Salem School in Baden-Württemberg. 'Salem cannot remain neutral,' Hahn had written to his former pupils. He asked them to choose. If they were members of the SA or the SS they must leave, or break with Salem. Hahn was thrown into jail.[10] The following month, Corder Catchpool, who ran British Quaker relief efforts in Berlin, was the first Briton to be arrested by the Nazis, prompting questions in the House of Commons in London. His crime was to show public support for Jews who had been targeted by the Nazis. Interrogated in the Gestapo headquarters in Alexanderplatz in Berlin, Catchpool insisted he was 'a friend of Germany'. His Gestapo interrogator told him he 'had made insufficient effort to understand our Great National Revolution' – a very similar charge to the claims made against Anna by her informant.[11]

For Tante Anna, the model community that she had created was far more than just a school. At Herrlingen, Anna had turned conventional thinking on education on its head to create an ideal environment for children from all backgrounds to grow and thrive. Her school was more like a big family than an institution and yet it enabled her pupils to aspire to the very highest levels of attainment. The ideas and principles that guided her efforts were the culmination of her life's work.

Tante Anna would not allow fear to interfere with her plans, even as people were disappearing off the streets for expressing opposition to the Nazi regime. No one must suspect that a momentous adventure was in progress. One way or another, she resolved to do the impossible and secretly smuggle the school out of the country, right under the noses of the Nazi authorities.

*

Anna had been born in Ulm in 1879, the first child of Fanny and Leopold Essinger. The Essinger family expanded rapidly and for eighteen years Fanny was invariably either pregnant or feeding a new baby and Anna was expected to help. It was the convention that after each birth the mother should rest completely for six weeks, which added to the responsibilities of her oldest daughter. Every year or so there was a new arrival. After Anna came Marie, followed by Klara, William, Ida, Frederick, Max, Paula and finally, in 1896, Bertha. Anna's youthful-looking mother, who still wore her hair in plaits until she was well into her thirties, was prone to headaches and often turned for help to her capable oldest daughter, who devoted long hours to caring for her younger brothers and sisters.

Anna's father, Leopold, was better known in the family for his warm-hearted sociability and his work in the community than for his financial acumen. His insurance business, run from a local coffee house, produced a somewhat unpredictable income and money could be tight. As the family increased beyond the ability of this fickle income to provide a play-room, the children appropriated the attic and played among the washing lines meant for all the occupants of the building. Anna delighted in each growing toddler as they developed a character of their own: sensitive William liked to sit in a corner of the attic and read; Klara could be assertive; Frederick had a head for sums.[12]

The Essingers had lived in southern Germany for gener-ations. It is a measure of their standing as a Jewish family in the local community that in 1877 Anna's grandfather, Dr David Essinger, was invited to make a presentation during the 500-year celebrations of the famous church at Ulm. David Essinger donated a statue of the prophet, Jeremiah, along with the local Jewish businessman, Hermann Einstein, the father of Albert Einstein, who was born in Ulm in the same year as Anna. As Chief Medical Officer in Oberdorf, Bavaria, Anna's grandfather was highly regarded for treating the poor free of charge, although he was also allegedly involved in caring for mad King Ludwig II and had been awarded a doctorate for his efforts.

When Anna's grandparents visited Ulm they offered relief from her Cinderella role of domestic drudgery and opened a window on a wider world. Her grandfather, David, could bring Jewish biblical history alive, while her grandmother, Bertha, loved classical literature and even read Shakespeare in German to the children. Her repertoire of fairy tales, mystery and magic created an enchanted world that had the children enthralled. Ironically, it was the death of her beloved grandfather in 1899 that bought freedom from the domestic round for nineteen-year-old Anna. Her widowed American aunt, Regina Salzketter, came to help nurse David during his final illness and, recognising the onerous duties shouldered by her oldest niece, invited Anna to accompany her back to Nashville, Tennessee, after he passed away.

If Regina was hoping for a genial young companion on the American social scene, serious-minded Anna had other ideas. Tall, red-haired, and almost invariably dressed in sober colours, even as a young woman Anna conveyed an air of self-possession and intelligence, perhaps emphasised by her very necessary double-lensed spectacles. But those eyes were friendly and set in a face brimming with goodwill, which dispelled any first impressions of severity. Years of running the nursery for her mother had perhaps emphasised certain intrinsic qualities. Anna had a natural authority; she was the kind of woman who was unflappable in a crisis. Her discretion could be relied upon and she trusted her own judgement as though she had insights that eluded others. Anna wanted to make use of her life; to devote herself to a wider purpose. Perhaps feeling uncomfortable in the gossipy social whirl favoured by her aunt, with its unspoken but nonetheless unmistakable husband-hunting agenda, Anna longed for something more. Her mother's years of almost constant pregnancy had influenced her; she loved children but was in no hurry to have a family of her own. Thoroughly modern Anna wanted to understand, to question, to have a university education. Despite her severe short-sightedness, she set her heart on further study and suggested to her aunt that one of her younger sisters take over her role as companion, so that Anna was free to attend lectures at Wisconsin University.[13]

Wisconsin was no Midwest backwater but was at the hub of a progressive reform movement that was sweeping America. Industrialisation had brought dramatic change; railroads straddled the continent from coast to coast, automobiles rolled off the production lines in gleaming new factories in Detroit and skyscrapers reached some twenty storeys high in booming Chicago. But the benefits of such developments were not shared by all. At the University of Wisconsin, progressive thinkers were challenging the status quo. The 'Wisconsin idea' advocated by the university president, Charles van Hise, required 'the application of intelligence and reason to the problems of society'. He believed university research could be used to guide political thinking to improve the quality of life for all.

Inspired, Anna embarked on a degree in German studies at the University of Wisconsin, funding herself by teaching. After several years she had gained not only an undergraduate degree but also an MA in education. For Anna, education was the key to progress. She believed that by inspiring the next generation with all that was good, humanity could advance. But her youthful idealism was thrown into sharp relief in the late summer of 1914 with the outbreak of the Great War.

Suddenly there was such strong anti-German feeling that it was no longer possible for her to complete the doctorate that she had just embarked on. With German U-boats stalking the Atlantic it was too dangerous for her to return home, so she took work as a lecturer. Letters from her family brought little comfort. Two of her younger brothers, William and Max, excused from military service on account of their short-sightedness, had immediately volunteered as medical orderlies and been posted near Verdun. As stretcher-bearers on the front lines, both brothers witnessed the industrial-scale slaughter in the killing fields of Europe. In 1918 Max was himself mortally wounded while rescuing soldiers. Unable to save his brother, William was close to a nervous breakdown, traumatised by the horrors of the battlefield. Trapped in

America, Anna, the big sister who had always been on hand, was unable to help.

While in America, Anna became inspired by the ideas behind a little-known religious movement called the Quakers. She was drawn to their humanitarian and compassionate values and, when the war was over, she joined American Quakers in an ambitious post-war relief plan to help to feed schoolchildren in Germany. Herbert Hoover himself, the future American president and also a Quaker, supported the famous feeding programme or *'Quäkerspeisung'*.[14] Full of hope that she could help to make a difference, Anna returned home, but found her country unrecognisable.

Germany's emperor, the autocratic Kaiser Wilhelm II, had abdicated. The country was governed by the parliamentary regime of the Weimar Republic, but Germany's first experience of democracy was being forged in desperately harsh post-war living conditions. Following the Versailles Peace Treaty there were restrictions on German imports, including some foods, and diseases caused by hunger or malnutrition were rife. The Weimar Republic printed money to help pay war debts and meet the huge cost of reparations imposed on Germany under the terms of the treaty. The result was chronic hyperinflation, which saw the price of a loaf of bread rocket from two hundred and fifty marks in January 1923 to a staggering two hundred thousand million marks by November. The people seemed without hope, without a future.

The scale of the deprivation forced many working families into dependence on the Quaker feeding programme, which grew exponentially. 'Anna went to every town and called together the mayor, the teachers and the managers,' recorded her younger sister, Paula, 'and told them they would receive food and clothing without charge for their children if they could provide a kitchen and a cook.' It was a tremendous feat of organisation, something at which Anna soon discovered she excelled.[15] At its height, a thousand Quaker volunteers in Germany managed over two thousand kitchens, which fed a daily hot meal to a million schoolchildren, among them future Nazi leaders.[16]

As a Quaker liaison officer, Anna had the opportunity to visit hundreds of schools in southern Germany. She saw at first hand the limitations of traditional German teaching methods. For generations, teachers had been the unquestioned authority figure of the classroom, ruling with a rod of iron and a discipline that was almost military in its strictness, an echo perhaps of the militarism with which a united Germany had been forged in the nineteenth century. Teaching methods usually relied on the pupils learning traditional subjects by rote, regardless of a child's interest, with harsh punishment for failure.[17] Learning, it seemed, was not an adventure but a list of facts that must be remembered. For Anna, the system was based on instilling fear and conformity in the children. Why could teaching not be more child-centred, she wondered, encouraging children's instinctive curiosity and creativity? Gradually the idea of creating a new type of school began to preoccupy her, but could she do it?

Anna attended conferences of the New Education Fellowship, an international forum for educators exploring new approaches to teaching. She visited Odenwald in Heppenheim, one of a number of new progressive schools in Germany. Soon she was corresponding with a radical British educator, Alexander Sutherland (A. S.) Neill, who challenged centuries-old thinking about children. Dismissing the established wisdom that a child is fundamentally uncivilised and in need of training to fit into society, Neill believed in the child 'as a good, not an evil, being'. His aim was to cater for the child rather than force conformity to the school. Neill had tested out his ideas as co-director of a school in Dresden, but in 1923 he moved to England to create a school of his own – Summerhill. Neill saw freedom as key to a child's happiness, and so at his school exams and lessons were optional; there was no coercion. 'The absence of fear is the finest thing that can happen to a child,' he wrote. Summerhill itself was set up as a small democratic community where pupils could vote alongside teachers on the rules.[18]

The idea of creating a model community where teachers and pupils were on an equal footing appealed to Anna. She approved, too, of the idea of no set attainment levels. Each child should go at their own pace. The strong emphasis on practical activities as well as academic work also seemed to her to find the right balance. 'Children should know that physical and mental work are equally appreciated,' she thought.[19] But in other respects, she wondered if these British ideas went too far. Should lessons be completely optional? How would she establish discipline with no punishment? What was the difference between freedom and licence? Was there a balance to be struck in creating a truly child-centred approach that also helped each child to make the best choices? Instinctively she felt there would be a way to make this work.

Anna mulled over her ideas with her two younger sisters, who were both pursuing careers in childcare. Paula was now an experienced children's nurse, having trained for three years at the Kaiserin Victoria Hospital in Berlin. Klara had studied child development and attended lectures by radical new thinkers in Vienna such as Sigmund Freud and Alfred Adler. Freud's groundbreaking ideas on the unconscious mind and repression were bringing fresh insights to child development and the possible harm caused by punitive educational regimes. When Klara returned to Germany she had founded a children's home in Herrlingen, determined to help children from deprived backgrounds. As her twenty children began to reach school age, Klara wanted an education for them. She was not satisfied with the oppressively strict ethos of the local village school and challenged her oldest sister: 'You should put those ideas of yours into action.'

Anna hesitated, uncertain about taking on such a huge venture. She would be asking parents to entrust her with their children. Could she be certain she would be able to deal with their emotional needs as well as their education? Without using conventional rules and punishments, she would still need to meet the educational standards required to pass the *Abitur,* the exam required for university entrance in Germany. Everyone said she had a flair for organisation, but as head teacher she would carry ultimate responsibility: recruiting staff, raising funds, dealing with parents, finding pupils and setting the tone for the whole venture. Above all, she wanted to create a better future for the children; but what if she failed?

Klara forged ahead, finding 'a beautiful meadow' for the new school close to her children's home. She persuaded their brother, Frederick, to buy the land. Impatient with Anna's indecision, Klara even interviewed potential head teachers, favouring a master called Ludwig Wunder. The conflict between the sisters came to a head when the family gathered for their traditional birthday celebration for their mother, Fanny, and the conversation inevitably turned to the idea of a new school at Herrlingen. Anna raised concerns about Klara's potential headmaster. She had made a point of getting to know Wunder and was convinced he was the wrong choice – a judgement that proved astute when in the 1930s Wunder

26

joined the Nazi Party and founded a school based on Nazi ideology and what he called 'Hitler's magnificent achievements'.[20] Klara, in turn, demanded to know why her sister was hesitating.

Anna went to see the land Frederick had bought and could see the potential. It was a lovely spot bordered by woodland and a stream. She imagined the schoolhouse fitting in next to clumps of young pine trees whose aromatic perfume released by the sunshine drifted towards her. There would be beautiful grounds and she could take the pupils swimming in the nearby brook and on hiking trips into the mountains beyond. The schoolhouse itself she imagined being modelled on timber designs she had seen in America. There would be a large hall downstairs for meetings, concerts and plays, where she would open her children's eyes to the wonders of the arts and music; there must be music. Suddenly she felt decided. This struggle between confidence and caution had gone on too long. There should be a school here. It would be a great joy and a huge responsibility. It would be a life's work, *her* life's work.

'We were thrilled,' records Paula. The whole family gave Anna their backing. Frederick would finance the construction work. Anna's second brother, William, who ran a factory for decorative furnishings in Mannheim with their sister Marie, offered to fit the interiors. Paula wanted to join the staff as a nurse and 'housemother'. There was much discussion among the siblings about the school's design. Both Klara and Anna were equally forceful, but Anna was insistent on her vision. Eventually Anna, unable to compromise, said to Klara, 'You can give me the money. You can give me the building site, but I shall build the school my way and run the school my way.'[21]

One of the first people outside the family to hear of Anna's plans was a mathematician, Kathy Hamburg: 'indeed I was present at the whole birth of the idea,' she recalls. Kathy, who had worked at the progressive Odenwald school, hurried to Herrlingen to find out more. Anna happened to be unwell and obliged to rest. 'This gave us a chance to chat endlessly about the only subject in Anna's mind at the moment, which was the founding of a whole new type of school,' Kathy remembered. Kathy had given up her career teaching mathematics to devote her life to orphaned or illegitimate children and as Anna talked excitedly of her dream school, Kathy thought it would be the perfect place to send her seven adopted children. The two women mulled over every last detail, 'her ideas for the design of the bedrooms, the school rooms, the kitchen and the gardens,' wrote Kathy. They pored over catalogues of modern kitchen equipment together. Anna was convinced she was looking for a new kind of teacher, young recruits unaccustomed to traditional German ways. Above all, they wondered what kind of children would bring the venture to life and how they would inspire them. When Kathy left there was 'only one thought in my mind,' she said later, 'to have a share in Anna's experiment.' She moved to Herrlingen and enrolled her seven children in the school.[22]

On 1 May 1926 Anna opened the doors to her new school, Landschulheim Herrlingen. Records survive of the impressions of her first pupils. 'The atmosphere was relaxed right from the start,' recalled one pupil, Wolfgang Leonhard. 'The teachers were like friends only a little older.' Several of the new entrants were Kathy's adopted children and they nicknamed Anna 'Tante Anna' on account of the closeness of her friendship with their foster mother, Kathy. This soon became Anna's nickname throughout the school. 'She really was like an aunt to us,' recalled another pupil, Ruth Sohar, 'authoritarian but very motherly.' If ever there was a problem the children would go to Tante Anna's room. It was unprepossessing; flowers in pots crammed on the window ledges, the furniture homely and comfortable rather than smart. At the heart of it, Tante Anna herself, a voice of reason, who could guide the children without ever seeming to exercise power or raise her voice. 'She explained to you if you had done right or wrong and what was good,' continued Ruth, 'and it was her kindness that made you *feel* if you had done something bad.'

Somehow the atmosphere Anna created pervaded the school. Tante Anna was 'not in the least bit religious,' observed one of her first pupils, Susanne Trachsler. 'Not even Jewish.' Anna came from an assimilated Jewish family and did not place great emphasis on religious beliefs and practices, although she did adopt one custom she had observed in Quaker circles: before dinner, each child held hands with the pupils standing either side of them for a moment of silent reflection, the entire school briefly linked as one.

It was instilled in the children that they must help each other. Tante Anna managed to establish 'a kind of honour code,' continued Susanne. 'I don't know how she did it. The worst thing you could do was lie and cheat.' Children sometimes arrived from other schools who did behave badly. But Anna and the staff had no need to discipline them. 'The other pupils themselves treated them with such contempt that they stopped immediately,' Susanne recalled. 'We sort of educated each other.'

Anna's sister, often known as 'Tante Paula', the school nurse, enchanted any sick child with the so-called 'Märchenbett' –

fairy tale bed – 'the like of which I had never seen,' said one. It appeared to be a sofa but any unwary child who should happen to turn the lever on its side would find that it would spring to life. The upholstery turned itself over into 'a readymade bed, complete with brass bed-ends and lined with blue silk'. The extraordinary bed proved to be an ace card in dealing with any child who was downhearted or ailing. On the magic bed they found they could cross sparkling seas and starlit skies, no doubt learning some valuable lessons in the process.

Anna herself taught English in a small room on the first floor. She would bring in objects of interest to help along her popular lessons, although Wolfgang was most impressed when she rattled a tin of sweets before class. 'We really had fun,' he said. 'For me Herrlingen meant freedom. You learned what you really wanted to learn.' Reflecting years later on what Anna taught her, Susanne Trachsler said, 'intellectual curiosity, authority without violence, respect and solidarity, the courage to think for yourself, sport, foreign languages, to climb trees' and perhaps most important, *'joie de vivre'*. For Ruth Sohar, 'we didn't just learn Anna's progressive education. We learned to get along with each other. Every religion, every race, all kinds of people. We were like a big family.'[23]

*

As she was planning to smuggle her school out of the country in the spring of 1933, the post brought Anna frequent reminders of Hitler's increasingly sinister hold over their lives. She began to receive applications for work from experienced Jewish teachers who had been suddenly dismissed from their jobs. One in particular caught her eye, from a talented young teacher who had taught English and French for several years at a German state school in Berlin: Hanna Bergas.

Hanna later wrote in her memoirs of her astonishment at the 'force and speed' with which new Nazi laws were implemented. One day in early April the headmaster of her school had greeted her in his usual friendly way but then ordered her to report to his office immediately. As Hanna closed the door behind her, his tone of voice instantly told her something was wrong. He seemed both very serious and embarrassed as he forbade her to go to her classroom. As a Jew, she was no longer permitted to teach in a German school. Too stunned to take in his words, she made her way to the staffroom to gather her belongings. It was empty. No one had waited to say a friendly goodbye. She walked out alone through the school gates, suddenly overwhelmed by a feeling of bereavement. 'It was the funeral of my time teaching at a German state school,' she wrote.[24]

Hanna was one of thousands caught up in the changes made to the law within weeks of Hitler coming to power. Decades of progress in which Jews were integrated into German society were being dismantled. In April 1933, the Law for the Restoration of the Professional Civil Service effectively forced the Nazis' political opponents and Jews out of the civil service, including schools and universities. 'Non-Aryans', defined for the first time as those of 'non-Aryan' descent especially those with a Jewish parent or grandparent, were obliged to retire. The Law against the Overcrowding of German Schools and Universities strictly limited the proportion of new Jewish pupils in German schools to 1.5 per cent of the total enrolment. Many Jewish children in private schools were also forbidden to sit the *Abitur*, the exam for university entrance.[25] After seven years, Tante Anna's top class were ready to sit this crucial exam, but her Jewish pupils were denied that chance. Their opportunities were shrinking.

Tante Anna was the first person to respond to Hanna's job application. When they met in her office at Herrlingen in early May, the two women had an instant rapport. Anna perhaps saw in Hanna a younger version of herself. She appeared serious and dedicated, the kind of woman who could be trusted. Hanna was thin, her thick dark hair pulled back in a neat bun. She seemed under strain but had a magnetic quality. It was easy to believe in her absolutely. Anna felt confident enough in the younger woman to disclose her plans.

Anna revealed that she did not want to educate children in Nazi Germany. 'Of course, I do not either,' Hanna replied. Anna asked if she would be prepared to move abroad with the school. It was apparent to Hanna that Anna did not yet know where or how the school would move, or even to which country, but 'she asked me whether I was ready to join her venture.' Hanna did not hesitate. 'I told her that I shared her ideas.' Soon it was settled. Hanna would teach on probation at Landschulheim Herrlingen over the summer while Anna prepared the big move.[26]

America seemed the obvious choice of location for the school, as Anna had contacts there and understood the educational system. However, in the 1930s it took two weeks to cross the Atlantic and parents had no desire to send their children so far away. So Anna travelled across Europe, searching in Switzerland, then Sweden and Denmark. By June she was seeking help in Britain, determined to find a way of raising the funds, overcoming immigration problems and getting her school out of Germany. She began a series of lectures in London to alert people to the crisis in Nazi Germany. 'The English at that time had not the slightest idea of the situation in Germany,' wrote Paula later, but Anna found a knowledgeable audience in Quaker and Jewish circles. As soon as Hitler came to power, British Jewish leaders had created the Jewish Refugees Committee to assist persecuted Jews in Germany, led by a London stockbroker, Otto Schiff. British Quakers, too, had responded immediately by forming a German Emergency Committee, which was run by the indomitable Bertha Bracey. Anna and Bertha had much in common. Both had worked for the *Quäkerspeisung* feeding programme in the 1920s, and through the network of Quaker relief workers abroad, such as Corder Catchpool in Berlin, Anna found Bertha was very familiar with the grave dangers she described. With Bertha's help, Anna was soon introduced to an anonymous Quaker backer who was prepared to help with financing her venture.[27]

It is arguably a measure of Anna's confidence and ability that on her trips to England in the summer of 1933 she attracted a distinguished panel of backers: Sir Herbert Samuel, the leader of the Liberal Party and a former home secretary; eminent lawyer and academic, and former attorney general of Mandatory Palestine, Norman Bentwich, and his wife, Helen, who had family connections to the banking dynasty of Samuel Montagu; Mrs Corbett-Fisher, an advocate of women's rights, and the Marchioness of Reading, wife of former foreign secretary Lord Reading. All agreed to create a special 'School Council' under the chairmanship of Bentwich, to help Anna by raising funds and finding a suitable site for her school. At last her plans were taking shape.[28]

When Anna returned to Germany she found ominous developments on her very doorstep in Ulm. On 15 July 1933 there was a huge bonfire of the works of eminent Jewish scholars and writers in Ulm Minster square. Once a haven for tourists marvelling at the tallest stone steeple in the world, now the church square was filled with an unruly mob, roaring their approval as the works of Albert Einstein, Sigmund Freud, Karl Marx and others went up in flames. Einstein had publicly rejected Nazism and surrendered his German passport. 'As long as I have the opportunity, I will only reside in a country ruled by political freedom, tolerance and equality of all citizens before the law,' he wrote on 28 March 1933, while travelling in Europe. Almost immediately, the street named after Einstein in Ulm was renamed '*Fichtestrasse*' by the Nazi authorities and his cottage was raided.[29] The bonfire of Jewish works was just round the corner from Wienhof Square, where Anna's mother was still living. The image of the burning books so close to her childhood home, the fury of the crowd whipped up by Nazi rhetoric, mingled with Anna's renewed fears for her family.

Germany was becoming uncertain, unpredictable, but Anna pressed ahead, arranging small gatherings over the summer in Stuttgart, Berlin and Mannheim for her pupils' parents. She could not rule out that someone might report her – a careless word could do it – but cautiously she revealed her plans and, to her relief, found a warm reception. 'Most of the parents were thrilled at the idea,' recorded Paula; they feared what the future might hold for their children. Almost all of the Jewish parents entrusted their children to Anna, as well as several of the non-Jewish ones. 'More parents signed up than children we could take with us,' Paula wrote. Over the summer, teachers were on hand to advise parents and prepare the children. Anna had recommended that any child who wished to come should pack for a minimum of two years. Hanna tried to inspire the children with stories about England and teach them the language. Anna herself flew back to London a couple of times to liaise with members of her new School Council and report back on progress to her staff in Herrlingen.

While finalising the escape plans, Anna also had to make arrangements for her existing school in Herrlingen and this soon saw her involved in navigating a bureaucratic minefield with the authorities in Württemberg. Fortunately for Anna, the letter of denunciation sent earlier in the year had not led to any reprisal – the educational authorities in Württemberg had not yet been replaced by Nazi Party members. Anna had worked hard over the years at building up a good relationship with local officials, and they appear to have taken no action over Helman Speer's letter of denunciation.[30] Even so, for the first time, Anna found herself in a position where she had to be less than frank with the educational authorities.

Anna hoped that Herrlingen School could become a private Jewish school to help persecuted children, but was anxious to avoid provoking suspicion. It was no longer permitted to open a new secondary school, but an existing school could continue in a different direction. As a result, Anna had to find a new head teacher quickly to avoid having to close her original school. In order to create the impression that she was only leaving for a short sabbatical, she placed an advertisement in the local papers for a temporary head-master. She also had to change the curriculum, since Jewish education had to be more vocational. Anna hurriedly applied for a licence in compliance with all these rules, which may have helped her fool the authorities about the scale of her planned escape.

Finding a head teacher prepared to take on the challenge in Nazi Germany was no easy task. In Württemberg, the educational authorities had already closed many Jewish primary schools and it was unclear what kind of future Landschulheim Herrlingen would have as a Jewish school. Whoever took over would also have to find new pupils and staff. Most of them were leaving with Anna, although her sister, Klara, and friend, Kathy Hamburg, had decided to stay behind with their children. Several suitable candidates turned Anna down. Finally, she heard of a dedicated Jewish teacher called Hugo Rosenthal, who had chosen to remain in Germany at this time 'to help on the spot' with the crisis in Jewish education. Tante Anna invited him to meet her.

Hugo Rosenthal was a man of deep inner commitment. Although Anna was convinced she could no longer raise children 'in honesty and freedom' in Germany, Rosenthal had come to a different view. The oppression of Jewish children in German schools was wrong and the Jewish community must stand its ground. Generations of German Jews had tried to integrate into German culture and synthesise 'Judaism with European humanism', and where had this got them, Rosenthal asked. It was time to go back to their roots and convey 'to our youth the incomparable heritage of the Jewish spirit and knowledge'. Rosenthal wanted to give oppressed Jewish children something to hold on to under the onslaught of condemnation, and help them 'face the future with determination'. Anna asked him whether he would take over the running of the school. It was very short notice for such a large undertaking and he did not know whether he could raise the funds. Nonetheless, Rosenthal agreed.[31]

In early September as Anna and her trusted staff were finalising their secret escape plans, they found Hitler once again on their doorstep. They had not expected this. Another Nazi rally was planned in Ulm. This was bad news for Anna and the team. They had so little time left and it would only take one person to inform on them. To Anna it was as though the city of Ulm was suddenly engulfed in collective madness. Giant swastikas were hung across the city, heralding Hitler's arrival. A poem on 5 September 1933 in the local paper, the *Ulmer Tagblatt*, captured the mood, breathlessly welcoming the Führer as though God himself was descending on the town.

> Welcome German Chancellor
> The Danube city greets you
> In which the Great Führer
> Was sent by God...
>
> Welcome Adolf Hitler,
> You modest Great Hero
> Justice and German character
> Conquer the World.

'With lightning speed the news flew through the streets and alleys,' enthused the *Ulmer Tagblatt*. The masses rushed to greet him, 'to see the man whose mission it was, to create a new Germany'. Anna saw that all the Ulm papers appeared to be outdoing each other in a bid to win Nazi approval, no doubt fearing reprisals from the regional Nazi officials in charge of local press. It was alarming to realise how quickly freedom of the press had disappeared. The Ulm papers transformed Hitler into an almost mythical figure. For the reporter on the *Ulmer Sturm*, his plane did not even land: 'for the bringer of salvation it *floats* down'. The loyalty with which the local people waited 'is evidence that this man is loved here . . . Indescribable joy could be seen on people's faces.' An even larger crowd than before, six thousand strong, surged into the church square to hear Hitler speak. 'A thunderous storm of sound emerges from the alleys,' reported the *Ulmer Sturm*, 'a thousand-fold it rings out across the streets, Heil Führer, *Heil!*'[32]

As Hitler left Ulm on the road to Blaubeuren to view the military manoeuvres of the 5th Division, his convoy passed directly through Herrlingen village, not far from Anna's school. A crescendo of sound marked Hitler's progress as the convoy of high-powered cars drove at speed. Then he was gone. The small groups of teachers, busy with details, breathed more easily – though not for long, as that evening the Führer returned to the Hotel Russischer Hof. The impatient crowd demanded to see him again. Eventually Hitler stood in the window for several minutes. Thunderous calls of 'Heil' and rowdy singing of the German national anthem, 'Deutschlandlied', and the Nazi Party anthem, 'Horst Wessel Lied', continued until late in the night, like a solid wall of sound.

The burning of the Jewish books, the oppressive restrictions for Jewish teachers and children, the arrests of innocent citizens, the sight of the dreaded Brownshirts swarming through Ulm spoiling for trouble; for Anna the school's escape could not come soon enough. She would lead the way with an advance party of six teachers and six senior boys and girls to make preparations in England for the arrival of the others. Sixty-five children would follow two weeks later. She had decided that they would travel out of Germany in three separate groups, each masquerading as day trippers on a picnic with a member of staff. The religious affairs teacher, Martin Schwarz, was to pick up a child at each station along the Rhine from Basel. At the same time, Anna's sister, Paula, would set out from Munich to Herrlingen and on to Stuttgart and Mannheim, collecting pupils on the way. Meanwhile the new teacher, Hanna Bergas, would be leading a third group through north Germany from Breslau via Berlin.[33]

In the final days, Anna had pored over train timetables and routes, double-checked everyone had the right paperwork, liaised with parents and briefed the children on how to behave on the journey. There were also painful farewells. Her large, close-knit family was being split up. She had to leave her mother in Ulm in the care of her younger sister, Ida. With the exception of Paula, who was coming to England, and her youngest sister, Bertha, who was in France with her husband, all her brothers and sisters were remaining behind. William and Marie felt tied by their furnishings business to stay in Mannheim. Frederick, too, had business interests. Klara had chosen to keep her children in the school at Herrlingen.

Two weeks after Hitler's rally, Anna's advance party set out. She had deceived the authorities and by her actions she was revealing her lack of support for Nazi methods and ideology. Innocent MPs, politicians, Jews and priests were languishing in concentration camps without charge or redress. How would her own cover story of a short sabbatical stand up before the Gestapo if it became clear an entire school was following her? Would they have grounds to charge her with treason against the German state? Anna's eyes scanned each station for any sign of anything unusual, but she had been making preparations for months and the journey passed without incident. They reached England safely and by 5 October, Anna was ready to implement the second stage of her plan.

Years later, Hanna Bergas could remember her impressions of that day. On the platform of the Zoologischer Garten station in Berlin, ten boys and girls were waiting. Ten was a notable number. Would it attract attention? Only a few parents had come to say goodbye. Feelings were taut. It was difficult to appear normal, to pretend that this was just an ordinary day trip. No one dared show any emotion. 'It was a quiet subdued leave-taking,' Hanna wrote. 'Much thought and talk had been spent on this moment in previous weeks and now everybody was controlled.' Her own elderly mother was also on the platform and Hanna felt the wrench keenly, wondering when they would meet again.[34] A very uncertain future lay before them. If just one person had talked, it was hard to know what might happen. Would the thuggish Brownshirts storm the train, frighten the children and cause trouble? Had anyone given the Gestapo advance warning? Would a child accidentally give the game away? However much the young ones wanted to help, they could still forget.

The tension was palpable as the train made its way west to the border. This was the supreme test. At the border station they could hear the sounds of the shouted instructions, and caught sight of armed guards on the platform. Their papers were inspected. Finally the whistle blew and the train moved forwards, gathered speed and then travelled on into Luxembourg. The children began to relax.

When they reached the docks at Ostend, the children in Hanna's group suddenly caught sight of Paula, already waiting with another contingent of their classmates. Soon the third group arrived. Spirits rose at once. The children, so subdued at the start of the day, began to feel it was 'a tremendous adventure,' observed Paula. Everyone had managed to slip out of Nazi Germany successfully. By the time they boarded the ferry for the Channel crossing they were 'thoroughly lively, interested and very noisy,' Hanna recorded. When they sailed into Dover she found the children 'were more fascinated by three fat red buses waiting for us than the famous White Cliffs.' There beside them on the docks was Tante Anna, thrilled to see them, standing with two members of her School Council as she waited to escort her pupils on the final leg of the journey.

They wound their way through the Kent countryside, the children fascinated by the cone-shaped oast houses and the large numbers of chimneys on the low red-brick houses. The early autumn sunshine changed the spirit of the adventure. This was the garden of England and it looked beautiful. It looked at peace. At last they turned off the main road into quiet country lanes and the buses finally came to a standstill in front of what appeared to be a mansion, partially obscured behind a high, thick green hedge. They entered through an imposing gateway, Hanna thought: 'two red brick pillars enthroned with two large balls of white stone'. Improbably, there before them was a gracious manor house. Hanna took in the tall, square sash windows, wisteria tumbling around them, a rose garden and parklands where the children could play. It was quintessentially English and picture-perfect.[35]

At the heart of it all was Anna, who seemed to be everywhere, making sure everyone settled in. She had put everything into preparing for this moment. 'Those days of cleaning and getting ready for the reception of the children will never be forgotten by all who helped,' she wrote.[36] But now their exodus was assured. She led her children across the threshold into the grand and spacious entrance hall. To one side was a large assembly room, which Anna and her team had filled with long tables gaily covered in yellow tablecloths and set ready for dinner. Beyond this were various doors that branched out from the hall in all directions and further down, an impressive 'festive looking broad staircase with a carved wooden bannister' leading invitingly upstairs, where a hundred beds were ready and the children found rooms with their friends. It was clear from the children's whoops and screams of delight that this was the real thing. They were in England. They were safe; and what a place to be safe in: a sort of school palace.

In a matter of moments 'the house swarmed with children all through its three storeys,' exploring their new home.[37] At last Tante Anna could create her model school in freedom, a community where her staff and children would thrive. It wasn't long before she and the children decided their school must have a new name, one that would welcome their new future in England. It would be called after its historic buildings: 'Bunce Court School'.

2

'[Bunce Court] school falls short of the usual requirements'

British school inspectors

For the first few weeks the excitement of what Anna's staff and pupils had achieved was like an invisible glow that spread throughout Bunce Court, imbuing all their efforts with a sense of optimism and hope. They had escaped. The enemy was formidable but they had done it. They could create their own future unshackled by the poisonous hate-filled agenda unfolding in Nazi Germany and all the uncertainties that came in its wake. 'Oh, the joy of coming to a large country house that contained nothing but sand-wiches, three long tables and a hundred beds . . .' Hanna Bergas recalled in a speech years later. They felt like pioneers. Everything was a novelty, even sleeping in a dormitory for the first time. For a few weeks the curriculum was all but forgotten as staff and children threw themselves into turning the manor into their home.

'The discoveries we made,' says Hanna. 'Swallows on the wallpaper, English nursery rhymes such as "Bye Bye Baby Bunting, Father goes a-hunting" . . . cornflakes and cereals generally, secret escapades to the cellar where I remembered eating puffed rice all morning instead of washing up . . . the village shop "Warren Street", with its never-ending supply of Mars Bars, chocolate biscuits and bacon, apples in the orchard, Canterbury, theatricals, conversations in English with tradespeople . . .' Pupils, too, remember the magic of those early weeks. 'What a time we had!' wrote one older girl, Maria Dehn. Nobody minded the hard work. 'We felt ourselves to be pioneers collaborating to provide for a great new need.' She was so happy that, looking back, she feels that any visitor coming to the school 'would have thought, "They seem to know what they are living for"'.[1]

For Tante Anna, this was her chance to create the school she had held in her mind for so long. Bunce Court was to be a secure and loving home where each child felt completely accepted, as though part of a big family. It must be a place where joy reigned and actions were not guided by fear and punishment. She aimed to build on the ideas she had used to create her original school in Herrlingen, but there were key differences. Anna had always placed equal importance on the practical side of life as to academic study, but at Bunce Court it was a necessity as a means of sustaining the school. There was no money for domestic staff. Each afternoon, after the sacred 'rest-hour', the children joined in to do the chores, just as they would at home. Tante Anna's prospectus from that autumn shows many photographs of the children helping out in the grounds with gardening, carpentry or feeding their new flock of chickens, all with the radiant glow of youthful health and vigour. 'As a principle of the school,' she wrote, 'every child has to take his part in doing some of the practical work necessary in the running of a large house.'[2]

More important still, Anna was keen to integrate her school into the British educational system. To do this, Bunce Court had to meet the requirements of exacting British school inspectors and win formal recognition by the British Board of Education. If approved, it would be easier to attract British pupils to Bunce Court and bring in much-needed fees, making the school's future more secure. It would also help her German pupils assimilate into the British way of life. Their lives were full of uncertainties, their futures, whether in Britain or Germany, unknown. Tante Anna stressed the importance of integration and English was spoken at all times in the school, except on Fridays. A great deal would rest on the British inspectors. Without their support, Tante Anna was in a catch-22; it would be hard to attract British children and make the school more financially viable. As soon as they were settled in, she wrote to the local authority and the Board of Education inviting them to inspect the school.[3]

But it was Home Office officials who turned up at the school first, to check everyone's passports and register the teachers and children. 'The British government did not cause us any trouble,' Paula wrote, but they did stipulate that within six months half the staff must be British. Tante Anna managed to make two very successful appointments almost immediately. A young Montessori teacher called Gywnne Badsworth came to look after the very youngest pupils in a converted cottage in the grounds. Anna was delighted to see Gwynne's gentle manner with the children. 'Everybody loved Gywnne,' observed Hanna, 'she was so understanding and warm.' Norman Wormleighton, or 'Wormy', as he soon became known, was the good-looking new English teacher, who joined from the recently formed Dartington Hall School, a progressive school in Devon established on similar lines to A. S. Neill's Summerhill School. Wormy was said to be pleased to find a greater sense of discipline in the German refugee school.

Tante Anna found the English staff joined the Germans in trying to help with the children's emotional concerns.

Nine-year-old Eric Bourne was typical of the first wave of pupils arriving at Bunce Court in the immediate aftermath of Hitler coming to power. He remembers the moment he arrived at the local train station at Lenham. 'The door flies open and the wind drives rain into your face. You tumble out onto the slippery platform . . . you notice the shining wet rails disappearing into the darkness.' The sound of a telephone reminded him of the nearness of life, 'but then hearing voices you relapse. They are talking a strange tongue, and you are in a foreign country. There is, some-where, a queer, dragging feeling of homelessness.' Eric believes there is no English word that does justice to the full German meaning of the loss of '*Heimat*' – or homeland – as a child, 'and the emotional pull which *Heimat* exercises on the German mind'. For Eric, it was a profound feeling of uprootedness that went well beyond homesickness or missing one's home country, as though all his emotional ties had been severed. Eric believes all the children at the school in 1933 were suffering in varying degrees from the loss of '*Heimat*'.[4]

Eric soon discovered he could raise any worries with the teachers. Sometimes it was a relief to talk about his family, especially his father, Robert, whom he adored. Robert was a left-wing journalist who had a remarkable ability to produce 'controversial, even inflammatory articles at the drop of a hat,' wrote his admiring son. Among his many transgressions in the eyes of Nazi officials, Robert had taken it upon himself to write to President von Hindenburg in 1932 advising him to arrest Hitler. As soon as Hitler came to power, Robert had fled to Paris. Eric suffered the splitting up of his family in a few short weeks, but he found other pupils in a similar plight.[5] 'I think I had the distinction of being the most homesick boy there for some time,' recalled another pupil, Gerry Schloss. 'I vividly recall Tante Anna trying to help me overcome my homesickness by frequently talking to me with concerned care in her room upstairs.'[6]

'We were certain that a real home could never be replaced,' Tante Anna observed, but she would do all in her power to create a loving atmosphere. Each day in the late afternoon, she and her team met to discuss any problems over tea and toast. Together the teachers mulled over how to create that feeling of warmth and security that Tante Anna saw as 'essential to the growth of these uprooted children'.[7] Hanna found emotional problems usually surfaced in the evening as the children were winding down from the day. With the shortage of bathrooms, 'going-to-bed-time stretched over two hours, staggered according to age,' she wrote. 'We got lots of stories about "how we did it at home"', and this created openings to discuss deeper feelings. 'Many ideas, wishes, longings and worries came to the fore before finally one sat on a girl's bed saying "goodnight" occasionally with a kiss'.[8]

Despite the enthusiasm of the early weeks, as the cold autumn weather drew in, they ran into a serious problem. It rapidly became clear that the wisteria-clad 'school palace' was deficient in every up-to-date convenience. 'We were spoilt at Herrlingen,' wrote Paula regretfully. 'Everything was modern and the best.' English manor houses, by contrast, were 'expensive and too primitive,' she observed, 'with no electric lights, too little water, hardly any lavatories and petrol lamps for lighting.'[9] The owner of Bunce Court, Lady Olga Manning, who had leased the property to the school, had not lived in it for several years. The rambling manor had character but little else. Bunce Court was not connected to the Kent electricity mains; pupils remember the stuttering 'putt putt putt' of the engine room and a curious 'gas machine' next to an old tool shed. Neither did the trick. With no gas and limited oil-fired electricity, it was a struggle to heat forty rooms over three floors and harder still to heat the outbuildings that were hastily adapted to house the older boys. They depended on shifting portable paraffin stoves from room to room and open coal fires. The water supply, too, was insufficient. Even the large and apparently welcoming Aga in the kitchen had a mind of its own.

In Herrlingen, Tante Anna had been able to rely on local help, but in England she found that initially people were distrustful. Why had a German school settled in their midst? In 1933 there was no understanding of the dangers of Nazism that Anna described; quite the reverse. People had heard that Hitler was lifting Germany out of the great depression and working an economic miracle. They were puzzled as to why Anna had felt under pressure to bring children out of Germany and saw no reason to get involved.[10] Tante Anna's keen desire to integrate her school into the British way of life and 'build bridges in foreign lands' was not going smoothly.

But she did succeed in making one crucial appointment. A local GP, Dr Terence Porter, 'a gentleman in his best years,' observed Paula, 'offered to treat us and our children for a whole year without charge. A considerable present.' Dr Porter's contribution proved critical. One boy recalled chill November days that brought cold winds whipping in from the east with the power to penetrate layers of clothing, 'blowing down my back'. The handsome old trees in the grounds seemed to be permanently covered in a thick mantle of hoar frost. Some of the children in the unheated dormitories on the top floor were so cold they suffered from chilblains. Suddenly Tante Anna and her team found themselves battling a serious health emergency.

In late November a few of the children became ill with sore throats and fever. Tante Anna and Paula rapidly improvised quarantine measures to deal with what seemed to be a severe bout of flu. Isolating with the children, Paula was 'greatly shocked' when one older pupil, Max Kantorovitz, 'appeared to develop symptoms of paralysis'. Dr Porter came at once. In a matter of hours, Max had such severe muscle weakness he could no longer move. Grimly, Dr Porter told Anna the worst possible news. As Paula feared, this was indeed 'infantile paralysis': the dreaded polio.[11]

The days that followed were filled with anxiety and dread. Max was a much-loved boy who had been with the school for six years. But in the 1930s, infectious diseases could be the scourge of childhood: diphtheria, scarlet fever, measles and polio. Polio could kill a child or leave them crippled for life. It was infectious and there was no vaccine to protect the other children. Nor was there a cure. The incubation period was six weeks. If any of the other children had caught polio, Dr Porter explained gravely, it could take six weeks for the symptoms to show. There was even a risk the disease could have spread beyond the school into the local community.

Bunce Court was immediately put into lockdown. Food and other supplies were left at the gates. Visiting parents were obliged to have meetings outside as quarantine measures were extended. Any pupils who developed symptoms had to be isolated somehow, despite the lack of space. Dr Porter, assisted by Paula, Tante Anna and other staff, did everything in his power to help. It was the worst possible situation. A child could die. At the centre of it all was one popular teenage boy whose life was hanging by a thread and whose weak limbs could barely move.[12]

*

For Tante Anna, the shock of what happened blotted out all the good things. Max was transferred to hospital but, tragically, his three-day struggle ended in his death.

The worst that Tante Anna could imagine had happened. She knew Max's parents personally and they had entrusted her with their child. There was much soul-searching. Could she have done things differently? Had she taken on too much? Bunce Court remained in lockdown for weeks. Despite the close supervision of Dr Porter, although there were no further polio infections, they dealt with a few cases of diphtheria and scarlet fever. 'It was a grave winter indeed until we were certain the rest of the children were safe,' she wrote later.[13] As soon as they were out of lockdown, she started on plans to build an isolation ward at some distance from the main house. The sanatorium was to be run by Paula and would enable them to isolate an infectious child in any future emergency.

It is perhaps not surprising that when British inspectors came out early in 1934, to look at the 'spatial and sanitary conditions', they were not impressed. Their report does not survive, but a later inspection points out that 'the school falls short of the usual requirements'. This was arguably unduly harsh since the average village school in Kent at the time had outside lavatories and sinks and infectious diseases were rife. Nonetheless, exacting inspectors made a detailed tally of the baths and water closets at the German school and did not like what they found. 'Arrangements for washing are of a limited and makeshift kind,' they observed. 'For twenty boys in the long dormitory there are three baths in a former garage, which also contains a sink and some pans,' although they acknowledged there were six showers also available to these boys. The junior boys in the main building 'share the use of two baths and four washbasins with those of the staff who live on the second floor'. For the girls and female staff, 'there are only ten basins and two baths' although they did concede that 'it proves possible for each girl to have a hot bath every day and members of staff after the girls have gone to bed'. All this gave the school a bad mark.

The inspectors were also puzzled by the discipline of the school, 'being that of a large family rather than that of an institution'. Instead of seeing the benefits for refugee children in a homely environment, they saw only the downsides. 'Pupils go about the house freely and use as day rooms, not only the classrooms and library, but also the rooms of the staff, including the Headmistress's own room,' they wrote incredulously. One classroom, they noted, was in a garage, and the science room was relegated to an outbuilding. The inspectors did approve of Gywnne's cottage for the juniors, although the fact that there were no on-site catering facilities did not escape them. Breakfast and high tea were brought down from the main house – another bad mark.[14] The generosity of spirit that lay behind the charitable venture seemed to elude them as the school was reduced in withering remarks to its closet, catering and washing facilities. It seemed that the inspectors considered that these Germans were merely playing at schools.

The inspectors also had reason to take Anna to task on her compliance with the British authority's demands that within six months, half the staff must be British. Anna had advertised for teachers and received a number of applications, but struggled to find suitable staff, especially during lockdown. Several of those she had interviewed did not appear to understand the special problems faced by Jewish refugee children, or even why they had to leave Nazi Germany, and lacked the empathy and imagination that she was looking for. But from the point of view of the inspectors, Anna's plans to create a model school with no resources were unrealistic, perhaps even impossible.

Tante Anna was not going to admit defeat lightly. Children, staff and parents were looking to her for leadership and she would not let them down. Her determination to secure the future of Bunce Court may also have been influenced by the growing number of desperate queries she received from both parents and teachers anxious to leave Germany. No one else attempted to smuggle an entire school out of Germany, but Bertha Bracey, who ran the Quaker German Emergency Committee in London, asked Anna to endorse the start-up of another Jewish refugee school in Britain. With Bertha's help, in 1934 the German educator Hilde Lion opened Stoatley Rough near Haslemere as 'a temporary experiment', with just seven pupils and three staff. Both Anna and Bertha were on the school committee.[15] Meanwhile, Kurt Hahn, the Jewish founder of the famous Salem School who had been briefly imprisoned by the Nazis, had escaped to England with the support of prominent friends including the British prime minister, Ramsay MacDonald. Starting with just two pupils, Hahn began to recreate his Salem system at his new school: Gordonstoun in Scotland.[16]

Tante Anna proved skilled at inspiring her staff with her vision for Bunce Court. She had that rare combination of 'a sense of adventure and of order combined', Hanna Bergas wrote later, 'the power of quick decision making, a readiness for steady responsibility and a true devotion to the children'.[17]

But not everyone appreciated Tante Anna's strong personality. One new teacher, Hans Meyer, a medical student from Mainz, who had been forced to leave university when Hitler came to power, found her too quick to judgement. Hans had included a photograph with his application from Germany that showed him daringly balancing his nephew on his hands. It caught Anna's eye. 'Oh, we must have him,' she declared impulsively. But when Hans arrived, not only did he not meet her high academic expectations, it was unclear what subject he could teach. Hans could also be short-tempered. Tante Anna could barely conceal her disappointment. She started Hans in the school office, but discovered he could only type with two fingers. Determined to find a way to fit in, Hans was soon helping in the garden, on the sports field and in the carpentry workshop.[18]

With the arrival of spring, Tante Anna found that the manor and its gracious twenty-five acres of grounds came into its own. After a worrying winter, to work outside in the warming sun with nature promising much was an unadmitted pleasure. The mathematics teacher, Adolf Prag, 'was just as likely to be found repairing the roof or painting our innumerable window frames' as teaching multiplication tables, observed one pupil.[19] Other staff created plans with the children to make the school self-sufficient in fruit and vegetables. Fired up with the possibilities, the pupils mended greenhouses and glass frames and prepared the vegetable garden for seeding. Outbuildings were adapted to enlarge their flock of free-range chickens. Even the younger pupils joined in the efforts to raise funds. One child remembers making 'cut out hardwood elephants with stick-on plywood ears and a ropy tail for sale at 2/6d a time'. In spite of the school's lack of money, he felt 'unaware of being a refugee or disadvantaged in any way whatsoever'.[20]

Tante Anna renewed her efforts to integrate the school into the local area. To deepen the children's knowledge of English literature she arranged with the county council to send a van at least once a month with over a thousand English books to choose from, in addition to the books the children could choose from the staff library and her own private collection. She invited guest speakers from very varied backgrounds to broaden the children's horizons: the League of Nations, the Workers' Education Association and even the British Post Office. On one occasion the local postman turned up to give a talk, the postmaster having declined. The postman had no experience of public speaking and 'felt a bundle of nerves before an endless sea of children's faces', but his talk proved such a success he was soon invited as a speaker to other venues.

Anna and the children decided to hold a big open day in the summer of 1934 to thank their sponsors and show the local people – and hopefully the exacting school inspectors – what they could do. The older children wanted to stage a play to entertain their guests and Anna recommended an ambitious Greek comedy, perhaps deliberately turning her back on German literature. She would instead introduce the children to drama from the time of the birth of democracy, with *Peace* by Aristophanes. It was a satire in which the character Peace has been driven away by corrupt politicians profiteering from war, and imprisoned in the House of the Gods; but, happily, all ends well as the people of Greece themselves find a way to rescue Peace. Anna also had an ambitious plan for the little ones. Complete with a trumpet, drums, rattles and other toys, as well as a great deal of help from the staff, they formed a junior orchestra to give a playful rendition of the *Toy Symphony*.

By late spring there was much excitement about the coming open day. The older boys and girls had been transforming the grounds for weeks. They restored the overgrown tennis courts and cleared a wide tree-lined path leading to a new sports field, marked out with an athletics track and football pitch. Many other children were happily preparing costumes, masks and props for the school play. The actors were busy with rehearsals. It was to be a live performance in front of over two hundred and fifty people, including members of the Jewish Refugees Committee and distinguished members of the School Council such as Sir Herbert Samuel, who would give the opening address. 'At Home' invitations were proudly sent out for 15 July. English accents were rehearsed. Music was practised. Lawns were mowed. Flowers decorated the house. Everything was to be perfect for the big day.

The play went without a hitch. Then it was the turn of the junior orchestra, who took up their places for the *Toy Symphony*. 'The children's score sheets had been fastened to their backs, so they could be read by the person behind,' recalls Paula, 'when a gust of wind blew all the papers into the pond.' The audience was enchanted when the little ones continued to play as if nothing had happened.[21] Afterwards children served teas and home-made cakes on the colourful tables set out in the grounds, while others proudly showed their guests around. Visitors could see for themselves the flourishing vegetable garden, the restored greenhouses and cold frames all now overflowing with summer produce, the growing flock of chickens, the new formal flower beds and the beautiful rose garden. In the dappled afternoon sunlight the crowd of people on Bunce Court's lawn created the impression of a centuries-old English summer fete.

Even when the splendid day was over and many feats some had privately thought impossible were accomplished, the intoxicating glamour of the event lingered, investing all with magical extra inches in height that lasted at least a week. Local people began to take a keen interest in the school. Some parents made enquiries about sending their children as day pupils. Others offered to take the refugee children out to tea, for a picnic, or even for a short holiday to give them a taste of British family life. The local Women's Appeal Committee offered to fund three new classrooms in a new building in the grounds, freeing up more space in the house.

As for the children, the excitement was infectious. They decided to stage an even bigger event the following year. This time they would build their own proper stage. There would be no more music sheets blowing in the pond. They would create a grand outdoor amphitheatre with seating for three hundred guests. A spot was chosen against a backdrop of handsome cedar trees. Why stop there? Perhaps they could design electric lighting, too? They even planned to dig their own swimming pool and create a gym. In all the optimism there seemed no limits to what they could achieve together. Tante Anna was delighted. The people of Kent were giving the refugee children a warm welcome and the children were responding. These were the very bridges she had hoped to build.[22] For Anna it was a reward to savour; handsome payment indeed for work she loved.

But Her Majesty's school inspectors did not see the triumph of that day. They had declined Tante Anna's invitation. In the autumn of 1934 she renewed her efforts, applying again for inspection by the Board of Education 'for the purpose of becoming a Recognised School'. Once again, the inspectors declined to visit. 'The Board is unwilling to conduct Full Inspections of new schools until they have had time to become firmly established,' wrote the inspector, Mr Hankin, who considered 'it was much too early to think of inspection [for Recognition] at present'. Tante Anna pointed out that her school had been thriving for nine years in Germany before moving to Britain, but this seems to have cut no ice. The inspectors were sticklers for the rules and appeared to have a lack of insight into the crisis in education in Nazi Germany. 'Unless they can attract English pupils as well, the school will presumably cease to function as soon as the supply of children from Germany peters out . . .' observed Hankin unsympathetically on 5 February 1935. From the point of view of the inspectors, Anna's plans to create a model school with such limited resources were unrealistic, perhaps even impossible.[23] Some believed it was only a matter of time before the school must close. As a foreigner in a foreign country, with no money, for Tante Anna it was beginning to look like a Herculean feat.

*

As Bunce Court was attempting to integrate into British ways, Tante Anna's original school at Herrlingen was facing a painful expulsion from life in Nazi Germany. A staggering forty-two new laws that restricted the rights of German Jews were introduced during 1933 alone.[24] For Herrlingen's head-master, Hugo Rosenthal, the German referendum held on 19 August 1934 brought another unimaginable blow. By a huge landslide, the German people voted to merge the powers of the president with those of the chancellor following the death of President von Hindenburg. Adolf Hitler's transformation to absolute dictator was complete. There was now no constitutional check on his power.

Against this ominous backdrop, Hugo Rosenthal and his wife, Judith, were becoming convinced their school at Herrlingen had no future; or a few years, at most. Even so, they planned to dedicate themselves to helping Jewish children seeking an educational refuge for as long as possible. They found many of their new pupils were struggling with feelings of inferiority after suffering antisemitic attacks in their home towns. Children of assimilated Jewish families were also effectively cut off from German culture and yet knew little of Jewish culture either. Rosenthal felt these children existed in a kind of 'cultural vacuum', and he wanted to give them something back of their 'centuries-old community'. He added Hebrew, Bible studies and knowledge of Jewish festivals and traditions to the curriculum. His aim was to create a feeling of optimism, of 'rebuilding amid destruction'. He called it 'education for courage'.[25]

As Rosenthal enlarged Herrlingen as a Jewish school, he was painstaking in his diplomacy with the educational authorities. Local officials increasingly found themselves in a tricky position, obliged to stick to the letter of new antisemitic laws. One petty issue arose almost immediately over the position of Tante Anna's loyal friend, Kathy Hamburg, and her seven adopted children. Kathy had supported Herrlingen School since its inception, but several of her children at the school were not Jewish, a fact that came to exercise the minds of the authorities in Stuttgart. The presence of these supposedly 'Aryan' children at the school meant that, 'it follows that the description of the school as a "*Jewish* Landschulheim"￼ is impermissible,' wrote Mr Bracher from the Ministerial Department for Higher Education, Stuttgart, in November 1933. 'It must cease with immediate effect.' Rosenthal took great care not to commit any such glaring blunders as he patiently submitted to inspections of the school. The authorities had the power to close the school down.[26]

Apart from navigating the quicksand of Nazi bureaucracy, the school faced episodes of hostility from local Nazi supporters. One day Rosenthal found his pupils were no longer permitted to bathe in their favourite spot in the nearby River Blau. They searched the river for places where notices had not yet appeared restricting the presence of Jews. When they went on country hikes, his pupils were banned from youth hostels. Teachers began to face problems with landlords who were under mounting pressure not to rent rooms to Jews. On another occasion, a group of Hitler Youth marched towards the school, chanting provocatively, 'To Arms, Comrades!' Herrlingen pupils responded spontaneously with a rousing Jewish chorus, 'March to Palestine!' For a brief moment it was unclear what might happen. Then the Hitler Youth marched on. The threat passed.

Rosenthal always urged diplomacy not confrontation. Taking advantage of the school's secluded spot, he managed to keep the children away from trouble. His wife Judith, a former concert pianist who led the school's music department, helped to set the peaceful tone. 'Her piano playing contributed substantially to the serene atmosphere,' observed one pupil, Ruth Sharon. Another child, Joseph Ewen, considered 'it was our good fortune to spend the years of our youth in a place unmarked by that which was taking place outside the bounds of our little village'. It was only later he began to question whether he was taking part 'in a fool's paradise, insulated from that which went on around us'.[27]

While private schools in Germany such as Herrlingen were able to keep the Nazi world at bay – at least for the time being – both Hugo Rosenthal and Tante Anna knew that the vast majority of Jewish children in German state schools were being exposed to the full force of the Nazi ideology. Germany appeared to be descending day by day into barbarism. Who was there to protect Jewish children in Germany from this harsh new reality?

3

'No match for the Raging Mob'

Seven-year-old Leslie Brent, Germany, 1933

The vast majority of Jewish schoolchildren in Germany were beyond the reach of the kind of sanctuary provided by teachers like Tante Anna or Hugo Rosenthal. In 1933 there were more than 60,000 Jewish schoolchildren in German state schools who had no means of removing themselves from disturbing changes around them. Among them was Leslie Brent, whose experiences were typical of many Jewish children. Growing up in the small town of Köslin near the Baltic coast in northern Germany, for seven-year-old Leslie life changed dramatically in 1933 as the grown-up world suddenly became unpredictable, unanswerable and filled with odd threats.

Even without fully understanding the significance of the forest of swastika flags that appeared almost overnight, the change of public mood felt 'pretty alienating'. Flags festooned the streets, except on the few Jewish shops and homes, marking them out as different. The feeling of being shunned was also new. People had once been so friendly to Leslie's family, but now 'it was very striking when we went out, neighbours and family friends would avoid us'. His father had always politely raised his homburg as a greeting but increasingly the convention was to give the *Heil Hitler* salute.

People would 'pretend to cross the road' to avoid any awkwardness. For Leslie this was 'very extraordinary'. Everything had changed in such a subtle way without a given signal, without a word said. Why had no one told him?[1]

Leslie's first taste of real fear came at his grandmother's house. His grandmother, Oma, was an object of fascination and dread because she suffered from a disfiguring skin disease. The odour of her medication permeated her flat. But that evening in spring 1933 any thoughts of his grandmother's ailment were eclipsed. As Leslie was playing with his older sister, Eva, they heard a great tumult outside; the sound of heavy marching boots, drumbeats marking time. The street below was empty, but they watched from their vantage point behind the curtain until the thunderous noise drew closer and closer and finally the marchers came into view. It was the SA, the formidable brown-shirted *Sturmabteilung*, their flaming torches casting deep shadows. Leslie watched trans-fixed. He had seen nothing like this before in the quiet Köslin streets. The 'horrible German song' they chanted made no sense. 'When Jewish blood spurts from the knife then all is really well'. It was not just the words of the song that struck terror. It was the sense of purpose of the crowd, the feeling of mob violence. 'For the first time, I realised something very odd was going on,' he recalls. Without warning, the grown-up world was suddenly grotesque, like a nightmare. Was it just associated with the dark?[2]

But then in the daylight, equally incomprehensible was the sudden boycott of his uncle and grandfather's long-established shops in town. On 1 April that year, the Brownshirts stood guard outside Jewish businesses, looking for a fight. Inexplicably to Leslie, they had the authority to stop customers going inside. Leslie was also unaware that his father, Arthur, a travelling salesman, had begun to lose commissions, though he sensed that his father seemed under strain, that he was working harder, travelling longer distances.

Arthur's family had been part of the small Jewish community at Köslin going back generations to the early nineteenth century. He had fought in the First World War and been awarded for bravery in rescuing German soldiers under fire. Leslie remembers his father took to wearing a label that indicated he was a bearer of the Iron Cross, a proud badge of his unquestioning loyalty to Germany. Arthur was one of 18,000 German Jews awarded the Iron Cross who thought he had a measure of protection from Nazi antisemitic extremes – after all, President Paul von Hindenburg himself had intervened as the civil service law was drafted, to exempt First World War veterans who had served at the front from dismissal from their employment. Whatever Arthur's fears, he kept them to himself, wanting to protect his children from anxiety. 'The extraordinary thing is that my parents never talked to me about the political situation,' Leslie recalls, though perhaps Eva, who was two and a half years older, knew more. 'I expect my sister was more fully aware of what was going on around her, but I was totally unaware. They kept me in the dark.'

Eva seemed to Leslie to encompass all the intelligence and mystery of being a little older. With her lively, inquisitive manner and long brown hair, Leslie remembers, she was 'very pretty and highly strung'. He delighted in a secret language she taught him, 'with repeated syllables, nothing very subtle but it did enable us to speak privately'. From their block of flats they had a view across the valley to another apartment block. Eva created an imaginary world for Leslie filled with exotic 'mandarins' from far-flung places like China or

Manchuria, and he would watch from across the valley, fascinated. 'We imagined all kinds of things happening there.' He saw Eva as much more sophisticated and grown-up than himself, although she would throw occasional tantrums 'and storm out of the house and my mother and I followed her with beating hearts to persuade her to return'. In retrospect, he believes Eva was far more aware of the dire political situation than he was, and occasionally in conflict with her parents. 'I lived in a kind of bubble.'[3]

One hot day Eva and Leslie had a quarrel and he stole money from her purse for an ice cream. 'It was about the equivalent of two pence today,' but he knew it was wrong. Recalling this some eighty-five years later, the episode is as vivid for Leslie as though it happened yesterday and his eyes fill with tears. 'I've never been able to apologise to her.' Leslie still struggles even at the age of ninety-four, with feelings of guilt that he survived. He still feels he owes his sister something that can never be mended.

How could a young boy put together all the disconnected events and work out what they might mean? One day Arthur was taken for questioning at the local police station. After a few hours, Leslie went down to see what was happening. He waited disconsolately outside, not daring to knock. Hours passed in the cold. Darkness fell. Leslie found himself watching the carbide lamp swinging in the breeze. Why, of all people, was his father – a pillar of the community, liked by everyone – at the police station? A small boy could not understand; but he learned to fear.

At last his father emerged into the darkness, apparently unhurt. Arthur revealed nothing of his prolonged interrogation. Determined to make things seem entirely normal, he bought his son a large chocolate ice cream on the way home.

It was only looking back later that Leslie understood his father was in triple jeopardy as a social democrat, a Freemason and, above all, a Jew.

Family life became a haven of safety and protection. Leslie's mother, Charlotte, was plump and comely. Her sunny nature seemed to fill the rooms of their home and as a young boy he remembers snuggling on her lap in the evening to hear stories. Often when she put her children to bed she would sing a soothing Brahms lullaby, and she taught them a bedtime prayer: 'Dear God, I beg you to lead and protect me, so that when I am grown up I can help others.' Leslie loved to help her on Friday afternoons with the weekly ritual of preparing for the Sabbath. They did the baking together, the homely room soon dense with the smell of freshly baked bread. Afterwards, Leslie would scrub down the wooden kitchen table and cover it with a special embroidered tablecloth. His parents were practising Jews, although not Orthodox. Each Saturday, Leslie joined his father for morning service at the imposing domed synagogue at Köslin.

Arthur was an excellent pianist and for Leslie the evocative sound of the music is indelibly associated with memories of his early childhood. 'There was always music,' he remembers. Arthur played Schubert and Beethoven on his much-loved grand piano, which occupied a prime position in the drawing room. His particular favourite was Mendelssohn's *Songs Without Words*. The soothing sounds of the piano, the orderly rhythm of the repeated refrain, the delight in a tune in a different key or with a different instrument; all this seemed to weave its melodious way through family life. Eva and Charlotte could also play and Leslie sang duets with his father. Arthur joined the local men's choir and played the magnificent organ in the synagogue. An elderly man used to do the pumping, but sometimes it became too much for him and Leslie would hurry to take over before the sound of the organ became too flat. The music must continue.[4]

By the summer of 1935, there had been a marked increase in antisemitic violence, not just from Nazi officialdom but from the grassroots. It was as though Hitler had given ordinary people permission to turn on their Jewish neighbours with obsessive zeal. In Köslin the Hitler cult, which treated him as godlike, seemed all-pervasive. When boys who Leslie once knew joined the *Hitler Jugend* or Hitler Youth, and girls joined the *Bund Deutscher Mädel* or the League of German Girls, he saw how passionately committed they became to the Nazi viewpoint. Violence was never far away when Hitler Youth marched through town chanting anti-Jewish songs. Leslie learned to keep out of their way. But during services in the grand Köslin synagogue, this was not so easy. Hitler Youth would congregate outside and throw stones. Windows were broken, the shattering glass falling on the congregation. Eventually the Jewish community were driven out of their synagogue and services were held in a private home. Offensive signs began to appear: 'Jews enter village at own risk' or 'Anyone dealing with Jews will be thrown out'. How long would it be before Jewish families were driven out of town altogether?

Leslie had heard something of Hitler's speeches and rants against the Jews on his uncle's radio in the office of his draper's shop. Even the poor quality and crackling of the set could not conceal Hitler's fervour at the Nazi Party congress at Nuremberg in September 1935 and the tumultuous roar of approval of the vast crowd. Leslie wondered what the crowd was cheering for so enthusiastically. It wasn't really a cheer; it was one long note made by many voices.

What did it mean? His uncle gave nothing away and Leslie was afraid – his uncle always explained things. A shiver of fear touched the back of his neck. At the end of the Nazi Party congress, something new was announced. Over the coming days, his uncle began to refer to 'the Nuremberg laws' as though a great injustice had been dealt. Leslie grasped that these laws marked a turning point, although talk of changes to the law did not mean much to a young child. He does remember the shock and disbelief that, a few months later, ran through Köslin's Jewish community when one local Jew was punished for an affair with an 'Aryan' woman with months of hard labour.[5]

With Arthur's business declining rapidly, Leslie's family had to give up the apartment with a view across the valley and take a smaller flat by the railway station. Leslie remembers that his father's library of books had to go, an entire wall of books. The grand piano, too! No more Brahms and Schubert. There was no room. Outwardly, his father remained optimistic. Arthur was one of hundreds of thousands of German Jews who found the situation hard to read in the early years of Hitler's dictatorship. In 1933, the state-sponsored boycott of Jewish businesses and a succession of antisemitic laws had marked a decisive early step in the Nazi oppression of the Jews, but 1934 was relatively quiet. Some Jewish families who had emigrated returned, believing the difficulties would blow over.

Leslie loved to meet Arthur off the train from their new flat by the station. His father was always pleased to see him. Things would get better, he reassured his son. There was nothing to fear.

*

Tante Anna was beginning to notice a change in her younger brother William on his sales trips to England. His brief visits to Bunce Court were always a welcome chance to catch up on the news from home, but by the mid-1930s, Anna noticed that he was becoming thin and strained, a slightly stooping figure, as though buckling under an impossible load. She knew that her brother had never fully recovered from his experiences in the First World War. On top of this, William revealed, he was facing a nightmarish new problem. The decorative furnishing business that he ran with their sister, Marie, in Mannheim, was being stolen by the Nazis.

Tante Anna herself had been getting letters from distressed Jewish parents in Germany who could no longer afford to pay for their children at Bunce Court. Their livelihoods, too, were being stolen or destroyed. The school had always carried ten or twelve children whose parents did not pay the fees of around eighty pounds per year, but this number was rising worryingly fast. As William talked through what had happened to him, she could see just how hard-working Jewish families were becoming caught in a Nazi trap.

William's worries had begun in 1933, shortly after the Jewish boycott. One morning he arrived at his factory in Mannheim to find a yellow circle surrounded by a black square had been daubed on the driveway in the night, marking the firm out as a Jewish business. Nazi-supporting employees began to turn up for work in Nazi uniform, loath to take orders from Jewish managers. Customers became fearful of buying from a Jewish firm. In time, their chief supplier, a wood merchant called Huth & Co, led by a well-known local Nazi, Herr Goebels (no relation to the propaganda minister, Goebbels), became an unscrupulous competitor, refusing to supply William's company with wood without a huge discount on their finished goods in return. Within two years, William and Marie's once-booming business had no future and Goebels offered to take over their business at a very low price. With an unmistakable note of fear in his voice, William conveyed to his sister how he had found himself treading a fine line not to cross Goebels; the dangers of doing so had been spelled out quite clearly. At any stage, Goebels 'could have lifted a little finger to despatch my father to Dachau concentration camp,' William's daughter, Dorle, wrote later. A local Nazi was effectively stealing the firm.

William was ordered to stay on as chief European salesman to disguise the change in ownership. Herr Goebels did not want to lose any foreign customers who might object to doing business with the Nazis. To ensure his compliance, neither William's wife, Hennie, nor his son, Hermann, had permission to leave Mannheim. Outwardly, William had to give the impression that everything was fine, but in reality he was both angry and frightened. By 1935, he was convinced that he must give up the factory and devote himself to getting his family out. 'But we had no permission to leave Germany or to emigrate to England,' wrote Dorle. Visits back to Germany after a sales trip became increasingly fraught, 'each time taking his life into his own hands,' continued Dorle.[6]

William and Anna talked over the problems. Anna knew that many of her children's parents were battling similar injustices: Jewish doctors and dentists were not permitted to take 'Aryan' patients; shopkeepers and small businessmen found their custom diminishing fast; many professionals were dismissed from their jobs. Those who saw emigration as the solution, like William, found themselves trapped. Most countries had strict immigration quotas and did not welcome impoverished Jewish immigrants from Germany. At the same time, the Nazis were making it increasingly hard to take any capital or even household goods abroad. A 'Flight Tax', originally introduced in 1931 to ensure that emigrants pay twenty-five per cent of their capital to leave the country, rose dramatically under the Nazis. Jews were targeted, frequently finding their assets confiscated and only released at the discretion of the Nazi government. For the vast majority of Jews, leaving the country increasingly meant losing almost everything they had.[7]

William also confided to Anna his grave worries for the safety of his family. Although he, his wife and his son were trapped, he hoped to send his daughter, Dorle, to Bunce Court as soon as possible. Dorle was unhappy in her German state school. She had told him of the compulsory 'race education' sessions in which Dorle's science teacher told the class that 'Aryans' were the master race, as though it were proven fact. New textbooks were issued with charts comparing alleged 'Aryan' or Nordic characteristics to Jewish traits. Children were taught that Jews had different faces, with characteristic noses, lips, ears and even chins. In the classroom, pupils' head sizes or eye colour were compared as issues of 'racial hygiene' were discussed. The key message of these 'racial awareness' classes was to make the children believe that the Jews in their midst were inferior, akin to '*Ungeziefer*': vermin.[8]

Even as early as June 1933 Tante Anna had read in the *New Statesman* that the entire German curriculum was being subverted by Nazi ideas. 'Art must incite to national passion. Literature is to be purely patriotic,' it reported. History was reinterpreted as a struggle between races, with Germany's enemy identified as the Jews. Geography was taken over by Nazi ideas of 'living space' for the German people. Arithmetic, too, could have a racial bias, with pupils being asked to do calculations on, for example, how many blond people there were in Germany. Even religious instruction did not escape the new ideology. 'Hitler has been sent by God to the German people,' one headmaster allegedly announced at school assembly.[9] The pupils had to show they were absorbing these ideas in their homework, with essays on such subjects as 'Jews are our misfortune'. Education was becoming an entire 'thought-world' of Nazi ideology, observed another headmaster. Any teacher who dared reveal their disagreement risked arrest if they were reported to the Gestapo. William found his daughter, Dorle, was miserable, trapped in a world where other children swallowed false theories wholesale and became vicious and cruel.

William had tried to relieve the pressures on his daughter by sending her for summer breaks at Anna's original school at Herrlingen, where Hugo Rosenthal was making a success of the venture. Within two years, Rosenthal had managed to attract a hundred Jewish pupils. There were extra classrooms and a much-needed sickbay to help with the diphtheria epidemic that was sweeping across southern Germany. But in 1935, Rosenthal faced serious setbacks as the educational authorities in Stuttgart brought private schools in line with Nazi ideas on race. Any 'Aryan' pupils at Herrlingen School had to be transferred immediately to other schools.

This edict had devastating implications for Kathy Hamburg, the first person outside Anna's family who had backed her vision. Kathy was obliged to split up her children, suffering 'the traumatic liquidation' of her large adopted family, according to one pupil. Her 'Aryan' children went to the local village school while her Jewish children eventually emigrated to Palestine.[10] Anna's sister, Klara, too, was removing her children from Herrlingen School. She was making arrangements to take them with her to Palestine, where she planned to start up a new children's home. William had news of other family members. Their mother Fanny, now frail and elderly, was still being cared for by another younger sister, Ida, in Ulm. He hoped Anna could find a way to bring them to safety at Bunce Court.

William was urging all family members to emigrate because of a dramatic escalation over the summer of 1935 in the violence against Jews. On 28 June their local Jewish-owned swimming pool in Mannheim was violently 'cleansed' of Jews; hundreds of Nazi supporters marched on the baths, chanting Hitler songs and attacking swimmers 'with army boots and broken furniture' according to one press report. Men were stripped to see if they were Jews, and beaten; many, Jewish or not, ran away naked. The local police did nothing.[11] Similar scenes were repeated across Germany that summer. As before, the Nazi leadership wanted it to appear as though the German people themselves had turned on the Jews, but in practice, SA troops and Nazi thugs were whipped up into a frenzy by propaganda that talked of Jews 'contaminating' public swimming baths and of 'race defilement'.[12]

William's daughter, Dorle, had suffered another traumatic incident that summer. Forbidden to use the local baths, she and her friends went for an outing to swim in the local river, accompanied by Lily Ascher, a local Jewish youth leader. But the peaceful river was deceptive and one of the girls, Alma, went for a swim and was soon in difficulty. Lily struggled to try to rescue her. There were 'plenty of strong men' along the riverbank that day, observed Dorle, but no one came to their aid. Alma disappeared beneath the water. They called the emergency services only to discover that they, too, no longer responded to Jews. Alma's body was found a few days later. Lily was so distressed by the tragedy that she committed suicide a short while later.[13]

As William feared, the violence over the summer was a pretext to introduce extensive antisemitic legislation. At the end of the Nazi Party rally in Nuremberg on 15 September, at a special meeting of the Reichstag, Hitler announced his bombshell: new Nuremberg laws that had far-reaching effects for Jews in Germany. At a stroke, Jews were no longer 'citizens', but 'subjects', stripped of their political and civic rights, along with other minorities deemed 'non-Aryan'. In addition, they were forbidden to marry or have a sexual relationship with 'Aryans'. German Jews, even those who had lived in the country for generations, were now an underclass, increasingly outside the protection of the law. 'The anti-Jewish legislation of the Third Reich represents a regression to the medieval policy with regard to Jews,' stormed the *Manchester Guardian* on 20 September. For Tante Anna, what made this even harder to understand was the apparent lack of opposition to the Nuremberg laws in her home country. There was no uproar. Where had the voices of millions of ordinary, decent Germans gone?

When Anna next saw William, he was shaken by a family emergency that autumn that drove home the insidious impact of Hitler's racial theories. Shortly after the announcement of the Nuremberg laws, his son, Hermann, was diagnosed with diphtheria. Hermann was not permitted entry into the local hospital so William and Hennie nursed him at home. Hermann was seriously ill when they were contacted by a research group at Heidelberg University.

The scientists were experimenting with new diphtheria antitoxins that had not yet been tested on humans. The authorities were prepared to permit Hermann to be used as a guinea pig for the new antitoxin since the scientists reasoned that, as a Jew, he 'was a convenient intermediate step between an animal and a human being,' Dorle recorded later. For William and Hennie it was an agonising decision. Other children had died in the epidemic – but what kind of experimental care would the scientists test out on their 'subhuman' son? Eventually they agreed to try the new drug. Against all the odds, Hermann survived, although he was still weak months later, his eyes seeming huge in his strikingly pale, gaunt face.[14]

For Tante Anna, William's account was a shock. She had heard Hitler describe Jews as '*Untermenschen*' or 'subhuman' but it was hard to grasp that respected, truth-seeking scientists had, in all seriousness, applied the same term to her own nephew. Did they believe what they had put on their research application? Or was this the only way to get their research approved? Whether the scientists believed the lie or chose to be complicit, Anna was filled with foreboding.

*

In the midst of a renewed wave of antisemitism at the time of the Nuremberg laws, ten-year-old Leslie progressed to the state secondary school, or '*Mittelschule*', in Köslin. His form master, Dr Gaul, was dedicated to the Nazi cause and often appeared in class in his Brownshirt uniform, which Leslie associated with the Jewish blood song; with the menace of uncontrollable violence. 'This was to be the man responsible for my departure from Köslin,' he recalls. The man who would drive him from his family.

Leslie tried hard to do well, but it never worked. Every boy in the school soon knew him to be a Jew and nothing he could do would alter that. He became a target. Snowballs, even stones, were thrown at 'the Jew boy' and he often had reason to flee to a friend's house on the way home to dress a bleeding wound. Sometimes it was hard to escape and he would arrive home 'in a pretty distressed state'. It was even harder to recover from the mental abuse. One day in 1936 Leslie arrived at school to find the accusing words 'All Christians are liars and swindlers' chalked on the blackboard. His teacher insisted Leslie was responsible, ignoring his pleas of innocence.[15]

Leslie felt the injustice keenly. Even as a child, he knew 'the teacher must have done it'. He was trapped in some weird loop of logic whereby he was always cast as the villain even if those in authority had invented his crime. Leslie was shy, hard-working, conscientious and, frustratingly for the teacher, innocent of this. He was also the boy who had just won the hundred-metre race on sports day, a triumph that was duly ignored. Now he was made to 'stand in the corner, facing a wall', while his Nazi teacher delivered an abusive diatribe denouncing 'dirty, filthy Jews and what they got up to' in front of the whole class.

Leslie's father, Arthur, had reached a point of utter despair. It was agonising to see his only son constantly marked out as inferior, victimised by playground bullies and a thuggish teacher alike. Was his son to miss out on an education altogether? Leslie never complained, but appeared older than his years, self-contained, guarded with his feelings. Arthur wondered what this unjust victimisation was doing to his state of mind. Leslie had no idea why he was now 'bad' and he had no way of knowing that his experience was being repeated all over Germany. 'I didn't know it was happening elsewhere,' he recalls. For some reason his sister was not singled out. He was alone.[16]

Arthur had one last hope. There was a large Jewish orphanage in Berlin in a suburb called Pankow. He happened to know the director of the orphanage, who was from Köslin, Dr Kurt Crohn. Arthur decided to entrust his only son to Crohn's care, convinced that in the big city there was a chance a Jewish boy would attract less attention. Leslie was devastated to leave home but there seemed to be no other choice. 'It was very traumatic,' he recalls.

His father took him to a huge, gaunt building in a Berlin suburb. It seemed to stand in a mysterious world of its own making. The blank windows offered nothing. Inside, the long echoing corridors distorted the sound of the human voice. Leslie felt intimidated but bravely tried to disguise his sense of desolation. He knew his father was upset to leave him there. 'Don't worry. You're a Sunday's child. You'll make your way all right,' his father tried to reassure him. On many occasions Leslie would try to summon those words of comfort as though they could bestow special protection, but they were small consolation. As a young boy with no sister or parents close at hand he now felt utterly lost.[17]

Leslie found himself surrounded by genuine orphans and others like himself, who had been driven from their homes in other parts of Germany. He began to realise that he was not alone. The abuse that had forced him from his family was affecting others, too. Jewish schoolchildren from state schools had been vilified in a multitude of cruel ways: ordered out of class and then summoned and questioned on the lesson they had missed to 'prove' their stupidity, or made to eat their lunch in the toilet because they were 'dirty Jews'.[18]

Repeated persecution had instilled in them that they were part of an 'odious race' with 'devious minds' and that they were 'enemies of the people'. Leslie felt he had almost internalised the endless denigration. 'I took it for granted as a fact,' he recalls. By the time they reached the orphanage, some boys had become seriously disturbed. Leslie remembers children throwing tantrums or screaming hysterically, out of control; behaviours that he had never seen before. It was unnerving. There were children who had parents in concentration camps. Others had nothing; no one to care whether they lived or died.

For Leslie, the absence of the all-encompassing warmth and love of family life was like a deep physical pain. It felt as though he was broken and unmendable. But the director, Dr Crohn, who had himself been orphaned in childhood, understood the traumas and went out of his way to try to settle his troubled young charges. Leslie remembers one evening when he said goodnight, Dr Crohn stroked his hair gently. It was a fleeting gesture, gone in a second, but it filled Leslie with hope. This was a token of affection such as a parent might give and he felt comforted by it, as though he did matter after all.

One day Dr Crohn took a group of boys including Leslie to a concert in Berlin to hear Mendelsohn's *Elijah*. Looking back, Leslie marvels that the performance of this intensely Jewish work, by a Jewish composer, performed by a Jewish choir in the Oranienburgerstrasse synagogue in the heart of Berlin, was permitted. It was his first concert. There before him was a full symphony orchestra as well as a very large choir. Around him was an audience of hundreds in this richly ornamental setting built in ancient Moorish style. The lights dimmed and as the music started Leslie was profoundly stirred, held completely in the magical, all-encompassing sea of sound. The vast scale of the work and the magnificent chorus had a huge impact, the voices mingling as they soared into the great dome and reverberated around the great hall.[19]

Leslie listened attentively. It was sublime; like one passionate *cri de cœur* from the Jewish community of Berlin to the soul of Germany for the restoration of peace and humanity. There must still be hope. Listening to the music he felt enraptured, alive with joy.

*

Tante Anna was finding that of all the major British papers, she could most trust the *Manchester Guardian* for news of the escalating persecution in Nazi Germany. Reporting on the concentration camp system on 20 September 1935, shortly after the announcement of the Nuremberg laws, the *Guardian* concluded, 'there has been no improvement in the lot of prisoners . . . All the protest from the outside world has made no difference. Some of the prisoners have been in Dachau for two and a half years . . .' The prisoners had no prospect of release. The *Guardian* also hinted at a change in the type of prisoner; in addition to the political opposition such as communists and social democrats, there were 'Jews, tramps and ordinary criminals . . . The Jews include thirty who returned to Germany this year thinking it must be safe . . . the treatment of Jews is particularly terrible'.[20]

By the mid-1930s the concentration camp system was indeed changing. The many ad hoc camps that had sprung up in 1933, largely for the mass incarceration of Hitler's political enemies, were being closed or replaced. The concentration camp system was now under the control of the ruthless Heinrich Himmler, who, as head of the paramilitary SS or *Schutzstaffel,* and the dreaded Gestapo, or secret police, was rapidly forging a path for himself as one of the most powerful men in the Third Reich. The son of a Catholic schoolmaster, on first impressions Himmler could seem innocuous, almost dull. Yet this was the man who was centralising the concentration camp system with Dachau as the prototype, developing a system of forced labour in the camps and beginning to apply Nazi ideas on race and social engineering. With the political opposition crushed, Himmler aimed to tackle 'the enemy within'. This included those the Nazis deemed 'socially undesirable' such as homosexuals, the homeless and habitual criminals and especially those deemed 'racially degenerate': the Jews.[21]

Tante Anna was able to gain further insights into the changes in the camps through the network of British Quakers who still operated in Nazi Germany. Quakers were still endeavouring to negotiate the release of prisoners, or at least provide much-needed liaison. Corder Catchpool, who had already been arrested once by the Gestapo, and his colleague, William Hughes, were among those volunteers pressing Nazi officials for access to the camps. They were inundated with appeals from those whose relatives were imprisoned and knew of the brutality. Prisoners could be sent to 'the punishment cells' for any trivial misdemeanour and held for months on end. Those in the cells could suffer floggings and treatment so inhumane that some died, and the prisoners who returned were barely recognisable, often with festering wounds.[22]

In February 1935, Catchpool and Hughes were finally permitted to visit Dachau and to meet some prisoners, though never without the presence of guards. The Nazis were keen to show the Quakers features such as the prison library and, after some negotiation, they were permitted to see unoccupied punishment cells. They were shown 'small, dark cubicles equipped with leg irons,' recorded Catchpool. Although the SS were careful in what they revealed during the visit, the Quaker reports back to Bertha Bracey of the German Emergency Committee in London in the mid-1930s convey the evil they encountered.[23] Bertha Bracey agonised over whether to make their reports public, but held back for fear of harm to any named prisoners or that access might be denied for the British Quakers in Germany. Nonetheless, she passed on her information to the British Foreign Office.

In April 1935, Corder Catchpool was interrogated for a second time by the Gestapo in Berlin. 'You are deliberately undermining the purposes of the punishment we are directing against those who do not support the state,' he was warned. Catchpole defended himself by pointing out that he had never attempted to influence German people's views towards the Nazis and that he was dedicated to achieving Anglo-German friendship. The Quaker work was becoming dangerous, even for British nationals. Some of his colleagues were advised in no uncertain terms to leave the country.[24]

It was not long before Tante Anna had first-hand knowledge of the brutality in the concentration camps through her own family. In 1936 William succeeded in getting his daughter, Dorle, out of the country to Bunce Court. Tante Anna was relieved to see her twelve-year-old niece at last. She 'embraced and kissed me,' Dorle remembers, and proudly introduced her to everyone. Dorle felt embarrassed, not least because she had told her travelling companions that her name was Marianne, in honour of her best friend, Marianne Weil.

It took time before Tante Anna understood the special significance of Marianne for her niece. Before she left

Mannheim, Dorle had been playing one afternoon in her best friend's apartment. Marianne's father had been arrested and sent to Dachau concentration camp just a few days before. There was a knock on the door and Marianne's mother opened it to see a man dressed 'like a postman' carrying a large parcel. She signed the receipt and carried her package inside. A parcel was unexpected and exciting. Everyone gathered around to watch as she opened it.

It was difficult to open, giving time for extravagant expectations to develop. At first it was hard to comprehend what they were seeing. The wrappings of sacking did not inspire. It was nothing of any value: just a box of ashes. Slowly they understood. 'It was all that remained of her husband,' wrote Dorle.

There was no warning. No explanation. No account of what had happened. Mr Weil had been a well man just days before, and now his remains had been handed over like an ordinary, everyday object. Marianne and her mother were beside themselves with grief and shock. For Dorle, the sheer horror of that day would never leave her.[25]

4

'The Gestapo arrived early one morning'

Eleven-year-old Karl Grossfield, Austria, 1938

At Bunce Court, one solitary pupil, Eric Bourne, took it upon himself to defend the school against the rising tide of fascism. He marched around the school's borders with a replica of a rifle at the ready, poised 'to fire at any fascist who might have infiltrated the peaceful Kentish countryside'. To his twelve-year-old imagination, the rising fascist threat of 1936 was transformed into ever-present danger.

The older pupils took it in turns to read a single copy of each of the newspapers. They learned in alarm of Hitler's triumph in March 1936 as his army marched west into the demilitarised Rhineland, in flagrant violation of the Treaty of Versailles. His actions prompted such wild jubilation in the streets of Germany, 'it was as though Hitler had captured not just the Rhineland, but the German soul,' one pupil wrote later.[1] The rise of fascism in Europe continued to cast a long shadow. In May, the Italian fascist dictator, Benito Mussolini, gained control of Abyssinia in Africa. By July, fascist aggression had spread to Spain. Mussolini and Hitler backed the fascist leader, General Francisco Franco, against the Spanish republican government and the country erupted in civil war. Britain took no action against the fascist dictators.

But at Bunce Court, like some medieval knight errant, Eric was poised to act with honour as he prepared to defend the school's freedom. The current British prime minister, Stanley Baldwin, may not have understood the threat, but Eric most certainly did. Hitler was the man who had driven his father from Germany and split up his family. Eric policed the grounds, his make-believe uniform soon supplemented by a real Spanish republican soldier's tasselled cap, his most prized trophy from his father. The school, 'to its credit,' Eric writes, tolerated this eccentric behaviour 'until his fervour died down naturally'.[2]

For Tante Anna, the children's imaginary games often revealed their deepest fears. When 'valiant fighters from the Boy's Floor' engaged in 'Cottage Wars' or invaded each other's woodland camps they often acted out the threats that they had experienced in Nazi Germany.[3] With the menace of Hitler looming large over their lives, Tante Anna knew she must build strong roots in England. She could not contemplate the idea of sending a single child back 'to the conditions which obtain in Germany,' observed her niece, Dorle. Bunce Court must not fail. Whatever the future held, the school was the springboard from which the children would launch themselves on their adult lives. Tante Anna was determined to win the approval of British inspectors for the work they were doing and build the school's financial security. Looking back years later, Eric came to marvel at the richness of their experience at the school when they had so little. 'Bunce Court was a complex amalgam of humanism, the Quaker faith, liberal values and Judaism, brought together by the mind of a woman whose one purpose in life seemed to be to serve children,' he wrote. But what made this truly exceptional, he continued, was that all this happened while Bunce Court 'was in a permanent state of near bankruptcy'.[4]

Tante Anna was wrestling week by week with a severe shortage of funds. The deepening crisis for Jewish families in Germany was having severe repercussions. By the mid-1930s some parents had had a lifetime of hard-won assets seized or, like Eric's parents, were struggling to re-establish themselves in another country; others were in concentration camps. In addition, a growing number of new German parents wanted to send their children to Bunce Court but had no means of paying. Just the process of transferring money to educate German children abroad 'is beset with difficulties and uncertainties', observed Bertha Bracey, who tried to help. 'These are beyond our control and the most persistent efforts to find a solution have . . . in many cases failed altogether'.[5] Meanwhile worried parents in the neighbouring countries of Austria, France and Belgium began to seek places for their children at Bunce Court but could not guarantee payment. Anna turned to the School Council for help, but members were opposed to taking too many children 'without definite financial arrangements'. Tante Anna was finding it 'humanly hard to bear'.[6]

In February 1937, Tante Anna wrote again to the British school inspectors inviting them to visit. Bunce Court now had ten English pupils, she pointed out, 'and it seems more and more important to become a recognised school'. Sensing their hesitancy, she asked 'whether it would make a difference in their decision if we succeeded in buying the property?' The records show that almost four years after her arrival, the British inspectors were still unwilling to make a 'Full Inspection for the purposes of Recognition'. 'I see very little proof in these figures that the supply of pupils is likely to be sufficient to maintain a reasonably large school,' Mr Hankin wrote on 31 May 1937 to the Chief Inspector of

Schools, Mr Duckworth. 'There is no reason to think that Germany will continue to export children, hence I feel the Full Inspection ought to be postponed for another year or two until its future is more secured . . .'[7]

Tante Anna's struggle to keep the school afloat was completely reliant on the goodwill of her staff, since she could pay them little more than pocket money. It is perhaps a measure of Anna's passion for her cause that by 1937, she had drawn around her a full team of eleven teachers of high calibre, almost achieving the equal balance that British inspectors required, with six German and five British members of staff. Some of her talented staff received tempting offers elsewhere, such as Hanna Bergas. Hanna's cousin, Helmut Schneider, was creating a school of his own in the Italian Alps and wanted her to help run it. For Hanna, it was an agonising choice. She was close to her cousin but Tante Anna was creating something unique: Bunce Court was a vocation, an inspirational way of life that could transform children's lives.

Tante Anna's unusual mission was even attracting staff from Germany who were not in danger of antisemitism, such as the new school cook, Gretel Heidt, who according to one pupil 'detested the Nazis'.[8] Gretel, her blond hair neatly tied back in a bun, was very petite and slim, but her larger-than-life presence was felt throughout the school. Her cooking was exceptional but so too was her temper. She could throw extraordinary tantrums in short order. Should any luckless child on kitchen duty fail to meet her high standards of food preparation or cleanliness they could find themselves at the sharp end of a volatile outburst.

Far from this counting against her, Tante Anna soon found Gretel was immensely popular. The children were queuing up to help her. Nothing was more exciting than to work in the kitchen, the scullery, the bread pantry, the milk pantry, the main pantry . . . The temperamental cook proved to be warm-hearted and cheerful, with a deep interest in the children. Whenever she had the means, there was a tantalising aroma of doughnuts or some other baking emanating from the kitchen. One boy remembers waiting by the kitchen window to ask, 'Is there cream today?' If you were lucky, he says, 'she would hand out the ladle and you could lick the spoon if she had finished cooking.' As she grew into something of a mother figure for the children, Gretel won her own special nickname: 'Heidtsche'.[9] But however talented, even Heidtsche could not conjure up meals without supplies. Despite her dedicated team, Tante Anna was fast reaching the point where the continued existence of the school was in doubt, 'in the face of almost insurmountable difficulties'.[10] The larder was down to one sack of cocoa.

Tante Anna threw herself into an extensive fundraising lecture tour to raise awareness of her refugee school. With her thick spectacles and homely air she may not have had the confident look of the professional speaker, but there was something about her unselfish vision and determination to help the refugee children that inspired her audience. She won support from refugee charities in London and sometimes complete strangers came forward to help. At the end of one talk, Anna was approached by an elegant Anglo-American, Iris Origo, who was married to an Italian count. Iris had recently lost her seven-year-old only son to meningitis and was keen to help suffering children. Fired by Anna's ideas, the countess offered to act as guarantor for ten refugee children to attend Bunce Court. 'In short order a cheque arrived from her for 1,500 English pounds,' wrote Paula.[11] For Anna, such moments made all the difference.

Tante Anna could also take heart from the children's responses. After months of the staff giving everything they could to the school, the children wanted to give something back. The novel concept of teachers being 'off-duty' was finally introduced, Hanna Bergas recalled. At last, they could enjoy a day off. 'We had been available to the children all the time which was of course good, even necessary to create a home,' she wrote. 'Finally it became possible to read, to write a letter or go away for a few hours.'

The children decided to do even more for those who cared for them and voted to test 'self-government' for a day. They would run the school while all the teachers took a complete break away, except for a nurse in the isolation hut. The pupils created their own constitution for Bunce Court, 'modelled on the Weimar Republic crossed with the House of Commons,' recalled one boy, Peter Stoll. Having seen what their country looked like without democracy, they were keen to give everyone a voice and a vote. 'Motions were moved and debated with considerable eloquence, however for some mysterious reason they were always defeated,' continued Stoll. Nonetheless, the boys and girls planned their day in charge down to the last detail: who would teach, who would supervise the practical tasks, even 'who would arbitrate possible quarrels,' observed Hanna. 'When we returned the children were elated, but obviously exhausted as they sat down with us bubbling over with stories of their day,' she wrote. Democracy was hard work.

The children not only took on their daily chores uncomplainingly, they relished the work of enhancing their school and were impatient for more projects. One idea that fired up all the pupils was the creation of their own open-air theatre to entertain their sponsors. The children chose a site near the tennis courts set against a handsome row of cedars and helped the teachers draw the architectural plans, but, recalled Tante Anna, 'no one could imagine how difficult it would be to remove the necessary cubic feet of earth'. Mountains of earth had to be carted away before the terracing could begin: a large semicircle for the audience, five rows high, providing seating for three hundred guests. 'It took almost a year to complete this huge job,' she wrote. Despite this, digging the amphitheatre became the most favourite of the afternoon tasks. The very idea of it caught the children's imagination. Any child who was brave enough could claim the stage, dazzle the audience and get a standing ovation for a few glorious minutes.

The whole school was caught up in the flurry of excitement for their first open day with their own amphitheatre. Rehearsals were in full swing for *The Birds* by Aristophanes. 'Costumes, props, electric lighting, and all technical necessities were planned and made by the boys and girls,' wrote Tante Anna. When the big day came all three hundred seats were filled. Tante Anna introduced the chairman of the School Council, Norman Bentwich, to open the proceedings. As the play began, Hanna Bergas was enchanted: 'What could have been more natural and delightful than seeing these fantastically dressed bird-children fluttering, hopping and crawling out of bushes and trees which formed the curtain.'[12]

Encouraged by what they could achieve together, the children planned to dig a swimming pool and began to raise funds for their venture by organising sponsored events at the school. A class of fifteen-year-olds decided to keep pigs, with a view to making the school even more self-sufficient. The growing herd of pigs, fed entirely on kitchen waste, soon made a profit, not to mention supplying the school with one of the children's favourite kind of German sausage, *Würstchen*. The class in charge of the pigs was soon in a position to buy the school a car, duly nicknamed the '*Würstchen* car'.[13]

News of the refugee school's adventures perhaps reached the inspectors, and there might have been unwelcome talk; in any case, in July 1937 the Chief Inspector of Schools no less, H.M. Inspector Mr C.I.M. Duckworth, decided to investigate the Bunce Court rumours. With more animals than children and excavations in the grounds, this school sounded far from textbook. In early October, a panel of experts duly arrived for a 'Full Inspection'.

Over the course of a week, Mr J. Hales, Mr A. Kerslake and Miss A. Philip interviewed children and staff and took notes of everything that went on in the school. They saw the open-air theatre, the carefully cultivated vegetable garden, the huge flock of five hundred chickens, the growing herd of pigs – all tended by the children – not to mention the repairs to the fabric of the school itself. Under the guidance of Hans Meyer and other teachers, the children had fitted wardrobes and cupboards in their bedrooms, converted a shed into a gym, laid tennis courts and an athletics track. In addition the children talked of polishing the floors, washing the windows and stoking the fires, as well as 'a grand "clean-up" of the whole school' on Friday afternoons. Was this 'Dotheboys Hall'? 'Did you do practical work over in Germany too?' one incredulous inspector asked a young boy. 'Yes, sir,' he replied earnestly. 'But there, it was part of our education. Here it is a necessity.'[14]

The inspectors wanted to satisfy themselves that this was not harmful to the pupils' schoolwork. They observed the teaching and saw the incongruous mixture of informality and discipline. The headmistress had raised funds for three new classrooms in the grounds with large doors that opened out onto the lawn, the classes in the garden adding to the casual air. All lessons were more like seminars, taking the form of a conversation between the children and the teacher, with usually just six or seven pupils in each. Despite the 'sound and stimulating teaching', which was arousing a 'lively keenness' in the pupils, the inspectors observed dismissively that 'the writing in the exercise books is slipshod and untidy'. But even they could not fault the exam pass rate.

Tante Anna proudly showed them the school record. At the end of their first year, thirteen boys and girls had been ready to sit the British final examination, the School Certificate. They had had just a year to master their subjects in the English language. Nine had passed, three with distinction. 'This gave us great courage,' Tante Anna explained to the inspectors. Since then they had not looked back, with successive final-year children passing the School Certificate with good marks. The inspectors were surprised to find that on top of all their academic and practical achievements, the children seemed to be very knowledgeable on the arts, too, chattering happily of plays, recitals, art history, painting and above all music. During their visit, 'the whole school collected on the staircase and in the hall one evening and listened eagerly to a recital of classical music.'[15]

How was the quietly spoken headmistress doing it? There was no governing body. The whole responsibility rested on her. Nor was there any formal system of keeping order and discipline. Even something seriously naughty, Eric explained solemnly, attracted no worse a punishment than 'missing dessert at mealtimes'. Yet the inspectors found the children were very self-disciplined, with a sense of purpose and clear school routine; in fact their day started at 7 a.m. in all weathers with a gruelling round of exercise on the lawn. Despite this, boys like Eric talked happily of the great freedom at the school; Eric described Bunce Court as 'his true home and family'. The headmistress, too, appeared something of a contradiction. Modest and quick to highlight the efforts of her dedicated staff though she was, it was also clear that she didn't miss much. No detail of the school was beneath her notice. She had not written any paper on the philosophy of her school. Nor could she point to any formula, although she was very fond of a particular quote from Ruskin: 'The entire object of true education is to make people not merely do the right things, but enjoy the right things, not merely industrious, but to love industry, not merely learned, but to love knowledge, not merely pure, but to love purity, not merely just, but to hunger and thirst after justice.'[16]

The experienced inspectors were 'amazed by what could be done in spite of very limited facilities,' Tante Anna observed. They could see for themselves that these children who had arrived in Britain with no English were passing exams, learning important life skills, putting on plays and helping to run their own school. More importantly perhaps, they also saw how the children were all infused with the idea of working hard, doing well and giving something back, despite the emotional pain of being far from home and without their parents. Even former pupils, who turned up with sleeping bags in early October to celebrate the school's fourth anniversary in Britain, expressed strong positive feelings for Bunce Court. There was no denying that the once-shabby English manor house was now a haven for refugee children.

At last the British inspectors were won round. 'The school may leave much to be desired in its inadequate resources,' they concluded, but they admired 'the spirit' of Bunce Court. Anna's personality 'plays a big role in giving the school its attractive character'. Despite its unusual methods and lack of funds, Tante Anna's refugee school was formally recognised as 'efficient' by the Board of Education, holding its own alongside other top Kent schools such as Maidstone Grammar and the Rochester Cathedral Grammar.[17] The inspectors left convinced, 'as I always had been' wrote Anna, 'that it was far more the personality, the liveliness and the interest of the teacher' than the resources around them 'that made things work so well'. It was a triumph. Tante Anna had successfully integrated Bunce Court School into the British educational system while retaining its essential uniqueness.

She did not see the inspectors' unpublished comments. 'The headmistress is a most capable woman and fine character. Driven from two countries (US and Germany) for political reasons, she betrays no thought of complaint on her own account but gives herself entirely to work for the children and the school. She is large minded and philosophic but also practical and can deal with large problems and small details. She reigns in a calm undemonstrative way over the entire establishment, including six men teachers (four of them English) and all appear loyal to her.'[18]

Not long after Tante Anna's great success with the British inspectors, shocking developments on the continent served to underline the very purpose of Bunce Court. They would have devastating consequences for her original school at Herrlingen.

*

Eleven-year-old Karl Grossfield, who lived in Vienna, did not, at first, understand the significance on 12 March 1938 when Nazi troops crossed into Austria. Without a shot being fired, Austria as an independent country was wiped off the map of Europe. 'Hitler is breaking the bonds of the Versailles Treaty one by one,' reported Pathé. 'Today comes another mighty moment as Hitler carries Nazi expansion across the borders of Germany into the land of his birth . . .' The annexation, or *Anschluss*, of Austria brought seven million German-speaking people into the Third Reich and pro-Nazi crowds packed the streets to cheer the military cavalcade. Even children waved little swastika flags or ran alongside the endless stream of trucks. Hitler's reception in Austria became a victory parade. When he drove into Vienna on 15 March, it took three lines of troops to hold back the jubilant population that crammed onto the wide boulevards. Austria had been swallowed up into Greater Germany. It was a move that plunged Austria's 200,000 Jews into crisis. Nazi supporters within Austria had been stoking hatred of the Jews for several years and with annexation, an antisemitic frenzy was unleashed. Within hours, Jews were being hunted down.

In the sleepy suburb of Lainz, four miles from the centre of Vienna, schoolboy Karl had no sense of the danger moving ever closer. The radio, which had been playing Viennese waltzes, suddenly blared out endless Nazi songs and speeches instead, but to Karl it had no meaning. His father Marcus, the eternal optimist, reassured him. 'This will all blow over,' he said. 'It's just short-term.' His mother, Miriam, also saw no reason for alarm. 'Looking back,' says Karl, 'it was a disastrous day for our family.'

It did not take long for the Nazis to reach the suburbs. Early one morning there was loud knocking on their front door that woke the family. Karl had no sense of fear. Everything happened so fast and was 'very calm'.

There was a stranger at the door. To Karl's eyes, he seemed quite ordinary. The stranger explained that he had come for Karl's father, who was to leave immediately 'for his own protection'. Karl does not remember his father making a fuss or seeming frightened. He got dressed and was gone with the stranger. It was only much later that Karl understood this was the Gestapo and realised what a shock it must have been for his father, who had trusted all would be well. 'But that was wholly wrong because lawyers, like my father, were the most hated group among the Jews,' he explains. He remembers being told that his father was in a concentration camp, 'but that didn't mean anything. I had no clear image of a concentration camp in my mind.' Innocent and trusting, with no experience of racial hatred, he was sure his forceful Jewish mother would put this right.[19]

But Austrian mothers like Miriam were up against a new phase in the escalation of Nazi violence against the Jews. Austrian Jews had to adapt almost overnight to anti-semitic laws that in Germany had been introduced over five years. The changes were introduced with ruthless efficiency against a backdrop of terror and mob fury. Sinister disappearances started at once, removing Jewish citizens like Marcus Grossfield, who dared not protest as they were taken to destinations from which they did not always return. Invariably the dreaded knock on the door came at night. In less than a week, a staggering 70,000 people in Austria had been imprisoned, mostly the political opposition and Jews. A disused railway station in Vienna was hurriedly turned into a temporary concentration camp.[20] By daylight, among the swastikas and Nazi banners that festooned Vienna's wide boulevards, there were the telltale signs of night-time violence: burned-out buildings where once there had been Jewish shops or businesses. The scale of antisemitic violence unleashed in Vienna was like 'opening the gates of the underworld,' according to one observer.

Behind the targeted mass arrests was one of the most sinister organisations in the Nazi hierarchy: the German Security Service, or SD, the shadowy intelligence arm of the SS. Heinrich Himmler had charged a former naval officer, Reinhard Heydrich, to develop and lead the SD; he was a man of such driven ruthlessness even Hitler was said to call him 'the man with the iron heart'. Heydrich's SD agents had arrived in Vienna equipped with a list of Nazi 'enemies' that had been carefully compiled in advance, including the addresses and assets of many prominent and wealthy Jews. By August, Heydrich had tasked his deputy, Adolf Eichmann, to run the Central Office for Jewish Emigration in the Rothschild Palais in Vienna. This SD agency functioned as a 'conveyer belt' system, forcibly stripping Jews of their assets before granting the necessary emigration papers. It was state-organised theft, run like a well-oiled machine. 'It all went like an assembly line,' Eichmann boasted to his superiors. Terrified Jews were summoned to the Nazi Central Office and, with callous efficiency, made to sign over their assets to the German Reich so that everything appeared legal and correct. The ever-present fear of concentration camps focused minds.[21]

In retrospect, Karl sees shining through those months in Vienna the remarkable fortitude and spirit of his mother. The daughter of a rabbi, Miriam Grossfield had a natural authority and commanded respect. Determined to save her family, she discreetly explored every avenue of escape for her four children, though she herself would not leave without her husband – she 'was very much concerned with getting him out,' says Karl.

In front of her children, Miriam was always calm. 'She did not encourage us to feel frightened,' recalls Karl. All the shops in their suburb now displayed Nazi flags but he still went to the sweet shop. 'To us it was just a difference of decoration,' he says. He took in his stride being ordered to leave his school and attend a Jewish school instead. There were changes at home, too. Miriam tried to prepare her children for whatever might lie ahead. They all had high expectations of going to university, and Karl remembers her explaining that this was now closed to them. 'You must learn a trade,' she said. 'Always remember it's important to get qualifications so that your trade can be recognised.' She engaged a shoe repairer and a chocolate maker to teach them. 'I remember the iced chocolate we made. It was absolutely delicious,' recalls Karl, who was then still unaware of the danger. He remained innocent as Miriam solemnly warned them that the family might have to be split up. They would almost certainly have to emigrate. Karl adapted to all the changes. 'It did not occur to me that any of this was unusual,' he recalls. 'I took the world as it was.'

Not long after the disappearance of his father, Karl was at home alone with his thirteen-year-old sister Erica when there was another knock on the door. The Nazis had come for Erica. When Karl's fifteen-year-old brother, Herbert, returned, 'he was horrified that Erica had gone'. Herbert went searching for her. There was a commotion out on the streets and he found Erica at the centre of it, on her hands and knees, being forced to scrub the pavement with other Jews. Herbert offered himself in her place, only to be ordered to clean the streets, too.[22]

The scrubbing of the streets became an iconic image of the ritual humiliation of Vienna's Jews. Some were ordered to put on their Sunday best and found themselves kicked or beaten with horsewhips until they fell in the dirty water. Others were required to clean public toilets. Jews could be forced to dip their cloths 'into buckets of hydrochloric acid with their bare hands,' recalled one Austrian schoolgirl. 'The Nazis whipped up all the primitive instincts of the masses.' Old men could be forced to do strenuous exercises before they fell on the pavement, their humiliation entertainment for the jeering crowd, who would shout abuse such as '*Saujud*', 'Jew pig', as they spat at the victims or even threw stones and dirt.[23] 'Absolute fear ran through everybody,' wrote one Jewish resident. 'You cannot understand it unless you have experienced it. The fear of walking the streets, the fear of every door . . .'[24]

Hours elapsed before Karl's brother and sister returned. 'Erica wasn't frightened,' Karl thought, but he does remember her describing the reaction of the onlookers. It was as though Vienna had forgotten overnight that Jewish people were former neighbours and friends. Erica saw one friendly shopkeeper who cried to see the Jewish schoolchildren humiliated in this way, but others in the crowd were silent. No one dared come to their aid.

*

Tante Anna soon had first-hand accounts of events in Austria from those at the forefront of relief efforts. 'Germans troops poured into the city . . . like the Goths bursting into ancient Rome,' observed Norman Bentwich. 'Jews killed in the streets, the sense of utter hopelessness . . .' Ignoring Foreign Office warnings, Bentwich had set off to Vienna shortly after the *Anschluss* hoping to help the Jewish community and was stunned at what he found. He heard Hermann Göring, one of the most powerful men in Germany, proclaim 'to a howling audience' that Vienna should be made '"*Judenrein* (Free of Jews). We don't like Jews; they don't like us. They shall go."' Turned out of house and home, subject to arbitrary arrest at any hour of day or night, there was panic in the Jewish population. 'Suicide took its daily toll,' Bentwich recorded, 'and thousands were threatened with starvation.' People besieged the consulates in the hope of escape. The queue outside the American embassy alone was a quarter of a mile long. Those waiting in line were easy targets for SS round-ups or the random violence of the SA. The position was 'more catastrophic even than we had judged,' Bentwich concluded.[25]

News of the horror unfolding in Austria spread to the Jewish community in Germany. Tante Anna's original school in Herrlingen was not that far from the Austrian border and day after day, parents called Hugo Rosenthal to withdraw their children, fearing they, too, would become trapped. Student numbers plummeted. 'After the German invasion of Austria, the new term started with more than twenty empty places,' Rosenthal wrote. In the following months 'our roll-calls became a kind of measure of the rate of Jewish emigration'. By the summer of 1938 Herrlingen was down to twenty-five pupils, from over a hundred the year before.

Hugo Rosenthal and his wife, Judith, recognised that it was only a matter of time before the school would have to close. 'The island of refuge' that they had hoped to build was beginning to feel more like a 'ghetto on the hill'. Rosenthal had no intention of leaving until his last remaining children had found a way to safety. 'We must not give in to despair,' he wrote. He now felt strongly that 'we must continue our work as long as we are given any opportunity to do so.'[26] But living without hope was not living. Tante Anna felt helpless hearing such words. She was anxious to help, but how was this to be achieved?

Intense pressure to find more places at Bunce Court was coming from all directions. Tante Anna's loyal ally, Hanna Bergas, had eventually resigned her position at Bunce Court to help her cousin, Helmut Schneider, create a new school at Vigiljoch in the Italian Alps. Even in this remote mountain spot, Hanna did not escape the turmoil created by Hitler. She had only just settled into her new position when the Italian school was also plunged into crisis. Not long after the *Anschluss,* Hitler paid a week-long state visit to Mussolini in Italy. The world looked on as in early May 1938 the two fascist dictators, strutting like Caesars, paraded their friendship and solidarity from the grand palaces of Rome. Following Hitler's visit, Mussolini also introduced racial laws against the Jews. All Jews who had arrived in Italy after 1919 had to leave by June 1939. As the school's director, Helmut Schneider 'had to present himself *every day* at the local municipal office,' Hanna recorded in her memoirs; this was a trek of several hours down the mountainside. Hanna and her cousin knew their Italian venture now had no future.

Hanna was deeply touched to receive a letter from Tante Anna. She knew that many German teachers were also applying for work at Bunce Court and 'the choice from among applicants was great', but Tante Anna had not forgotten Hanna's dedicated work. 'There will always be a place for you at Bunce Court,' she reassured her. Anna also offered places for five children from the Italian school. Anna wanted to help Helmut Schneider, too, but this was not so easy.

While Hanna's entry permit for 'gainful employment' was still valid, Anna wrote, with the flood of immigrants to Britain the rules had changed and work permits were only being given to 'domestic' workers. She could only promise Schneider work as a gardener. But it was a lifeline. 'These were most valuable offers,' Hanna wrote, 'that we accepted with profound gratitude.'[27]

As the refugee crisis on the continent deepened, there were anxious conversations among the teachers at Bunce Court. What did the Austrian *Anschluss* mean for parents trapped in Germany? Was it safe for the children to go home in the holidays? European countries were tightening their border controls and protesting to Germany over the sudden illegal influx of impoverished Jews. Although Britain had introduced a visa system after the *Anschluss* which had the effect of increasing the number of refugees admitted, most countries had strict immigration quotas and Jews in Greater Germany were becoming trapped. The world was rapidly becoming divided into two parts, 'places where they [Jews] can not live, and places where they can not enter,' one Jewish leader, Chaim Weizmann, had famously declared.[28] In June 1938, the American president, Franklin D. Roosevelt, seemed like a saviour when he proposed an international conference to find a solution to Europe's refugee problem. The conference 'would recognise the urgency of emigrations,' claimed Roosevelt, and acknowledge the dire plight of Austrian and German Jews.

There were 'almost Messianic hopes,' observed Norman Bentwich, who joined the delegates of thirty-two countries who descended on the French spa town of Évian on 6 July for the conference. The setting on the shores of Lake Geneva was enchanting. The hopes were extravagant. But days passed, meetings dragged on; nothing was resolved. Government representatives feared an antisemitic backlash in their own countries, and others pointed out that Nazi emigration rules that stripped Jews of all they possessed forced them to become a burden on the taxpayer of any host country. The British, intent on a policy of appeasement, argued that increasing immigration quotas might actually encourage further Nazi violence against the Jews.[29]

Tante Anna followed the debacle at Évian with mounting disbelief. 'No progress,' reported the *Manchester Guardian* on 9 July. 'Conference members have been disappointingly cautious and negative.' Delegates were wary of upsetting the German government in a climate of impending war. The Americans did make one concession, agreeing to simplify their bureaucracy so that the US quota of 30,000 German immigrants each year could be more easily fulfilled. With the exception of the Dominican Republic, all other countries refused to relax immigration rules or even tightened them further. Of the thirty-two countries that sent delegates, not one created a significant new opening for the refugees.[30] Tante Anna felt the strain for her staff and children alike, who 'feared for the lives of those they loved abroad,' she wrote.

Tante Anna was determined to find a way to expand Bunce Court and threw herself into another round of fundraising, hoping to build a large extension. During 1938 as pupil numbers increased rapidly, Tante Anna had extra practical help in the capable form of her younger sister, Bertha. Bertha had joined the school as the unpaid school matron in return for free schooling for her children and it fell to her to find more space within the existing accommodation. Bertha's room overlooking the gardens became 'the nerve centre of

Bunce Court,' observed her niece, Dorle. Everything was presided over with discreet efficiency, from the state of the linen cupboards to darning socks and stitching repairs in worn clothes.

Among the new arrivals, Tante Anna was pleased to welcome her nephew Hermann, now reunited with his sister, Dorle. Their father, William, had finally managed to escape the clutches of the Gestapo in Mannheim and settle in London. Hermann – the boy who only recently had been classified as 'subhuman' in Germany for the purposes of having experimental diphtheria treatment – blossomed at Bunce Court, every inch the normal schoolboy in the rough and tumble of the children's games.[31]

New beginnings, new life; it almost seemed a miracle. The children had such a capacity to adapt. As Tante Anna walked around the grounds she saw children enthusiastically clearing the grounds and moving shrubs where the foundations for the new dormitories were to be built. Another new boy, fifteen-year-old Richard Sonnenfeldt, led an enterprising team of older pupils to bring electricity to Gwynne's nursery, which was still only lit with candles and kerosene lamps, under the supervision of the maths teacher. 'Had we not been young with exciting new lives, we would have been paralysed with fear,' Richard wrote later in his memoirs; Bunce Court 'was the only England I knew and it became a spiritual home I never had known existed, a home I loved then and have loved ever since.'[32]

*

The vast majority of Jewish families in the Third Reich who had once trusted that the German people or foreign powers would rein in Hitler's ambitions were now finding they were losing control over their fate. Among them were Leslie Brent's parents, Arthur and Charlotte, who were driven out of Köslin during 1938 because life 'had become untenable,' Leslie observes. Twelve-year-old Leslie was still living in the orphanage at Pankow in Berlin and his parents joined him there, to be nearer their son and hoping to escape attention in the large city. They were able to visit Leslie at the orphanage at weekends, bringing his sister, Eva, too. Leslie was always thrilled to see them. These precious moments when they could be together were anticipated all week. But unspoken fears and their strained circumstances invaded the family reunions, although Leslie's parents concealed their difficulties, trying hard 'to behave normally'.

At the time, Leslie did not understand the extent of their troubles. By the late 1930s, his parents were 'totally impoverished,' he explains. His father had given up his business and taken work in a timber factory despite pitiably low wages. Their flat in Berlin was tiny. 'I can only marvel at their bravery and fortitude.'[33] Efforts to find someone overseas who would vouch for them, sponsoring their visa applications, had all but come to nothing. Arthur had written to every possible contact in Britain and America explaining his family's predicament; no one was able to help. For all the fine words and moral outrage of other countries, none would open their doors. Arthur and Charlotte could see that the failure of other countries to respond to the Jewish refugee emergency was almost like a vindication for Hitler. Triumphant headlines in the Nazi Party newspaper, *Völkischer Beobachter*, summed up the gloating perspective of the Nazi leadership. The 'Jewish problem' was not Germany's fault. 'Nobody wants them.'[34]

The European crisis that erupted over the late summer of 1938 proved to be a further crushing blow. Having annexed Austria, Hitler extended his territorial demands. He wanted the Sudetenland, a wide strip of Czechoslovakia that bordered Germany and Austria, home to a further three million German-speakers. German troops massed at the Czechoslovakian border. The Czech army mobilised, relying on Czechoslovakia's alliance with France and on military support from Britain. Europe was catapulted to the brink of war. The newsreels conveyed the imminent threat. There was the all-powerful dictator in the vast square at the Nuremberg rally of September 1938, glorying in the creation of Greater Germany and claiming the Sudetenland, too. The triumphant crowd roared their ovation: 'We will follow our leader, we will follow our leader . . .'

For Arthur and countless others like him, the British response dashed all hopes of checking Hitler. By now, Neville Chamberlain had taken over as British prime minister and he remained committed to appeasement. Hitler took brink-manship to new heights, threatening war. In London, gas masks were distributed and trenches dug. In Berlin, on 27 September there was a vast military parade. Crisis meetings culminated on 29 September in Munich. Britain, France and Italy ceded the Sudetenland to Hitler. Europe had a reprieve but at the cost of caving in to the dictator's demands. This may have been peace 'with honour' for Neville Chamberlain in Britain, but for people like Arthur, the Munich Agreement not only betrayed the Czechs, but strengthened Hitler's hand, empowering the forces of tyranny. The Rhineland, Austria, and now the Sudetenland; for many in Germany, Hitler was infallible, a godlike figure.

Trapped in Berlin, Leslie's family was finding that their

hopes of a way out were fast becoming extinguished. Like so many other trapped Jewish families, it was impossible for them to know what to do or where to go. The threat of further violence against Jews was everywhere. One evening in the early autumn of 1938 it became clear to Arthur that even the orphanage sanctuary he had found for his son was no longer safe. A large mob of Hitler Youth and Nazi thugs gathered outside the Pankow orphanage, spoiling for a fight, chanting obscenities against Jews. Inside, Leslie and his friend, Fred, heard the sound of the heavy front doors under attack. Despite heavy battering they did not give way. Then they heard the sounds of the rabble surging to the back of the building. Older boys rushed to defend the back gate. Surely it could not hold?

Fred urged Leslie to hide. Escape was impossible. The noise below froze thought. 'Let's go to the top,' Fred cried, running up the stairs. Fred revealed his secret hiding place, squeezed under the rafters of the roof, where it seemed to Leslie he had hidden before, almost certainly to break the rules and smoke. The two boys climbed in and lay stock-still in the darkness listening to the ominous sounds. Even their breathing sounded too loud.

The back gates soon gave way. The rabble were streaming through the rear courtyard. The noises now were inside the Jewish orphanage. The sound of things breaking was so close at hand it was as though everything was being smashed and broken. First the basement, then the ground floor . . . Leslie and Fred listened 'with beating hearts', not daring to move, as the appalling sounds of the orphanage being ransacked below drew ever nearer. [35]

5

'I did not trust a soul'

*Thirteen-year-old Ruth Boronow, on Kristallnacht,
Germany, 1938*

The attack on the Jewish orphanage at Pankow in Berlin where Leslie Brent was staying proved to be a mere dress rehearsal for an event without parallel in 1930s Germany, one which proved to be an irrevocable turning point for Jews in the Third Reich. The ink was barely dry on the Munich Agreement, expanding Greater Germany's south-eastern border into Czechoslovakia, when trouble brewing on Germany's eastern border with Poland came to a head. The crisis was precipitated by the Nazi leadership, who turned on Jews in Germany of Polish descent.

On 28 October 1938, schoolgirl Mia Schaff had just celebrated her seventh birthday when her safe, happy world collapsed. 'It was about four a.m. in the morning. There was a knock on the door,' she recalls. She heard unfamiliar voices inside the flat. Strangers were talking to her parents. 'I remember standing up and calling out, "What's going on?"' Mia sensed there was something very wrong.

Her father, Oscar, appeared. 'He gave me a hug,' she remembers. For a fleeting moment all seemed to be well but then 'he said goodbye, told me to be a good girl, and went.' Through the hallway, she glimpsed two men waiting to escort her father away. Later she learned it was the Gestapo. Suddenly he was gone. 'I was crying. I was sobbing. I was a great one for crying,' Mia remembers.

Although they lived in Berlin, Mia's father, Oscar Schaff, came originally from a large Polish Jewish family. He had moved to Germany as a young man and proved so successful in business that he now owned two large apartment blocks in a fashionable part of town. After his disappearance Mia's mother, Ida, tried urgently to trace him. To a seven-year-old child what had happened was incomprehensible. If strangers could come in the night for her father, would her mother vanish, too? The world was suddenly very frightening. Mia and her older siblings became 'always afraid, very, very, very nervous children'. After their father's disappearance, Ida kept her children indoors. 'My mother locked us in on many occasions and told us not to answer the door.' But even the locked door was not enough. They were always listening, although they didn't know what for. That made it worse.[1]

Mia's father was caught up in the next brutal escalation in Nazi antisemitic policy. Without warning, in late October 1938 the Gestapo ordered over 12,000 Polish-born Jews in Germany from their homes, herded them into trains at gunpoint and dumped them at the Polish border near Zbaszyn. But Polish border guards were under orders to prevent them entering the country. Anticipating a flood of refugees from the Third Reich, the Polish government had already taken pre-emptive measures, stripping Jewish Poles who had settled in Germany and Austria of their Polish citizenship. More than eight thousand Jews became trapped at the German–Polish boundary in no man's land, many stripped of all they had, with no means of finding food and shelter. After being evicted from his home, Oscar Schaff found himself forbidden to return to the life he had created in Germany.

It took time before Mia's family learned of Oscar's fate, but there was one teenage German Jew of Polish descent who knew exactly what was happening and was intent on revenge. Seventeen-year-old Herschel Grynszpan in Paris simmered with rage at the injustice heaped on his family. His sister, Berta, and parents were among thousands trapped at the Polish–German border without food or shelter in freezing rain, the conditions so desperate that a few were driven to suicide. Herschel bought a pistol and on 7 November went to the German embassy in Paris, posing as a messenger with a package to deliver. 'In the name of twelve thousand persecuted Jews,' Gynszpan cried as he shot a German diplomat, Ernst vom Rath.[2]

As vom Rath's life hung in the balance the fate of thousands of Jews across the Third Reich was being planned. The Nazi leadership had long been seeking a pretext for a violent pogrom against the Jews, and when vom Rath died of his injuries at 5.30 p.m. on 9 November, Joseph Goebbels, Reich minister for propaganda, swung into action. Goebbels turned the random act of desperation of one distressed Jewish teenager into part of an international Jewish conspiracy. The Jews were 'murderers', Goebbels proclaimed, as he insisted vom Rath's death was orchestrated 'by World Jewry'. Nazi revenge was swift and brutal. The next few days would prove a watershed for Jews across the Third Reich.[3]

*

In Berlin at the Pankow orphanage, thirteen-year-old Leslie Brent knew little of the orgy of destruction unfolding around him. But Dr Kurt Crohn, the director of the Pankow orphanage, was expecting trouble. He was a man of great humanity who had dedicated his life to looking after the orphans under his care; it was hard for him to know how he could best protect his young charges. There had been a sense of foreboding in the city for days as vom Rath clung to life. Nazi newspapers had stoked up the hatred, promising that 'Jews will get what they deserve'. In the hours following vom Rath's death, Dr Crohn glanced out anxiously from the uppermost windows of the Pankow orphanage, but it was hard to tell if anything was amiss. There was an eerie silence.

At around 1 a.m. on 10 November the uproar began. Dr Crohn saw gangs of Brownshirts and their supporters roaming the street below, many armed with weapons, truncheons, axes, daggers or even guns. The marauding gangs were smoking stolen cigarettes and carrying plundered goods away. Jewish shops in the nearby thoroughfare were being smashed and looted. As Dr Crohn made his rounds to check the orphanage was secure, the children in his care were still sleeping soundly. He had nowhere safe to take them. They had already come under attack only a few weeks before, but this time the violence against the Jews would be on a different scale.

Dr Crohn was soon alerted to attacks on other orphanages in Berlin. At the Auerbach orphanage, staff received an ominous warning. 'Something bad will happen tonight.' Not long after this, storm troopers battered down the door of the Auerbach orphanage intent on arson. 'Out. We are setting fire to the building,' they shouted. The terrified younger children were unable to leave quickly. The Nazi thugs had cans of petrol and it was only with great difficulty that some of the staff and older boys managed to convince them that any blaze would spread to neighbouring buildings. The mob eventually retreated, still intent on destruction. Secretly they blew out the sanctuary light in the synagogue and opened the gas valves. An explosion was only narrowly avoided when the children smelled gas. As the night progressed, Crohn learned of attacks on the Jewish orphanages of Ahawah and Reichenheim as well as the children's home in Fehrberlinstrasse. An attack on Pankow seemed imminent.

The Jewish community had a warning system to spread word of trouble but, during the night of 9–10 November, this was disrupted. Something was breaking the chain of communication. Jewish people were disappearing. There was a manhunt under way. The Gestapo, the SA and the Berlin police were targeting Jewish men and boys over the age of sixteen. They were being arrested in their homes. It was hard to make sense of what was going on. Hundreds were being taken away. This was a mass arrest. All the while the Brownshirts and Hitler Youth continued to incite the crowds. After looting shops and businesses the armed gangs turned their fury on Jewish homes, breaking in and terrorising the inhabitants, destroying anything they could: china, furniture, windows, mirrors, gramophones, even musical instruments. By the pale light of the morning of 10 November, foreign journalists were reporting that thirty synagogues were burning across Berlin. There were even reports that Jews had been murdered in the night.[4]

The pogrom continued that day in broad daylight. Storm troopers on motorcycles revved through Berlin throwing stones to smash the windows of Jewish shops, paving the way for a marauding spree by ordinary German citizens. By early afternoon in the fashionable shopping district a crowd of thousands had gathered outside Israel's Department Store, one of Germany's oldest and largest stores. It was owned by the family of the Jewish businessman and philanthropist, Wilfrid Israel, who was heavily involved in relief work to help those escaping Nazi persecution. Now his own employees fled as the Nazi thugs attacked, stealing and plundering before the applauding multitude. During the late afternoon at the Pankow orphanage, staff saw a long line of police trucks driving out of town. Over three thousand men and teenage boys had been arrested during the night. They were being transferred by the police to Sachsenhausen concentration camp twenty-two miles north of Berlin.

Dr Crohn and the orphans in his care were caught up in the brutal pogrom unleashed on Jews across Greater Germany that became known, in a cynical understatement devised by Goebbels, as Kristallnacht: the 'night of broken glass'. But this was much more than the breaking of shop windows. Thirty thousand Jewish men were sent to concentration camps, mainly Dachau, Buchenwald and Sachsenhausen. A thousand synagogues were set on fire and over seven and a half thousand Jewish shops destroyed. It was a pogrom the like of which Dr Crohn had never seen in his lifetime; an explosion of hatred and sadistic rage against Jews that was hard to comprehend.[5]

In the German press, Dr Crohn read that this was a 'spontaneous uprising' of the German people against the Jews, but those who had witnessed the attacks knew the entire apparatus of the Nazi Party was involved: the brown-shirted SA, the black-shirted SS, the Gestapo and the Hitler Youth. Their violence was actively supported by the Berlin police, who were under orders from the city's police chief, Count von Helldorff, a well-known Nazi, formerly head of the Berlin SA and a friend of Goebbels. There was only one reported incident where the

Berlin police intervened. Oblivious to its sacred spaces and Moorish beauty, Storm troopers broke in to the magnificent Neue Synagogue on the Oranienburgerstrasse – the very place where Dr Crohn had taken his young charges to see *Elijah* the year before – smashing its seats and lighting a bonfire. The flames were destroying the vestibule when one lone officer, the area police chief, Lieutenant Wilhelm Krützfeld, persuaded the arsonists the synagogue was a protected landmark and summoned the fire brigade, later receiving a strong censure for his pains from Count Helldorff himself.[6]

Dr Crohn kept his charges under curfew. When thirteen-year-old Leslie Brent finally did venture out, the city had sprung back to life as though nothing had happened; but evidence of the violence was eerily visible. Jews themselves were being made to clear up the mess of shattered glass and looted merchandise that littered the pavements outside their homes and shops. Here and there, Leslie came across the blackened shell of a building. His main anxiety was for his parents and sister and it was a relief to find their tiny flat in a run-down part of Berlin had not been a target and Arthur, Charlotte and Eva were still safe. But the family soon learned of the destruction in their home town. Köslin's grand synagogue had been set on fire.[7]

Across town in central Berlin, seven-year-old Mia Schaff and her siblings had rarely left the family home since their father's arrest two weeks earlier. Despite such precautions, like Dr Crohn, her mother, too, was unable to shield her children from the impact of Kristallnacht. After that night the draper's shop on the ground floor of their building, once so busy and bright, now stood silent, in darkness. They learned that the owners, the elderly Jewish couple Mr and Mrs Davidson, had committed suicide. Life in a constant state of fear was no life at all and the Davidsons had found a way out with an overdose. Mia had never heard of such a thing. She shrank closer to her big brother and sister. What horror could have happened that drove the Davidsons to see no hope, no future? Was the world coming to an end, she wondered? It was hard for a seven-year-old to understand. The Davidsons were just two out of over three hundred suicides across the Third Reich that night.[8]

The wave of destruction took place in every town across Germany. Fourteen-year-old Ruth Boronow has never forgotten the sheer terror of that night in Breslau in eastern Germany. It began for her when the Gestapo suddenly arrested her father. She had no idea where he was being taken. Her mother sent Ruth out to warn friends to leave home at once before the Gestapo arrived.

Outside in the streets, Ruth found herself in an unrecognisable world. Breslau was transformed. There was a terrible roar as fire consumed familiar houses. Jewish shops were being looted. The angry crowd surged out of control, her father's former patients among them. Ruth ran blindly, turning a corner only to see the synagogue on fire. She had grown streetwise in Hitler's Germany. 'I used to stand like that [she indicates Nazi salute] like all the others, otherwise they would take you straight away. They were ruthless.' This time she understood at once that it was very different. The seething mob acted as though of one mind, surging through the streets, their flaming torches casting a red glow. Suddenly there she was, in the middle of the chaos, a defenceless target. Even with the passage of eighty years, Ruth's voice changes as she conveys the terror of that night. 'I was frightened. Anything could happen. You did not trust a soul, not a soul . . . They could do *anything.*'[9]

Even those who narrowly avoided the violence heard it and understood its power. Eight-year-old Susie Davids in Wuppertal Elberfeld near Düsseldorf spent the night cowering in the darkness, listening to the attacks around her. Susie and her family had been ordered to move house a few days before Kristallnacht. 'There was a new rule that Jews must not live with non-Jews,' she recalls. Their new home in an all-Jewish block proved to be a prime target. That night they heard angry shouted orders as the Nazi Brownshirts entered their building. Her parents turned off all the lights and they shrank back into the darkness. The thudding of many heavy boots continued up the stairs to the top floors. Susie remembers her mother 'signalling me to be absolutely silent whilst we heard banging and crashing in the two flats above.' There could be no doubting the extreme violence going on upstairs. When they heard boots coming down again, they knew that at any moment their door might burst open, but, miraculously, the sounds just receded down the stairs. They lay still all night in the dark, not daring to move, not daring to sleep. The next morning they learned that Jewish neighbours had looked out for their family, telling the Gestapo that the flat below had been empty for ages while their own flats were so badly wrecked, Susie remembers 'the contents crunching under my feet'. After Kristallnacht she was not allowed to return to school. 'Our parents refused to send us,' she continues. 'In fact they never let us out of the house again.' As for her father, his reprieve was temporary. 'After a couple of weeks, the Gestapo got wise,' she says.[10] They tracked him down and he was sent to Dachau.

Fourteen-year-old Heinz Redwood in Hamburg has a vivid memory of arriving at school on 10 November to see the synagogue burning. 'The skeleton was still there, but it was badly burned. It couldn't be used any more.' He immediately thought of his parents.

Four years earlier, Heinz had come home from school to find both his parents missing. The Gestapo had been particularly interested in his mother, Alice Ekert. Although she was not Jewish, she was a target as a satirical writer for the political journal, *Die Weltbühne* (*The World Stage*) – one of many publications banned by the Nazis. Alice and her husband, Leo, had been denounced by their own maid, who had acted as a Gestapo spy, and they were held in concentration camps for months. During Kristallnacht, Heinz hurried home, not knowing what to expect. Opening the front door, he was astonished to find them safe. 'Why they had not been re-arrested we've never been able to find out . . . It was one real piece of luck.' Almost all the Jewish men in Hamburg were arrested that day and later imprisoned in Sachsenhausen concentration camp. For teenage Heinz Redwood, Kristallnacht was the breaking point when 'I realised the reality of the situation. We could not stay in Germany.'[11]

The brutal violence extended to Austria in Greater Germany. In Vienna, Karl Grossfield's father had already been arrested and sent to Buchenwald. When twelve-year-old Karl did venture out with his mother, they found their local shop was largely destroyed. Across town in the sixteenth district, six-year-old schoolgirl Helen Urbach was frightened to see a burning synagogue. The vast majority of Vienna's synagogues came under violent attack. Some were blown up with explosives, others sprayed with petrol before they burst into flame. Helen's father had disappeared, in a desperate bid to avoid the Gestapo.[12] Ten thousand Jewish men were arrested in Vienna alone. The majority of Jewish businesses were wrecked or stolen. Many Jews were forced to hand over the keys to their homes and businesses, their livelihoods snatched away by Nazi officers in a few terrifying minutes. The violence in Austria was extreme; in Innsbruck a special SS murder commando killed some Jewish leaders in front of their families. 'A feeling of fear pervaded the very air,' wrote one witness. The long-established Jewish way of life in Austria was all but destroyed.[13]

For Karl and Helen in Vienna, like Leslie and Mia in Berlin, Ruth in Breslau, Heinz in Hamburg and countless Jewish children across the Third Reich, it was like waking up in a new world. It was impossible to know what might happen next. Innocent parents were deemed criminals, forced into hiding or carted off to a place so fearful that grown-ups would not discuss it. Those who returned from this 'other place' were inexplicably altered: their heads shaved, their bodies injured, their spirits broken. Whatever occurred there was so terrible it was invariably whispered about behind closed doors. One child has a vivid impression of not recognising her father when he finally returned from a concentration camp. His extreme pain and untreated wounds were a shocking sight and her parents retreated for hours into the bathroom. She was not allowed to see what had happened to him. Even young men who went to this 'other place' looked like old men – if they returned. But many did not come back. Family homes became places of extreme tension, waiting for news. Mothers who had once seemed happy and light-hearted were now in constant dread.

Many Jewish children experienced being turned out of their homes. Their parents were suddenly powerless, forced to hand over their keys. Any child who dared to say the obvious, to stand his ground and protest at the glaring injustice, would be quickly silenced by worried parents and ushered out. 'You see that tree?' retorted one Nazi to a confused youngster. If he and his Jewish companions were not gone by the afternoon, 'we'll hang you all up there.' In the unequal struggle against violent, armed gangs, children sometimes grabbed anything they could keep as a weapon; even knives and forks. Everything happened so fast, emotions could not keep pace with the unfolding danger. Many children describe being overpowered by new feelings of terror, anger and helplessness. One child describes being stricken with anxiety, refusing to leave his mother's side, even to go to the bathroom. The omnipotent Nazi enemy seemed possessed of infinite powers. The telephone wires could be tapped. A family maid or a once-friendly neighbour could be a Gestapo spy. Anything could be taken from you at a moment's notice. Not just your parents, perhaps even your own life. One girl spotted on the street remembers hearing the cry go up, 'Oh, there's a Jew. Let's throw her on the fire as well!'[14]

*

At Bunce Court, Tante Anna saw the horrific newspaper reports on what was happening in her home country. At last, the Nazi leadership stood condemned by the full force of the British press. 'A Black Day for Germany,' stormed *The Times* on 11 November 1938. 'The scenes of systemic plunder and destruction have seldom had their equal in a civilised country since the Middle Ages.'

The British press was unsparing in its reports of gruesome crimes. In Berlin alone, according to the *Daily Telegraph* on 11 November, one Jewish man was trampled to death, four others were lynched by the mob, and the caretaker of one

Berlin synagogue 'is believed to have been burnt, with his family, to death.'[15] One ill-fated Jew in Aschaffenburg was allegedly abducted from his home in the night, tied to a tree and used as target practice until dead.[16]

On 10 November at the height of the pogrom, the Sudetenland in Czechoslovakia became part of Greater Germany in accordance with the Munich Agreement. The Jews in the Sudetenland paid a terrible price for Chamberlain's 'peace in our time'. The next night the Nazis drove many hundreds of Sudeten Jews from their homes to the new border with Czechoslovakia, 'where they were forced to crawl on their hands and knees over the frontier,' reported the *Daily Telegraph*. Across the Third Reich the death toll of Jewish citizens climbed to ninety-one, although unofficial estimates suggest the true figure was over a thousand.[17] More than seventy Jewish prisoners in the newly expanded Buchenwald concentration camp did not survive the night of 8 November, revealed the *Manchester Guardian*. Some were beaten so severely, even the police 'turned their backs, unable to bear the cries.'[18]

Tante Anna worried for her mother, Fanny, and sister, Ida, who had not yet been able to leave Germany, although incredibly they had managed to avoid the violence in Ulm. Nazi storm troopers had crowded into the peaceful town squares of Anna's youth and attacked Jewish houses and shops in the town centre. Brandishing their torches, they set light to the synagogue in Weinhof Square, directly opposite the Essingers' childhood home.[19] Anna knew the local rabbi, Dr Julius Cohn, personally. He and his colleagues were forced to parade in circles around the fountain in the square as the Nazis beat them with rifles. Dr Cohn was singled out for particularly vicious treatment and, according to one account, barely escaped with his life. He was 'repeatedly dunked into the fountain until he almost drowned'.[20] Even Anna, known for her calmness, was hard-pressed to keep her feelings under control as she thought of his bravery and felt utterly helpless.

As for her original school at Herrlingen, with its timber-framed buildings, she knew it would be an easy target. There were reports of other Jewish schools being destroyed, such as the boarding school at Caputh near Potsdam.[21] But to her relief, an attack on Herrlingen School never came. The morning after Kristallnacht, Hugo Rosenthal and his wife saw just one shiny black car approaching down the drive. They knew it was the Gestapo. Judith was terrified, fearing they had come for her husband. She half expected to hear the sounds of attack but instead, the doorbell rang. Hugo Rosenthal answered. The Gestapo official simply thrust a letter into his hand.

It was from the criminal investigator of the secret state police. 'For the protection of the People and the State,' Rosenthal read, 'I prohibit with immediate effect the publication of the periodical, *Herrlinger Leben*.'[22] This unexpectedly trivial command was hard to take in. The *Herrlinger Leben* was the school magazine. Its contents were utterly innocuous; accounts of the children's activities and letters from former pupils, many of whom had settled happily abroad. To this day, no one knows why the Herrlingen School got off so lightly on Kristallnacht. 'It is very, very strange,' observes Ulm historian Hansjörg Greimal. 'After all, the mayor of Herrlingen was a Nazi. Some things really cannot be explained.'[23]

Equally inexplicable to Tante Anna was how towns and cities across the Third Reich spontaneously erupted in such extreme antisemitic violence on the same night. According to the *Manchester Guardian,* Joseph Goebbels, the propaganda minister, 'emphatically denied that the demonstrations were organised by the government', a denial that was widely repeated by the senior Nazis. This was not credible. All the press reports pointed to the conclusion that the pogrom was instigated by the Nazi government. Records, including Goebbels's own diary, now reveal the role of Hitler himself in authorising the pogrom. After meeting with Hitler on 9 November, a few hours after Ernst vom Rath's death, 'I immediately give the necessary instructions to the Police and the Party,' Goebbels entered in his diary. 'All are instantly on the phones. Now the people will act . . . The Führer has ordered that 20–30,000 Jews should immediately be arrested.' He made it plain he wanted to see 'a blood-red [glare] in the sky'. Goebbels was gleeful at the scale of the response. 'Bravo! Bravo!' he wrote when he saw the windowpanes smashed in Munich, and he relished the sight of the synagogues burning 'like big old cabins'. As for Berlin, in his view, 'all proceeded fantastically'.[24]

But Tante Anna could see from the numerous reports in the press that ordinary people had also joined in the violent spree. It was as though the worst aspects of human nature were being unleashed in German society and, approved by the state, given free rein. This was the very opposite of everything she was fighting for. In the aftermath of the Great War, she had seen a career in education as a way of transforming society for the better, for preparing people from all walks of life to get along together. The cruelties of Kristallnacht demonstrated the reverse. Five years of racial lessons in German schools was teaching a young generation to believe that violence would make Germany great. How far would this go? The fires were not yet out on the smouldering remains of the synagogues when the Nazi government openly condoned the attacks on the Jews, announcing that no one involved would be charged. Hermann Göring, chief of the German air force, revealed the final vengeful twist: Jews themselves must pay the immense cost of repairing the damage done to their properties and shops, a staggering one billion Reichsmarks.

The staff at Bunce Court tried to shield pupils from the shocking news, but telegrams from relatives began to arrive from Germany. Fathers who had been running businesses and shops just a few days before were now reduced to a name on a sheet of paper somewhere in the concentration camp system of the Third Reich.

Among those pupils worried about what this meant was the new boy, Richard Sonnenfeldt. Only a few months before, his mother, Gertrud, had been driven to contemplating a family suicide. As a doctor she had the necessary drugs in the surgery, she had explained. 'We would just go peacefully to sleep together.' Richard couldn't believe it. He remembered feeling very grown-up as he dismissed the idea out of hand. Drawing on every possible contact, Gertrud had managed to accomplish what she thought was impossible: she got her sons to England. But shortly after Kristallnacht, Richard received a telegram from her revealing that his father was in a concentration camp. Richard consulted the teachers. His mother had written in veiled terms – how could he draft a reply to her without placing her in danger? She had been stripped of everything: the family business, their home, her children and now her husband; she was staring at 'a frightening void,' he thought. Richard feared she was at risk of ending up in a concentration camp, too.[25] Tante Anna guided her pupils with the careful wording of telegrams so that they did not endanger their parents in Germany. She was always on hand to comfort any grieving child. 'Staff and children alike feared for the lives of their dear ones abroad,' she wrote.

All over the school heated discussions took place. What more could be done? For months there had been heart-rending advertisements in the *Jewish Chronicle*. 'Please help me bring out of Berlin two children, ten years old – very urgent case . . .' or 'Which family would give a home to two Viennese children, girls, aged 14 & 10, very well educated . . .' Now the desperation of parents was acute.[26] Those Jews in Germany who had clung to the belief that Nazism would come to an end 'saw at last how wrong they had been,' Hanna Bergas recorded in her memoirs. They made desperate attempts to get out, 'or at least get their children out,' she continued. The phone in Tante Anna's office was ringing almost constantly.

In the staffroom, Tante Anna and the teachers discussed their ambitious expansion plans for Bunce Court. Tante Anna had already added a timber-framed building in the grounds as a dormitory for twenty boys. With the help of an architect, she now planned large extensions on either side of the Boys' House in the hope of doubling her pupil numbers and taking an extra one hundred children. The whole school joined in the fundraising effort. Even the children who had plans for a school swimming pool came to see Tante Anna. They had made enough money to pay for another pupil's entry to England, they explained solemnly. By a unanimous vote, they wanted to donate this to help another child rather than complete the pool. Tante Anna spoke to influential members of the School Council. 'Anna was among the first to offer to take in young refugees,' recalled one prominent relief volunteer, Elaine Blond, the daughter of Michael Marks, who founded Marks & Spencer.[27] Everyone shared Tante Anna's belief, 'the only important thing now was to save life.'[28]

Jewish and other religious leaders were urgently seeking to change British government refugee policy. The German Jewish businessman, Wilfrid Israel, whose family department store in Berlin had been vandalised during Kristallnacht, had cabled his contacts in London explaining the despair of Jewish parents in Germany. If it wasn't possible to save entire families, surely they could rescue the children? More than 70,000 Jewish children were estimated to be in danger in Germany and Austria – many of them fatherless or orphaned – not to mention thousands more in the Sudetenland. If they did not leave the Third Reich they might die, cruelly, anonymously. That was the simple sum. Just another nameless group of Jews in the way of Hitler's mad plans. The crisis called for 'extraordinary measures', he urged.[29]

Wilfrid Israel's appeal was quickly escalated. On 15 November, five days after Kristallnacht, a Jewish delegation led by Viscount Herbert Samuel raised the fate of Jewish children in the Third Reich with the prime minister, Neville Chamberlain. Samuel pointed out that the Jewish refugee committees were prepared to bear the cost of saving the children. But Chamberlain was non-committal. If his government raised the issue with Hitler, he reasoned, it could make the plight of German Jews worse. Nothing was agreed.[30]

The issue was discussed the next day in cabinet. Leading members of the British government, far removed from the terror on the ground in Germany, calmly discussed the possibilities of freeing up space for Jewish refugees somewhere in the British Empire as though they had control of the world. The secretary of state for the colonies pointed out the problems in Kenya, Rhodesia, Tanganyika and even British

Guiana; then there was the question of whether the dominions of Australia, Canada or South Africa could do more. If Britain could find a way to take the lead, pointed out the foreign secretary, Lord Halifax, it might force the Americans 'to take some positive action . . .'[31]

With the British government sympathetic but still deliberating, Wilfrid Israel turned to the Quakers in London for help. It was considered too dangerous for Jews of any nationality to travel to Germany after Kristallnacht, but British Quakers could witness the scale of the problem at first hand and report back to the British government. Anna's friend, Bertha Bracey, head of the Quaker German Emergency Committee, set out for Berlin at once with a small team.[32]

Bertha and her team did not go to the Berlin Quaker office. 'We considered it was unfair to risk the involvement of German Friends,' Bertha wrote later, knowing that some Quakers who had helped German Jews had been arrested and thrown into concentration camps. Guided by Wilfrid Israel, her team split up across Germany to meet Jewish women leaders who were running relief efforts while their husbands were in concentration camps. From Prussia, Saxony, Silesia, Central Germany and the Rhineland: all the mothers had the same agonised plea. They were prepared for the ultimate sacrifice to give their children a chance to survive. Their overriding thought: to say goodbye, possibly for ever, to their precious children, desperately trusting in strangers to create a miracle.[33] For Tante Anna, who heard what was happening through the Quaker network, it was hard to imagine the tormented state of mind that would lead to such a decision.

On 21 November, Bertha Bracey and one member of her team, Ben Greene, returned to London in time to join

Viscount Samuel with the home secretary, Sir Samuel Hoare, before a parliamentary debate on refugee policy scheduled for later that night. They presented their shocking findings. 'I could not help thinking what a terrible dilemma it was to the Jewish parents in Germany to have to choose between sending their children to a foreign country, into the unknown, and continuing to live in the terrible conditions to which they are now reduced in Germany,' Samuel Hoare announced to the House of Commons afterwards. 'I saw this morning one of the representatives of the Quaker organizations, who . . . had only arrived in England this morning from a visit to Germany. He told me that the Jewish parents were almost unanimously in favour of facing this parting with their children and taking the risks of their children going to a foreign country, rather than keeping them with them to face the unknown dangers with which they are faced in Germany . . .' Britain *must* open its doors to the children, he argued. Parliament was won round. That very evening the government gave approval for refugee children to come.[34]

Suddenly the country woke up to the plight of Europe's Jews. The impact of Kristallnacht 'went through Great Britain like an electric current,' observed one relief worker. Former prime minister Stanley Baldwin made a national appeal on the radio. 'I ask you to come to the aid of victims, not of any catastrophe in the natural world,' he said, 'but an explosion of Man's inhumanity to Man.' Across the country, volunteers stepped forward. Sponsors offered to provide funds. Regional and local committees sprung up. 'It was a quite fantastic thing . . . In every little town, every village in England they said, '"we must save the children".'[35]

Almost overnight, the desire to help the children became a national effort. Norman Bentwich and his wife, Helen, proposed the creation of a new organisation to coordinate the efforts of all relief agencies, which soon became known as the Refugee Children's Movement or RCM. The RCM brought together all the leading Jewish organisations, Quaker and Christian agencies and many other relief organisations such as the Women's Appeal Committee. Members of Bunce Court's School Council had key responsibilities. Viscount Samuel acted initially as co-chairman of the RCM and the Marchioness of Reading became deputy chairman. Samuel worked alongside Sir Wyndham Deedes, an accomplished administrator who already ran a rescue enterprise called Children's Inter-Aid. Before them: the formidable task of rescuing the children from the Nazis.[36]

Norman Bentwich began planning the route to bring the children across Europe and liaising with the authorities in Holland and Germany. Other volunteers set about fundraising and recruiting an army of helpers. Others still began the process of seeking foster homes. Meanwhile relief workers went to Germany to work on the ground with Wilfrid Israel and other Jewish leaders to start the urgent selection process. They were soon overwhelmed with heartbreaking queries. Volunteers had to decide which children were at greatest risk, obtain the necessary approvals from the Nazi authorities and find homes in Britain for these young refugees.

Back in London, the RCM was urgently seeking a large reception camp where they could house the children immediately while they tried to find more permanent homes and hostels. They alighted on two holiday camps on the east coast: Dovercourt, near Harwich in Essex, and an overflow camp at Pakefield near Lowestoft, Suffolk. Helen and Norman Bentwich turned to Tante Anna, known as the respected head of a refugee school in England, and Anna offered to take charge of the camp.[37] Her task: to convert the former Butlin's holiday camps, within days, into reception camps for the refugee children.

Tante Anna quickly reorganised Bunce Court so that she could release core staff. 'Six of us, together with some former helpers and some of the older children went to Dovercourt to receive the children,' she wrote later. Anna chose her trusted lieutenant, Hanna Bergas, to accompany her, as well as a key member of the kitchen staff, who was to set up arrangements to feed hundreds of children.[38]

The Bunce Court team arrived at Dovercourt in early December 1938 to find the camp had an air of desolation. The North Sea air was bracing. The rows of wooden cabins in the half light of winter were stripped of all comforts and nothing worked in this cold little citadel. There was one large room that they could use for teaching, but no pencils and paper; not even a blackboard. Anna was acclaimed for her organisational skills, but this would stretch them to the very limit. At stake were the lives of countless children in urgent need of rescue. 'Anna thought the place was horrible,' observed Elaine Blond, who would soon become co-director of the RCM.[39] But there was no time to lose. 'We had scarcely got the cabins ready,' recalled Hanna, 'when the first bewildered group of children arrived.'[40]

6

'The children were used to having everything taken away . . .'

Hanna Bergas, Dovercourt, Essex, England, 1938

For Dr Kurt Crohn at the Berlin Pankow orphanage it was hard, at first, to believe the rumours circulating in the city towards the end of November. After all this time, one of the great powers would open its doors. There had been countless rumours before; all of them came to nothing. This time it was different. There was a sense of urgency. The first train to Britain was due to leave Berlin in a couple of days.

Dr Crohn was determined to help the children under his care to escape, but he soon found that those from the Berlin orphanages that had come under attack on Kristallnacht were a higher priority, along with children whose parents were in concentration camps and teenage boys, who were themselves at immediate risk of imprisonment.[1] The relief workers in Berlin were overwhelmed with urgent cases. Even so, Dr Crohn managed to reserve a few places for children from the Pankow orphanage and hurried to make the arrangements. Each child would need a completed two-part identity card issued by the British Home Office, a health certificate and a photograph. He liaised with parents and made his selection; among them were thirteen-year-old Leslie Brent and his friend, Fred Gerstl.

Leslie's last days in Berlin passed in a blur. 'It was quite worrying because . . . I didn't know where I was going except to England,' he remembers. 'I had no inkling of what the future held.' He had the comfort of knowing he would be travelling with his friend Fred, but this changed at the last minute when it was found there were too many children booked on the train and Dr Crohn had to reduce his allocation. Fred's name was removed from the list, 'presumably because, being half-Jewish, he was considered to be less at risk,' says Leslie.[2]

The whole family gathered for Leslie's final evening on 30 November at his parents' flat. The one-room apartment was filled with his aunts and uncles, his beloved parents and his sister, Eva. Eva was training to be a nurse at the Jewish hospital. Leslie couldn't quite understand why she wasn't coming with him, and assumed she would be following on another train. It all seemed unreal. He was leaving his life behind. He could only absorb impressions. With tears in her eyes, Leslie's mother gave him the family violin, a symbol of their unquestioned belonging to each other, and a suitcase of beautifully stitched clothes. His father was full of words of reassurance: they would all join him in England soon. He gave his word . . .

The next day Leslie's parents took him to the Anhalter Bahnhof station in Berlin. 'My parents tried to put on a stiff upper lip of course and not to cry as so many other parents did.' Leslie stood close to them on the platform, as if they could stay like this for ever, rooted to the spot. His mother was quiet, almost in shock. Leslie tried to control a feeling of utter desolation. He understood that he was supposedly the lucky one, that 'some great act of kindness had been extended to me.' But rationality alone could not dispel that lurching sense of fear and abandonment. There was chaos; a crush of people including over two hundred children, cold-hearted Nazi guards with their guns trying to get parents back behind a barrier, the noise and smoke from the steam train. Leslie found it 'very bewildering'.[3]

All too soon the children had to board the train. One child later recorded the moment of parting. He tried to turn back to wave to his parents but an SS officer in a black uniform 'rushed towards me, "You Jewish swine. One more sign or word from you and we shall keep you here." And so I stood at the window of the train . . . suddenly overcome with a maiming certainty that I would never see my mother and my father again. There they stood, lonely and with the sadness of death . . . Can the world ever justify the pain that burned in my father's eyes? . . . As the train pulled out of the station I leaned my face against the cold glass of the window and wept bitterly.'[4]

Leslie found himself in a compartment with children he did not know. Many were too shocked to respond, emotions frozen by this strange new world. Those who were crying, were crying silent tears. 'It was very, very quiet,' he remembers. 'We were told to be on our best behaviour on the train. They did not want us to run into any trouble with the guards . . .' German police patrolled the train and the fear was palpable. Few dared say a word and when they did, 'they spoke in whispers'.

The journey was long and it was hard to know exactly where they were. They stopped at Hamburg. Another group of subdued children joined the train. After many hours the landscape seemed to be changing, becoming flatter. From the window they could see many German troops. Leslie assumed their train was approaching the border. Outside, the marching soldiers instilled a sense of fear. Everyone was on edge. There was a grating sound as the train ground to a halt. Dreaded SS guards boarded the train. They searched through the children's cases checking that none of the children had any gold or silver in any form with them. Some children knew their parents had hidden little trophies such as jewellery and were in terror of them being found. There was a rumour that if anyone had broken the rules, the whole transport would be sent back. But in Leslie's compartment the customs inspection passed without incident.

After waiting an interminably long time the train started to move and was gathering speed when, once again, it came to an unexpected halt. It was impossible to tell if they had escaped Germany. Some children feared they were about to be turned back. Inside the carriage there was a marked rise in tension. Uniformed guards appeared. From the window they glimpsed a man being led off the train. What was going on? The train moved forwards and then stopped yet again.

Through the window Leslie saw they were at a station. Women on the platform were smiling at them. 'We were not used to it. No one ever smiled at us in Germany . . .' It dawned on him that perhaps they had done it. Could this be Holland? Sure enough, the women boarded the train and began to dish out treats: drinks, fruit, sandwiches, biscuits and chocolate. 'Suddenly it was a complete transformation,' Leslie recalls. 'We couldn't believe it. It was absolutely wonderful . . . we felt free.' The Dutch women overbrimming with kindly warmth became 'an abiding memory' for Leslie. 'It was the first time we were ever treated as individuals in public.' They later learned that the man escorted from the train had been a German spy, arrested by Dutch guards. A photograph of Leslie taken on his arrival in Holland reveals the strain on his face; the anxiety of a child alone in a world that was hard to read.[5]

It was evening before the children arrived at the Hook of Holland. They could smell the salt air of the North Sea and hear the seagulls circling as they boarded the ferry *De Praag*, its vast hulk looming over them as they mounted the ramp. The children were sent to their bunks but many were so seasick in a turbulent night crossing that they got little sleep. 'It must have been one of the roughest of nights,' recalled thirteen-year-old Gerd Nathan from Hamburg. 'It was terrible.' He was already feeling desperately homesick when the child in the bunk below him was physically sick, 'and that of course triggered me off'.

By the pale wintry light of early morning on 2 December 1938, they came into harbour at Parkeston Quay in Harwich. Waiting for the children were the refugee organisers, keen to welcome them and speed up disembarkation. A queue formed as each child waited for their name to be called. They each had a label round their neck with their name and address, and their identity cards were endorsed by the immigration officer. Leslie caught sight of a British policeman. He was struck by the strange helmet and even more surprised to see the policeman smiling at them. 'This was very extraordinary. The police were friendly.' But despite the valiant efforts of those at the dock that morning, many in the straggling group of children found tears were not far away. 'Never has a sadder boatload of passengers filed through the customs barrier at Harwich,' observed the *Eastern Daily Press*.[6]

Leslie was directed onto a double-decker bus that drove the children through Harwich and on for a couple of miles by the coast. They arrived at a large entranceway marked out by a wooden frame, 'Warners Holiday Camp' cheerily painted on top. There was an avenue of tall trees and a glimpse of chalets and the sea beyond. But it was not blue seas and skies that greeted them and the welcome embrace of a family holiday but an endless grey North Sea that at some indefinable point merged with an infinite sky. The children clambered off the bus and were welcomed to Dovercourt Reception Camp.

'Hundreds of children streamed into the camp,' recalls Hanna Bergas, 'children who were strangers to each other, to the adults who accompanied them, strangers to those who received them in strange surroundings.' Tante Anna and the staff were keen to provide loving reassurance. Most of the children had experienced 'bad treatment, even brutality' in their country of origin, and were 'full of anxieties and fears . . . distrust and suspicion'. Hanna wanted them to feel 'that people here would be kind to them.' Their first step was to give them a good meal and settle them into their sleeping quarters.[7]

The children were anxious to be reunited with their pack-ages. Small tokens from home assumed immense significance. They were 'used to having everything taken away from them' and could be 'extremely restless until their little possessions were under their care,' Hanna noted. Reunited with his suit-case, Leslie found his mother had thought of everything. 'There were a couple of photographs . . . All my shirts, underwear, towels, she had sewn on the initials L.B. There was even a flannel . . .' It is a mark of what all this meant to him that even fifty years later he still had the same flannel, saved as a treasured memento.

Leslie was allocated a chalet, which he shared with two other boys. Then the staff arranged the children into small groups and told them what the camp would be like, what to expect and 'we explained that we would help them with their English,' recalled Hanna. The photographer asked the children to raise their arms in a cheer. Some did manage a smile, others were more uncertain. They looked at the camera as instructed, arms wavering, not quite raised, many still in the best clothes their mothers had provided. There was a heavy frost on the grass and a chill in the air; the place had the incongruous feel of all holiday camps out of season. Fear showed on young faces. This bleak camp could not be the promised place. What would happen to them?

Leslie tried to adapt to his new English surroundings. Kippers, tea and porridge were all part of his curious introduction to British life. English lessons started on the second day but there were no teaching aids, not even a blackboard, and the children all had different levels of skill. A few lessons were held in the larger dormitories but in the absence of anywhere else to congregate, several classes were held simultaneously in the large hall. 'It was a challenge to a teacher's imagination,' wrote Hanna, 'to communicate knowledge entirely from within.' Even more challenging was the noise volume; in addition to the busy classes, the piano in the hall was in almost constant use. Hanna found it best to encourage each child to talk about themselves and their families. Another volunteer assistant describes trying to make a game out of teaching the English names of basic objects: 'a spoon, fork, knife, sugar, milk . . . they learned very fast.'

'Dovercourt Bay was mothered – there is no other word for it – by the formidable Anna Essinger,' observed Elaine Blond, of the Refugee Children's Movement. Anna's team 'introduced a semblance of decent living'.[8] In an effort to alleviate the children's feelings of loneliness and homesickness, activities during the day were followed by evening entertainments. Leslie can remember learning popular English songs from the music hall, like 'Tipperary', 'The Lambeth Walk' and 'Daisy, Daisy'. 'I liked singing so I joined a small choir,' he says. To ease the shortage of staff, Tante Anna placed advertisements for student assistants, knowing she was reliant on the goodwill of any volunteers since she could not pay them more than one pound per week. Fortunately, the constant lack of supplies was eased by some generous donations. The Dunlop Rubber Company provided hot-water bottles for each child and Marks & Spencer gave blankets and children's outdoor clothing. As word spread, local people volunteered to help with day trips and home visits. Leslie never forgot his welcome into an English home. 'I was invited to tea by an elderly English gentleman. He lived in a very fine detached house and I saw my first English open fireplace with a roaring fire.' In Germany they had tiled stoves, not open fires. 'It was my first bit of Englishness really . . . It impressed me enormously,' he recalls, along with the tea and toasted crumpets.[9]

But Tante Anna found her hopes of recreating the welcoming, homely atmosphere of a 'Bunce Court by the sea' were thwarted by the conditions at Dovercourt and the ever-growing numbers of children. The overspill camp at Pakefield, sixty-five miles further up the coast in Suffolk, was also soon full. Inevitably, Dovercourt had the feel of a transit camp, with endless arrivals and departures. The pressure to find homes for the children quickly in order that more could be rescued from the continent was relentless. Tante Anna much preferred to place children in hostels or schools, rather than allocating them to unknown foster parents, and demand for Bunce Court was huge. 'Soon there were one hundred and twenty children and we could not have taken more without being overcrowded,' observed Hanna Bergas. Plans were under way to build extensions but an appeal to supporters from Bunce Court's treasurer, Mrs Saloman, highlights the additional crises in funding they faced after Kristallnacht. Saloman explained that the headmistress was 'almost daily compelled to refuse applications from parents who would make any sacrifice to send their children out of the Third Reich. The school is already too full, and its financial position more and more disturbing . . .' Saloman appealed for more 'Friends' of the school to help build up a fund so that they could rescue more children from the continent.[10]

Under pressure to find homes urgently, the Refugee Children's Committee tried to raise awareness of the children's plight. This led to a succession of visitors who wanted to look around Dovercourt: local politicians and dignitaries, journalists, even a team from the BBC. Leslie was excited to be chosen for a BBC interview. 'My English was quite passable,' he recalls, 'ironically, thanks to my Nazi teacher in Köslin.' But when he found himself before the microphone, he felt momentarily confused. Knowing the radio broadcast was important to encourage volunteers to foster the children, he was keen to make a good impression. Far more significant, Leslie hoped that his parents might hear him. The odds were against it – he knew it was difficult for German Jews to keep their radios – but there was just an outside chance that they might recognise his voice and take heart. He imagined having a conversation with them, actually talking to them alone. As Leslie juggled with all these thoughts, the producer came to his rescue and asked him to describe a typical day in the camp.

'A bell rings at eight and we have to get up,' Leslie began. His English was clear despite the marked German accent.

'We have a good English breakfast, which we enjoy. First we didn't eat porridge,' he explained, 'but now we like it.' After breakfast the children were given their letters from home 'and we are all very happy.' This was followed by two hours of English lessons and then 'we can make what we like . . . we go to the sea which is wonderful or we play English games of football.' He described going to see the very latest Disney film, *Snow White and the Seven Dwarfs,* in the local picture house. In Germany, Jewish children were banned from the cinema and this was a new experience. 'We were all delighted,' he said. There was even ice cream. As for his ambitions, he wanted 'to speak English good and then I would like to be a cook.' Even as he spoke, he was thinking of his mother and her home cooking. 'We are all very happy to be in England,' he finished.

The programme, called *Children in Flight,* helped to spread the word around Britain, prompting more potential foster parents to come to Dovercourt to choose a child. But Tante Anna became increasingly concerned that the selection process was an additional stress for the refugees in her care. Each Sunday they were prepared for 'the cattle market', as Leslie called it. 'We all had to be dressed up, displayed as it were . . .'[11] The day began with a thorough wash, a haircut and then clean clothes. The children emerged by lunchtime thoroughly well-scrubbed, if somewhat subdued. Then their ordeal started.

Potential parents walked around the dining tables to view the children. Although nothing was said, the children understood perfectly well what was happening and became anxious. 'We felt a bit like monkeys in a zoo,' recalls one. Sometimes a child was called out to be interviewed by a prospective family. By Sunday evening, children learned their fate on the camp tannoy as the names of those selected were announced. 'Many a pretty little girl and her belongings were packed into the car of the family who were to become her foster parents,' wrote Hanna, while those left behind faced 'prolonged uncertainty.' The children repeatedly rejected by prospective British parents began to suffer, feeling anxious, even traumatised. What awful unseen stigma lay over them that they could attract so little interest? Tante Anna worried the cattle market was doing more harm than good. She raised the matter with the Refugee Children's Movement – there had to be a more sensitive way of finding homes for the children.[12]

There were also conflicts brewing within the RCM over how the refugees should be treated. The Marchioness of Reading, a leading light within the RCM, believed that the child refugees 'were not to be pampered,' observed Elaine Blond furiously. As the daughter of Michael Marks, originally a Russian-Polish immigrant, it jarred with Elaine that the marchioness 'judged every problem within the narrow conventions of her class', viewing refugees as from some lower social strata. Elaine could scarcely conceal her fury when she learned the marchioness had actually turned down coupons from the government to buy the refugee children new clothes, believing it more suitable for the children to have second-hand.[13]

All the while, more and more children flooded into the camp each week from Germany, Austria, Poland and then Czechoslovakia. Dovercourt was soon a Tower of Babel, its corridors babbling with the different languages of hundreds of disconsolate refugee children. 'We barely had time to adjust before the camp became impossibly crowded,' Leslie recalls. 'The noise was pretty deafening.' Soon there were one thousand children in a camp designed to hold no more than five hundred.

To compound the problems, the endless rain turned to snow, which blanketed the ground. That winter proved to be one of the coldest on record in Britain. The Dovercourt chalets became ice-houses. 'We froze to death,' says Leslie. The dining hall was made out of glass and snow drifted between the panes onto the children's plates. Water in the pipes turned to ice so it was no longer possible to wash or use the toilets. The jugs of water laid out for breakfast froze over overnight. Leslie remembers huddling for hours with the other children around the few 'smelly stoves' in the great hall, everyone in their overcoats – which they did not remove even to go to bed. The volunteers could only encourage the children to do exercises to keep warm. Before long there was colourful talk of one or two children losing fingers and toes to frostbite in the overspill camp – rumours that came to nothing.

Tante Anna did not want the elements to defeat her. If the camps failed it would severely hamper the race to get children out of the Third Reich. She knew how British winter weather could confound the best of intentions and keeping the children safe was uppermost in her mind. But even Tante Anna's organisational skills were no match for the uncharitable North Sea. One night at Pakefield, the rain combined with 'a storm at high tide [that] brought the sea crashing into their chalets,' recorded Elaine Blond. Many children in the flooded camp had to be evacuated, along with those in the lower chalets at Dovercourt. After the night-time rescue, the bewildered children were hurriedly rehoused in local schools. Defeat was staring Anna in the face.

For Leslie, the bitter cold and the transitory nature of the camp pushed that feeling of home ever further away. He longed for news of his family. It was his first Christmas away from his mother and father. He thought of the fun they used to have together in Köslin: the beautiful singing in the synagogue, the games with Eva in the snow, his father bringing home a Christmas tree and occasionally dressing up as Father Christmas as he gave presents to everyone in their block. In Berlin now, it would be out of the question for Arthur to do such a thing.

Any secret hopes of seeing those dear, familiar faces in England soon were fading. Leslie knew Arthur was doing all he could to get them out of Germany, but with Christmas 1938 approaching, there was still no word.[14]

*

While the first Kindertransports were under way from Germany in early December, the first from Austria had run into an obstacle. Norman Bentwich had turned to the formidable Gertrude Wijsmuller-Meijer to negotiate permission with Nazi officials in Vienna. Wijsmuller-Meijer, wife of a Dutch banker, was renowned for her refugee work. For years she had helped Jewish people escape from Nazi Germany, even allegedly once smuggling a Jewish child over the German border under her skirts. But when she arrived in Vienna on 3 December, she was promptly arrested and thrown into jail.

Mrs Wijsmuller-Meijer passionately believed in the rightness of her cause. Every day that she languished in jail was precious time lost. 'I knocked on my cell door to explain that I was not Jewish,' she recorded later. The loudly protesting Mrs Wijsmuller-Meijer gave the guards a piece of her mind, insisting she would let the foreign press know how the Nazis dealt with visiting 'Aryans'. Eventually orders came for her release, whereupon the fearless Mrs Wijsmuller-Meijer immediately demanded an appointment with the notorious Adolf Eichmann.

Two days elapsed before she was brought before Eichmann in his sumptuous offices in the Rothschild Palais. Newly promoted to SS *Obersturmbannführer* in recognition of his ruthless enforcement of Jewish emigration, Eichmann was seated on a raised platform at one end of the palatial room, surrounded by all the intimidating paraphernalia of Nazi authority. He had the air of a man at the peak of his command.

Mrs Wijsmuller-Meijer stood her ground. She explained she had permission from the English government for 10,000 children to come to London.

'Have you got a letter from the English government?' Eichmann asked.

'No,' she replied.

He did not take her seriously.

'Now we'll make the joke of a lifetime,' he announced to those in the room. 'This woman does not have a letter from the English government which confirms that she is permitted to bring children into Britain. We will put together a transport of six hundred children and they must cross the frontier on Saturday midday then Mrs Wijsmuller will show how she can bring children into the country.' They both knew he was putting her on the spot. He effectively gave her a deadline that was so tight the organisational feat was impossible. Set up the transport of six hundred children from scratch in a few days or you will lose your permission.[15]

Anyone other than the doughty Mrs Wijsmuller-Meijer might not have taken on the task. She contacted Jewish youth and women's movements and soon teams of volunteers were working on the selection process and paperwork for each child. The news soon reached Karl Grossfield's mother, Miriam, in the outskirts of Vienna. This was the chance she had been desperately hoping for.

At midnight on 10 December, with Eichmann's deadline fast approaching, the station in Vienna was packed with children. Despite the very short notice, Karl felt prepared. His mother had explained the situation but now the moment was upon them, he could see 'she was very sad'. Miriam appeared calm and dignified but Karl knew 'she would have retained her tears until later.' Their family had been torn apart in the nine months since the *Anschluss*. Karl's father, Marcus, was still in Buchenwald, with no word of his release. His two older brothers had successfully emigrated to Palestine. Now he and his sister, Erica, had to leave their mother behind. Miriam would not think of leaving Vienna without her husband.

Taking courage from his mother's fighting spirit, Karl treated it all as an adventure. He was going to a promised land where Jews were not treated as criminals and where his sister would not be ordered to scrub the streets. Karl cannot recall the long journey across Europe or his arrival in England. His first memory is of the crowded reception centre at Dovercourt. 'What I remember most [is that] they arranged very good entertainments for the evenings,' he says. Even eighty years later, his eyes light up with amusement.

Before long, the controversial cattle market separated Karl from Erica, who was chosen by a family. In due course, another family offered to take Karl. 'There was a certain Mrs Smith who for various reasons thought I might be suitable but by the time I reached London, she had changed her mind,' he recalls. Karl found himself stranded in the refugee headquarters. He remembers an earnest, whispered discussion about what to do with this boy. 'Do we send him back to Dovercourt?' he heard one woman say. It was late and Miss Jelf, the Secretary of the Pinner Committee for

Refugees, offered to settle the matter. She would take him in for a few days.

'Now my story becomes very unusual,' recalls Karl with delight. He was taken to a rather grand house in Pinner and to an ornate dining room immaculately laid out for three people: Miss Jelf, her father, Sir Ernest Jelf – and Karl, the slightly dishevelled refugee boy, seated between them. Karl was amazed. The English ate in grandeur. 'There were three silver knives on one side, three silver forks on the other and a fork and spoon in front as well as three glasses. The servants who brought in the food called me "Master Karl".' It was quite a baffling contrast to simple meals in Vienna. Karl watched his hosts most carefully 'and tried to copy as fast as I could'.

Karl's stay with Miss Jelf settled happily into a few weeks, until the servants rebelled at having to wait on a refugee boy. Miss Jelf's neighbour, who 'happened to be the son of an earl', offered to help out. The earl's garden included two tennis courts, and Karl recalls he had a chance to learn tennis. Above all, at the earl's house, he remembers the dining room. 'It was fully hand painted.' Karl had never seen such opulence.[16]

While Karl could write home with heart-warming news for his mother about his remarkable reception in England, for most refugees it was a different story. There were new arrivals at Dovercourt almost daily, with many children 'confused, some intimidated, some even defiant out of ignorance about what was happening to them,' observed Hanna. Tante Anna remained convinced that Dovercourt's cattle market must be stopped. 'Public sympathy was raised to a high pitch,' she wrote later. Many potential foster parents volunteered, but there were not enough staff at Dovercourt to monitor all the placements. Many foster homes were not properly vetted and she feared that vulnerable children might find themselves in unsuitable homes or that they had been taken in as cheap domestic help. With the constant influx of new children, arrangements were so hurried, 'none of us knew the children; in many cases not even the bare facts of their backgrounds; and hardly anyone knew the families who offered to take them into their homes,' she wrote later. Tante Anna's disagreement with the Refugee Children's Movement over the weekly 'cattle market' escalated into a painful clash of views.[17]

The Refugee Children's Movement did accept that there were problems at Dovercourt. Organisers conceded that they had difficulty matching each child with a family of a similar background. One internal report went so far as to acknowledge the camps were little more than 'slave markets', where foster parents, however well-meaning, went to select one child 'but unconsciously did harm to many by looking them over and rejecting them'. Indeed, one girl, when her name was announced on the camp tannoy, cried out, '*Ich bin verkauft . . .*' ('I am sold'). But for all this, there was no other way of solving the essential problem: to save more children they had to empty the reception camps quickly. Volunteers on the ground in Greater Germany responsible for making the selections for the Kindertransports were facing panic from parents desperate to get their children to safety. Tante Anna did not succeed in stopping the hurried foster placements, but she did eventually bring an end to the 'cattle market'. The matching of children and potential foster parents was carried out more discreetly, through private interviews rather than the dreaded Sunday parade.[18]

Even so, for the children remaining at Dovercourt it was a forlorn winter. The strain began to tell. Overstretched staff were not always able to maintain discipline. 'A grotesque thing happened one day,' wrote Hanna. 'Children from Hamburg behaved with hostility towards some from Vienna and vice versa, each group boasting about how much better its home town was.' Almost unbelievably, a knife fight broke out, 'and we had difficulty establishing the peace between them.'[19] Then there was the day when a few older boys found their way to Harwich's version of a red-light district, a particular misfortune since their adventures coincided with a visit from the chief rabbi, the biblical scholar Joseph Hertz. The chief rabbi also expressed concern about why the boys were playing football on the Sabbath and why it was not proving possible to match Orthodox Jewish children with a similar cultural background in Britain. Tante Anna conceded on the football but there was nothing she could do about the marked shortage of volunteer foster parents from Orthodox Jewish backgrounds. Many of the children arriving on Kindertransport were from assimilated or non-practising Jewish backgrounds but this did not stop one fundamentalist rabbi managing to delay a train full of children due to leave Germany on the Sabbath, prompting frustration among the RCM volunteers.

Tante Anna was concerned that if bad publicity leaked about Dovercourt this could thwart their efforts to gain public support. Not everyone was enthusiastic about opening Britain's doors to a large number of Jewish refugees. A memo to the chief general inspector, Mr Roundell, at the Department of Health reveals they 'have had a good many enquiries about the refugee children from Germany and the possibility of their spreading disease.' The chief inspector and a women's inspector, Miss Montagnon, turned up at Dovercourt in short order, since the risk of contagious disease was inevitably highest in the camps. Tante Anna was in London and Hanna Bergas showed them round. Their visit was the first of a veritable army of inspectors and eminent visitors including catering inspectors to ensure dietary needs were being met, as well as a further visit from the Ministry of Health that happened to coincide with a day when the water supply was frozen solid.[20]

The daunting task before Tante Anna almost became too much for her. The warmongering stance of Hitler's government, the race to save children in time, the sheer scale of their trauma, the conflicting views of the organisers as well as the inevitable compromises needed to empty the camps quickly: all this took its toll. According to one friend, even years later, she would not talk about her difficult months there.

For most children, as for Leslie, letters from their parents kept them going. 'The emphasis was always on their coming over to England,' Leslie remembers. Looking back he does not know whether his parents believed in this, 'but they hoped.' He tried to picture his mother, father and Eva in their tiny flat, waiting for news of their journey to England. It surely wouldn't be long?[21]

Leslie became friends with an older boy, Gabi Adler, a volunteer from Bunce Court. One day Gabi told Leslie all about his school, conjuring up a picture of a wonderful place in beautiful grounds where the children had fun.

'Would you like to go there?' Gabi asked Leslie.

'It sounds lovely,' came Leslie's polite reply.

It was hard to imagine a school that was so different to anything he had known, and Leslie thought no more about it. A few days later, he was running through a door when he bumped into 'the by no means negligible figure of a lady who seemed to be so short-sighted as to be almost blind.'

The lenses of her glasses were very thick and it was hard to see her eyes.

Tante Anna lifted up Leslie's face by a shock of hair and said, 'And *whoo* are you?'

On learning his name she asked if he would like to come to her school, Bunce Court. 'Yes please,' he stammered. And that was it. A chance meeting that, he wrote years later, would affect 'my survival, development and career very profoundly.'[22]

7

'The only important thing was to save life'

Tante Anna, on Kindertransport, 1939

In January 1939, Leslie Brent travelled through London with a few other children on their way to Bunce Court. Accompanied by some older pupils from the school, at Victoria station they boarded a steam train and Leslie sank back into soft padded seats, so unlike the uncomfortable wooden seats in German trains, and watched the countryside drift by through the windows. Once outside London, there was a sheet of white snow as far as the eye could see, blotting out the scattered farmhouses. A taxi was waiting to collect them from Lenham station and soon the children were winding down narrow lanes, thick with snow, deep into the Kent countryside. As they arrived at a grand manor house, half obscured behind a high hedge covered in heavy snow-drifts, Leslie's spirits rose. To him, the place looked 'magical', like something you read about in books.

For Leslie, the friendly welcome he received at Bunce Court could not have made more of a contrast to the oppression of his German schools. Pupils showed him around the main house and took him to his dormitory on the third floor. Through the window, he could see more children having fun outside. Leslie's explorations of the grounds revealed an ornamental pond that was frozen solid, a carpentry workshop, a rose garden neatly pruned for the winter, a large amphitheatre almost concealed by the blanket of snow . . . Beyond the grounds were extensive playing fields that merged with the surrounding farmland. As the sun glittered through bare trees onto drifts of snow the place had an air of enchantment, he thought, 'like a fairyland'. The pure white space of land and sky where no creature moved had him breathless. Surely nothing bad could happen to him here?[1]

Leslie soon learned that the ruler of this little private kingdom, the headmistress, Anna Essinger, was spending much of her time at Dovercourt. When Leslie did see her at the school it was clear that everyone seemed to take their cue from her. Tante Anna had an aura around her; she was both a little forbidding and immensely kind. This ambiguity in her character was heightened by her double-lensed glasses, which made it hard to see the expression in her eyes, although her manner and her greeting were always warm. Leslie noticed there were some children who treasured being invited to tea in Tante Anna's rooms. It was 'a treat' to have breakfast with Tante Anna, observed one German refugee, Walter Block.[2] Others held back from 'sitting at her table in the dining room', fearing 'you had to have good table manners and all of that,' remembers Leslie. When the noise in the hall reached a certain height 'she used to ring a little bell and say, Silence *pleeease . . .'* Such attributes, which soon became very familiar, predictable even, seemed to endear her to her pupils. As with Tante Anna – or sometimes just 'TA' – and her sister, Tante Paula, all the teachers, Leslie found, had a nickname. Hanna Bergas, who he had already met at Dovercourt, was known as 'HB', her cousin, Helmut Schneider, who taught maths and music, was 'Schneidy' and the sports master, Hans Meyer, was 'Meyerlein'.

Leslie joined in the practical tasks during the afternoons and was also introduced to the brilliant cook 'Heidtsche', whose 'spectacular tantrums' came as quite a surprise. Her angry torrent in a Hessian dialect could often be heard on approach to the kitchen. 'She was not averse to throwing the odd frying pan around the place if a child behaved really badly,' he noticed. When dishing up she could also be in 'a very excitable, nervous state, trying to serve hot food for so many.'³ Other children soon allayed his doubts. Fourteen-year-old Eric Bourne, now an old-timer who had long since outgrown his armed patrol of the school, was full of reassurance. In his view, Heidtsche was 'one of the pillars of Bunce Court and the personification of the statement that a dog's bark is worse than his bite.' The 'war' between the children and the cook that preceded every meal 'was a regular routine and always peacefully settled by the time food was served.'⁴

Putting aside his initial wariness to accept an invitation to join Heidtsche in her room for tea, Leslie soon found comfort in the cook's motherly interest and attention, along with the warmth of the tea and home-made cake. It felt like 'a great treat . . . an indication that she liked us.' Heidtsche appeared to be intimately bound up in the emotional life of the school. Leslie felt drawn to her, although she could not have been more of a contrast to his own gentle mother. As he settled in, he began to feel that the volatile cook 'radiated an uncomplicated motherliness and warmth' and he was quite happy to be allocated work in the kitchen.

The carpentry workshop was the province of Hans Meyer, who lived in Greet Cottage, a couple of miles across the fields, with his warm-hearted wife, Hannah, the geography teacher, known as 'HaGo'. They had recently had a baby boy, Joseph, whose pram was invariably parked somewhere near the kitchen under the supervision of Heidtsche when classes were in progress. Hans's early morning gymnastics were not universally popular but in the workshop he came into his own and Leslie found him 'endlessly patient'.

Leslie had much to report to his parents when he wrote that week. His father's comforting words that he was in some inexplicable way extra lucky as a 'Sunday's child' seemed to be coming true. With the promising prospect of settling into an English boarding school, he began to feel his good fortune.

At the end of the first week Leslie joined the other children, who had filled the large hall and crammed up the handsome stairs to hear a musical recital. All eyes were on a young woman with dark hair and an intense manner who was preparing to play the violin. Leslie learned that she was Lotte Kalischer, who ran the school's large music department. As she took her place she was joined by Schneidy, on the grand piano.

A 'sacred silence' descended, as was the case whenever Lotte and Schneidy played together, observed one pupil later. It was clear to Leslie that the Friday evening recital was eagerly anticipated.

Beethoven's *Spring* sonata.

Leslie felt transported. Music at last; he gave a silent cheer for the wonder of it, for the way it could evoke something good in his memory. Lotte's beautiful playing seemed to express all the tumult of emotions that he was feeling, to say everything that needed to be said . . . He felt almost at home. 'I felt liberated from all the hate and persecution I had encountered in Germany . . . I *was* happy.'[5]

*

At Dovercourt in the early spring of 1939, Tante Anna saw at first hand the intensifying pressures on the Refugee Children's Movement. Seventy volunteers were now working from the RCM's new headquarters in Bloomsbury House in central London to save as many children as they could. In December alone they had successfully brought almost two thousand children from the Third Reich to safety, but there were tens of thousands more, all desperate for a chance to escape. Every day letters poured into Bloomsbury House from parents on the continent begging for help. Many 'were so touchingly written that it required a hard heart to consign them to files and indices,' wrote one hard-pressed relief worker. Each one seemed to be a deserving case.[6]

Mia Schaff has a vivid memory of those nightmarish months in Berlin, when she was eight years old. Mia's Polish-born father, Oscar, had been forcibly dumped at the Polish border just before Kristallnacht. Since then, he had only been permitted home once. Mia overheard her parents talking in hushed tones about attempting to cross a border without papers. She strained to hear any word. 'My father was the eternal optimist,' Mia recalls. 'He was saying we'll get through all right.' There were snatched conversations about how to escape. It came to nothing. Within days, the Gestapo had ordered Oscar back to Poland.

Mia's mother, Ida, pursued every avenue to get her children to safety, but the odds were against her. The RCM had a backlog of more than ten thousand cases of potential child refugees. Britain appealed to America to open its doors, but a proposed US bill to admit 20,000 German Jewish refugee children became entangled in congressional bureaucracy. Among the objections raised by opponents of the bill was that admitting children without their parents was against

God's law.[7] Ida found no one was able to help them. The weeks slipped by without them getting a prized place on Kindertransport. 'It was a very very strange time,' says Mia. 'I can't really describe it to you. We were afraid to go out . . .'[8]

Some families did manage to flee across the borders of the Third Reich, but even then they were not out of danger. In Vienna, six-year-old schoolgirl Helen Urbach felt she sank into an abyss after Kristallnacht. Her once-doting father, Otto, was still in hiding from the Gestapo. Her mother, Eti, managed to flee to England as a domestic worker. Before leaving, she obtained a place for Helen on the second Kindertransport out of Vienna. Days before the departure, Helen fell ill with chickenpox. She was too ill to travel. Helen couldn't join her mother after all.

Otto embarked on a daring plan. One night, without warning he ushered Helen and her cousins quietly into a big black car. He was among thousands who slipped unofficially across the Austrian border. 'We children were told to be very, very quiet,' Helen remembers. Tension ran high. They drove for hours. Otto managed to avoid the checkpoints and reach Brussels. He hoped to arrange emigration from abroad, but a couple of weeks later there was a knock on the door. It was the Belgian police. They ordered Helen and her father back to Vienna 'because we did not have any papers,' she remembers. Helen does not know who gave them away. She remembers only her father's fathomless desperation.

Shortly after returning to Vienna, for Helen the worst happened. Her father, too, disappeared. Both her parents had now gone. Helen has no memory of what happened next. 'The whole thing is a blank,' she says. It was only later that she understood why her father had to leave her. For him, Vienna was a death sentence. It was only a matter of time before he was caught by the Gestapo. One night he slipped out of Vienna to France with his own mother, despite having to abandon his daughter. Helen has no memory of the painful weeks that followed, when she was seemingly abandoned by both her parents.[9]

In cities across the Third Reich, the relief volunteers were faced with the impossible task of deciding who should get a precious place on Kindertransport. They saw at first hand the deteriorating conditions for Jewish families: teenage boys disappearing off the streets into concentration camps, families made homeless overnight. All the while, Hitler's rhetoric was increasingly menacing. He blamed the Jews for any war. If 'international Jewish financiers' caused another world war, he ranted, it would prompt 'the annihilation of the Jewish race in Europe'.

But it was Hitler's next move that stunned Europe and shattered the fragile peace agreed at Munich. On 15 March 1939 German tanks crossed the Sudetenland border to seize the rest of Czechoslovakia. The following day, Hitler arrived in Prague and the swastika flag fluttered over its ancient castle. It was the end of Czechoslovakia as an independent country.[10]

At Bunce Court, Tante Anna and the older pupils heard of this horrifying watershed in German aggression on the wireless. When Hitler's troops had marched into the Rhineland and seized Austria and the Sudetenland, he had been able to claim that he was seeking only to reunite German-speaking peoples. Now German troops had seized non-German territory, bringing seven million Czechs into the Third Reich. Britain and France still did nothing. But in the House of Commons, prime minister Neville Chamberlain seemed a broken man, his trust in the word of Hitler now looking foolishly misguided. Finally, on 17 March, he conceded that

Hitler was seeking war, attempting 'to dominate the world by force'. People were ready now to listen to the leading anti-appeasement member of parliament, for so long dismissed as a warmonger: Winston Churchill. 'Vast areas of home defence need to be prepared against attack from the sky,' Churchill urged. It was hard to know what might happen next. 'Hitler now looks towards Romania, the Black Sea, Turkey and beyond, the Ukraine, Poland and Soviet Russia,' Tante Anna read in the *Manchester Guardian* on 16 March, 'or he might look west to Holland, Switzerland, France and Britain.'

The Nazi's 'second rape of Czechoslovakia', observed Norman Bentwich, also deepened the refugee crisis. Overnight, a further 118,000 Jews in Czechoslovakia were brought into the Nazi net.[11] The RCM was so hard-pressed for staff and funds that it did not have the resources to mount a rescue of children from Czechoslovakia in addition to those from Austria and Germany. Kindertransports from Prague were being hastily arranged by another team of volunteers including London stockbroker Nicholas Winton, and schoolteacher Trevor Chadwick. Across Europe, volunteers were racing to save as many children as possible in a climate of impending war. Just two weeks after dismantling the rest of Czechoslovakia, Hitler threatened Poland. He demanded the free city of Danzig, the surrounding corridor of Polish land and '*Lebensraum*' ('living space') in the east.

Against this ominous backdrop, there was a sudden crisis at Bunce Court; the school's very existence was suddenly called into doubt. The owner of Bunce Court, Lady Olga Manning, decided not to renew the lease on the manor house, perhaps fearing her income could be jeopardised if war broke out. Tante Anna was effectively given an ultimatum. 'Unless the school is shortly purchased by the school authorities, she

[Lady Manning] will put it in the hands of her agents for sale,' reads a memo in the school files.

It seemed an insoluble problem. Agents came to the property to value it. The handsome manor, the twenty-six acres of grounds with the cottage, workshops and other buildings was valued by Messrs. Daniel Smith Oakley & Garrard at the princely sum of £5,000.[12] Tante Anna did not have access to such funds. New children were arriving by the day. It was inconceivable to her that she should turn any of them away, but she knew that all those who had helped her set up the school in the beginning were stretched to the limit helping children escape from the continent.

Tante Anna walked around her beloved grounds trying to find a solution. In March the RCM closed Dovercourt, which had served its purpose as an emergency reception camp. Freed from responsibility for the camps, Tante Anna could focus on this new crisis. In the six years since she arrived, Bunce Court had been transformed. Every part of it was put to good use. The main house was lovingly restored and all the ramshackle outbuildings had been repaired and turned into classrooms or dormitories. The grounds provided enough to make the school self-sufficient, with the flourishing five-acre vegetable garden, the flock of chickens and herd of pigs, not to mention the growing hive of bees. Anna's plans to take in as many children as possible would be thrown into jeopardy if she had to leave all this behind. And she was no longer young. Increasingly her eyes failed her. Was she taking on more than she could manage?

Tante Anna knew Bunce Court was just one small piece in a huge relief effort. Even so, it was unthinkable that she not play her part. The school's future might be uncertain but she could not falter in her efforts now. Tante Anna put her ambitious plans to double the size of her school on hold, and focused instead on how she could secure its future and build a more modest extension. She took on trust that somehow there would be a way to solve the financial problems. Paula admired her oldest sister who 'carried responsibility for all the children'. For her, Anna appeared to possess some inner core of steel that drove her to do more without ever seeming to buckle under the pressure. She had an ability to see what was important and not worry about the rest. 'We were constantly short of money and bookkeeping was near impossible,' wrote Paula. Even so, she had no doubt that her sister would find a way to keep her school afloat.[13]

*

Quite apart from the uncertainties over funding, Tante Anna recognised that there would be difficulties integrating this second wave of traumatised children into Bunce Court. In the spring of 1939, the school expanded at 'an alarming rate,' observed old-timer, Eric Bourne. He felt the family-like atmosphere and 'relatively tranquil routine' of Bunce Court's early years was 'rudely and crudely disrupted' by the sudden influx of strangers. Eric found himself looking back with nostalgia on 'the golden years' before Kristallnacht. Many of the new pupils were 'frightened and bewildered . . . all of them uncertain of the fate of their parents, all in trepidation at finding themselves in a foreign land . . .'[14] For Tante Anna, it was as though their childhood 'was stolen from them'. Somehow, she and the staff had to find a way to give it back.

Tante Anna believed that children were very adaptable, but many of the new arrivals had first-hand experience of extremely traumatic incidents, which intensified their anxiety. There was a wide range of emotional problems. Fourteen-year-old Ruth Boronow was one of several girls who refused to cooperate when they arrived at Bunce Court. For Ruth, the terrors of Kristallnacht in Breslau were still raw and fresh. The shock of seeing her home town burning and her mental anguish over the disappearance of her father combined with indefinable fears. Ruth knew of a distant relative who had taken his own life. 'He'd had enough. He was frightened of everything.' Ruth's father had eventually been released from Buchenwald concentration camp on condition that he sign over his assets to the Nazis and take his family out of the country.

Even with official approval, for Ruth the excruciating and long-drawn-out process of obtaining permission to leave Germany proved as frightening as Kristallnacht. She helped her mother make a list of the few possessions they were allowed to take with them. 'You had to get permission for everything. You had to wait for affidavits.' She felt tormented by delays at each stage. 'You had to pay them to go out,' continues Ruth. At first, Ruth remembers Nazi officials going into Jewish homes to choose what they wanted. 'There came a time they just wanted it all brought to them.' A new decree required Jews to surrender all personal items of value including any jewellery, gold, silver or platinum. Ruth's mother was ordered to deliver the family silver, 'anything we possessed', to a designated collection point. 'It's quite disgusting when you think of it, they were just looting.'

One chilly day in February, Ruth and her mother walked through the Breslau streets carrying their cutlery. The experience was surreal. Unlike the mob fury of Kristallnacht, this time there was silence as the Jews carried their belongings to the Nazi depot. Ruth was overwhelmed by the feeling of coldness as the people watched them go by. She felt singled out, condemned, in some way dirty and criminal. 'We must have been seen by many people who were not Jewish,' she says. 'These *rich* Jews – that's how they feel. *Rich* . . . They were jealous. I think that's how it was.' Nothing escaped the Nazis' interest, even their shoes. 'We used to rub each other's shoes with water to make them look less new,' Ruth remembers. 'Otherwise they would take them.' Ruth helped her Jewish neighbours to rub their shoes, too. 'It was just normal for us . . . We left with what we could carry.' Hounded from the country, stripped from her old life, she came to hate Nazi Germany. 'I do remember *spitting* on Germany as we left,' she says. Even though Ruth was one of the fortunate few who managed to escape with her parents, the prolonged ordeal of their departure felt ever-present. When Ruth finally reached Bunce Court, she did not wish to be parted from her mother and father in London and was in a rebellious mood.

Ruth was one of several teenage girls who expressed their distress by refusing to take part in school life. After her flight from Germany, Ruth was disappointed to find herself sent away to school. 'Oh I was naughty. I had gone meshugge [crazy]. I didn't want to learn any more,' she remembers. 'I thought it was too much work.' Tante Anna had her own unique way of handling each crisis. She told Ruth: 'This is the form you belong to if you wish, but you don't have to go to school if you don't want to.' Whatever her choice, though, Ruth would still have to make a contribution to the running of the school. Her task was to clean the windows. Ruth held out against joining the lessons although the window cleaning had no appeal either. 'It was summertime and I thought I'm not doing this any longer if I can possibly help it.' She believes her protest stemmed in part from being separated from her mother. 'I was frightened of being alone without her,' says Ruth.

Tante Anna was very sympathetic, but firm. She pointed out that Ruth was 'one of the lucky ones who still had parents'. In order not to add to the distress of the others, she wanted Ruth to ask permission before she visited her mother. 'Tante Anna very seldom said "yes",' Ruth remembers. At first her strict rule was hard to accept. But Tante Anna recognised the acute stress for children whose parents were still trapped in the Third Reich. As Ruth reluctantly cleaned the windows she pondered on the problems faced by other children and Tante Anna's words. Each day the other pupils came back from classes, apparently united by a bond of camaraderie. Ruth began to feel excluded and decided to join in. 'I soon found out that I was wrong. I picked up that you have got to know something,' she says. 'You can't just mess about. I was being stupid. If you didn't want to learn anything – you will go for the rest of your life like that.'[15]

Ruth was one of the few who knew her parents were safe. For many, homesickness was almost visceral. New boy Michael Trede remembers feeling homesick for months. He saved his pocket money to buy sweets 'as a present for my mother – should I ever see her again.' With intense worries about relatives left behind, 'no wonder so many children were in a constant state of emergency,' he observed. For Michael the homesickness was worse at night. For others, it felt acute all day long. Leslie Brent remembers the suffering of his room-mate, thirteen-year-old Gerd Nathan. Gerd was an only child whose father had long since died and he was accustomed to being 'the man of the house' for his mother. Gerd was beside himself to see her again. He worried about her alone in Hamburg. Each night, Leslie heard Gerd crying in the dormitory. One day, Gerd tried to escape. He walked out of school, along the road toward Faversham, confused, but with a desperate hope that he could somehow rejoin his mother. A kindly policeman brought him back to Bunce Court, where Tante Anna did her best to comfort him. Leslie, too, tried to encourage his friend. Slowly it worked. Gerd responded to the exuberant friendship of the school.[16]

Leslie understood the pain of longing to hear news of parents' emigration – news that never seemed to come. Months after Leslie's arrival in England his father, Arthur, had written that he had finally heard back from the American embassy. They had a number in the queue: 68,000! 'With such a high number one can wait years for permission to emigrate,' Arthur admitted. Arthur was evidently making repeated efforts to help his daughter escape from Germany. 'With Eva too, it doesn't seem to work out,' he wrote. 'So you see it is not as easy as it was with you, little boy.' Leslie longed for his sister to join him. Words and explanations were empty things. It was hard to remember faces that were once so easily available to him. His family were now just numbers.[17]

For many new pupils, the traumas were hard to express. British day boy Douglas Boyd remembers catching glimpses of the new pupils' anxieties indirectly. 'When we played games of smashing up each other's camps, my best friend, Tommy Heidelmann, mentioned that soldiers had burned his house.' On another occasion the boarders were making jokes 'about not wanting the bunk below one fifteen-year-old boy who wet his bed.' As a child from an English background untouched by Nazi tyranny, it was only later Douglas understood 'the terrible things' that had happened to his classmates. For older children like Eric Bourne, who helped to settle in this second wave of children, 'we were all brought face to face with the ugliness and viciousness of racism.' The newcomers changed 'the nature of our community by introducing a sense of hopelessness where there had once been tranquillity and optimism.' It was not only the end of their childhood, he thought, 'it may have also been for some of us.'[18]

Tante Anna knew that sometimes the children's emotional pain could produce real physical symptoms. One boy, Michael Messer, who arrived before Kristallnacht, was particularly traumatised by his parents' departure. When they left him at Bunce Court they had told him they would see him the next day. But they did not come. Not that day, nor the next or the day after. Michael found out later his parents had emigrated; perhaps they had thought it easier not to tell him. Not long after their departure, Michael began to suffer seizures and was diagnosed with epilepsy. He moved into Paula's isolation wing under her tender supervision. 'His seizures were frightening and they were dangerous in that he might fall out of a tree if he was in one – so he was not allowed to climb trees,' recalled his friend, Michael Roemer. It took several years of care before his seizures disappeared. Although there was no proof of a psychological basis to his illness, his friends suspected his epilepsy was tied to childhood suffering.[19]

Hans Meyer recalls another child who responded to his inner turmoil by flying into frenzied rages. On one particularly bad occasion, Hans 'tried to restrain the boy with a firm but loving embrace,' observed pupil Michael Trede. The boy spat right back in his face. 'Yes – go ahead and spit. Let everything out,' Hans said. The boy carried on spitting until he could no more. Then he started to weep, uncontrollable tears. It was as though he was 'liberated', wrote Michael Trede years later. 'The embrace of the teacher became less firm but all the more loving.' The boy never flew into rages again.[20]

Of all the emotional problems, arguably Tante Anna's greatest challenge came in the form of the talented, irrepressible, larger-than-life Gerard Hoffnung – who as an adult become famous as a cartoonist and impresario. In the spring of 1939, thirteen-year-old Gerard from Berlin was rapidly becoming a serious headache for Tante Anna. In the confusion of new arrivals, he stood out straight away. 'You couldn't miss him,' says Leslie. He was 'big even as a boy, with a very deep, clear voice and he made his opinions known in no uncertain manner. He would not take no for an answer.' Although he came from an 'impressive' German background with wealth and connections, 'he was very keen to be British, very corpulent and very funny,' Leslie observed. 'An outsize personality.'

Gerard had already discovered that he had a fantastic talent for entertaining the other children. 'Gerard did the most marvellous things,' says his admiring classmate, Hanni. 'His imagination was remarkable.' She remembers him creating a ghost lair in the boys' wing 'where if you went in you paid a penny' for him to terrify the other children with his fantastical horror stories. In class, among his many crimes, he would sit behind Hanni, 'blowing paper through a straw onto my neck'. He could be 'very, very naughty'.[21] On another occasion a teacher doing the night round was shocked to come across a boy covered in blood lying outside her door. As she bent down to help, the boy 'stood up, nodded, and walked away'. It was only then that she realised it was, of course, Gerard, his pyjamas soaked in red ink.

Gerard's mother, Hilde Hoffnung, believed that her talented son suffered from an overactive imagination, almost certainly augmented by disturbing events in Nazi Germany. 'He only obeys after he has exhausted us,' she conceded. 'He is frightened because, through his imagination, he is drawn to everything that is sensational, thereby he himself intensifies the anxiety, until in the end he is scared by his own grimaces.' Unruly Gerard took comfort from being the centre of attention. He played his saxophone very loudly anywhere he chose, a habit that 'drove the headmistress to distraction'.[22] But all the children loved Gerard. 'He was one of those very few real eccentrics,' observed Leslie. 'The school just could not accommodate that.' Tante Anna did not believe in punishment but the ill-disciplined Gerard was not open to persuasion. It was as though Gerard's larger-than-life personality could not be contained, even within a school as free and liberal as Bunce Court. Serious-minded Tante Anna appeared to have met her match.[23]

*

The spring of 1939, as Bunce Court was expanding rapidly, marked the end for the original Herrlingen School. Its future had been sealed by Kristallnacht and its aftermath. The school could not survive the violence against the Jewish community in Germany. To assist parents trying to emigrate, Hugo Rosenthal managed to keep the school open until 1 April before closing the gates for the last time, supervised by Nazi officials who took the school keys and personally escorted him and his wife to Ulm station. Fearing for their safety, Hugo and Judith Rosenthal went into hiding in the small village of Lautern.

The threat of war was in the air. To celebrate Hitler's fiftieth birthday on 20 April 1939 there was a massive military parade in Berlin, heavy artillery on display flaunting German power. The following month, the 'Rome–Berlin Axis' between Germany and Italy was officially announced, an alliance between Europe's fascist dictators known as the 'Pact of Steel'. All the while, antisemitic hostility escalated. Having delayed their departure to help others, Hugo and Judith Rosenthal now struggled to obtain their own exit visas to Palestine. Their sons, who had gone ahead, feared they had left it too late.[24]

Tante Anna helped Rosenthal by offering places where she could to Herrlingen staff and children and was also greatly relieved in May 1939 when her mother, Fanny, and sister, Ida, finally joined her in England. Meanwhile the Gestapo turned her former school at Herrlingen into a forced Jewish retirement home. Over the summer of 1939, elderly Jews from all over the state were taken from their homes and compulsorily rehoused in the empty school, which was just one of many forced Jewish homes for the elderly. Unknown to Tante Anna, among them was her own 88-year-old Uncle Jacob, who was taken there on 28 July. Archives in the Herrlingen museum reveal that the elderly Jews were often 'terrorised, intimidated and coerced' into leaving their homes. Blamed by the Nazis for 'the World War and the collapse of Germany in 1918', the elderly Jews now had to pay for 'their crime'. Effectively a prisoner in the old school, Uncle Jacob and others faced a bleak future: their children exiled, their assets confiscated, their very existence in the hands of a hostile Nazi bureaucracy.[25]

While her former school was being taken over by the Nazis, Tante Anna was making progress in her plans to secure the future of Bunce Court. After much discussion, the School Council concluded that if Tante Anna could raise enough in donations it might be possible for the school to obtain a mortgage and buy the manor from Lady Manning. This would create more security for the child refugees; a welcoming home for them whatever happened in Europe. Tante Anna was already running the school 'on practically nothing', Leslie found out later, and once more 'she had to go begging for money'.[26]

While trying to raise the necessary funds, Tante Anna had had another idea to find extra space for child refugees immediately. She appealed for local support and soon had a heartening response. Dr Porter, who had guided the school through the polio crisis of their first winter in England, told them about an empty former hospital five miles away at Faversham. With the help of 'our very understanding Dr Porter,' observed Paula admiringly, they persuaded the local council to let them use a large annexe in this hospital, known as Kennaways. But there was much work to do before the hospital buildings could be used by the children. Meanwhile, a Kent landowner, Lord Chilston, also came forward. He had an old farmhouse the children could use, known as Dane Court, a few miles away at Chilham. When he showed her round, Tante Anna was disappointed to find the farmhouse was very run-down. 'Would he allow his grandchildren to live there?' she asked cheekily. The obliging Lord Chilston promised not only to have linoleum laid on all the floors but to install electricity and heating. He was as good as his word and by late spring 1939, Dane Court was ready for occupation as a temporary junior school, providing an extra thirty places.[27]

Tante Anna put Gywnne Badsworth in charge of the new junior school, accompanied by Lucie Schachne, who had joined from Herrlingen. Gywnne was finding that many of her new younger pupils did not yet grasp the implications of being separated from their families. They couldn't comprehend what had happened to them. Parents sometimes had not explained the full significance of a precious son or daughter's journey or considered that their children were too young to understand. Among Gwynne's young charges was eight-year-old Frank Auerbach, who later became a renowned painter and who has never talked publicly about parting from his parents. His parents, Max and Charlotte Auerbach, had agonised over sending their treasured son abroad. With the threat of a European war in the air, finally – just before his eighth birthday – they had accepted the place at Bunce Court offered through Iris Origo, the Italian aristocrat. In April, they took Frank to Hamburg.

A photograph of Frank at the time shows an attractive boy with a dark mop of curls. Charlotte and Max had had to endure the pain of seeing their only child walk up the gangplank, accompanied by two other children who were going to Bunce Court. The carefully packed treasures in Frank's suitcase are a measure of the depths of Charlotte's unspoken fears. She had marked clothes for when he grew bigger with a neatly embroidered cross for later use. Tablecloths and sheets, for when he was grown-up, she had stitched with two crosses. With childlike innocence, Frank had no notion that he might never see his mother again.

Frank describes himself as 'rather quiet and nervous' when he arrived at Bunce Court, but after his cloistered life in Berlin, he felt a strange sense of freedom. On his very first afternoon Frank found himself under playful attack by other boys, who promptly locked the shy new arrival in a shed. Despite the unfriendly start, he 'felt curiously at home'. When he moved to Dane Court, Frank warmed to his housemother,

Gywnne. The atmosphere Gwynne created was homely and informal. The children kept pets and explored the woods around the farmhouse. He remembers evening bath times with her and the bedtime story with everyone gathered round. Despite Lord Chilston's repairs, plaster occasionally fell off the walls, which pupils duly patched over with pages from the *Picture Post*. Nurtured by Gywnne and her team, Frank was soon fluent in English, had mastered the steps of country dancing and joined the Wolf Cubs. In effect, 'without any conscious effort, we were anglicised,' Frank wrote later.[28]

Leslie Brent, too, was adapting to his new life in Britain. Tante Anna was keen for the children to learn about their host country and, wherever possible, matched each child to an English family for special day visits and the occasional holiday. She introduced Leslie to a kindly young couple from Basingstoke, Mr and Mrs Baulch, who had no children of their own. Mr Baulch worked on the railways and both were extremely welcoming. Even so, Leslie was always happy to get back to Bunce Court, where the staff were becoming like friends.

Apart from the tempestuous Heidtsche in the kitchen, Leslie warmed to Hans Meyer, who he found to be 'a very caring and understanding housefather'. He was getting to know Hanna Bergas, who helped devise the curriculum. 'HB was an intellectual woman, very clever and also lovely. I was very fond of her.' In the evenings HB sometimes gave talks on the history of art. 'I remember she talked about the French impressionists. She showed us pictures and told us what they were about and how they came to be painted.' After years of being excluded from cinemas, galleries, any kind of culture, like many of the children Leslie wanted to know what he had been missing. He found HB's talks 'inspiring'. As he came to appreciate the staff, he also realised that many of them had problems of their own. HB's cousin, Schneidy, the pianist, had had a nervous collapse trying to leave Germany before he accepted the lifeline of working for Tante Anna.

English lessons soon held a particular fascination for Leslie because they were given by Norman Wormlington, 'Wormy', who in his eyes was what they were aspiring to be: 'a real English gentleman'. His Englishness was in part bound up with his restrained manner. He was very cultured, gentle and polite but for Leslie there was also something unknowable about Wormy. Unlike some of the German staff, he managed to be both 'very loving and kind but quite distant at the same time'. He had an air of informality, perhaps emphasised by the sandals and corduroys that he almost invariably wore. Above all he had a passion for the English language. He could amuse the German boys 'with all these wonderful English idioms that no one recognises any more such as "you can take a horse to water, but you can't make it drink".' Wormy loved poetry, especially Romantics such as Wordsworth, and Shakespeare's sonnets, and could hold the class spellbound if he read them out loud. He was highly respected, Leslie recalls, 'a very, very good teacher'.

In contrast to the mild-mannered Wormy, Leslie found the talented staff in the large music department more of a puzzle. They were led by Lotte Kalischer, who appeared to Leslie as highly strung as her violin. 'I couldn't get on with her . . . and didn't take very easily to the violin which in retrospect am extremely sad about.' His own violin had special significance as it was a gift from his mother. He was happy to report back home to Arthur and Charlotte that he was learning to play and was keen to make progress. But Lotte was prone to tantrums 'when things went wrong'. She required something beyond excellence 'and she found me to be a less than brilliant student.' Leslie's father advised him to practise more but he struggled. Even so, he was inspired by Lotte's evening recitals. Lotte's talent was beyond question. 'These were wonderful occasions that lifted the spirits,' he says.[29]

'The fantastic musical scene' was also one of the highlights for Leslie's new friend, Heinz Redwood. Heinz, too, decided that Lotte was 'a remarkable person'. Each weekend, her musical friends visited from London to play chamber music in the hall at Bunce Court. Heinz remembers their concerts 'as the most outstanding thing about the atmosphere at Bunce Court'. For him, it was not just the exquisite beauty of the music that resounded through the gracious rooms of the old manor. It was the fact that the musicians had come all the way from London to play. This was far removed from his closed-in life in Hamburg, excluded from everything. 'It gave us the feeling that there was an outside world and a whole range of musical adventures we could go through,' he says. Through the music he began to feel 'there was a whole exciting world' out there to explore. Heinz had already come up against Tante Anna's gravitas as he had challenged her on such important matters as pocket money. Now he was beginning to see that she had created a 'unique and orderly situation' as far removed from the chaos of Germany as it was possible to imagine.[30]

Lotte was in charge of the school's next big performance, planned for the open day of summer 1939: *The Magic Flute*. A great many of the school's benefactors and the refugee organisers who had been instrumental in the rescue of the children would be invited. Tante Anna was keen to include as many of the new pupils as possible. Singing together would perhaps help to lift their spirits, she hoped, and introduce many of them to lives filled with music. She placed such a high value on this, it was as though 'ordinary life was blended with arts and music,' observed pupil Walter Block. But turning Mozart's masterpiece into a little piece of magic with amateur performers and the proudly named 'Bunce Court Symphony Orchestra' was hugely ambitious and, on occasion, strained Lotte's patience to the limit.

Lotte cast herself and Wormy in the leading roles and many older children had singing parts. 'I was one of the three ladies,' recalls former pupil Judith Adler, 'and I can sing this part – and some others – to this day.'[31] Leslie was thrilled when he secured a role as one of the Moorish slaves and was pitched into the fun of rehearsals with his new friends, Heinz Redwood, Ernst Weinberg and Eric Bourne. Lotte devoted herself to the task of creating a fairy-tale world with her pupil singers and, despite her impatience, had the ability to 'persuade a donkey to sing if he only tried,' observed Eric. 'For weeks the melodies of The Magic Flute seemed to be on everyone's lips.' Despite the imminent threat of war and oppressive personal worries, 'we all went opera mad and even sang to each other in the course of our work.'[32]

The open day of June 1939 was one of those quintessentially English events, somehow outside time, where it was almost possible to forget the frightening headlines and the threat of war. The weather may not have been perfect, Hitler may have been making ever more strident demands, but Tante Anna's prized lawns at Bunce Court were mowed to smooth perfection. Chairs, tables and sunshades decked the grounds. One budding reporter for the school magazine even saw enthusiasts 'putting finishing touches to the windows and paintwork' just before the school gates opened. Everything was 'in apple pie order' as the designated car park officials, 'still slinging ties around their necks', rushed to their posts in the field when the rumour spread that the first car had arrived, early.

A short speech by Anna was followed by an address from Norman Bentwich, who 'expressed his hopes for the continuation and growth of the school and its influence'. Then came teatime on the lawn, with a feast of home-made cakes and sandwiches made by Heidtsche and the children. At last, it was the longed-for moment. Everyone gathered in the amphitheatre. Without warning, the music soared above the silent fields, telling its tale of hatred and goodness and finally love. The magic of beautiful endings cast its spell. The clapping was generous. The praise unending. Wormy's colourful Papageno became a talking point. In fact, Lotte's production was deemed such a triumph that the Reverend Dr Johnson – known as the 'Red Dean' of Canterbury on account of his strong left-wing views – invited the children to give a repeat performance in Canterbury Cathedral itself later in the autumn for charity.

As for Tante Anna, during the afternoon she found time to escort select visitors to the carpentry workshop where 'a scale model of the proposed extensions were on view,' according to the school magazine. She had modified her ambitious original plan and now hoped to accommodate an extra sixty children. No opportunity for fundraising was missed. Even some of the children's artwork and handiwork was on sale for the first time. In discreet conversation, Anna's list of illustrious patrons also continued to grow: His Grace the Archbishop of York, Brigadier-General Sir Wyndham Deedes, the Right Honourable Lord Eustace Percy, the Viscountess Samuel...[33] By the time she finally waved goodbye to her three hundred guests, Tante Anna had succeeded in raising enough funds to convince the School Council that they could now raise a mortgage to buy Bunce Court and secure its future.

*

By the summer of 1939, Hitler's strident demands for the free city of Danzig had made the prospect of a Nazi invasion of Poland imminent. Britain and France prepared to stand by Poland. Across Europe, people prepared for war. There was little time left for the Kindertransports. By July, the RCM had transported several thousand children to Britain from Germany and Austria. The Polish Refugee Fund in London arranged the escape of three trains of children from Poland. Kindertransports were also still running from Prague, organised from London by relief volunteers who had been forced to leave Czechoslovakia. But tens of thousands of destitute parents and children remained trapped, their futures increasingly bleak.

Eight-year-old Mia Schaff was still waiting inside the family's Berlin apartment. It was July before her mother, Ida, finally succeeded in getting a place on Kindertransport for Mia and her older sister, Alice. 'The day before she took us out shopping. All new clothes, suitcases, she bought me a watch . . .' Mia remembers. 'Next morning we had to be at the station at six a.m. She wasn't allowed to come onto the platform with us.' Nazi officials ordered the parents behind a barrier. Mia and Alice stood close to their mother and brother, waiting fearfully. Anhalter Bahnhof station was like a battlefield, crammed with people in confusion: children crying, parents struggling to hold back their emotion. Then came the moment that felt like walking off a cliff. 'They called our names,' says Mia. 'My sister took my hand.' Mia found herself walking towards the barrier with Alice, leaving her mother behind. Her thirteen-year-old sister led her away onto the platform. 'It was all like a very bad dream.'

Ida had been strong but the sight of her two beautiful young daughters being swallowed up in the crowds was too painful to bear. She hailed a taxi with her son and raced to the next station stop at Charlottenburg. 'We looked out the window and there was my mother running down the platform,' recalls Mia. 'She beat the train and saw us one last time. That was the only time I remember crying. She said "don't cry . . ."' But there were no words that could travel the gulf separating mother and daughter now, that could reach across like a comforting arm and stop the madness. Mia tried in vain to conceal her distress from her mother. 'I said I was being squashed because everyone was leaning out the window . . .' she said, trying to be brave. Many times in later years Mia reflected on her mother's courage that day. 'On top of which I don't suppose my poor mother had any sleep that night because she was packing.'

Ida would not rest until she had saved all her children. She managed to secure a place for her son, John, on one of the last Kindertransports from Berlin. In England, her oldest daughter, thirteen-year-old Alice, had promised her mother she would keep her younger brother and sister with her, but well-meaning grown-ups intervened. Before long the three children were sent out of London and separated, each placed with a different family. Mia found herself going from one home to another. 'I may not have been an easy child. I don't know. Certainly I wasn't happy. Nobody wanted a little girl who spoke no English.' Her mother soon wrote to reassure them. There was good news at last. Her visa had arrived. It was not long to wait. She was due to leave Germany on 10 September 1939. They would be reunited.[34]

But Europe's refugees were being swept along in a tide of events so much larger than themselves. Then came the bombshell: on 23 August Germany had signed a non-aggression pact with the Soviet Union. 'The pact will clearly make it easier for Germany to carry out her aggressive plans in Europe,' explained the *Manchester Guardian* on 25 August. There were reports that German troops and tanks were massing along the Polish frontier. The people of this country 'are confronted with the imminent peril of war,' warned Neville Chamberlain.

Across Britain, the prospect of attack from the air brought unknown terrors. Civilians would be on the front line. Air Raid Precaution schemes were set up and gas masks distributed. Sandbags piled high outside buildings transformed inner cities. Mothers registered their children for evacuation to the countryside. Anti-aircraft guns were manned and manoeuvred into position. At night, the beams of searchlights probed the dark sky while people hurried to black out their windows. 'Many shops have run out of suitable dark cloths,' reported the *Manchester Guardian* on 30 August. 'Any shops that sell tinned food have also had an enormous rush of customers.'[35]

At Bunce Court, Tante Anna had succeeded in taking in sixty more children, most from the Kindertransports. As the remaining new pupils arrived for the start of the autumn term, Eric remembers Matron, Anna's youngest sister Bertha, 'forever wandering about looking for unoccupied beds'. With the new arrivals the school was very short of space. Among the newcomers was Karl Grossfield from Vienna, whose generous welcome by the wealthier members of the Pinner refugee committee had finally come to an end. He arrived at Bunce Court with his older sister, Erica, who joined the same class as Leslie. Karl had been waiting for news of his mother, Miriam, who still would not leave Vienna without her husband. In late August he finally learned his parents had escaped together. 'It was like the films,' says Karl. 'They left Austria with a suitcase.' His parents even smuggled a case packed with Skoda cameras through customs so they were not destitute as they began a new life in Palestine.[36] Richard Sonnenfeldt, too, was fortunate. A year ago his mother had been contemplating a family suicide, but now he heard his parents had managed to flee to neutral Sweden. Tante Anna was relieved to get word that Hugo and Judith Rosenthal had also managed to slip out of Germany via Switzerland and were reunited with their sons in Palestine. But most children, including Leslie, were still waiting for news of their parents; news that never came.

With war perhaps just hours away, the relief agencies in Europe's capitals were still battling to save more children. Borders were closing. Communications with the Gestapo were breaking down. Despite this, miraculously on 1 September 1939 one last Kindertransport managed to leave Germany amidst urgent reports that Hitler had already invaded Poland. Some 9,354 children had now reached the safety of England. In Prague, one hundred and eighty more were also preparing to leave. Their panicky exodus became fraught. There were interminable delays. Parents waited anxiously, the moment of parting painfully prolonged. Finally, the Gestapo refused permission for the train to leave. Almost all these children are thought to have later perished in concentration camps.[37]

On those fateful days at the beginning of September, Leslie

Brent was still on holiday with his 'English family', the Baulchs. During the summer of 1939 they had offered to adopt him. Leslie appreciated their kindness but felt confused because he loved his own parents. With Germany at war with Poland, he was straining every sinew for news of them. 'I did not regard myself as an orphan,' he says. He resolved to seek Tante Anna's advice. On 3 September, in this troubled frame of mind, Leslie has a vivid memory of sitting with the Baulchs listening to the radio. They were waiting to hear the British prime minister. The clock struck eleven. Neville Chamberlain's grave voice seemed to fill the small living room with his ominous words. Hitler was not prepared to withdraw from Poland, announced the prime minister, 'and consequently this country is at war with Germany.'

Even though war was expected, Chamberlain's words still came as a profound shock. 'Everyone was terribly upset . . .' recalls Leslie. The Baulchs had to report to the Territorial Army barracks immediately. They drove him in their little Austin 7 back to Bunce Court. It was a beautiful sunny Sunday and that made it worse. Leslie felt desperately vulnerable in the car. He half expected war to come swiftly at any minute. As they circled around London, he saw diggers excavating great mounds of soil in the fields. Almost certainly the earth was for sandbags for protection from bombs, explained Mr Baulch. Leslie kept peering out at the sky, looking for enemy planes. When they approached the Kent Downs, there were huge grey barrage balloons, floating like giant hulks suspended in the sky. It didn't seem enough. 'I thought bombs could drop at any time,' Leslie remembers. 'It was a horrendous thought.'[38]

That morning in Bunce Court, Tante Anna was joined by the staff and a sombre group of top-formers who crammed into her room to hear the prime minister's announcement. Britain, the country of their refuge, was at war with Germany. German and Austrian pupils were technically now in 'enemy territory'. Some pupils had not yet returned from holidays in Germany. 'God only knows what fate befell them,' Richard Sonnenfeldt wrote later.

The staff and older children threw themselves into urgent activities that might help distract the younger ones. Richard led a group building shelters. 'We dug madly,' Richard remembers. They chopped trees to make the timbers for the roofs and disguised them from the air with earth. It was a welcome diversion for anxious children, although 'quite ridiculous', Richard admitted to himself, since the school was hardly likely to attract a bomb. Even so, the children saw a squadron of RAF planes in the distance flying low across Kent towards France. Biggin Hill, one of the 'last ditch' fighter stations, was just forty-five miles away. Pupil Michael Roemer remembers three planes directly over their cottage in the grounds. '"Germans!" cried one of the boys. Of course, they were not Germans. They were Spitfires,' he says. The staff busily distributed gas masks and taught the children how to wear them. Everyone was jumpy. There was fear of a poison gas attack or even a parachute drop. One or two older children were designated as air raid wardens and issued with special helmets.[39]

Nothing could quite detract from the numbing sense of fear felt by most children who had parents now trapped in the Third Reich. When Leslie reached Bunce Court, there was no comforting letter from his parents. They were cut off. It was as though the bottom had fallen out of his world. He could picture them, Arthur, Charlotte and Eva, in their Berlin flat and only wonder what war might mean. His parents were now in 'enemy territory'. It felt unreal. 'It was a bad feeling . . .' He was separated from them 'in a wholly unpredictable way'.[40]

Over the coming days Tante Anna read of the horrors of the German Blitzkrieg unleashed on Poland. This 'lightning war' was a new kind of hell as Germany's military arsenal was let loose on an unimaginable scale simultaneously by air, land and sea. All their efforts to save children in Germany, Austria and Czechoslovakia appeared to be dwarfed by this appalling cataclysm. There were three and a half million Jews in Poland, the largest population in all of Europe. It was hard to imagine how many more children were about to be caught up in the horror.

Part Two

―――

September 1939–July 1948

8

'How stupid to cry when the next minute I would be dead . . .'

Nine-year-old Sam Oliner, Poland, 1939

Friday, 1 September 1939. For seven-year-old Sidney Finkel that's when it began. The end of his childhood and the beginning of the events that could not be spoken of. Hitler's invasion of Poland.

Sidney remembers a stream of valiant fighting talk on the radio, but any Polish optimism was rapidly overtaken. In Piotrkow near Lodz, in central Poland, Sidney felt the awesome might of the German Blitzkrieg: the all-out lightning war unleashed on the country by air, land and sea. Piotrkow was some 250 miles from the German border but by 2 September the skies darkened with German bombers. Sidney remembers rushing for cover with his family to a crowded cellar where the air was stale and the ground trembled as hundreds of bombs dropped above. It was his first taste of all-consuming terror.[1]

When Sidney and his family dared to emerge, they found everyone was fleeing. They joined the exodus on foot, carrying what they could. Sidney's father, Laib, inspired confidence; he knew what to do. He led his family six miles to Sulejow, the village where he had been born. When they arrived, there was a comforting sense of normality. Friends and neighbours were reunited. The sun was shining. Sidney found a ball and began to play.[2]

Then, as if from nowhere, Sidney was enveloped in an all-embracing, sucking, screeching noise that bore down on him. Without warning, the world around him went up in flames. The wooden buildings of the old village turned into bonfires. Sidney was standing in the middle of what seemed to be walls of fire. It was a scene from hell. People, cattle, pets were ablaze like living torches, still running . . .[3]

It was such a total transformation from the peaceful village scene seconds before that Sidney could not make sense of it. This could not be real. It was beyond anything he could even imagine. Later he understood that these were low-flying *stukas*, German dive-bombers, dropping incendiaries that fell from the sky. At the time, Sidney stood rooted to the ground. His legs could have been made of stone. He could not stop staring up at the sky. The planes came so low that Sidney could see the German pilots take aim with their machine guns, concentrating hard, seemingly oblivious to the panic and chaos they inflicted below. Still, he could not move.[4]

Then he heard his mother's voice. Faiga threw herself over him. He could feel her wet tears as she buried her face in his neck and kissed him. He felt comforted until he felt her stir. She left him to protect his twelve-year-old sister, Frania, who could not stop screaming. Sidney wanted to follow, but remained paralysed as though held in a vice. All his senses shouted out the danger: the searing heat from the flames, the blood-curdling screams, the repellent smell of burning skin. Intense fear, unlike anything he had ever felt before, transformed his body into an immovable weight.[5]

When the bombing stopped, Sidney realised he was still alive. He half raised himself and found he was lying at the centre of a massacre. Of all the horrible impressions, it was the nauseating stench of burning flesh that overpowered anything else. 'You never forget that smell,' he says.[6] Sidney found he could stand. Then quite suddenly he was running blindly over the dead and dying, almost without seeing them, his eyes scanning the village for any sign of his family. Nothing.

Sidney had gone some distance before he heard his name being called. He turned. There was his father, Laib. His father was a strong man, with the air of unquestioned authority that came from his years of working in the flour mill, sawmill and timber yard he had built up from scratch, from years of giving orders and expecting them to be followed. Even in this catastrophic setting, the very sight of his father brought relief. Laib swept his youngest son into his arms and held him tight all the way to the forest. Even then he did not let go. They pressed on to the centre of the forest where villagers had congregated.[7] Sidney wanted to know what had happened to his mother and the rest of the family. He knew his oldest brother, Isaac, was fighting with the Polish army. His oldest sister, Ronia, had probably escaped with her husband. But where were his mother and two younger sisters, Lola and Frania? His father did not know.

Three days passed before Sidney and his father ventured back to the village of Sulejow. The scene before them was gruesome. People were digging a mass grave to bury some three thousand bodies. More terrifying still was the sight of those still half alive, many burned or indescribably injured. Sidney and his father searched among them for his mother and Lola and Frania, until someone told them they had been seen fleeing on a cart.[8]

Sidney and his father went back to their home town, Piotrkow, on someone's open wagon. Even as they approached, the smoke drifting over the town told them it had been badly bombed. They made their way through a maze of wreckage-strewn streets to find their apartment. The block was ripped in two. One side, improbably, was still upright, the other a pile of rubble. They no longer had a home.[9]

Laib had worked hard all his life to provide for his family. Before the financial crash of the early 1930s, 'he was almost a millionaire and the next day he was a poor man,' according to his oldest son, Isaac.[10] He had rebuilt his businesses from scratch, but now the prospect of a second annihilation proved too much. Sidney saw his father staring blankly at the wreckage of their home, their personal belongings spewing out over the torn fabric of the building and onto the street. For the first time, his all-powerful father had tears in his eyes.

They took refuge in Laib's sister's house, which was still standing. Sidney's uncle told him what had happened. The German army had been in Piotrkow for several days. No one had known what to expect. When the Germans had occupied the town in the First World War they had not singled out the Jews. This time it was very different. Over his aunt's kitchen table, long-held fears about Hitler's brutal treatment of Jews began to take on an ominous new reality. There had been random killings and beatings. Jewish men had disappeared from the street. It was rumoured they had been sent to a labour camp. More than a quarter of the entire population of Piotrkow was Jewish. One of the first acts of the German army was to burn down the town's Jewish quarter. Jews were shot as they ran from the flames that lit up the skies over the city.[11]

*

One hundred and eighty miles south-east in Dukla, southern Poland, nine-year-old Sam Oliner remembers the day the German army marched through town. When war broke out he was separated from his family, having been sent away to Hebrew school, or cheder. For days there had been intense fighting. Alone in the crammed cellar of someone he barely knew, he tried to interpret the sounds of battle above. He heard the screech of planes diving low, the thudding of heavy bombardment and, close at hand, the yak-yak of retaliatory fire, coming, improbably it seemed, from Dukla's city hall. The noise of the battle outside was indistinguishable from noise inside the cellar. He was crammed in the darkness with a crowd of strangers whose fear was so intense he thought he could smell it.[12]

Eventually the fighting stopped. The Polish army retreated. Sam heard the advancing German army before he saw it. 'It was frightening to hear a tremendous march,' he remembers.[13] By the light of a narrow cellar window that opened onto the main road, he could make out the wheels of foreign vehicles driving by. In this poor district of Poland peasants counted themselves lucky to have a horse and cart, but the Germans had a seemingly endless cavalcade of vehicles of war. Sam could smell the gasoline as he scrambled out of the cellar and joined the Poles who lined the road to watch the extraordinary sight of the conquering army. To a young boy, the German soldiers seemed very strange. They were all alike, their faces without expression, hard and uncommunicative. It was as though each German soldier was moulded into a part of one almighty force, joined in some invisible way, 'like the links of a never-ending chain'.[14] There were so many of them it took two whole days before the chain had passed by.

Dukla was transformed. The changes were not just physical, with wrecked buildings and the dead unburied in the streets. For Sam it was like finding himself in a different country. Soon after the German occupation, bizarre anti-Jewish rumours began to spread. It was said that Jews were stockpiling food and raping Polish women. A strong sense of threat grew not just from the Nazis, but the local population, who turned on their former neighbours.

One night Sam was eating supper with a Jewish family in Dukla when there was a hammering on the front door. Poles were looting Jewish homes. They watched fearfully as the front door shook with each blow. Then the noise stopped. Through the window they could see there was a free-for-all; the looters had smashed their way into the house opposite. Sam saw people he knew running from the Jewish house clutching their stolen trophies, little more than cooking pots, lamp oil and basic supplies such as sugar or salt. It was the poor stealing from the poor, but with a fury and sense of entitlement that Sam had not seen before.

Far from intervening to keep order, when the Poles cried '*Jude, Jude*' the Nazi soldiers would help them smash down the doors of Jewish houses. On another occasion, Sam watched from a hidden vantage point as he saw Nazi soldiers attack an elderly Jew in his home. They yanked his long beard and beat him with a pistol. Sam saw the blood as the man fell to the floor. 'With nine-year-old eyes I was shaken by this sight,' he recalls. 'I just couldn't understand why they would do this – I mean, he hadn't done anything.'[15]

As a child it was hard to understand the full scale of the tragedy that was engulfing his homeland. Much of what he knew rested on anecdote and word of mouth. Now, looking back on his nine-year-old self, he sees that he was a mere speck on the landscape, caught in the almighty clash of two vast armies. On 17 September 1939, the Soviet army invaded from the east. Poland was under attack from both sides. By 6 October, Poland had ceased to exist. His homeland was divided; Germany annexed western Poland and Danzig and the Soviet Union seized the eastern territory. Poland's three and a half million Jews had good reason to fear what would happen next.

One day Sam's maternal grandmother, Reisel, came to take him back to her farm in Zyndranowa, twelve miles south of Dukla, high up in the mountains near the Czechoslovakian border. As their wagon approached the log cabin, Sam's older sister, Feigele, ran out and rushed to hug him. Feigele had heard rumours of the attacks on Jews and had feared Sam wasn't safe in Dukla. Their father, Aron, and brother, Moishe, were not at the farm. Despite the protection of her grand-parents and uncles, Feigele felt frightened without them.[16]

Since the death of their mother, Jaffa, two years before the war, their family had split into two camps. Sam could never forget the terrible day in 1937 when his father had carried his mother out of the log cabin. She was ill and seemed weak and frail as a rag doll as he placed her on the straw on the back of the cart. No one would tell Sam where they were going. He had watched as the cart retreated from view, worried for his mother. This had never happened before. It didn't occur to him he would not see his mother again. When Grandmother Reisel told him a few weeks later that his mother had died, seven-year-old Sam had been unable to grasp the idea. 'What do you mean she's dead?' he asked. 'She's dead for a little while maybe. When is she coming back?' His grandmother gave him a hug.[17] She was crying and did not like to contradict his idea that 'death is only for a little while'. The months came and went and still Sam was sure his mother would come back.

After the horrors he experienced in Dukla in September 1939, Sam settled back into the routine of his grandparents' farm, taking comfort from caring for the animals. His father was not at the farm. Following a centuries-old tradition, Aron had visited the matchmaker and remarried a younger woman called Ester, and they had settled in a village called Bielanka, twenty-five miles away. But Sam did not feel comfortable with Ester. Something was missing. She was no replacement for his own precious, warm-hearted mother.

Sam didn't tell his grandparents about the antisemitic violence he had witnessed in Dukla. 'I coped with the fear by denial,' he says. 'I would pretend I hadn't seen this stuff.' It was easier to deny that he had seen these things.[18] But even in this isolated spot, the rumours reached them. They heard the Nazis were looking for Jews and demanding food from the farms. High up in the Carpathian Mountains, for Sam it was almost possible to feel safe.

One day Sam saw a car winding up the track towards their cabin. He realised at once it was a German car. No Polish peasant had a car. Quick-thinking and practical, he hurried round the back to get the chickens out of the yard, fearing the German soldiers would take them for food. Sam also tied up the dog – he had heard that the Nazis would shoot any dog that attacked or even barked. Peering round the side of the house, he glimpsed the dreaded Nazis at close quarters. One of them waited in the car. The other four went to the front door and demanded to know whether this was a Jewish home. His grandfather confirmed that it was and they pushed past him and went inside.

Sam joined his grandparents in the kitchen. The Nazis

pushed his grandfather up against the oven until his clothes singed, demanding gold and money. When he explained he had none, they knocked him to the floor. His grandmother tried to help him up but he was unsteady. The Nazis prepared to fire. Sam and his grandparents cowered helplessly, backed against the kitchen wall. 'I was certain I was going to die,' he recalled.[19] His quick thinking deserted him. He struggled to breathe. There was an unrecognisable noise in the room that he realised was the sound of his own sobbing. He wanted to live. His grandparents were pleading with the Nazis for them to let the child live. He shivered with fear. At the same time, he thought quite rationally, 'how stupid to cry when the next moment I would be dead'.[20] The Nazi in charge did not seem to hear their pleas. His face was impassive. There was a click as he released the catch on his gun.

Just then the Nazis heard a commotion in the yard and ran outside. Through the window, Sam saw the Nazi driver was trying to kiss his sister. Feigele was about four years older than Sam and pretty, with her creamy skin and dark hair. He had already noticed the effect she seemed to have on men. The driver held her down against the car. He had torn her shirt as he tried to kiss her. The Nazi officer ordered him to let her go. Feigele fled but was caught by one of the other Nazis, who pinned her against the barn as he ordered her to report to Gestapo headquarters in Dukla.

As the Nazis' car disappeared from view, the family gathered in the kitchen. No one could speak. The shock was too great. Their relief at being left alone was short-lived once Feigele revealed what the Nazis had demanded. It was now clear that the intruders were from the merciless Gestapo. The very name inspired terror. Over the following days the tension in the house was unbearable. No one wanted Feigele to go to the Gestapo headquarters but Sam's grandparents feared reprisals. Would they lose their farm? Should they run away? Where could they go? If Feigele disappeared to her father's house at Bielanka, would the Gestapo return and kill everyone else? Eventually, no longer capable of rational thought, his grandparents decided Feigele must do as instructed. Sam should drive his sister in the wagon to the Gestapo headquarters.[21]

For Sam, the proud feeling of being grown-up enough to drive the horse and cart all the way to Dukla was overwhelmed by a sense of foreboding. His sister's silence was interspersed with brave but unconvincing attempts to reassure him that she was fine. They reached Dukla and were directed to the headquarters of the Gestapo, the former mayor's villa. The guard fetched another Nazi official, Finke, who to Sam's astonishment greeted them warmly. Finke seemed surprised to see them. He had forgotten all about what he had said to Feigele. He smiled at Sam, gave him some sweets and told him to wait outside and guard their horse. Sam was frightened. He hated leaving his sister. He also felt very silly. Finke had forgotten his order and 'we had walked into the jaws of the lion like two dumb rabbits.'[22]

The minutes dragged by. Sam circled the horse. An hour passed and more. Eventually Feigele emerged. She looked unhurt, but was in tears and wouldn't speak all the way home. The next day Sam overheard his grandmother saying that she was 'very much afraid that Feigele had been raped' by several of the Nazis at the headquarters.[23]

Since the war began, nine-year-old Sam had been finding that his childhood had disappeared. 'There wasn't much time to grow up in,' he said later.[24] His schooling was over. He had narrowly escaped being shot at close range. What weighed even more heavily was that he had been powerless to protect his sister – not from some playground bully, but from the Gestapo.

✳

In the opening weeks of the war, thousands of Jews fled east towards Soviet Russia, hoping the Polish army would stop the relentless advance of Nazis. Among them was three-year-old Anna Rose and her family. Anna remembers the terrible uproar of the day they left Krakow in southern Poland. There was a tumultuous noise coming from outside their apartment. Anna stepped out onto the balcony and looked down on to bedlam in the street below. The traffic was at a standstill, the road crammed with people bearing cases, bedding, even furniture; anything they could hold or push in a cart. At a distance was a different sound, a sound Anna had not heard before: thunderous, monotonous and very threatening. 'The Nazis,' the grown-ups said. 'We must leave at once.' By 6 September the German army had occupied Krakow.

The sounds of the Blitzkrieg were never far behind and sometimes overtook them as their snaking column of refugees became caught in German strafing. 'I had no idea what was going on,' Anna says. Her life of comfort with devoted parents was transformed so suddenly 'I just sort of shut down.'[25] At one point, her father, Jan, suddenly emerged from the crowd, having found it impossible to rejoin his regiment. 'The German army is sweeping through western Poland,' he said. It took almost three weeks to flee three hundred kilometres nearly 200 miles east. The Rose family reached Ostrog on the Russian border but were caught up in a new catastrophe.[26]

That night they woke to find that the building they had pitched camp in for the night seemed to be shaking. There was an unfamiliar noise outside. Peering out in the darkness, Anna and her older brother, Arthur, saw long columns of soldiers trudging through the streets, dressed in brown uniforms, bearing rifles. There seemed no end to this sinister sight. From their high window, they saw the canvas roofs of military vehicles, cannon rolling by and officers on horseback. The soldiers bore the red flag: the Soviet Red Army entering Poland from the east. Arthur watched, mesmerised. For Anna's parents the alarming implications of the pact Hitler had made with Stalin just before the war were becoming clear. The Russians were invading and occupying the eastern half of Poland. They were trapped.

There were so many unknowns. With the brutal state repression of Stalin's Russia, it was hard to imagine what the arrival of the Red Army would mean for Polish Jews. Anna's father was certain they were safer in the Soviet zone but Anna's grandmother was terrified of the Soviets and wanted to go back to Krakow, fearing arrest or deportation. Anna recognised the tone of agitation and despair in the grown-ups' voices but did not understand. Her overwhelming impression was of the change in her parents' behaviour. 'All of a sudden I realised my parents were very angry, they were quarrelling, they were disciplining us – much more than before.' Something crucial had shifted, 'I didn't know why.'[27] She had no way of understanding their new nightmare world. Poland was wiped off the map of Europe, its spoils divided between Nazi Germany and the Soviet Union.

Living in the Soviet-occupied zone, the Rose family found a room to rent in Lvov, but their life was restricted and Anna's father disappeared for long periods. Anna found the puzzle of the grown-up world ever more confusing. Her parents wanted her to swear that she would never talk of her father being a lawyer. Why was it bad to be a lawyer? It had been good in Poland. Still more mystifying, why was it bad to be a Jew? 'I walked around in a fog of confusion.'[28] Her deep-seated fears mingled with a sense of uncertainty. Nothing was the same.

Anna was too young to understand that the Soviet secret service, the notorious NKVD, known for its ruthless purges, was hunting down the professional classes and intellectuals. As a lawyer and a Polish army officer, Anna's father was deemed an 'enemy of the people', at risk of being sent to Soviet camps or even shot. In Joseph Stalin's Russia, foreign intellectuals and military officers were potential subversives; better off in Siberia, better still dead.

In their relentless search for 'undesirables', the Soviets laid a trap. The NKVD polled the refugees, ostensibly to ascertain if any wished to return to the German sector. Anna's father suspected this was a ploy. He urged everyone in the family to state that they wished to stay in the Soviet zone but Anna's grandmother did not follow his advice. She left with Anna's half-sister, Liana, who was ordered to leave under suspicion of being a Nazi sympathiser.

A few weeks later a letter arrived, not from Krakow in Poland, but from Siberia. The Soviet train had not taken Anna's grandmother and half-sister west, but east to a labour camp in Omsk. Anna did not know of the desperately harsh conditions there. But she did see her father painstakingly cut out a secret cavity in a large book by Vladimir Lenin. He concealed her mother's gold and jewellery in the space, wrapped the book carefully and posted it to his mother-in-law in Siberia. This was something else Anna understood she must never, never mention in nursery school in this alarming new world of hidden spies and deadly denunciations. It was a sort of game of death. What could be spoken of? If you got it wrong, somebody died or disappeared.[29]

*

On 8 October, just two days after the Nazis annexed western Poland, seven-year-old Sidney Finkel and his family were among the first to experience a watershed in their barbaric treatment of the Jews. Barely a month after the trauma of living through the Nazi Blitzkrieg, notices were posted through the town ordering the Jews of Piotrkow in central Poland into a small area within the town, now renamed 'the Ghetto'. This was war-torn Poland's very first Nazi ghetto.[30]

Sidney's family were allocated a couple of rooms in his former school: one room and a small kitchen for the whole family. The close confinement was hard. There was no running water and toilets were shared by many families. But Sidney's mother and sister Frania, who had become separated during the bombing, rejoined them in the ghetto. Sidney can still picture his mother in their shabby new home, sewing the obligatory 'J' on his jacket to denote that he was a Jew. Sidney's oldest sister, 23-year-old year old Ronia, and her husband were also driven into the ghetto although, since they were married, they lived in a different room. Before long, 20,000 Jews were crammed into a space once occupied by just 5,000 Poles.[31]

The deprivations soon piled up. Sidney's father, Laib, had his assets confiscated, including his profitable flour mill and sawmill. Everything he had laboured for was now gone. Foreseeing problems, he had already sold his timber yard to a sympathetic non-Jewish business associate and the precious

funds raised by this were all he had to provide for his family.
At first it was possible to escape the ghetto during the day
for up to two hours. As time passed, there were tighter restrictions until no one was permitted to leave. Everyone had to
be inside their cramped quarters by 5 p.m. Signs marked
'Ghetto' with an image of a human skull were placed around
the border. 'I don't think there was a fence,' Sidney recalls.
'It was just, no one was allowed to leave.'[32] Anyone caught
breaking the rules could be shot.

Smuggling was rife, despite the risk of death if caught.
Sidney's parents became involved with a smuggler, but he
robbed them of their savings. Sidney was alarmed by the
depths of his parents' despair.

Keen to be of use, he volunteered with his friend, Harry,
to work at the local Hortensia Glass Works. The industrial
setting around a vast furnace was no place for a young boy.
One day, as Sidney helped to unload large sacks, he ran into
trouble. Instead of carefully lowering the weighty cargo, the
youth unloading the van threw a sack at Sidney, who was
knocked off balance. The heavy sack fell to the floor. This
caught the eye of the Nazi officer supervising the works. The
officer marched Sidney to the centre of the square and took
out his gun. Savouring the hold he had over a small, terrified
boy, he toyed with Sidney as he slowly prepared to pull the
trigger. There seemed to be an interminably long moment as
Sidney waited. The end never came. One of the Jewish leaders
happened to pass by and recognised Sidney. He had the
courage to reason with the Nazi foreman. Sidney found his
life was spared and he fled.[33]

Many months elapsed before they were joined in the ghetto
by Sidney's older brother, twenty-five-year-old Isaac. He had

been shot fighting with the Polish army. Despite life-threatening injuries and burns he had recovered and found his way back to Piotrkow, where he was ordered into the ghetto. The family was overjoyed to see him. 'It was a very happy moment – we only thought we are alive and we are together,' said Isaac.[34] Sidney felt much safer with the protection of his capable older brother. He had seen a change come over his father since his businesses were taken from him. 'My father was by that point almost a beaten man,' says Sidney.[35] As a wounded ex-prisoner of war, Isaac was allowed to leave the ghetto for treatment by the Red Cross for his injuries, which gave him a chance to make crucial contacts outside the ghetto who could help them with food and medicines and restore some kind of control over their lives.

'Every day we read a different story about someone being arrested and taken away,' recalls Isaac. The disappearances became so common that it was almost accepted as part of daily life.[36] One day their own sister, Ronia, disappeared. The days passed and no one could explain to Sidney where she had vanished to. He searched the ghetto. She was nowhere.

Ronia was Sidney's favourite sister. She was nearly twenty years older than him and he loved her like a mother. Warm-hearted Ronia had always been able to stand up to their father when his temper got the better of him and Sidney saw her as clever and, in retrospect, politically astute. Perhaps she had seen the dangers of German antisemitism more clearly than their parents. At one stage before the war she had planned to emigrate to Palestine with friends, but their father had opposed the idea. Sidney remembers Ronia arranging donations of food and blankets for the Jews dumped by the Nazis at the Polish border. Shortly before the war, she had fallen in love and married.

'How stupid to cry when the next minute I would be dead . . .'

Despite the restrictions of ghetto life, Ronia had actually been happy the last time Sidney had seen her. Her first baby was nearly due and she was excited. Polish friends helped her when her time came, smuggling her out of the ghetto into the Catholic hospital. Sidney learned that the birth was successful. Ronia had a little boy and he was now an uncle. But where were they?[37]

For days he could make no sense of what happened. No one could tell him where Ronia had gone. Months had passed before her husband finally revealed what had happened. The Gestapo had found out that there was a Jew in the Catholic hospital. Without hesitation they came and grabbed the newborn baby and threw him from the window. Then they took Ronia, still recovering from childbirth, to the cemetery for Jews, where they shot her.[38]

Sidney was inconsolable. He collapsed on the floor, sobbing. His mother and father were also weeping uncontrollably, but he could bear no one near him. He wanted *her*. 'I crawled under the bed and cried. That's the most I ever cried.'[39] He never cried again, he recalls, even on a long journey that would take him to concentration camps and several times when he was within an inch of death. That softer side of him was dead already. There would be nothing as beautiful as Ronia in his life for a long, long time.[40]

Sidney could have no idea as he sobbed under the bed from their crowded room in the ghetto that his country was at just the start of a process that would see the entire Jewish population herded into ghettos like animals.

9

'We were shocked when they came for the cook . . .'

Fifteen-year-old Heinz Redwood, Bunce Court, May 1940

In England at Bunce Court, pupils queued up to read articles that Tante Anna posted on the noticeboard about the progress of the war. 'Britain's fight to save the world' was much vaunted in the papers in September 1939, but Britain and France seemed to do little to help Poland.[1] The devastating Blitzkrieg crushed the country with brutal swiftness. For anxious pupils, whose own flight from Germany was a recent memory, it was hard to know what this swift destruction of an entire country could mean. Would Britain face a Blitzkrieg like Poland? Could enemy parachutists suddenly land in the vicinity? Could German bombers wipe out whole cities and bring the British to surrender? The safe distance between themselves and the Nazi regime shrank in the face of such unknowns.

The war brought urgent changes to the daily routine of the school. As matron, Bertha led everyone in a hurried effort to sew blackout curtains for the many Georgian windows. 'Not the slightest glimmer of light was to penetrate from the outside,' wrote Hanna Bergas. 'We were close to the coast.'[2] The children became accustomed to finding their way in dim passages and helping with the evening 'curtain patrol'.

Occasionally the night sky lit up with bright searchlights. 'It was somehow horribly beautiful,' recalls Hans Meyer; the beams were an eerie warning of the prospect of enemy planes. Hans was responsible for practising the ARP — Air Raid Precaution — exercises with the children, for ensuring that everyone's gas mask fitted well and rehearsing the fire drill. 'We all gracefully glided down the fire escape from the boys' floor,' remembered Eric Bourne, including the staff. Hans's wife, Hannah, who the children nicknamed 'HaGo', insisted on making the drill more like a real emergency by rescuing a load of favourite toys as she manoeuvred herself down. Even the deep chime of the school bell fell silent, designated for use only as an alarm for an invasion or the dropping of enemy parachutists.

All too soon, it felt as though the war was directly over-head. 'There was the first air-raid when we all sat in the dimly lit dining hall at about 3 a.m. and HaGo read to us,' Eric remembers, 'nobody was listening very much, it just gave the appearance of normality.'[3] But everyone knew 'normality' was a phantom. The next step might bring disaster. It seemed to be always night; sunny days were a mirage. In the first autumn downpour the bunkers the children had dug in the grounds filled with water and had to be cleared.

It was no longer possible for the pupils to receive letters directly from their families in Germany or Austria and the short monthly messages facilitated by the Red Cross told them little. Leslie Brent became accustomed to going to the town hall to collect the Red Cross forms. Only twenty-five words were allowed and he could see that his parents, Arthur and Charlotte, in Berlin, were being careful not to offend German censors. 'Beloved boy. We are happy about your message. We are well. Practise the violin . . .' wrote his father. Leslie was equally cautious in his replies. 'Am well and cheerful. Do not worry. Kisses for all . . .'⁴ Before the war he had dared to hope that he would see them in England; that Eva would follow on another Kindertransport. Such dreams were now channelled through the slender lifeline offered by the Red Cross forms. The staccato messages, never stating real feelings, were nonetheless imbued with a multitude of possible meanings as children tried to read between the lines.⁵

In their deliberately upbeat messages, Arthur and Charlotte gave no hint of an inexplicable family tragedy: Leslie's grandmother had vanished without trace. Whatever avenues Charlotte pursued to find her mother, Oma, the trail went cold. It was incomprehensible. Although her mother suffered from a painful and incurable skin condition, she was otherwise well, and it was completely out of character for her to disappear. Eventually Charlotte learned that her mother had been sent to 'a so-called Old Age People's Home,' says Leslie. It was only years later he understood it was 'probably an extermination home'. Grandmother Oma was never seen again.⁶

Grandmother Oma was almost certainly an early victim of the Nazis' terrifying 'Aktion T4': their first official extermination programme, innocuously named after its headquarters in Tiergartenstrasse 4 in Berlin. Anyone with a chronic disability or an incurable physical or mental illness could be deemed 'life unworthy of life'. The patient's religion and ethnicity was also taken into account and as an elderly Jew with a chronic skin disease, Grandmother Oma would have been a target. The Nazis endeavoured to conceal the true fate of the disappearing patients by the use of 'Charitable Ambulance Buses' manned by members of the SS wearing medical white coats. The patients were usually taken first to major hospitals to disguise their true destination: *Sonderbehandlung* Centres or 'Special Treatment Centres'. There they were murdered; the Nazis called it a 'mercy killing'. As early as 1940, the T4 programme was trialling the Nazis' first experiments in killing by using gas.[7]

Just how much Charlotte was able to piece together of her mother's fate is not clear from the records. Leslie had no idea of his grandmother's disappearance in the Red Cross messages he received from his parents. It was only later he understood the terrible despair of their war years in Berlin. Almost a year had elapsed since he had last seen his parents and his sister and there were times when he still felt the intense pain of separation. He found he could turn to the staff, even though many of them 'were suffering themselves,' he observed. 'They were very conscious that we children were carrying this burden.'[8]

Quite apart from fears for their families abroad, both the pupils and staff found the war directly affected their own lives in Britain. The British government classified the 70,000 Germans and Austrians living in Britain as 'enemy aliens'. By late September 1939, the Aliens Department of the Home Office had set up tribunals across the country to assess the potential security risk of each 'enemy alien' over the age of sixteen. Those classified as 'Category A' were deemed a high security risk and were to be interned. 'Category B' was considered suspect and subject to certain restrictions. The vast majority of Jewish refugees found themselves ranked as 'Category C': no threat and exempt from internment.

Nonetheless, Tante Anna was acutely sensitive to local anti-German feeling. 'Please speak English' signs sprung up across Bunce Court. German would go down badly in the area. 'I found it strange, even eerie, that no one answered when I spoke German,' wrote new boy, Walter Kaufmann. He was in awe of one classmate who had been in the school only eighteen months but 'spoke English like an Englishman'. The *Oxford English Dictionary* 'was his Bible and he solved English crossword puzzles with ease.' This paragon pointed out to Walter that 'German is for Germans. We are outcasts and don't belong.' Walter defied the rules one day while walking in the grounds with one of his teachers. Tante Anna flung her office window wide. 'English, Walter Kaufmann, please!' she called out 'shrilly'. Walter was taken aback by her sharp hearing.[9] (There was not much that eluded Tante Anna, although a few children did successfully break the restrictions on leaving the school grounds to visit Mr Smith in the village shop 'Warren Street'. Sweets, chocolate, or a Wall's ice cream from his pushcart tricycle were all part of the irresistible allure.)

Recognising the children's many worries in wartime, Tante Anna was keen to avoid more disruption by splitting them up again, but in late September Kennaways, the large annexe in a former hospital, was ready to form a second outpost of the school. The temporary junior school Tante Anna had already created at Dane Court was thriving and now Anna promoted Hanna Bergas to take charge of an additional thirty pupils at Kennaways. Hanna was accompanied by her cousin, Schneidy, and a third teacher who rapidly acquired the nickname 'Shushi' on account of her habit of trying to settle the children at night with a 'Shush . . .'

'The primitive, long-abandoned hospital was an empty, rather obsolete place,' observed Hanna. She and the children explored the three buildings in their annexe. One seemed to be a former wash house and none of them had any electricity or heating. 'We carried our lamps around from this room to that, as we did not have one for each room,' she remembers. The place was deserted but they heard a creaking sound coming from one of the buildings. To the children's delight, a cat streaked out. Adopted as 'a resident cat', it was soon 'loved by everyone,' wrote Hanna, and acquired a German-sounding nickname, 'Hannchen'.[10] But not even the purring bundle of fur could compensate for the intense cold. 'I remember the moist bedclothes,' recalls one pupil, Judith Adler, 'and the effort it took to decide to go to the bathroom in candlelight.' They became very dependent on the 'Icebear', an elderly man who arrived very early each morning to stoke the stove in the main house, fill the lamps with kerosene and keep them warm and lit.[11]

The children tried to make the best of it, but Hanna recognised that in their isolated spot, engulfed by the 'deep darkness' of the blackout each evening, the children might feel frightened. As the autumn evenings drew in, they invariably huddled together around the kerosene lamp on the table in the common room as she read out a story. When the younger ones were settled, the ever-serious-minded Hanna invited the older girls to her room to discuss literature, 'and we got acquainted with some fine pieces of writing in these sessions,' she wrote. Her last task of the day was to go 'from room to room and house to house equipped with a flashlight to check whether a gas mask was near the bed of every child and to say goodnight which sometimes entailed long conversations to soothe fears concerning the war.'[12]

One pupil, Ernst Weinberg, gives a different account of the night-time routine in a rhyme:

Although we should be fast asleep
We all into the open creep
To walk about and watch the moon
Annoying Schneider in his room

Until on stealthy foot and hush
From shadows dark appears Miss 'Shush'
We all a sudden quickly sped
To safety, comfort, warmth, to bed.[13]

Back at the main school, with the large number of new pupils and the strained circumstances of war, Tante Anna was reliant on everyone pulling together. But there was one boy who seemed unable to see the point: Gerard Hoffnung. One Sunday morning, even Tante Anna reached breaking point. She had asked him not to disturb the other children by playing his saxophone at all hours *inside* the school. That morning she became aware that a crowd of children had gathered outside, staring up at a figure high up on a dormitory window. To her horror, there was Gerard, precariously perched on a top-floor window ledge, 'legs dangling out of the window, playing his saxophone . . .' observed Leslie. Technically, he was playing his saxophone *outside* the school – just – but he was making no attempt to live up to the spirit of her words. Tante Anna had had enough.[14]

His actions prompted much soul-searching. Here was a very talented child undoing that precious thread of goodwill and cooperation that she relied upon to run the school. What's more, Gerard was a danger to himself. Finally, Tante Anna concluded that she couldn't manage him. Gerard was expelled, the only child in the school's history to achieve this distinction. To the secret disappointment of many pupils, Gerard's uncle arrived to take him away. He was sent to Highgate

School in London. 'We later heard they couldn't cope with him either,' according to Leslie Brent. 'He was a very extraordinary person.'[15]

In contrast to the uncontrollable Gerard, Leslie was one of many children who came into his own at Bunce Court. Tante Anna delighted in his progress. Unlike the isolation he felt in his German schools, here Leslie found himself in a happy circle of like-minded friends such as Eric Bourne and Karl Grossfield's older sister, Erica, who joined him organising sporting events. Another older pupil took a shine to Leslie and decided to build him a bicycle 'out of bits and pieces that were lying around'. It was a real boneshaker, with 'brakes that worked up to a point,' he remembers. Leslie used his bike to visit Hans and Hannah Meyer in Greet Cottage. The narrow lane had high hedgerows and with the unreliable brakes, 'we just had to take a chance. We'd go round the bend hoping a car wouldn't come.' Feeling the rush of wind in his face as he sped downhill was exhilarating, miles away from his cloistered, restricted life as a Jew in Germany.[16]

Performing *The Magic Flute* in Canterbury Cathedral itself was another highlight for Leslie and his new-found friends that autumn term. Here they were, clapped and cheered by an enthusiastic British public at the very heart of the Anglican establishment and given a warm welcome by the 'Red Dean'. There may have been a war on, they may have been classed as 'aliens', but they felt they belonged. Excited by the occasion, Leslie and his friends took advantage of the interval to explore. They wandered around Canterbury Cathedral dressed in their costumes as Moorish slaves, feeling wonderfully free, just like normal children with no fear of encountering violence. They reached the crypt. 'We walked in through a large creaking gate,' Leslie recalls. Suddenly it swung shut behind them. 'We were locked in. Trapped in the crypt.' The play was due to restart. 'We had to shout very, very loudly,' Leslie recalls. They got back just in time, their lark apparently unnoticed by Tante Anna.[17]

As he adapted to life as an English schoolboy, Leslie found the deeply ingrained fears of violence and persecution receded and he could begin to enjoy a new intellectual freedom. The classes were very different to those in his previous school in Köslin where the teacher had imposed his hateful Nazi ideology on the pupils. Here questions were encouraged. The teachers wanted to know what he thought and were happy to discuss ideas. Suddenly there seemed so much to find out. The absence of any imposed ideology or adherence to fixed beliefs extended to religion. This, too, was a revelation for Leslie. Even at home, his mother and father had taken the weekly rituals of the Jewish faith very seriously. Helping his mother on Friday afternoons, the services on the Sabbath with his father; all this was a treasured part of his early childhood. Yet here, the pupils were free to follow any religion, or none at all. This was all the more surprising because the school was partly reliant on Jewish generosity and most of the children came from Jewish families, although many were from assimilated backgrounds. He later learned that Tante Anna was criticised for not doing more to encourage Jewish culture or faith.[18]

Tante Anna herself was not religious. Years later, one former pupil explained what she was trying to achieve. Her goal 'was to prepare us for life,' observed Martin Lubowski. 'She never intended to show us the exact way. Everyone had to decide for themselves.' Her openness to any possibility extended to her views on the children's future. 'She was no fanatic Zionist. She did not prepare us for Palestine. Nor did she prepare us for a possible return to Germany,' Martin continues. Placing a strong emphasis on assimilation, she tried to give children the building blocks to create their own futures, 'and when we reached seventeen or eighteen, she left us to work it out for ourselves.'[19] It was essential for Tante Anna that she created freedom for her children; no ideology, no fixed beliefs, not even personal goals should be imposed on them. They must choose for themselves. There was something unique about the atmosphere she created in the school, explains another pupil, Maria Peters. 'It was *wonderful*,' she observed. Everyone was aspiring to do their best but in a non-competitive way. She remembers 'the complete absence of the stress of competition and *personal* ambition.'[20]

Leslie blossomed under this approach. Of all the subjects, he felt most drawn to natural science. The biology lessons were taken by a gentle unassuming Englishman called Dennis Brind, who for unknown reasons went by the nickname of 'Maggy'. Maggy could captivate the class as he illuminated the natural world. Leslie still remembers being riveted by a lesson on the biology of the rabbit as Maggie revealed in exquisite detail what it takes to make a living creature live. It seemed a miracle. Mr Peckover, a conscientious objector who was in charge of the colony of bees, also awakened Leslie's interest in nature. No one was allowed to assist Mr Peckover, but one day, perhaps prompted by Tante Anna, he asked for Leslie's help. Mr Peckover was an unassuming man with a limp who lived in a small hut in the grounds and was making honey on quite a scale for the whole school. He had begun his apiary by transferring a hive of bees from under the east-end gables of the roof and expanded it with a swarm he collected off a hedge. Leslie felt very honoured to be singled out to help. 'You had to put on a net and get into the beehive and of course, I was fascinated by the way the honey was extracted from the comb like a big sponge.' On another occasion the bees were swarming. Leslie watched 'spellbound', as the swarm settled down in a nearby tree and he captured it in a net to form another colony. 'The whole thing was utterly intriguing.'[21]

If a practical but thoroughly modern, questioning approach to study underpinned the intellectual life of the school, there was one area of equal interest to the teenage pupils that was unaccountably taboo: sex. For all Tante Anna's warmth and skill as head teacher, when it came to any question of a sexual nature she could be bafflingly obscure and old-fashioned. Her advice to any adolescent boy seeking her opinion on such matters could have come straight out of the pages of an Edwardian manual. 'When you feel the urge come over you, take a shower . . . a cold shower,' Leslie recalls. Later he reflected on the responsibility she might have felt. Bunce Court was unusual for the time as a co-educational school. He is unaware of there being any pregnancies throughout its entire history. 'This is all the more remarkable,' he says, 'because there was no sex education as such.' Instinctively, Tante Anna was not a person to open up on her private feelings and on personal matters she could be strait-laced. News of one incident spread quickly round the school. Tante Anna happened to be doing the evening round of checks. She opened the door to the bathroom to see a boy slouching on the toilet. 'Sit up straight, boy . . .' she is alleged to have said, to the great amusement of the children as the story shot around school.[22]

As Leslie adapted to school life he felt his relationship with 'the teachers was so good, so intimate' that the trauma of being away from home was considerably eased. He enjoyed the Gramophone Club, which congregated in Wormy's room, and came to love the temperamental cook, Heidtsche: 'she became a kind of mother to me,' says Leslie. He was also drawn to Hanna Bergas, who he felt was so wise. If Heidtsche was his 'emotional mother', the serious-minded Hanna was fast becoming 'my intellectual mother.'[23] According to his lifelong friend Karl, 'Leslie took off once he got to Bunce Court.' No longer the outcast from the orphanage, 'he was outstanding at school'. The reticent, withdrawn boy from Nazi Germany had become outgoing and friendly, even a good sportsman. Karl believes Leslie became 'the most popular boy in the school'.[24]

By the early spring of 1940, the long-planned new buildings in the grounds were complete. The timber-framed wings set at right angles to the Boys' House may not have provided the hundred places Tante Anna had first envisaged, but it was possible to bring back the sixty pupils from Kennaways and Dane Court.[25] The children raced to explore the new buildings. There was much excitement as they discovered extra dormitories, smart new bathrooms and even the luxury of a few private bedrooms. 'These were highly valued,' says Leslie. The fortunate boys allocated one of these 'could make his home'.[26] The children were accustomed to using an old-fashioned blocker to polish the many wooden floors in Bunce Court and it wasn't long before there was a competition to see which boy had the best-blocked bedroom.

Tante Anna was delighted with the reunion. She felt the equilibrium of the school was becoming re-established. Their future at Bunce Court looked secure. They owned their own premises and her 'big family', which had 'grown so much larger during the year of separation,' she observed, 'now lived together once more'.[27] Leslie felt Tante Anna organised her school in a way 'that was paradise'. The children were happy, he says. 'I think most people thought it was paradise.'

*

In the spring of 1940, the threat of a larger land war was in the air. The Blitzkrieg on Poland had been followed by the phoney war, or 'Sitzkreig', as the children called it, over the bitterly cold winter months, where there was a stand-off on the western front. At Bunce Court the children invented games imagining the actions of the troops at the German Siegfried and the French Maginot defensive lines. It was the custom each week for one of the older children to give a talk. Sixteen-year-old Richard Sonnenfeldt remembers one day in March when it was his turn to speak. He had read the papers and explained fears of a wider war in western Europe. The Germans could launch an attack, 'march into Holland and Belgium', outflank the French defences at the Maginot line 'and make it to the Channel.' The younger children were 'spellbound and horrified'. Such a prospect was no longer a game. It would be cataclysmic.[28]

It was a quiet Easter at Bunce Court. Some of the children went to stay with their 'British families'. The weather was mild, the spring glorious. The daffodils were out on the lawns and bluebells in the nearby wood held out promise for May. It was almost possible to imagine there was no war. But on 9 April, all this changed.

Tante Anna had switched on the BBC news on the radio in her room. Suddenly the words of the newscaster commanded her full attention. The Nazis had invaded Denmark and Norway. The phoney war was at an abrupt end. Denmark capitulated in just a few hours and over the coming weeks,

British failings in the Norwegian campaign were widely reported. Since moving to England Tante Anna had felt her school was out of reach of the Nazis, but that feeling of invulnerability was becoming seriously shaken. The disastrous blunders of the Norwegian campaign led to a crisis in British leadership. There was no knowing what Hitler might do next.

On 10 May, older pupils joined Tante Anna to hear the BBC news, expecting to hear who might take over from Neville Chamberlain as prime minister. But the grave, understated voice of the announcer was talking about something else. Everyone listened in frozen silence. The words were hard to take in: 'German forces have invaded Holland, Belgium and Luxembourg by air and by land . . . The invasion began at dawn with large numbers of aeroplanes attacking the main aerodromes and landing troops . . .' Western Europe was being torn apart by the German Blitzkrieg. The reporter talked of the panzers, 'the iron fists', that were destroying the old order. 'Then, spurred on dive-bombers, cold bloodedly but effectively, whole populations set in motion . . .'[29] All hell was let loose on the continent.

For Tante Anna everything in her room was the same: the same worn carpet, the same comfortable armchairs, the plants on the window ledge; but the world had shifted on its axis. She tried to gather herself to find words of reassurance for anxious children, some of whom had parents waiting for re-emigration in Belgium, Luxembourg or France who were now caught in the storm. Many pupils had only recently escaped from the Nazis through the Low Countries. They could remember the train stations where kindly Dutch women had greeted them, the ports where officials had helped them embark. It was hard to comprehend that all this was now engulfed by war. They learned that Chamberlain had resigned and Winston Churchill was the new prime minister. 'My enthusiasm was unbounded,' wrote Richard Sonnenfeldt when he first heard Churchill speak.[30] But Churchill faced a crisis the like of which no prime minister had faced before or since.

Day after day came news of the lightning speed of the Nazi Blitzkrieg unleashed on western Europe. On 15 May the Netherlands surrendered. There were reports that the Germans had broken through into France. The battle lines moved so fast the situation was very confused. By 20 May German panzers had reached the French coast at Abbeville. The next day they were at the port of Boulogne just twenty miles from Calais. As the countries of western Europe fell one by one to the Nazi onslaught, Britain, the country of their refuge, was beginning to look small and isolated. Poland, Denmark, Luxembourg and the Netherlands had fallen. How long before the capitulation of Belgium, Norway, perhaps even France, too?

At Bunce Court the children were horrified by the Nazi conquests. 'We all felt a numbing fear that German para-chutists or fifth columnists could conquer England in a blink,' continued Richard Sonnenfeldt. He had a vivid memory of Germany's 'jackbooted hordes' of SS and SA troopers and its 'steel helmeted robot-like soldiers'. The victorious German army, bloated on success, was just twenty miles from the Kent coast across the Channel. 'I had imagined I would be secure for ever,' continued Richard. 'Now the Nazis were at the doorstep.'[31] Eric Bourne remembers vividly 'the red glow on the eastern horizon where Nazi armies, on the threshold of our refuge, were driving the allies into the sea.'[32] With the school a passionate hotbed of anti-Nazi feeling, what happened next caught everyone by surprise. 'It was a severe blow to the whole school,' wrote Tante Anna.[33]

Very early one morning in mid-May 1940, there was a knock on the door at Bunce Court. Roused from her sleep, Tante Anna found the police at the door. They had come to arrest all male German teachers and pupils over sixteen, explained the senior officer politely. The home secretary was rounding up all 'enemy aliens' and consigning them to internment camps 'under the provisions of Regulation 18b'. Staff began to emerge from their rooms. 'We were told as the "enemy" we might collaborate with the Germans!' Hanna wrote incredulously.[34]

Tante Anna pointed out that they were Jewish refugees in flight from the Nazis but it was no use. The police had their orders. Britain had been in the grip of spy fever for days. Anti-German feeling was rife. British newspapers had been carrying stories about a pro-Nazi 'fifth column' already operating secretly in England. There was intense fear of betrayal from within. Leading the charge against German immigrants was the British diplomat, Sir Nevile Bland. 'The paltriest kitchen maid,' Bland proclaimed, could be a dangerous spy. 'Every German or Austrian servant, however superficially charming, could be a real and grave menace. When Hitler so decides [to invade], there will be satellites of the monster *all over the country*.'[35] Many thought the Netherlands had fallen so fast because German parachutists had been helped from behind Dutch lines. Even the way laundry was strung out on washing lines might contain a secret code for enemy planes. Dangerous Nazis could be in disguise as Jewish refugees. Category C enemy aliens who had fled to Britain to escape the Nazis were now deemed a potential risk, explained the police. Germans and Austrians in the coastal areas of the south-east at high risk of invasion were to be interned imme-diately under Churchill's order to 'collar the lot'.[36]

Sixteen-year-old Richard Sonnenfeldt remembers being woken at 6 a.m. by the history master, Mr Horowitz. He was told he must dress and pack immediately. He was going to an internment camp. Richard was stunned. He grabbed a few treasured possessions, clothes, a passport and his favourite fountain pen, and joined the others on the waiting police bus, including his housemaster, Hans Meyer. He couldn't believe what was happening. There must be some mistake, he thought. Whisked away from the security of school, with no opportunity to say goodbye to his sleeping younger brother, he felt his life once again was thrown into turmoil as Bunce Court retreated rapidly from view. 'I thought how ironic it was, my saviours and protectors, the British, were now imprisoning me,' he wrote later, 'when the Nazis had put my father into concentration camp just eighteen months earlier.' With his complete faith in the notion of British fair play, Richard reeled against finding himself a prisoner of 'my beloved English'. He began drafting long, protesting letters to 'His Majesty the King and Prime Minister Churchill about the grave error they had committed by interning me, a Jew, who was eager to fight the Germans.'[37]

Anna immediately started a campaign for the release of her staff and pupils. Apart from Richard Sonnenfeldt and Hans Meyer, seven of her top-form pupils had been taken by the British police along with Hanna Bergas' cousin, Schneidy, Walter Isaacson or 'Saxo', who had joined from Herrlingen to teach biblical history, the school's dentist, poultry keeper and gardeners. 'I should be willing to vouch for the loyalty of all these people,' she wrote to the Council of German Jewry.[38] Tante Anna felt her children were under siege from both sides, British and German. She was already doing all she could to trace parents caught up in the Nazi invasion in Holland, Luxembourg and Belgium. Ernst Weinberg's parents were now missing along with several others. She appealed for help to Jewish organisations and the Home Office, enclosing details of parents' last known addresses. 'The children are very brave in spite of their worrying . . .' she wrote. 'It is impossible for us to obtain any information regarding their whereabouts . . .' came the reply from the Council of German Jewry.[39]

Western Europe was a maelstrom, reeling from the obliterating German Blitzkrieg. On 28 May, Belgium surrendered. The British army was being evacuated from Dunkirk under heavy attack. Churchill warned of 'hard and heavy tidings'.[40] At this grave moment in late May 1940, the police returned to Bunce Court. This time they came for the 'alien' women. They took the beloved cook, Heidtsche, and three sixteen-year-old girls. 'We were shocked,' recalls Heinz Redwood, fifteen at the time. Why were the British interested in their cook? 'It was incredibly unjust.' The pupils viewed it as 'an act of enormous kindness' that Heidtsche had chosen to come and help in a refugee school. She was not Jewish and did not have to leave Germany. 'She certainly put herself really at risk by coming to England,' Heinz continues. 'We were really shocked that of all the people who had come to our help that she should be interned.'[41] The standard of cooking at the school 'dropped precipitously,' Leslie recalls. For some pupils, the absence of Heidtsche 'changed the entire character of the place'.

Soon came news of more arrests, including Tante Anna's own brother, William. After the forced sale of his interior decoration business to the Nazis he was trying to start again as a jeweller in central London. 'He couldn't believe his luck,' one pupil recalled later. A London bobby had come to his house full of apologies. 'I'm terribly sorry, sir . . .' the policeman began politely. His attitude formed such a striking contrast to William's frightening experiences with the Gestapo that he accepted the situation. Along with many thousands of others, including Heidtsche, he found himself effectively imprisoned on the Isle of Man.[42]

Tante Anna did manage to trace many of her former pupils and staff, such as Heidtsche, to boarding houses and hotels on the Isle of Man. The camps were surrounded by barbed wire and no amount of British politeness could quite dispel the sense of injustice and helplessness they felt at finding themselves prisoners, detained for an unknown length of time. Married couples were initially separated into different camps and refugees were sometimes sharing quarters with Nazi supporters as though there was no difference between them. But Tante Anna could not find Hans Meyer, Richard Sonnenfeldt and a few other pupils on the lists for the Isle of Man. She was horrified. The children had been taken away because they had only just turned sixteen and as a result had not appeared before a tribunal where they could establish their loyalty. She made repeated enquiries at the Home Office and the War Office. They seemed to have disappeared.

Meanwhile for many at Bunce Court, seeing their classmates taken away brought fears flooding back. 'It was five weeks before my sixteenth birthday,' recalls Heinz Redwood. His parents had been taken away by the Gestapo. What was the difference? Was internment like concentration camp? His friends and teachers had been imprisoned without trial. 'If you were in a protected area and were over sixteen you were in trouble,' he thought. 'We were essentially stateless.'

Heinz Redwood went to see Tante Anna. 'What happens in middle of June when I'm sixteen?' he asked. 'Will I be arrested too?'

'No you won't,' Tante Anna replied. She spoke with the kind of reassuring authority that gave Heinz peace of mind. She explained that she was doing all in her power to stop further arrests, 'and if I don't get this done in time for your birthday, we will arrange for you to go to another school outside the protected area so you won't be arrested.' Heinz felt immense relief. 'She really stood by me in an amazing way which I never forgot. My attitude towards her totally changed.' Heinz knew Tante Anna was a woman of her word. When she said she was going to do something, 'I knew that this would happen.' From that point 'we became friends for life'.[43]

Even as Tante Anna was wrestling with the disappearance of some of her teachers, pupils and the cook, the school was overtaken by more bad news. With the Nazis just across the Channel everyone feared Britain would be next. The coastline along the English Channel was the most likely site of any invasion. Coastal defences were urgently needed. The Kent Downs became a protected military zone and Bunce Court was one of many properties requisitioned by the army. 'We were given three days' notice to leave the district,' Tante Anna wrote later. They had to give up their home.[44]

All Tante Anna's efforts to build security for the children had come to nothing. There was no choice. The entire school must close – or evacuate within three days. Some of her staff were at a loss at the prospect of a second exodus. It seemed 'incomprehensible', Hanna Bergas despaired, 'an over-whelming difficulty'.[45] Tante Anna would not consider closing the school. She had made commitments to the children and was not about to accept defeat. She must show the children that even a moment of crisis could be turned into something good. They were landed with another impossible task. Well – they would do it. They would make another school and it would be a success.

Tante Anna went to London 'with a heavy heart' and made urgent enquiries. A friend gave her a contact in Shropshire and she duly set off to the west of England. 'I knew no one but I had an introduction,' wrote Anna later. Her new contact in Shropshire 'made me feel at home and drove me about house hunting'. It was soon clear her optimism was misplaced. Every time they found a suitably large property they were invariably told 'it had just been requisitioned yesterday'.[46]

While Anna combed the west of England for a new home, the staff at Bunce Court started packing as fast as possible. The older pupils who understood what was happening saw Anna in a new light. 'Here was this half-blind woman touring the countryside trying to find another suitable building and suitable surroundings for us,' says Leslie. Heinz Redwood, too, was impressed. 'She was careering around England trying to find a place to move the school – on top of all this, she said she would see that I would not be arrested. It must have been hard.' Tante Anna understood, as refugees, 'we'd lost confidence in ourselves and what the future would hold. We were earmarked by authorities as "friendly enemy aliens" – there was a funny side to it – but it didn't seem funny at the time.'[47]

The Marchioness of Reading of the Refugee Children's Movement managed to use her position of influence to extend the school's notice by a few days, but despite this, there was only one place Anna could find in the time that would remotely fit the bill: a run-down manor house near Wem in

Shropshire known as Trench Hall. It had been empty for years, having once been the property of an old retired colonel of the Indian army and his seven servants. Tante Anna could see at once there would not be room for everyone. She would have no choice but to split up the big family temporarily once again. She contacted her friend, Hilde Lion, at Stoatley Rough School in Surrey, and Lion agreed to take fifteen of the younger children and their staff at short notice. With no time to lose, Anna thought, 'there was no alternative but to take Trench Hall'.[48]

Tante Anna saw Trench Hall on 8 June, signed the lease on 9 June, and 'engaged buses and lorries by phone and returned to Kent that evening'. On 10 June – the day Norway finally surrendered and Mussolini declared war on Britain and France – Tante Anna put her remaining German staff and children over sixteen, including Heinz Redwood, on a bus to Shropshire. They took with them 'sheets, blankets, one hundred and twenty mattresses and food for two days'. The following day, the younger pupils at Bunce Court piled into buses for the drive across Britain. 'People did not realise we were "enemy aliens",' Leslie recalls. 'They thought we were evacuees and treated us kindly, giving us apples and stuff everywhere we stopped.'[49] Even so, when they reached Trench Hall, Hanna found the bewildered children were 'more passive than we had ever seen them.'

Tante Anna remained behind to finish the packing. Dismantling the school at speed was heartbreaking work and overshadowed by momentous events on the continent. The free world in Europe was disintegrating under the fascist onslaught. Every news bulletin brought more shocking news. By 14 June, the Germans were in Paris. The fall of France seemed imminent. The Europe she knew was disappearing.

What would replace it? Reeling from the speed and significance of events, Tante Anna was determined to keep her mind focused on the practicalities as she was forced into immediate decisions. This was all she could do. She prayed it would be enough.

'Everything at Bunce Court was requisitioned except for the five-acre vegetable garden,' she recorded later. She found a gardener to raise whatever funds he could from the green vegetables and send the root vegetables on to Trench Hall. A buyer came forward for the school's stores of coke and crude oil, although he was unable to make immediate payment. With the army beginning to unload supplies on the lawn, she was forced into hurried decisions. She accepted a loss on 'all our poultry, pigs and their foodstuffs bought in advance'. Even more devastating, she had to leave most of the furniture 'and what is worse, our large library'. But with the prospect of an invasion imminent, Tante Anna did succeed in getting her school out of the danger zone on the south-east coast. By 17 June she was back in Shropshire making sure lessons resumed as normal at Trench Hall.[50] Two days later bombs were falling on the east coast of England, and on 22 June, the inconceivable happened: France fell to Germany. Britain stood alone.

It had taken Tante Anna just a week to move the entire school but it was soon apparent that under the tight deadline, she had had to overlook Trench Hall's many obvious drawbacks. The house was significantly smaller than Bunce Court and a large number of boys would have to sleep out in the stables. There were signs of past splendour, now long since overgrown or decayed. The place lacked even basic modern amenities. There was no electricity, 'the roof was in need of repair, the plumbing bad and the water supply inadequate,' observed Tante Anna.[51] The staff would have to take it in turns to operate a pump through the night to ensure there was water for everyone in the morning. In place of their thriving five-acre vegetable garden at Bunce Court, they had nothing but one acre of weeds, a glasshouse, broken frames and a neglected orchard. They did not even have their brilliant cook. Hanna Bergas remembers going to a local farmer to buy milk. 'It makes my blood boil to see Germans here,' the farmer replied angrily as he turned her away. They had to start from the very beginning. It was 'a new adventure, forced upon us,' Tante Anna would write later. But for all her fighting spirit, even she had moments of uncertainty.

Many of her pupils, such as Leslie Brent, had more pressing worries. The painfully staccato Red Cross messages from his parents in Berlin sounded bright but sometimes held an ominous subtext. Why had his father adopted a new middle name: 'Israel'? The newspapers carried occasional reports about atrocities against Jews in Poland. Would the fall of western Europe make things worse for the Jews? Leslie noticed that his parents changed address a great deal. 'Beloved boy. Our thoughts are always with you . . . May god protect you! . . . Remain God-fearing,' wrote his father. He sounded anxious. Did he know something? Leslie waited nervously each month for the precious twenty-five words that connected him to all he loved.[52]

10

'Everyone knew not to get on the death cars'

Ten-year-old Sidney Finkel, Poland, 1942

On 20 January 1942 a secret meeting was convened in Berlin that would have far-reaching consequences for Jewish families across Europe, including children in countries not occupied by the Nazis, such as Anna's pupils at Trench Hall. At a large villa in the Berlin suburb of Wannsee, Heinrich Himmler's deputy, Reinhard Heydrich, the man even Hitler thought had an iron heart, discussed the fate of eleven million Jews – a figure that anticipated gaining control over Jews in countries such as Britain as yet beyond Nazi influence. Gathered in the room were key state secretaries in the Nazi government, the bureaucrats and functionaries whose job it was to implement the orders. Adolf Eichmann, who worked for Heydrich, took the minutes, later amending them, as instructed, to obscure the full force of their meaning.[1] These minutes reveal that a key shift had occurred in the Nazi policy towards the Jews. The Nazi leadership had found their 'Final Solution of the Jewish question': extermination.

Before the war, Nazi policy towards the Jews had focused on emigration. The Wannsee conference brought together the appropriate heads of department to plan and coordinate mass murder. Jews from all across Europe would be subject to 'evacuation . . . to the East,' pronounced Heydrich. In camps in the east they would be separated into two groups. Those still capable of work would labour as Nazi slaves until they succumbed to the harsh conditions. The remainder, Heydrich implied, would be killed on arrival. The meeting ensured that all the heads of department understood the role they had to play in this state-organised, industrial-scale slaughter. The official policy of the Nazi regime had become genocide.[2]

It took six months for the consequences of this planning meeting to catch up with twelve-year-old Sam Oliner and his family in Nazi-occupied southern Poland. One day in June 1942, all the Jews in Sam's district were ordered into a ghetto formed at Bobowa. Anyone who failed to obey the order within three days would be counted as 'a fugitive' and shot on sight. As they approached, Sam was shocked to see a high barbed wire fence. It was new, the sharp points of metal glinting in the sunlight. He stopped and stared. There must be some mistake. Was this frightening prison the place where they were meant to go? They were losing their freedom and no one said a word. He was with his father, Aron, his step-mother, Ester, and his stepbrother and stepsister. Sam carried their clothes. Aron stumbled under a heavy load of bedding. Ester carried his baby stepsister and his infant stepbrother gripped a potato for their supper. They were ushered on inside by members of the '*Judenrat*', a council of Jewish elders appointed by the Nazis to keep order, effectively the Jewish police.

Sam and his family were led down dark alleyways milling with hundreds of people trying to find their new quarters. They were allocated a room, which was shared with Sam's paternal grandparents and another strange family. There was no toilet and no running water. The mattresses were made of straw. The stench and squalor were repulsive. Sam's father had still not spoken; he looked a ghostly pallid white. His grand-father's face, too, was blank, as though what was happening was meaningless. To Sam he 'looked like a dead man'.[3]

That night, Sam could not sleep. The woman from the other family seemed to be in pain. Gradually it became clear she was giving birth. There were various comings and goings as she struggled with labour in the darkness. Sam went to wait outside, watching the dawn. Even the sky seemed to be mud-coloured, as though splashed with murky water. The baby died. A small wooden box was fetched. The strange family's pitiful night-time drama underlined their sense of helplessness. They were captives.

Sam had no way of knowing that there were hundreds of similar makeshift ghettos already across Poland. The entire population of three and a half million Polish Jews were herded at gunpoint into captivity – their first staging post to the 'final solution'. Poland was in the process of being turned into a vast prison for 'expendable' Jews. Sam remembers, as a twelve-year-old child, feeling baffled as to why the Nazis would want to herd the Jews into ghettos. It made no sense. Homeless, stripped of all assets, survival itself became a struggle. Why? He remembers the paralysing terror, as the days turned into weeks, of not knowing what would happen next. There were so many uncertainties. Rumours were rampant. For him, it was as though a pall of intense fear hung over the ghetto, paralysing every action, stifling every thought.[4] The violence meted out by their captors was random and cruel, the worthlessness of Jewish lives in the ghetto underlined by the way the Nazis approached brutality like some kind of sport.

There was no knowing when the heavy gates to the Bobowa ghetto would open and Nazi soldiers, who appeared to Sam mere youths not much older than himself, would drive their trucks fast, deliberately targeting Jews as they zigzagged through the streets. Sometimes they shot at people randomly, or aimed at windows, showering those sheltering inside with glass. Another time, Sam was shocked to witness the brutal rape of a Jewish girl.

Jewish families had no means of defending themselves against such atrocities. They soon became even weaker as the ghetto was stripped of the young and the strong. One day the *Judenrat* spread word of a new Nazi order. All the young men were to gather in the market square. The *Judenrat* had been told that the youths were going on to a better life where they would be able to work. People were willing to believe this was true. They clung to the promises of the *Judenrat* as they said their goodbyes. The day came when the strong young men in the ghetto gathered in the square and piled into the Nazi military trucks. They were never seen, nor heard from, again. Not even one letter about their 'better life'.

Then the *Judenrat* was told of another new order. This time, it was the turn of the young women. The Nazis wanted all girls and women between the ages of fifteen and twenty-nine. Even as a child, Sam felt the *Judenrat* couldn't quite believe they were going to a better life outside, for they spoke with shame, terror in their eyes. Nonetheless, the people in the ghetto complied. What alternative was there? Sam felt that the departure of the young women brought on a new phase of utter despair.[5]

Sam felt overwhelmed by the sense of hopelessness. Death hung over the shabby, rubbish-strewn streets. The vacant looks of the inhabitants, the apparent gullibility of the *Judenrat*, the passive acceptance of any unreasonable or cruel demand: all this was stifling to a twelve-year-old child who wanted to live. One day he spotted a break in the perimeter fence. Leaving the ghetto was extremely dangerous. Any Jew caught outside was shot. But Sam could see at once that the broken wire created a hole just large enough for him to edge through. With his blond hair, pale skin and blue eyes he could surely pass for a Polish peasant boy for a few hours? How would anyone know? He would be careful not to give himself away. The prospect of freedom outside the ghetto became too tantalising. At the risk of death, he had to try.[6]

Beyond the perimeter, the taste of freedom was like a summer breeze. He roamed the beautiful summer countryside before slipping back unseen into the ghetto. As he gained confidence, Sam began stealing food and candles and bringing them back to his family. He became streetwise and skilled at thieving without being caught. He valiantly brought each trophy back home to the ghetto, each time craving some gesture of warmth or thanks from his family. There was none. No one acknowledged that he had risked his life to get a chicken or rabbit. His father, worn down into unresponsiveness, greeted his son's efforts with silence. Ester, too, seemed broken in spirit, her thoughts directed to her two younger children. Sam railed against their lack of warmth and affection. He tried to persuade himself that his grandmother, his sister Feigele and brother Moishe were still living in freedom at the farm in the mountains. He wished he hadn't left them to join his father. The very idea of seeing them again lifted his spirits.

Once when he escaped the ghetto, he met a Polish boy who knew what had happened to the Jewish girls. They were all given to the German army, the boy explained, who used

them as whores and if they were rebellious and not accom-
modating, they were sent to the crematorium. Sam wouldn't
believe it. He screamed a wild cry of agony and hit the boy
as hard as he could. 'I am Jewish,' he cried, 'you devil, you
scum . . .' Just then a Gestapo car appeared down the road.
He could be shot. Sam fled as fast as he could, his mind, his
whole being in terrible pain.

Sam thought he should tell his father what the boy had
said. His father still clung to the reassurance provided by the
Judenrat. These were after all, their Jewish leaders. Whenever
Sam attempted to question their views, his father seemed
angry. He would not be challenged. God was protecting them.
In his passivity, Sam thought he allowed himself to believe
this was true. With this new knowledge of the horrible fate
of the girls, he felt he must try once more to tell his father.
Tentatively he began: 'Dad, should we really believe the
Judenrat . . .'[7] He could get no further. Such ideas could cost
you your life. Angrily, Aron ordered his son to bed. Sam lay
in the darkness, crushed by the strength of his pent-up feelings. He loved his father; he didn't want to hurt him: but his
father could not be right. That was their last night together
as a family.

During the night of 13–14 August 1942, the Nazis rounded
up the inhabitants of Bobowa ghetto. In the confusion, when
his stepmother told him to run and hide, Sam felt she gave
him permission to leave. In that last frantic moment, as she
pinned her dark-circled eyes on him, he actually heard her
say 'I love you . . .'[8] Later that night and into the next day,
as Sam lay under the melting tarpaper, listening to the shouted
commands and screams, his terror mixed with gratitude
towards her. At last his stepmother had said the words he
longed to hear. Sam thought he loved her, too.

From his hidden vantage point on a ramshackle roof in Bobowa ghetto, it was hard to comprehend what he was witnessing. He did not yet have a word for this: 'the liquidation' of the ghetto. It took more than a day for the Nazis to herd all the Jews of the ghetto onto large military trucks. Even when they had cleared the streets, Sam could still hear the occasional gunshot and heart-rending cry. The murderous soldiers were methodically searching the houses with their vicious dogs for any survivors. Sam's senses were alive to the dangers. He knew only one thing: he must reach the perimeter fence unseen. He was being hunted.

Once beyond the boundary fence, Sam knew, if anyone suspected he was a Jew he was as good as dead. He moved fast, eyes scanning from left to right, in a state beyond hypervigilance. There was no knowing what was round the next corner. A black shiny Gestapo car? A former Polish neighbour who might recognise him as a Jew? At the sight of anyone, Sam discreetly headed in another direction. He had a big cap that he pulled over his face. He must avoid all eye contact.[9]

Mostly he moved at night, under cover of darkness. Whenever he could he rested, hiding in ditches and isolated barns. His future was bleak. Poland was now enemy territory. The Nazis would murder him. The Poles could turn him in for money. From his earlier forays out of the ghetto, he understood that there was one particularly vigilant Pole, a man called Krupa, who was making a good living by capturing Jews for the Nazis. A Jew was worth a pair of leather boots, perhaps even an overcoat or some money. It was said that Krupa sometimes maimed his prisoners for good measure before he turned them in.

Sam had no place to hide. He had to survive in plain sight. If he fell into the hands of a bounty hunter like Krupa, death was inevitable. Now he understood that death wasn't 'for a little while'. His mother wasn't coming back. He would not turn a corner and suddenly see her beloved face, however much he longed for her. Even so, he imagined she was looking out for him. Somewhere, somehow, she could see what happened and was fighting for him.

Alone in a hostile world, stripped of all those he loved, Sam had memory alone to bring back any feeling of human warmth. As he lay in ditches and cowered in dark corners in barns, hunger and fear burning inside him, he took comfort from remembering her. She might not be with him, but she was by his side.[10]

*

Although Anna Rose's family had fled to the Soviet zone in eastern Poland, eventually they, too, were unable to escape the Nazis. For almost two years they had lived under Soviet rule, but their lives became inextricably tied to the momentous events that would lead to the cold-blooded calculations at Wannsee.

On 22 June 1941, Hitler had broken his non-aggression pact with Stalin, attacking the Soviet Union with the largest invasion force in history. Five-year-old Anna and her eight-year-old brother, Arthur, saw the Russians fleeing Lvov. Once again, they witnessed the historic arrival of an invading army; this time the all-powerful German army. On 30 June Anna peered down on to an endless stream of tanks driving through Lvov, gun turrets open, German soldiers quietly viewing the city. This was a victorious army, bloated on success. Huge cannon rolled through the streets, cavalcades of motorbikes and military lorries, and soldiers marched in their thousands.

For two days the procession continued. Anna was frightened but Arthur was fascinated by their vehicles and their guns. A forest of swastikas appeared overnight and the city was renamed: Lemberg.[11]

As the children watched the German army march past, they had no way of understanding that the massive invasion they were witnessing would mark a step change in Nazi policy towards the Jews. Close behind the vast German army came the notorious SS death squads, or *Einsatzgruppen*. In Poland alone, the *Einsatzgruppen* by this point had killed 15,000 people, but in Russia the murder was to be on a different scale.[12] Four newly formed task forces were ordered by Reinhard Heydrich to root out their enemies: communist leaders and Jews 'in the service of the party or the state' – for Hitler, Judaism and Bolshevism were inextricably linked. By 8 July, Heydrich ordered the execution of all male Jews between the ages of fifteen and forty-five. Units of Einsatzgruppe C reached Lemberg on 2 July and in little over a month, several thousand Jews were executed.

Life under the Soviets had been desperately hard. Anna understood that she would not see her half-sister, Liana, again; she had died in the harsh conditions in Siberia. But even this loss paled next to the immediate danger they faced under the Nazis. German soldiers 'came and took away my mother as soon as they came in', she recalls. They rounded up many of the Jewish women. 'I just didn't believe that they could just walk in and take my mum away,' says Anna. Two anxious days passed before her mother, Irena, came back through the door. Without saying a word, everything about her conveyed the horrific ordeal that she had been through. 'She was in really bad shape . . . she looked totally wiped out,' recalls Anna. Her mother had been ordered by the Nazis to clean the barracks the Russians had abandoned.[13] This was a new reality where suddenly complete strangers could come in and seize your parents.

Within weeks the Rose family were ordered into a poor district in the north of the city near the railway line, which became the Lemberg Ghetto. As they approached the ghetto, Anna felt numb. She understood that this place would be worse than anything they had already endured. Hundreds of Jewish refugees jostled in the crowded streets. Lemberg became one of Poland's larger ghettos where eventually around 120,000 Jews were crammed into a small area, roughly a quarter of a mile long, once occupied by fewer than 30,000 people. 'It was horrific,' she recalls. 'I had never been near a slum. We were brought into a ramshackle, dirty, overcrowded environment filled with people who were totally traumatised.'[14] Some Jews never made it. As they filed their way under the Peltewna Street rail bridge into the ghetto, German troops gunned down 5,000 of the sick and elderly.

The life of the Rose family was reduced to one room in the ghetto, which was squalid and infested with vermin and cockroaches. 'I was covered with fleas and lice and my body and hair itched all the time,' Anna remembers. It was impossible to get clean. There was one water tap shared between dozens of people and Anna hated 'the daily humiliation of not being able to go to a toilet – having to use a chamber pot.' Although the air smelled bad, her father was forced to seal the windows with newspaper to keep them warm. Anna dreaded the night-time, when she could hear the rats moving around. 'It was the first time that I was not allowed to go out. I had to stay in this room most of the time.' Once in a while 'if Mother felt it was safe', they would go to a nearby field and pick sorrel to try to supplement their meagre rations. 'Food was so scarce we were always hungry.' Of all the deprivations, Anna found the hunger the hardest to deal with. 'It's totally physical. It's very hard to go to sleep if you are hungry all the time.'[15]

Trapped in the ghetto, it was hard for the Rose family to get news of events further east. Nazi tanks swept three hundred and fifty miles into the Soviet Union in just three weeks. There were problems of food supply, raising the prospect of starvation in Nazi-occupied Soviet Russia and Poland's larger ghettos. The Jewish women and children who had lost their breadwinners were particularly at risk and now the Nazis deemed them 'useless eaters', prompting a shift in policy that would shape 'the Final Solution'. During August 1941, Heinrich Himmler gave orders to the *Einsatzgruppen*: all Jewish women and children were to be shot. He increased the size of the Nazi death squads, which eventually reached 40,000 men.

The *Einsatzgruppen* drove Jews at gunpoint to open pits or ditches and made them strip and line up before being shot. The Jewish populations of entire villages along the eastern front were wiped out in such *'aktions'* that could last two or more days. In early August, Ostrog, the former Polish border town where the Rose family had first sought refuge, was the site of one such massacre. By 15 August, Heinrich Himmler was reviewing the work of death squads in Minsk, Belarus, when he was informed that the horrific mass executions were traumatising the German death squads themselves. Himmler wanted a different solution.[16]

Methods of killing using canisters of pure carbon monoxide had been trialled as early as 1940 in Germany as part of the T4 euthanasia programme. But Himmler could not see a way of transporting large quantities of bottled gas to the east in wartime. In 1941 the death squads carried out experiments in pumping exhaust gases from military vehicles into a sealed basement at a hospital near Minsk. Gas vans for killing were also developed.[17] At Auschwitz, a concentration camp in southern Poland undergoing massive expansion, tests were carried out that autumn using a chemical meant for insect infestations: 'Zyklon B', or cyanide. These and other gassing experiments showed it was possible to kill at scale without exposing the Nazi murderers directly to their victims.[18] In the spring of 1942, 15,000 Jews from Lemberg ghetto were among the first to be gassed at a new extermination camp at Belzec in south-east Poland. Exhaust gases were pumped through fake showerheads into sealed chambers disguised as shower rooms.

For Anna Rose in Lemberg ghetto, death was constantly in sight. Corpses were left in the street and a putrid smell permeated the air. Her imagination ran riot, with the whispered stories of disappearances and the brutal Nazi raids when soldiers with guns and snarling dogs drove Jews from their shabby homes into military vehicles, never to be seen again. 'When the trucks came, I would peek through the windows to see what was going on. I saw the trucks and the dogs. It was very, very scary because it was so brutal.'[19] Deportations and disease reduced the ghetto population by 25,000 in less than six months. Anna's world of safety shrank to the one room with her parents; and even here, life was uncertain. One thing stood out clearly in her mind: the Nazis were the source of unending misery.

So she was stunned when one night in September 1942, a German soldier appeared in their room with a sack. 'You have to get in,' whispered Anna's mother. 'Don't be afraid.'[20]

Anna was too shocked to reply. Her mother's order made no sense.

'I just must have known instinctively that my life depended on my obeying my mother and my father. That they were looking after me.' Her mother's hug gave her some reassurance. This was meant to happen. Her mother spoke in a low voice that conveyed urgency and brooked no contradiction. She must be very still and very silent. Sheer terror overcame her, but 'when I was told to get into that sack, I don't think I hesitated'.[21]

Unknown to Anna, her parents had bribed the German soldier to get their two children out of the ghetto. They had no way of knowing whether the soldier could be trusted or whether he might instead turn them in for the reward. This was the nightmarish predicament they faced that night as they let their children go with the enemy.

It was dark and hot inside the sack. The cloth was rough. Anna felt herself lifted up and thrown over the Nazi's shoulder like a sack of potatoes. She did not dare speak or cry out to her parents. She heard the ill-fitting door to their room close behind them. Then she was lowered onto something. She heard an engine start. Terrified and browbeaten, she knew only that she was on a Nazi vehicle being driven by a Nazi soldier. She had no idea where he was taking her or whether she would ever see her parents again.

✳

By the autumn of 1942, Sidney Finkel had been in Poland's first ghetto in Piotrkow for almost three years when unspeakable rumours began to circulate. Officially, the *Judenrat* claimed ghettos were being 'evacuated' because the people were being moved to better camps. Unofficially, the stories were too frightening and far-fetched to be believed. It was said that when the Jews were herded into the Nazi trucks in the ghettos they were taken to the railway and crammed into cattle trains. Crammed so tightly they couldn't breathe. One hundred and fifty people in a wagon that would normally hold thirty cattle. The trains went up the railway line to a place called Treblinka, not far from Warsaw. The people who disappeared into Treblinka were never seen or heard of again.[22]

The *Judenrat* in Piotrkow tried to calm the panic. These were just rumours. The people had gone to a new life further east. But the ominous stories kept coming. Local people reported that Treblinka camp itself was surprisingly small given the large number of trains that kept arriving there. Where had all the people gone? No food trains were ever seen going up the line to Treblinka. Could that mean the people who were sent there were no longer alive? Poles who lived near Treblinka reported a putrid smell that drifted from the camp, hanging in the air for days. One week in August 1942, local Poles saw a queue of cattle trains from the ghettos waiting outside the camp, and heard shooting.[23] As for what happened inside the camp, it was said Treblinka was 'a killing factory'. Murder on an industrial scale. Word spread: on no account should you get on the Nazi trucks. Ten-year-old Sidney understood they were 'death cars'.

But if Piotrkow ghetto was 'liquidated' the only way to escape the death cars was to have a work permit. Sidney's capable older brother, Isaac, tried every possible avenue. Permits were like gold dust. By the late summer of 1942 there were around 24,000 people in Piotrkow ghetto, yet the Nazis granted only 2,000 work permits. Isaac wanted to find work for their mother, father, and their two remaining sisters, Frania and Lola, as well as somewhere safe for Sidney. He was in no doubt of the urgency. There was talk of the ghetto being liquidated any day.[24] But women and children were not wanted in the labour camps. Isaac managed to get only two work permits, one for himself and one for his father. There was nothing left for the family but prayers. On Sunday 12 October, Sidney, Isaac and their father joined other families in prayer all day. Sidney remembers the overpowering anguish. They begged God to intervene. The prayers were an intense lamentation, a *cri de cœur* . . . Most in the congregation were crying, even his own father.

Tuesday 14 October. Sidney woke early to the sound of gunshots. The ghetto was surrounded by crack-shot Nazi soldiers using the Jews as target practice as a diversion while awaiting orders. To Sidney, they seemed like 'a highly trained group of murderers'.[25] The *Judenrat* directed people to the central square.

Sidney's parents warned him that the Nazis might split up the family. He wanted to stay with his mother 'no matter what', but his father and Isaac had work permits and planned to take charge of him. Sidney felt numb with grief as they joined the vast procession making their way with their meagre belongings to the reporting square. There was pandemonium. Children and babies were crying. There was the sound of gunshots. As they had feared, the SS was driving thousands of people into different lines. People were beaten or hounded by the dogs into submission.[26] Those with work permits had to move to one side.

The moment had come. Sidney had to leave his mother and two remaining sisters, Frania and Lola, who were ordered into a line of women and children. Sidney was in a state of shock. His mother was brave and she urged him to have courage, making him promise that he would do all in his power to stay alive. He was too overcome to speak. He longed to be with her. Isaac led him away. 'When they put us all in the different groups we didn't know where any of the groups were going to finish up,' wrote Isaac later. 'We were like animals and our only thought was to survive.'[27]

Later Sidney found out from his sister Lola what happened next to the women of the family. In the chaos of the square, Lola suddenly noticed the Nazi official who employed her as a maid. She begged him to spare them. He was prepared to help the sisters, but not their mother, Faiga. Lola pleaded and pleaded. She was in despair because Frania refused point-blank to abandon their mother. The Nazi officer became irritated. Their opportunity was slipping away. Frania simply could not turn her back on her mother. In the end, Faiga bravely pushed Frania away, urging her to go. Lola grabbed Frania's hand firmly and forced her to follow the official out of the square. The chaos of the square was behind them when suddenly Lola felt Frania slip her grip. She turned and saw Frania was weaving her way back through the crowd, searching for her mother. Lola never saw her sister or her mother again. She didn't even know whether they had the comfort of finding each other again before they were driven into the cattle cars.[28]

Meanwhile Sidney was standing in the line for the labour camp, hidden between his father and his older brother. Quite regularly there was the unmistakable sound of a shot and a cry as another person fell to the ground. Sidney did not dare look, but he heard the Nazis working their way up the line, the sounds of the gunshots getting closer. He clung to his father's back, rigid with fear. When the shots were almost upon them he saw what looked like a mess of body parts: brains, intestines, nothing human, but intensely human. Then he glimpsed the high riding boots and whip of the Nazi checking the line.

The Nazi soldier was standing right by them. Sidney's heart was beating so loudly he thought it must give him away. The official looked at his father's work permit. He seemed satisfied and gave orders to his father and his brother. When they did not walk on at once, he turned back. That's when he suddenly saw Sidney cowering between them.

Sidney felt a whip crack over his head. A surge of fear shot through him along with the lightning recognition that he had been spotted. Death would follow . . . He heard the Nazi's angry instructions. He was being ordered into a different line – almost certainly the line for the death trucks.[29]

*

At large in the Polish countryside in the early autumn of 1942, Sam Oliner grew up overnight. The twelve-year-old child was gone. Having escaped Bobowa ghetto by hiding under a roof, he was determined not to make a slip. He wondered if he was the only survivor. His feet seemed to know their own way to his grandfather's house. His clothes became very dirty and he was hungry and thirsty. It almost didn't surprise him that everything had been stolen, even the windows and doors.[30]

Sam felt at a loss to know where to go until he remembered a friend of his grandfather: a peasant woman called Balwina Piecuch. Could he trust her? Balwina lived several miles away in a small village called Bystra. It took him two days to find his way there, seeking cover every time he sensed danger.

He waited until nightfall before he knocked on her door, full of apprehension. Was this the right place? Would Balwina turn him in to the Gestapo? She was very poor and she could make money from doing so.

He could hear anxious voices inside. A woman was talking to her husband. A voice spoke on the other side of the door, asking for his name. Sam replied very softly. The voice asked him to speak up. Cautiously he repeated his name, more loudly.

The door opened. Balwina's plump figure was silhouetted by the light behind her. He could not see her face. It took her a moment to recognise him. Anxiously she looked around in the darkness and then ushered him in quickly and bolted the door. There was tension in her voice. 'What are you doing? It's very dangerous . . .'[31]

Sam tried to explain, but there was too much to say. Her husband puffed on his pipe, saying nothing, appraising the situation. Sam managed to convey what he knew. How he had become separated from his family, how everyone in the ghetto was herded on to trucks, how a farmer had told him they had all been machine-gunned at a mass grave. He thought he had lost his father, his grandfather, his stepmother . . . He began to cry. Balwina, too, had tears in her eyes. She took him in her arms and tried to comfort him.

Balwina explained the dangers. People knew that she was a friend of Sam's family. Neighbours might be watching the house in case she tried to help anyone. She had heard of house searches by the Gestapo. Even so, she would let Sam stay. She produced milk and bread and let him eat as much as he could. Then she settled him in her own son's room in the attic. Despite Balwina's great kindness, Sam struggled to fall asleep. His thoughts raced over all the possible dangers.[32]

When he surfaced the next day, Balwina began to cook him a hot breakfast and told him what she had found out. Her husband had been in the village and Balwina was evidently in some distress. Everything Sam had been told seemed to be true. There was talk in the village that all the Jews in Bobowa ghetto had been murdered and thrown into a mass grave. About twenty had escaped from the lorries and the Gestapo was searching the entire district.

Some hidden part of Sam's mind had allowed for hope. Now Balwina confirmed his worst fears. He began to cry again. The egg Balwina was cooking began to burn and Sam realised she was crying, too.

It suddenly occurred to Sam that he could not stay with Balwina. He would put her at risk. He thought of his grandmother's farm in the mountains. He told Balwina. He could go to her and be with his sister, Feigele, and his brother, too. For a moment a wonderful feeling of warmth and safety filled his mind as he pictured their isolated log cabin in the mountains, his grandmother's face breaking into smiles and Feigele rushing out to see him…

Tears were still rolling down Balwina's sun-beaten face.

'Oh Sam, don't you know what I am trying to say?' she cried. 'Do you want me to tell you?'[33]

Somehow Balwina managed to utter the words; dreadful words that seemed to tumble about the kitchen and still make no sense. She understood that there had been many ghettos in their region of southern Poland. All of them had had their 'final solution' – as it was being called. Balwina had discovered that Sam's mother's family – including his brother and sister – had been in a ghetto at Dukla. This, too, had been 'evacuated'. Balwina could not bring herself to use the German term she had heard: 'liquidated'.

Sam still did not understand, until Balwina's anguished cry said it all. No one had stood a chance, she said. 'Everyone that I know of is dead and the only Jews left alive are fugitives,' she sobbed, 'or in concentration camps like Auschwitz.'[34]

There in the kitchen, Sam learned he was an orphan. The Nazis were without mercy. He almost certainly had no family left at all. As they sobbed together, the bleakness of it all stretched out ahead of him. He was utterly alone in a hostile country.

Balwina started again with breakfast and began to form a plan. She would keep Sam in the attic until he was strong again. The Pole, Krupa, the notorious Jew-hunter, lived less than half a mile from her house. It was said that if he was suspicious someone was sheltering a Jew, he listened at their windows at night, waiting for any fugitive to emerge from their hiding place. Next day the Gestapo would be right there.[35] Balwina was certain it would not be safe for Sam to stay. She wanted him to change his identity, go to a village further away and pretend he was a Polish boy looking for work. This was his best chance. She would teach him Polish prayers. They would work out a cover story. They even agreed his new name: Jusek Polewski.

The day came when Sam had to leave. Just before dawn, barefoot, with nothing but the clothes on his back, he trudged down the dirt road from Bystra. It was some time before his terror subsided. He tried to get used to his new name and rehearsed his cover story in his mind. It took great courage for him to make enquiries in each passing village. But no one needed a stable boy. Sam felt utterly alone in a hostile world.

He slept in isolated barns. As he drifted to sleep, sometimes he allowed himself to believe that he was lost in a dream world. Anything could happen. He might wake up safe in

England or America. He would quickly dismiss it. Such thoughts could drive him crazy. It would never happen. His customary vigilance would rush back in. He was ever on guard, always ready to take off. With an existence hovering somewhere between life and sudden death, he felt he could never be anything. The Nazis had stolen his future.

*

On 14 October 1942, ten-year-old Sidney Finkel was standing in the central square of Piotrkow ghetto clinging behind his father, Laib, and brother, Isaac. He heard angry voices. He was discovered. To his utter astonishment, Isaac intervened. Sidney glimpsed him slip something into the Nazi officer's hand. He did not know whether it was money or some gem from Isaac's smuggling enterprise. Whatever the case, the bribe was all his life was now worth. Sidney was ordered with his father and brother to go to the wood barrel factory just outside the ghetto. It would not be the last time his life would be saved by his quick-thinking older brother.

Isaac's courage only bought a temporary reprieve. Straining to hear Laib and Isaac talking to the factory owners against the screeching backdrop of the woodcutting machinery, Sidney understood that he was not welcome. Work permits were not for children. If the Nazis found out, they would all be in danger. Once again, his father and Isaac fought for him. His father used to supply this company with wood and now he was having to beg for his son's life from his former customer, while working for him for nothing. The factory owner relented. Sidney could hide in the attic.[36]

Isolated for hours on end, Sidney struggled to deal with his feelings. His mother and sisters had vanished. His father and brother were effectively Jewish slaves. His father seemed bowed over with the strain. Laib had fallen a long way since the days when he was the proud owner of his own mills, taking good care of his family. Laib felt that his family's suffering was in part his fault. He had not foreseen the Nazi threat. His oldest daughter, Ronia, had tried to warn him and now she was dead; perhaps his wife and other daughters, too. This crushing blow diminished him further. There seemed no end in sight of the Nazis and their powers.

Isaac tried to build their morale. They had to survive one day at a time. But each day delivered fresh dangers. One day Isaac was stripped of all his remaining treasures by his former friends, who had enlisted in the Polish Secret Service and worked for the Nazis. Isaac had nothing left with which to bargain in the face of any horror that might be meted out. This was not long in coming. There was a new Nazi order. All those in hiding, including children, must be surrendered. Anyone without a work permit had no right to live. Isaac and his father managed to keep Sidney hidden but many were found and herded into the synagogue.

The gruesome atrocities that occurred in the synagogue after the liquidation of Piotrkow ghetto were relayed by the Polish workers in unsparing detail to the Jewish slave labourers. Some five hundred people were herded into the building. Without food and water for days, many died. Isaac heard that the babies were collected and 'put into large bowls', which were placed on a pyre in the synagogue where 'those babies were burned alive'.[37] A similarly horrific account was reported by a Jewish boy, Joshua Segal, who later escaped from the synagogue. The Nazi guards keeping watch outside had lit a fire. Suddenly one of the soldiers, who appeared drunk, tossed a baby over the fire and caught it in a large pan. 'I couldn't believe what I had seen,' Joshua wrote later. Again the guard 'tossed the baby in the air and caught it with the large pan. After the third toss the baby stopped crying and was still.' Joshua's shock was so great his body 'heaved in convulsions'. The five hundred Jews trapped in the synagogue were eventually driven to a nearby forest and machine-gunned into trenches that had been dug by the previous day's victims.[38]

When the 'evacuation' of Piotrkow ghetto was complete, the labourers at the wood barrel factory were moved back into an area now denoted as the little Ghetto. This was a small area of a few streets fenced off from the original site by barbed wire. As before, Sidney had to stay hidden all day. The searches continued for children, who were deemed 'useless eaters'. It was becoming increasingly dangerous to be a child. Laib and Isaac were astute in looking out for Sidney. They managed to get work in the wood factory in the Bugaj slave labour camp in Piotrkow, which enabled them to take Sidney into Bugaj, away from the immediate dangers of the little ghetto. 'Since he was not old enough to be a worker, he officially did not exist,' Isaac wrote. 'I had to hide him in the factory.' It was life on a knife-edge. There were frequent Nazi inspections with Sidney in danger each time. He became skilled at secreting himself in the best hiding places.

Sidney begged to pretend to be older and be allowed to work, but this soon led to trouble. While he was working he was bitten by a guard's dog and dropped a sack of potatoes. The commandant slowly reached for his gun and removed a bullet. He held it up for Sidney to see, speaking in a matter-of-fact way – 'this bullet is going to enter your head'[39] – as though he were a teacher explaining something quite simple in the classroom, except that his voice was heavy with sarcasm and for Sidney it was a matter of life and death. Sidney pleaded with the commandant, who toyed with him for some time, before thinking better of it and handing him in to the factory police, who beat him violently.

After many months word spread that they were to be moved on to another camp. The order came early one morning. Sidney was still asleep when Laib brought him a hot drink and told him to put on all the clothes he had. It was bitterly cold but everyone was ordered outside. Under SS guard they marched to the railway line by the factory. Sidney's heart plummeted. There were the cattle cars. He had heard about them and now he saw them. These were the cars that had taken his mother and sister. The death cars.

Sidney was taking in this horror when he became caught up in the uncontrollable forward surge of the crowd. Nazis with whips, guns and vicious dogs were herding everyone into the wagons. Sidney was swept away from Laib and Isaac by a tide of people. Helpless against the crush, driven relentlessly forward, he found himself in a car without them. Sidney was beside himself and could not stop screaming. He pushed against the flow to squeeze his way out until subdued into silence by the people around him, who insisted they would all be shot if he continued to cause a commotion. Sidney's legs gave way. He slumped on the wooden floor of the death car, sobbing.

Separated for the first time from the safety of his father and brother, Sidney was suffering panic beyond endurance. 'Crippling fear entered my body, fear that would stay with me for the rest of my life.'[40]

11

'It wasn't enough just to know . . .'

Twelve-year-old Harold Jackson, Trench Court, 1943

For Tante Anna the early months at Trench Hall were among the toughest that she faced. 'That we survived that summer is still a wonder to me,' she admitted later. She was responsible for the one hundred and twenty-five children and staff who tried to squeeze into the run-down hall. It was impossible to put from her mind that 'a very large number' of the children might now be orphans, 'since we have no assurance that their parents are still alive,' she wrote in August 1940.[1] Tante Anna made repeated enquiries through the Red Cross to try to trace parents, 'with little success so far'. The children's correspondence revealed their drastically changed circumstances. 'No more letters about lost Wellington boots,' observed Tante Anna, 'but about lost homes, countries and family members.'

Many of the children followed news of the war closely. There were fears of an imminent invasion. 'The Battle of France is over,' Winston Churchill declared in a momentous speech to the House of Commons on 18 June 1940. 'I expect the Battle of Britain is about to begin . . .' It was not as easy to obtain a daily newspaper in Shropshire as it had been in Kent. 'The BBC had a news summary every Sunday,' recalls pupil Michael Roemer. 'Tante Anna would let us come and hear it.'[2] The humiliating armistice terms for France, German landings in Guernsey and Jersey, any scrap of information about occupied territory: the children were full of questions. When they could, the staff pinned news articles on the notice-board. 'The Ministry of Information announced that there was no truth in the statements that German troops had landed in this country,' according to one bulletin of 1 July, 'or that parachutists had descended in the Midlands.'[3] But on 10 July, the German Luftwaffe intensified its attacks on Britain's Channel convoys. The Battle of Britain had begun.

Tante Anna tried to focus troubled minds on the present and rebuild a sense of optimism. The children were keen to 'carry on the life of the school as in Bunce Court,' observed Paula, but this was 'extremely difficult'. Not only did every drop of water have to be drawn from the Trench Hall well, but the coal stoves 'caused much aggravation and work'. The electricity was supposed to come from an ancient-looking machine in an outbuilding, which produced worrying noises and little else. Key staff such as the carpentry and sports master, Hans Meyer, and older boys who were best placed to help had disappeared. Nothing was growing in the grounds to supplement their limited rations and the new cook lacked Heidtsche's talent. 'She was a domestic science teacher who based her cooking on calories and there was never sufficient to eat,' continued Paula.[4] The children were hungry.

Eric Bourne remembers for the first fortnight everyone dedicated themselves to turning the dilapidated old hall into their new home, even those, like himself, due to sit their school leaving exams in July. It wasn't long before there was a bed for everybody and some kind of order was restored, with classrooms doubling up as bedrooms. Over the coming weeks, the pupils cleared and whitewashed the stables and the 'Saddler's Shoppe,' wrote Paula, 'where the boys' beds were put in three tiers high.'[5] This was deemed the top-ranked den for the oldest boys, explains Michael Roemer. Younger boys were in the main house, 'the Foxhole', followed by 'The Boys of the First Garage, the Second Garage and the Third Garage'. Some of the teachers slept in partitioned sheds originally intended for racehorses and a large chicken coop was plastered and converted into an additional bedroom. The engine room, with its long rows of old-fashioned batteries, was repaired to generate electricity and the children found a way to fit two more beds into its anteroom. Soon they had plans under way to convert the derelict cottage on the estate into a kindergarten so the little ones could return from Stoatley Rough. The children even found a sunken rose garden that could be turned into an open-air theatre.

Inevitably compromises had to be made. The stokehold in the yard doubled as a bathroom and washroom for the boys. No sooner were they clean than their feet were trailing in coal dust again. The small kitchen range was also a problem. It was large enough for the colonel's household, but not for a school. Tante Anna hoped to raise the funds to install a huge Aga.[6] Paula thought that Matron, Bertha, and her helpers had the most difficult time of it, 'because they had to provide for essential cleanliness'. She herself was heavily committed to caring for their elderly mother, Fanny, and sister, Ida, both of whom had fallen ill. As for the children, 'everything was accepted with understanding and good humour,' she observed. Absorbed in their tasks, 'the children were happy and closely attached as a family'.[7]

The children had the knack of turning the chores into a game. Bertha continued to set the cleaning rota as before and even the boisterous 'Saddler's Shoppe Boys' were tasked with cleaning their own dormitory every Friday. 'Before we start cleaning we have to fight a hard "Battle for the Buckets",' recalled one pupil, Werner Krebs, as there was 'rather a short ration'. Then the beds had to be maneuvered into the courtyard because the floor had to be scrubbed 'until it's beautifully red'. Cleaning the cupboards out almost invariably led to a rowdy 'Saddler's Shoppe meeting held in the rubbish heap' as belongings were reclaimed or discarded. When occasionally everything was done 'to everybody's satisfaction, we start singing in a chorus, "How clean is my Saddler's Shoppe".'[8]

The Battle of Britain intensified during August with attacks on the RAF itself, while 'we poor little innocent girls' of Trench Hall, observed Ursula Solmitz, had also 'been subject to heavy bombardments'. These were invariably carried out by the Saddler's Shoppe Boys, who hid behind hedges 'believing themselves to be invisible'. Heavy stones were thrown through the girls' window in the peaceful hours after bedtime. 'We did not stand for it! We had our revenge which ended the matter. Tough apple pies did the trick!' Some girls did not study history and while the boys were swatting, 'we quietly crept over the Saddler's Shoppe armed with a sack full of thistles and thread and needle. They must have had a pleasant night on the prickly projections . . . but were too proud to say a word about it.'[9]

Pupil Peter Stoll remembers making a game of mending the electrics. First, he tried to look the part. He 'set about with an old wooden work man's box which I found in the battery room'. Given the shortage of basic kit in the workshop such as buckets, inevitably a battle ensued. 'I had to convince people of the priority of my work,' and then he beat a hasty retreat before he could be found out. He improved the lighting in the sewing room and the stables and won accolades for solving the puzzle of how to avoid showing a light when the stokehold door was opened during blackout by devising a rather complicated switch. This feat earned him an admiring assistant and an upgrade in his nickname from the demeaning 'Baby' to the impressive 'Sparks'.[10]

But not all the chores were appreciated by the children. Getting life out of the boiler before everyone woke up was one of the more dreaded tasks. Fears of stoking mishaps 'even haunt my dreams,' confessed Leo, one of the Saddler's Shoppe Boys. He invariably overslept and had to race to light the kitchen stove and the stokehold boiler before getting-up time. 'With terrific fury I rush to the library forgetting to clear the ash. I choke it with peat and coal.' Leo invariably failed to beat the bell. 'It is dreadful . . . The water is cold. The boiler has gone out. While I clear out the whole mess I get the cheerful news that both stoves have gone out . . . I race to the library to relight the stove. In my fury I pour a gallon of paraffin into the stove since the firelighter has crumbled into black component parts. The whole room is smelling of paraffin . . . I am utterly exhausted and black in my face . . .' Worse still, 'everybody laughs at me!'[11]

Despite initial hostility in the locality for 'dirty Jerries', Tante Anna managed to persuade a local farmer to rent them a field. The children began planting but until their first crop, they were reliant on rations only. Some children couldn't wait. 'They felt they weren't getting enough food,' says Leslie Brent, 'and went to the fields, dug up sugar beet and ate it raw.' This was strictly forbidden. Tante Anna 'much encouraged good relations with local farmers,' he recalls, and the children were trusted to help out on several farms. At the neighbouring Moseleys' farm, the farmhand supervising the children was soon dubbed 'Chief of the Combined Field

Forces', although he much preferred to be called 'Archy'. The children ranked the Shropshire farmers into four categories. 'a) those that pay well. b) Those that give you good food. c) Those that don't do either. d) Those that do both,' recalled Tante Anna's nephew, Hermann. Although one farmer, Mr Croft, was rated 'C' he had the benefit of a land girl working for him who 'seems to be the great attraction of the countryside'. Leslie Brent remembers spending much time scything thistles and stripping cows.[12] Most farmers milked the cows by hand and there was invariably some milk left over. 'Times were hard so I was allowed to strip the cows to get the last drop of milk.'[13]

For all their efforts, Tante Anna found it hard to 'raise enough food to feed the children during that first year'. Records reveal the struggle she faced just to obtain enough milk. The children drank around sixteen gallons a day, at two shillings and two pence per gallon. She appealed to the Midlands Education Board for eligibility for the 'Milk in Schools Scheme', hoping for free or reduced-price milk. 'Some of our children have become orphans,' she explained, 'and we have lost contact with Belgium, Holland and France . . . We are working under great hardship . . . We live next door to a farmer whose milk is not even certified and whose stables are none too clean . . .' Unfortunately, due to the national shortage of milk, her appeal did not cut any ice with the board running the Milk Scheme. 'It seems clear that the Milk Scheme cannot apply unless an exception can be made,' came the official reply. 'We have not done so in this case.'[14]

All the while, Tante Anna continued her battle with the Home Office for the release of her interned staff and pupils. Over the summer of 1940 she pieced together the fate of the missing older boys and staff. They had been taken to the overcrowded Huyton camp near Liverpool, to await deportation to Canada. The SS *Arandora Star* departed from Liverpool with 1,200 internees on board, but was torpedoed on 2 July with the loss of hundreds of lives. Tante Anna's anxious enquiries to the Home Office were rerouted to the War Office and the Admiralty before she was able to establish that none of her pupils or staff had been on board. The Bunce Court group had been ordered onto another ship, the HMT *Dunera*, and on 10 July found themselves embarking on an ordeal that no one could have anticipated.

Over two thousand Category C enemy aliens, including Richard Sonnenfeldt and Hans Meyer, were confined on HMT *Dunera* with German soldiers captured in Norway and France. As they were chased down into a hold below the waterline by abusive guards with bayonets, Richard found his shock was soon replaced 'by fear bordering on panic'. The Jewish refugees were only separated from Nazi prisoners by a narrow passage with barbed wire, he wrote in his memoirs, but even more alarming were the 'feared and sadistic' British guards. They were poorly trained and assumed that all the prisoners were Nazi spies. 'They used to urinate in the porridge,' recorded one unhappy refugee. 'We all had dysentery. I think five people died.' Another remembered the guards breaking bottles on the deck and ordering prisoners to run barefoot over the broken glass.[15] 'We developed eagle eyes and quick motions to avoid cutting our feet,' Richard wrote. Combined with the dangers of torpedoes, he felt incarcerated in little more than 'a floating coffin'.[16] The horrific treatment of the prisoners did not come to light until the ship docked in Sydney, Australia in September. Tante Anna was astonished when letters from her former pupils began to arrive from the other side of the world. In the subsequent soldiers' court martial the HMT *Dunera* was described as an 'overcrowded Hell hole'.

Anxious to avoid any more internments, Tante Anna fought for her older pupils who turned sixteen that summer, such as Eric Bourne. Eric passed his school certificate, along with all the others who sat the exam that year, and was keen to stay on and help with the repairs at Trench Hall. 'The school had been my only and much-loved home for the preceding seven years,' he wrote. He knew little of the fate of his parents in France, except that his father had managed to flee from Paris. With a large number of parents missing, inevitably Tante Anna was taking on more parental responsibilities. One day she asked Eric to come to her room. She had managed to 'save me from being interned as an enemy alien,' Eric recalls, but he was required to make a personal contribution to the war effort. He was to be enrolled in a YMCA training farm in Oxfordshire. Eric was 'seriously disappointed' to learn that he must leave.[17]

A few were more fortunate. Heinz Redwood was one of just three children during the war who were able to stay to take the higher school certificate, the equivalent of A levels today. During the 1930s, Heinz's far-sighted father had sent money for his education to his younger brother in Australia. Heinz told Tante Anna he wanted to follow the advice of his beloved grandfather, Maximilian, and study chemistry at university. Birmingham's chemistry department had just won a prize for synthesising Vitamin C and Heinz set his heart on winning a place there.[18]

To his surprise, Tante Anna was not keen. In the early autumn of 1940, the Battle of Britain entered a dangerous new phase. Hitler's Luftwaffe had civilians in their sights. In the late afternoon of 7 September, hundreds of bombers and fighters darkened the sky over London. It was the start of the London Blitz: fifty-seven continuous nights of bombing. Cities in the industrial Midlands nearby were also heavily targeted, including Birmingham, just fifty miles away, and Coventry, where in one night 500 tons of high explosive all but destroyed the centre of the town. On another occasion the children saw 'a red glow along the sky towards the north,' recalls Michael Roemer. 'The whole sky was tinged red.' He thought it was Liverpool burning.[19]

Tante Anna felt strongly that as refugees, her older pupils should be making a contribution to their host country at such a critical time. Young people 'should be working on the land,' she told Heinz. 'We shouldn't be aiming at going to university.' But she relented once she understood the strength of Heinz's feelings. Heinz's grandfather had given him his first science set at a young age and had fired his imagination with chemistry experiments to encourage him to study the subject. Heinz was keen to fulfil his expectations. Tante Anna agreed that Heinz and two other pupils could study for their higher school certificate, working in the grounds for half the day for their board. Heinz was thrilled. Even so, he had a rebellious streak. 'I was critical about the headmistress . . . There was a row about the number of slices of bread we could eat. It was rationing after all. We had absolutely no idea that the financial situation of Bunce Court was extremely uncertain and of her struggle to maintain the school . . .'

Despite everyone's efforts, the strain of being a school for 'Aliens' in a country at war began to tell. Almost absurdly, conflicts came to a head over the trivial matter of a concert, with Heinz as ringleader. Tante Anna had arranged for British supply teachers to help over the summer, but this soon led to an unexpected row. The musical culture of the school, headed by the talented Lotte Kalischer, was exclusively classical, 'mainly German, Bach, Handel, Mozart, Beethoven,' recalls Heinz. Lotte and her team 'gave us a fantastic musical education but that was all they were interested in'. Modern music was out. 'Jazz too, was a swear word. You were totally in trouble if you liked that,' Heinz laughs. One of the British supply teachers took it upon himself to break with school tradition. He organised a performance of *Trial by Jury*, by Gilbert and Sullivan, a quintessentially British comic opera.

This satirical musical about the legal system had a riotous sense of fun quite unlike the stirring German classics to which the children were accustomed. The songs were funny, sometimes ludicrous, the whimsical plot a light-hearted attack on establishment hypocrisy. The production felt very British and the children loved it. But the German head of the music department was outraged. 'Things like that should not be performed at the school. It's quite unsuitable,' Lotte stormed crossly. Proud of his performance as the hypocritical judge, Heinz, as well as his fellow actors, became 'quite angry'. Lotte was quick to take offence. She made 'very adverse remarks,' recalls Heinz. The British comic opera was 'lightweight'. Their exchanges became heated. Eventually Lotte stormed, 'This Gilbert and Sullivan is not suitable' because it is '*rubbish*'.

Heinz decided that Lotte was wrong. He planned a full-scale rebellion and set up a circular letter to which 'everyone put their signatures in a circle, commenting on how much we did not agree with the musical policy of the school'. He sent it to Lotte, 'who of course was absolutely appalled'. Tension ran high. Was Gilbert and Sullivan a degradation? Was German music the best or were they just cultural snobs in the music department? There was a huge rift, as though all the tensions and frustrations of their circumstances at Trench Hall became invested in this argument over the music.

Tante Anna realised Heinz was behind the offending letter. She summoned him to her office. He expected her to talk about the musical policy of the school. To his astonishment, she raised something else entirely. 'When you disagree with something you should talk about it with the person concerned,' she said, 'not write anonymous satirical letters.' Heinz was taken aback. Tante Anna was not taking sides in the argument but she did object to the way he had handled his criticisms. 'It's fine to have a disagreement, but let's be out in the open about it,' she continued. Heinz reflected on what she said. His relationship with Tante Anna had been 'a bit up and down,' he admits. As a teenager he did not like to be told anything. 'I would weigh up almost anything I was told and decide whether I thought it was good or not.' As he pondered her advice, he conceded to himself it was 'quite impressive,' he says. 'That taught me a lesson for life.'

This encounter with Tante Anna, along with her support for his further studies, changed Heinz's attitude. He no longer saw the headmistress as someone 'who kept on telling you things', but rather as 'someone who is actually doing a wonderful job'. This view was underlined still further when she helped him with his university entrance a year later. Heinz passed his higher school certificate with flying colours and received his dream offer from Birmingham University's chemistry department – just at the point when he lost all contact with his parents in the Far East and his uncle in Australia had died and his aunt could send no more money until death duties were settled. Tante Anna contacted the university department to reassure them, 'you can be certain the studies will be paid for'. Her intervention made all the difference and Heinz embarked on his university career.[20]

Meanwhile Tante Anna's campaign for the release of her internees was bringing results. When the sinking of the SS *Arandora Star* and the inhumane treatment of refugees on the HMT *Dunera* came to light, the British public's attitudes towards internment changed sharply. Churchill did a U-turn and conceded that his policy of 'collar the lot' was 'a deplorable mistake' and agreed to review the cases of all the 'good Germans', including the refugees who had fled the Nazis. One of the first to return to Trench Hall was the much-loved cook, Heidtsche. Spirits rose immediately. Irresistible meals would return. 'She knew how to make the best of the rations,' says Leslie. The kitchen would once again be that borough of warmth at the centre of the house, with Heidtsche, symbol of security, expressing love in her own inimitable way.

During 1941, Hans Meyer also returned with one of the older boys, all the way from the Hay internment camp in New South Wales, Australia. There was much excitement as pupils showed them round their new home. Despite his 'highly dangerous and madcap' trip to Australia on HMT *Dunera*, Leslie noted, Hans was 'sanguine' about his treatment, without any hint of bitterness.[21] Hans could describe travelling across dangerous oceans at risk of enemy attack, HMT *Dunera's* encounter with a Nazi U-boat and the escalating hostilities in the Far East. His experiences brought alive the ever-expanding cataclysm that was engulfing the whole world.

On 7 December 1941, a few months after Hans's return to the school, the Japanese carried out a surprise attack on the American naval base at Pearl Harbor, Hawaii, and declared war on Britain and America. Children crowded round the school map to see the pin marking this alarming new development in a place no one had heard of on the other side of the world. The following day, America declared war on Japan. Three days later, Germany and America were at war. There were animated discussions in the classrooms. With American isolationism at an end, surely it was possible to hope that Nazism would now be defeated?

But during 1942 Germany and its allies, the Axis countries, continued to triumph across the world. By the summer of 1942, Hitler was at the height of his powers, his empire ever-expanding. The Third Reich reached across most of Europe to the English Channel. In North Africa, under General Erwin Rommel, the legendary 'Desert Fox', Axis forces fought their way into Egypt in June, threatening the Suez Canal and the Middle East. During July and August, Axis armies stormed across vast expanses of Soviet Russia, reaching the outskirts of Stalingrad in the south. In the Atlantic war, German U-boat wolf packs devastated Britain's convoy lifeline. Meanwhile, Germany's ally, Japan, had command of the Pacific, its troops gaining Singapore, the Dutch East Indies, the Philippines and Burma in quick succession and reaching almost to the Indian border.

The school in Shropshire remained a little haven of safety, but for how long? Bombing raids continued over British cities. There was speculation in the press that if Soviet Russia fell, the Nazis could return to invade. The unspoken fear that could not be dismissed was: what would happen to Jewish children and staff if Hitler did conquer Britain? Tante Anna tried to convey a sense of reassurance and continuity in the face of such unknowns, keeping those around her focused on the day-to-day challenges. The archives reveal a flurry of letters as she looked for donations to replace essentials left in Kent: books, an extra piano, even percussion instruments; 'if anyone has a tambourine or a drum at home,' she wrote hopefully to the school's supporters. She petitioned the Department of Health to approve a live-in 'Alien doctor' at the school, since the local doctor was finding the three-mile round trip from Wem 'is difficult for him considering the petrol,' she explained.[22] Against all the odds, Tante Anna also set her sights on expanding the school in order to help more children.

Tante Anna knew through the Refugee Children's Movement that not all the Kindertransport children hurriedly placed in foster homes in 1939 had settled well. If she could obtain supplies of timber, she could build another wooden house for extra dormitories and help them. Her efforts did not go unnoticed. Mr A.R. Marshall, of the Midlands Education Board in Staffordshire, understood the plight of the Jewish children. The headmistress 'has many applications for entry from both English and Alien [pupils],' he explained to the Midlands Board of Education. 'If she could obtain a hut of 60' by 20', she could house them.' He also asked for planking for the boys and the handyman master. The school 'is doing very fine work although working under adverse conditions and should receive all the support we can give it,' recommended Mr Marshall. 'How it manages to carry on with very few funds I cannot say but Miss Essinger is a "sticker".' He felt the Board of Education should help them in any way 'to put on this brave show'.[23]

The local Education Board was unable to help and so the request for timber was escalated to the Ministry of Works. But the work's department was hard-pressed to find building materials to repair bombed-out Britain and far too busy to concern itself with Boy Scouts' sheds. 'We can't do anything about it,' came the disappointing reply.[24]

*

Behind the flurry of news headlines, there was something else troubling Tante Anna over the course of 1942 that, at first, was rarely mentioned in the news. Something unconfirmed, unexplained, but deeply disturbing. The first clues to this new horror arrived at the school in the form of Red Cross messages.

Leslie Brent came to see her in October 1942 with an extremely worrying message from his father in Berlin. Arthur's usually even hand was uncharacteristically erratic; his message appeared to have been written in a very emotional state. They were going 'on a long journey', Arthur had written. Leslie had read and reread the twenty-five words. It made no sense. Why would his father not say where they were going? What could 'going on a long journey' mean, he asked Tante Anna. Why would his parents go away without giving him a new address? It was totally out of character. Up to this point, Leslie and his family had been in regular contact all year.

Leslie was no longer living at Trench Hall and had travelled some distance to seek Tante Anna's advice. Knowing of his interest in natural history, when he had passed his school certificate in early 1942 Tante Anna had tried to open a door to a scientific career for him, finding him a post as a laboratory assistant at the Birmingham Central Technical College. It was a modest beginning but with a chance of further study in the evenings. Although he was staying in Birmingham, Trench Hall remained Leslie's fixed point of reference. After work on Friday he often cycled the fifty miles to the school in Shropshire, hanging on to the back of lorries to help him up the hills. He thought nothing of the danger. He loved to get back to Trench Hall for the weekends. 'I was home!' he says.[25]

The messages Leslie had received from his mother and father since the war began could say little but proved a precious lifeline. 'Work is tremendous fun. Am learning a great deal,' he had told his parents in May 1941 when he passed his first chemistry exam in Birmingham. In June, he had sent news of a holiday visit to Trench Hall when he broke the school high jump record on sports day. His father sent regular reassuring replies. There in code, Leslie knew his family was still alive and getting by in Berlin in spite of the catastrophe unfolding around them. It was something to hold on to, an invisible anchor that profoundly affected his well-being. Arthur always started with 'Beloved [*Geliebter*] boy', but when he told his son they were going on a journey, the 'BELOVED' was written in capitals that were wildly uneven as though he could hardly hold the pen. His father advised him to write to an 'uncle' that Leslie did not know.[26]

Tante Anna did her best to comfort Leslie, concealing her deepest worries. There had been ominous reports in the papers. Over the summer, word had spread of mysterious deportations of Jews from Nazi-occupied countries, although it was not certain from the press where they were going or why. On 29 September 1942, the *Manchester Guardian* reported on 'the persecution and deportation' of Jews from Vichy France, which was pressured into increasing Nazi collaboration. 'What is the explanation of this evil measure, which has aroused universal repugnance?' asked the diplomatic correspondent of the *Guardian*. 'Why in any case should Germany want the Jews, including women and children?' The *Guardian*'s diplomatic editor speculated the 'major object was German military security', and noted that there was an increasing number of Gestapo agents in unoccupied France 'in the interest of security'.[27]

The Red Cross messages received by pupils such as Leslie about their parents 'going on a journey' appeared to be linked to the deportations. Reports of atrocities; deportations from Germany and France; the mysterious disappearance of relatives: what did it mean? There were an estimated nine million Jews in Europe. What was happening to them? Knowing what she did about Hitler's regime, peace of mind was not possible for Tante Anna.[28]

On 25 November 1942, a report published in the *New York Times* under the innocuous-sounding header 'Details Reaching Palestine' hinted at systematised mass murder. The article referred to 'the slaughter of Jews in Poland' and 'accounts of trainloads of adults and children taken to great crematoriums at Oswiecim [Auschwitz] near Krakow'. Their source was the Jewish Agency, a Zionist group in Palestine fostering immigration.[29] In the following weeks the British press, too, referred to the 'mass extermination of the Jews', citing similar reports from Polish and other sources. The *Manchester Guardian* on 15 December questioned why the Allies did not intervene: 'So far the British Government and the other United Nations have not even got to the point of protesting against the massacres,' stormed the *Guardian*'s political correspondent. Could not the British and American governments take steps to facilitate the migration of Jews in Poland to neutral Sweden? Could not more Jewish children be saved? Anthony Eden, the foreign secretary, should 'state the Government view of the Polish horrors'.[30]

The British government had in fact known since the invasion of Soviet Russia in June 1941 of the escalating atrocities against the Jews. British agents, the Polish government in exile, as well as Jewish sources, built up a steadily consistent picture of a change in Nazi policy towards the Jews from emigration before the war to containment in ghettos and camps to extermination. On 17 December 1942, Anthony Eden finally rose to make an announcement in the House of Commons. 'Reliable reports' from the Polish government in exile and others 'have recently reached His Majesty's Government regarding the barbarous and inhuman treatment to which Jews are being subjected in German occupied Europe,' Eden began. He condemned the Nazi authorities' 'bestial policy of cold-blooded extermination' of the Jews, who were being transported 'from all the occupied countries . . . in conditions of appalling horror and brutality to eastern Europe'. Eden identified Poland as 'the principal Nazi slaughterhouse'. The ghettos were being systematically emptied. 'The able-bodied are slowly worked to death in labour camps.' The remainder 'are deliberately massacred in mass executions'. His fearful disclosures carried weight. At the end of the debate, Members of the House stood in silence.[31]

Tante Anna heard the news of Anthony Eden's speech. There had been numerous reports of Nazi atrocities against Jews since the Nazis invaded Poland, but for many, such killing was indistinguishable from the horrors of war. This time it was different. The British government was confirming the transport and mass murder of Jews in Nazi-occupied countries. Although the details were not clear, Eden was effectively describing something systematic and continent-wide. The governments of Britain, America and the Soviet Union, and many others, united in condemning 'in the strongest possible terms this bestial policy of cold-blooded extermination' and made a 'solemn resolution to ensure that those responsible for these crimes shall not escape retribution'.[32]

Tante Anna had had great foresight in 1933, but never had she imagined that anything so inconceivably barbaric and inhumane could come to pass. It was, in the words of the

Archbishop of Canterbury, 'a horror beyond what the imagination can grasp'. Many of her staff were already grieving about the strange disappearance of relatives. Privately, as word spread, there were anxious discussions. How was it possible for this to happen? Did ordinary German people know about the deportations? Surely the Allies would take action? There were so many unanswered questions. Eden had said, 'I fear what we can do at this stage must inevitably be slight.' A statement from the Archbishop of Canterbury on New Year's Eve seemed to sum up the difficulties facing the Allies. 'It is a bitter grief that our nation can do so little to help but short of victory in the war, there is no way in which we can ourselves effect anything comparable to the need and the massacre goes on day by day.' The Archbishop could do little but 'offer prayers for the Jews of Germany . . . over whom the threat of extermination is hanging.'[33]

Tante Anna and her staff tried to protect the children from the horrifying news. Hans Meyer later described their approach. Decades on, he could still remember vividly the day Leslie told them about his Red Cross message from his father. 'My God, as soon as the letter arrived a hush fell. Of course, we knew about the camps . . .' he says. In order not to compound any pupil's anxieties, 'instead you tried to help them through the times of silence,' Hans remembers. 'Until they got used to the fact no letters would come. We got them used to silence. You didn't tell the children that their parents were in concentration camps and they would be killed. You really couldn't say your parents aren't alive any more. No one knew for sure. We knew they were in camps but we didn't know which ones or what happened to them. So we could neither raise children's hopes nor dash them.'[34]

Leslie found becoming accustomed to the silence was painful. November passed. Still no message. Then it was Christmas 1942. No news. He sent Red Cross messages to the 'uncle' his father had recommended but he, too, had heard nothing from Leslie's parents. 'All our relations have gone on a journey,' wrote his 'uncle' a few weeks later. Then his messages suddenly stopped, too. The silence was beyond endurance. Leslie began to suffer from a sharp pain in his chest. It surprised him that outwardly he could carry on as though nothing was wrong when the pain could be so intense. He found a doctor in Birmingham and explained his symptoms. The doctor did not even examine him. He pointed out to Leslie how anxiety alone could produce such a powerful sensation of pain and sent him away with a mild prescription. By day Leslie could get by, but at night when he closed his eyes he would see 'a long convoy of grey trucks' winding through a vast landscape and disappearing over the horizon. In his dreams it was always the same line of grey trucks, the same soldiers, the same angry skies. Eva? Arthur? Charlotte? Where had they gone?[35]

Tante Anna did all she could to trace missing parents through the refugee agencies and the Red Cross. More than ever, she was determined the school was to be a home for the children. Even those who had left, such as Leslie, should have a place of safety and comfort, a sanctuary to which they could return.

Years later Leslie tried to convey what this meant to him. 'People all over the world would find life almost unbearable if they had not an island to retire to in times of bodily and spiritual stress,' he wrote in the *Diagonal* magazine for former Bunce Courtians. 'It may be an island that is within us and not visible to the outside world; it may be external, perhaps within another person, possibly even an island in the true geographical sense . . . On such an island, men are free . . . free from all that enslaves us.' For Leslie, this island was the utopian place where 'the poor in spirit may find their "kingdom", the unloved his love . . . the persecuted will undoubtedly free himself from persecution, and the lone man his loneliness . . . For many of us old Bunce Courtians, the school has been and still is, an island such as I have described . . .' Leslie pointed out how many former pupils were drawn back to Bunce Court for holidays 'with almost monotonous regularity', or 'suddenly turned up' unexpectedly. He himself was irresistibly drawn back 'because everything the school embraced, I repeat *everything*, took you to an island where you felt free. An island that essentially never changed, which lived its own life unaffected by the tremors and upheavals around it, to which you could return as to a friend, knowing there was a place for you in its life . . .'[36]

*

With the departure of older pupils such as Leslie, Eric and Heinz, Tante Anna was in a position to admit more children. 'Thousands of children were saved,' she wrote of the Kindertransports, but mistakes were made. 'Mistakes that probably started by telling the children that they would have an easy life if they came away from their parents and over to England,' she thought. 'Mistakes by committees here who thought that the quicker these children could be absorbed into English families the better it would be for them and the community . . .'[37] Working with the Refugee Children's Committee, Tante Anna was now able to provide an alternative for some of these children.

Tante Anna knew that the brief notes she received on each case from the RCM could conceal layers of emotional trauma. Among those who arrived in this third wave of pupils was ten-year-old Mia Schaff, who had been moved repeatedly, going from one foster home to another. The loneliness she felt living with strangers in London and then Hertfordshire and the frequent unsettling changes compounded the trauma she had experienced in Germany. Her father had been taken by the Gestapo one night and had disappeared somewhere in Poland, and she had last seen her mother running down the platform at Charlottenburg station in Berlin in July 1939. In England, Mia had eventually found herself in the care of two kindly widows in Bishop's Stortford, Minnie Sheldrake and Minnie Ainger. Concerned at her solitary position in their elderly household and the long commute Mia faced each day to school, the two Minnies found a way to send her to Trench Hall.

By this time, Mia was lacking in confidence and felt very shy. The absence of her parents felt like an abandonment. Her mother, Ida, had promised to come to England on 10 September 1939, but never arrived. Her Red Cross messages from Berlin became more and more infrequent and eventually stopped altogether. A few months later, Mia learned through the Red Cross that her father was in Auschwitz. 'It didn't mean anything to me,' Mia recalls. 'Would it have meant anything to anyone in the war?' She was ten or eleven at the time. 'It was no different. I had no contact with my parents. I imagined myself to be an orphan nearly the whole time.' There were moments when Mia felt utterly bereft.

Initially, the sad little girl who turned up at Trench Hall thought her fellow pupils very self-assured and sophisticated. 'When I first went there – I just couldn't get it,' she says.

'Everyone had an opinion in that school.' She can still remember her first history lesson. The teacher, the intellectual Miss Clifford or 'Cliffie', a young teacher from New Zealand, set them an essay on 'American Isolation and Imperialism'. Mia had been learning about the Tudors and Stuarts in her English school. Now she had to write an essay 'on something where I didn't even understand the words.' She was far too shy to ask anyone. 'I wrote a lot of rubbish,' she remembers. When her homework came back, Cliffie had written, '"I don't think you quite understand." And I thought, you're right. I don't.' Cliffie helped Mia grasp the concepts under discussion. The lessons were more like a conversation, says Mia. 'Everyone was expected to chip in . . . I was only shy to start with. I soon got the hang of it.'[38]

Mia soon found that many in her class were without parents. She became best friends with Susie Davids, who was also an orphan. 'It was my great good luck to get to Trench Hall,' Susie recalls, 'because I was feeling extremely sorry for myself.' Although her parents had escaped to England before the war, they never recovered from their violent experiences in Germany. 'My father had a weak heart after Dachau,' Susie explains. He had suffered severe beatings. Although safe in England, one day he had a fatal heart attack. His sudden death proved too much for Susie's mother, who also died, six months later. An aunt took charge and sent Susie to Trench Hall. Susie soon found that 'many of the children were far worse off than me. They were losing their parents in concentration camps. My parents died in bed.' Knowing what happened to her mother and father and being able to comfort them as they died, she felt, in some small way spared her a little of the torment which others suffered.

Mia joined forces with her best friend Susie, who loved working in the kitchen. The girls started at six o'clock each morning. 'We'd help make the toast and stir the porridge,' recalls Mia. Susie remembers taking the food down to the cottage where Paula looked after the infants, 'who were all orphans I suppose,' she muses. Invariably they were rewarded with an extra cup of cocoa or coffee. 'Heidtsche's temper! Oh yes! If you didn't clean the saucepans properly God help you!' says Susie, but this did not seem to matter. She felt 'Heidtsche was wonderful. She loved her children. She loved the big boys who helped her. Some of the big saucepans were very heavy – she couldn't possibly pick them up.' United by their common experiences and their camaraderie, Mia and Susie thrived.[39]

The relative speed with which Kindertransport children from foster homes appear to have adapted to the school may be due partly to the support they gained from each other. They found friends from a similar cultural background who shared the same worries. The teachers, too, had greater experience. Tante Anna's team had become skilled at settling distressed pupils and helping them adapt to the disturbing changes in their lives; they knew how to create an environment that would reduce anxiety and pain; the imaginative focus on fun outdoors, much of which was critical to the running of the school: all this seems to have helped to calm troubled nerves, foster a sense of stability and purpose, and help each child feel of special value.

Settling in with the refugees from foster homes were new British pupils. Tante Anna was glad to increase her numbers of British children, not least because this brought some financial stability, but they often brought problems of their own. An English boy of eleven, Harold Jackson, never forgot his arrival at Trench Hall. The front door was opened by the matron, Bertha, who greeted Harold and his mother in German. Harold's jaw dropped. 'I was completely confused. We were fighting the Germans at the time so quite why I was going to school with them – I could not make out.'[40] In his mind, Germans were the enemy. Harold was convinced he was being punished.

Harold describes himself as 'a disturbed child'. His parents broke up when he was very little, and he has a vivid memory of being 'dumped'. Both his parents were members of the communist party and 'I kept being moved from one member of the communist party to another'. Growing up in strangers' homes, he felt an outsider and became something of a loner. That feeling of being excluded, 'not part of the whole thing', stalked his childhood. He describes himself as 'a daunting child' by the time he arrived at Trench Hall. Harold soon realised many of the children at the school were without parents. 'In that sense I was very much in tune with the refugee children because I felt more or less a refugee.'[41]

The teachers soon discovered that Harold had a flair for languages. Hanna Bergas helped him and soon he was so fluent in German he sometimes pretended to be German just for the sake of it, introducing himself with a German form of his name: 'Jacobson' rather than 'Jackson'. One day he was talking in German with a group of pupils as they dug potatoes out in a far field. By chance, there happened to be a group of German prisoners of war in the next field 'who heard us speaking German and decided it was some sort of dastardly plot'. The British guards brought the prisoners over to speak. 'The British soldiers were baffled by us,' Harold recalls. 'They just could not believe there were German youths at large in the countryside and thought it was some kind of clever ploy by the intelligence services.' No one realised that at least one of the pupils was a British boy pretending to be German for a lark. 'People just assumed I was German,' said Harold. There was a downside. Harold remembers the suspicions in the local district about the school. When he and other children left for the school holidays they would walk to Wem station. 'The local youths knew it was the end of term and they would gather and yell dirty Nazis.' Harold took the abuse in his stride as though he was German. 'I was a tough child.'[42]

The school held another unexpected interest for cynical Harold. One new British pupil was the beautiful Anna John, a granddaughter of the painter Augustus John. She and her younger sister, Natalie, were the 'two new genii at drawing and painting,' observed Hanna Bergas. 'Anna drew the most beautiful apples in the whole school.' For Harold, it was something else about Anna John that caught his attention. She stirred new and quite unexpected feelings. 'I was in love with her,' he says. Harold found he had much in common with Anna John. She, too, felt abandoned by her parents, who had separated when she and Natalie were very young and took little interest in their daughters. Anna had been sent away to boarding school at the tender age of five. 'My father was fed most royally by Heidtsche,' recalls Anna John, 'and decided immediately that we should now be deposited at Trench Hall. My sister and I were at a loss . . .'

Although Tante Anna created an atmosphere in her school that was light-hearted and fun, there were still firm boundaries. Anna John's experience of settling in at the school highlights how this was done. Anna had a bohemian disregard of authority and didn't recognise any limits. In her previous boarding school, the food had been inadequate and she had felt so hungry she regularly raided the larder. 'We used to cut the wire mesh from the outside, put our arm in and grab the food,' she explains. She didn't see anything wrong in stealing food, staff cigarettes or anything else to hand. 'We ran completely wild,' she recalls. 'Didn't recognise rules or anything. Certainly didn't stick to any.' When she reached Trench Hall, 'I didn't know anything about anything and broke all the rules.'

This invariably brought the new British girl with the long brown plaits into the elevated orbit of Tante Anna. Anna John recalls her saying, 'Come up and I'll have a talk to *you* . . .' There was something about the way she said 'you' that alerted Anna at once that she had been naughty. Indeed, Anna was soon left in no doubt. Tante Anna only had to look at her in a particular way and she would feel the full force of her transgressions. 'Tante Anna could dominate [a room] just by being there, without trying,' she recalls. 'If she just looked at you, you shrivelled into the floor.' Quite how she had this power Anna John could not quite discern. She knew Tante Anna was not really angry. 'Tante Anna gave a sweet smile, head slightly angled . . .' Sometimes she even seemed shy.

Tante Anna's room was the only one with a carpet and Anna John found herself 'on the carpet' with rather more frequency than was desirable, with Tante Anna trying to convey what aspect of her behaviour was at issue. Tante Anna would invariably say, 'You shouldn't be doing that. You wouldn't be doing that with your mother,' or 'you wouldn't do this at home'. Anna John was intimidated but still summoned the courage to stand up for herself. She retorted that she 'never saw her mother anyway and was never at home'. 'I felt I had lost my home,' she says. 'We had no badge of family life. Nowhere to go.' Tante Anna perhaps saw that Anna John 'felt at sea . . . and angry at her neglect'.

Anna John did not steal food at Trench Hall. 'Heidtsche was much too frightening. And we got good food anyway . . . I loved her, but I wouldn't say she was sweet. She was "Hitlerish" in the kitchen . . . She screamed and shouted a lot but her food was brilliant. We never even thought about it – just sat and enjoyed it. I've no idea how she did it.' Anna chose to give the hot-tempered cook a wide berth. She roamed and wandered wherever she liked, sometimes for miles. 'I'd run away . . . I just used to cross fields and look for horses because I always loved horses,' she recalls. When she wasn't roaming, she was invariably noisy. A cardinal sin. Back on the carpet.

In Tante Anna, Anna John was finally meeting some boundaries. She somehow 'made you feel part of everything,' she says. 'I felt I wasn't outside the place, we were all part of it. How she did it, I've no idea because she was quite severe sometimes. If you were naughty you got told, but she was never in any way bossy.' When Tante Anna had finished, 'she would invariably say with her lovely German accent, "You may go downstairs, but don't make so much noise next time".' Tante Anna made arrangements with a local school for Anna John to ride. Soon she was allowed to look after one of the ponies herself, grazing it on the edge of the hockey field. It was a little black New Forest pony that Anna nicknamed Rookie. She was thrilled. In retrospect, she thinks 'Tante Anna went the extra mile to deal with what a child wants . . .'

This did not stop Anna John occasionally getting into further scrapes. At Trench Hall there were 'expectations of us that I and my sister were not accustomed to and we took a while to understand it . . .' She relished slipping off to the bicycle sheds with her friends after the 9.30 p.m. lights out, where they were met by a group of boys. They would tour the countryside for hours into the night. On one occasion they were seen by a policeman, who tipped off Tante Anna. Anna John was once again on the carpet. Tante Anna made her feel 'I ought to know better'. As an English girl, with both her parents in the country, she felt 'a poor comparison' to the German children who were suffering, she recalls. 'She made you *own* your bad behaviour.'[43]

'I don't think Anna John was the naughtiest girl but she was the girl all the boys loved,' recalls Helen Urbach, a new pupil in the same class as Harold Jackson and Anna John. 'Anna was dark and very pretty – we were all jealous of her.' An only child originally from Vienna, Helen was thrilled to join in. 'We had midnight feasts. We would take the food from the kitchen somehow and meet the boys somewhere out of the building.' It was all a long way from the trauma she had suffered in Vienna when her mother moved abroad after Kristallnacht and her father fled to France. Even when she reached England on Kindertransport, Helen had struggled in different foster homes before she finally settled into a Church of England orphanage in Wiltshire. The nuns were kind but 'very poor and didn't have enough money to feed us,' observes Helen, 'so they would put us to bed early so that they didn't have to give us supper.'

At Trench Hall, Helen found herself released from the painful isolation she had felt in various foster homes. She slept in a large dormitory 'with five '"double deckers" – there were ten of us in there and we all had such a good time'. They were directly adjacent to Tante Anna's room; a tricky position. 'We were very naughty. She would often call us in and chastise us . . . We put glue on the handle of the door leading into our room hoping our housemother's fingers would get stuck to the handle. I don't think they ever did.' On ironing duty, Helen remembers 'sewing up the boys' pyjama bottoms so they couldn't get their feet through'. She, too, found herself called in with her best friend to see Tante Anna. 'We sat there quivering and she said we should behave better.'[44]

At Trench Hall Helen felt her classmates became brothers and sisters. It was the family she had always craved. Far from seeing Harold as an outsider, she remembers him as 'a lovely boy, very funny, very clever'. Harold, in turn, admired Anna John from afar; but no boy, however clever or witty, could compete with Rookie. 'I adored him,' says Anna John. For others, too, first romances blossomed behind Tante Anna's back. By the time they were teenagers, 'all the girls had a sort of – I wouldn't call it a relationship – they were crushes,' recalls Mia, with amusement. 'It was almost obligatory to have a little crush.' The first object of Mia's adoration was Frank Auerbach. She considered him 'good looking' but 'quite sarcastic'. It made no difference. 'Frank would not look at me twice,' she laughs. 'Certainly I went on walks with boys. The odd kiss – but nothing to what youngsters do today. How proper we all were.'

Tante Anna 'did not approve of girls dancing with boys,' Mia recalls. On one occasion, Mia thought the strait-laced headmistress even likened boy–girl dancing to 'prostitution'. Nonetheless, on a Saturday evening staff and children would sometimes organise dances, 'little hops', Mia calls them. 'I think we only had half a dozen records if that. I absolutely loved it.' She felt grateful to Bertha, who organised the duty rota. 'If she knew you had a crush on someone, she would make the duties so you could be together.'[45] But Tante Anna had a way of knowing if any budding relationship was going too far. She felt responsible for guiding pupils, and former pupils, not just in their careers, but in their private lives, too. Leslie soon found she did not hesitate to 'make her disapproval known'.

When he returned to Trench Hall, Leslie was always particularly pleased to see the teacher from New Zealand, Miss Clifford or 'Cliffie'. They would talk into the small hours and an attachment developed. When they began planning a weekend of cycling around Wales, Tante Anna made it quite clear that she thought the relationship was not suitable. The way she steered the children seemed 'almost effortless', recalls Harold. Often she did not need to say a word 'but you knew'.[46] The source of Tante Anna's incredible ability to have a mesmerising understanding of new, exciting or forbidden behaviour was never discovered. She was a dear innocent, but she knew everything.

*

Tante Anna found unexpected help at hand as she settled in her new pupils. The number of refugees released from internment steadily increased. Under government rules, once released these 'friendly enemy aliens' had to stay in the same place for the rest of the war. Tante Anna was quick to acquire staff of unparalleled calibre. 'At last, after all her struggles,' observed Harold, 'Tante Anna had got staff!'

One of the first to arrive at Trench Hall attracted considerable interest, not least because he took on the unenviable task of being the school's new stoker and boiler man: William Marckwald. Marckwald had been interned as a Category B enemy alien on the Isle of Man, having joined the Spanish

Civil War in support of the republicans against fascism. 'He did not fight,' explains his daughter, Nuri. 'He helped by doing translations.' The Quaker Friends Committee had recommended him to Tante Anna and she was relieved to find he took the dreaded boiler in his stride. 'It was a huge old-fashioned tiled contraption that might comfortably have provided for a normal household of eight,' Marckwald wrote in his memoirs, 'but for over one hundred and twenty people a day was a different proposition. The poor old beast did break down now and again.' Eleven stoves also came under his jurisdiction. 'Old crocks,' he observed, 'all much too small for the work they were supposed to do.' Marckwald could call upon a local builder and the failing boiler and stoves 'played a big part in many consultations' in which teachers, too, gathered round to offer words of wisdom. 'I often felt we were like a group of medical specialists over a patient.'[47]

As Marckwald stoked the boiler the children were surprised to hear him singing. They would gather round in amazement. Who was this star tending their boiler? 'He had the most wonderful tenor voice,' recalls Susie Davids. 'It was like listening to an opera singer to hear him when he was stoking the boiler. You would pay for that. The stokehole had a tiled floor that resounded. Acoustically it was absolutely amazing.'[48] Word soon spread that the new school boiler man who emerged from the dirty stokehold singing so beautifully was a significant talent: a former director at the prestigious Deutsches Theater in Frankfurt. It wasn't long before Marckwald promised to help with the school plays in every spare moment, alongside his duties as stoker and gardener.

During his internment on the Isle of Man, there had happened to be an English copy of *Othello* in Marckwald's camp. He knew the play by heart in German and with the help of an English-speaking friend, he had used it to learn English and had even formed a workshop in the camp to discuss the meaning of the play, recalls Nuri.[49] The children at Trench Hall soon found that he was an exciting and talented director to work with. 'He would go through every movement and every line with each of us until he was certain that we were getting the most out of it,' Harold recalls. 'We really got insight into the plays . . . He made us rehearse . . . until we had achieved the standards of the Deutsches Theater.'

After improvisations to find out what the children could do, Marckwald chose a romantic drama, *Lady Precious Stream,* for their first production. He quickly found that what mattered was not the quality of the performance 'but the bearing it had on each of the participants'. Bringing out their talents had dramatic effects on their confidence. One girl, Esther, did not shine at the school but she gave such a convincing performance 'the entire cast was quite speechless,' wrote Marckwald. 'It considerably altered her entire position in the school.' Another child, David, 'was a most awkward fellow. No one seemed able to be able to cope with him.' He had been allocated a part but refused to even try. Marckwald assumed 'he was simply afraid and had no confidence'. He adopted a policy of repeatedly praising him for whatever he did, while also assuring him he could do better. 'To my utter amazement at the next staff meeting several teachers came up to me and said, "What have you done with this boy? He is completely altered".'[50]

Marckwald's wife, a Spanish singer called Pilar, was hired as Heidtsche's deputy cook and he laboured in the fields in his spare time 'as we had to grow all the vegetables and potatoes for the school,' he continues. The children joined in and 'conversations while working were always extremely lively'. Harold remembers Marckwald had 'an absolute fund of horror stories' about the Spanish Civil War. On one occasion, Marckwald had been shocked to come across a collection of open coffins in which nuns were laid out. He told the children he happened to pass by later when rigor mortis had set in. It looked for all the world as though the nuns were sitting up! Far from being horrified at such macabre tales, 'we loved it,' says Harold.[51]

Inevitably the children's questions turned to news of the war. In November 1942, at last came good news of the North African War at a place called El Alamein in Egypt. The children had set up an imaginary Allied HQ at Trench Hall and the enthusiastic would-be map plotters hurried to display this decisive victory for the Allies. In February 1943, a new pin in the school map marked an even more historic watershed on the eastern front. Axis forces surrendered to the Red Army at Stalingrad in Soviet Russia. At last, the tide was turning. Hitler's troops were in retreat. Pupils enthusiastically plotted each momentous step as the areas under Nazi occupation began to shrink.

In May 1943, a few days after Axis troops were driven out of North Africa, older pupils listening to Tante Anna's wireless were electrified by news of the daring dam-busters raid. The RAF's night-time mission into Germany's industrial heartlands seemed a stroke of genius on the part of Bomber Command, and fired the imagination of the Saddler's Shoppe Boys. Over the summer of 1943 came more astonishing news; the Soviet army had won another critical victory over the Nazis in the largest tank battle in history at Kursk, south-west of Moscow. By early autumn, the Allied campaign in Italy was under way. At the school's weekly political evening, one pupil caught the mood when he dared to raise the question of post-war reconstruction. There must be an end in sight. Unfortunately, during political evenings 'the subject of the discussion was often forgotten while we talked,' recalled one pupil, 'and the chair had to remind people to keep to the point.'[52]

Despite continuing wartime shortages, in January 1944 Tante Anna finally succeeded in expanding the school. After a three-year campaign for timber, with help from her American friends she was able to buy two large poultry houses, which were stripped down for wood. The new Boys' House was completed in less than three months. 'This house was my heart's desire for a long time,' wrote Tante Anna, 'and the boys are happy in it.' The long-wished-for replacement Aga also arrived, thanks to a quite unexpected gift following one of her talks about the school in Birmingham.[53] All the while, top talent continued to arrive at Trench Hall from the internment camps, providing inspirational teaching.

Tante Anna recruited mathematics master, Mr Archenholt, who turned out to be a distinguished German astronomer. One day in the dining hall, he stood up to talk about sunspots, 'which were too large to be brought in,' he said, but he could demonstrate outside how to view them safely. The children were captivated.[54] The new music teacher, Greta Hirsch, had perfect pitch and enchanted the children by annotating birdsong. 'She could tell exactly what key and what note a bird was singing,' recalls Harold. Greta had previously worked with Ludwig Koch, the acclaimed wildlife recordist who is thought to have been the first in the world to make recordings of birdsong. One day Harold was sitting with Greta listening to the Hallé Symphony Orchestra on the radio. Yehudi Menuhin was playing a violin concerto. Harold suddenly realised Greta had the score in front of her and was making notes about how Menuhin played certain passages, 'which impressed me enormously,' he says. 'She showed me the subtleties of his interpretation.' The children responded to the talented staff around them. 'It wasn't enough just to know,' continues Harold, 'there was an extraordinary emphasis on the quality of our education.'[55]

For many of the Kindertransport pupils the school became 'home in every sense of the word,' says Susie.[56] British pupils such as Anna John also began to appreciate their new teachers. 'I was English, not a Jewish person out of the pogroms, yet I received from them exactly the same as they received . . . This feeling that this is where I belong. That these people like me. I don't need to be naughty any more. Here there was no need, because they loved us.' Looking back, Anna feels there was a largeness of spirit about the place. 'The whole school was about giving . . . There was very little at their disposal. It was all about the teachers giving what they could and it was a lot . . .'[57] The school condemned by Nazi authorities had become a beacon of good practice.

The 'Alien' school might no longer be viewed with suspicion by the locals, but it was still occasionally the object of British wit. Harold recalls one incident in the spring of 1944. There was a general feeling of optimism in the air and a great deal of activity at the local RAF airfield. Unknown to staff and pupils, the airfield was involved in preparations for D-Day. Harold recalls tremendous excitement one day when an RAF glider came down on the sports field at Trench Hall. Knowing he read the weekly magazine, the *Aeroplane*, and had a passion for aircraft, Tante Anna invited him to join her for tea with the station commander. Dora, a German member of the laundry staff, also happened to be in the room.

They were deep in discussion about how to get the damaged glider back to the airfield when suddenly a fighter plane flew over, very, very low.

Dora piped up, 'Oh, oh, I do hope that's one of ours.' Dora had a very thick German accent.

'No Ma'am, it was one of ours!' the station commander teased her politely.[58]

From democracy to dictatorship: Nazi forces parade in front of Hitler, 1933.

Boys and girls were indoctrinated in Nazi ideology through the
Hitler Youth and its affiliated organisations. Here a band of the Hitler Youth
marches through Neue Gasse in Nuremberg.

Children were given a day off school to celebrate the success of the Nazi Party in the elections on 5 March 1933.

Students sing the anthem of the Nazi Party, 'Horst-Wessel-Lied', in an elementary school in Berlin.

An illustration from a Nazi-inspired school book, *Trust No Fox on his Green Heath and No Jew on his Oath*, depicts Jewish children being taunted by 'Aryan' pupils and teachers as they are expelled from German state schools.

The Nazis rapidly imposed their ideology and 'race science' on the school curriculum. Here a teacher demonstrates alleged differences in face shape to his elementary students.

Two Jewish boys face their class in front of a blackboard bearing the Star of David and the caption 'The Jew is our greatest enemy. Beware of the Jews!'.

Headteacher Anna Essinger was known to her pupils as 'Tante Anna'.

Anna smuggled her school out of Nazi Germany – a feat no other head teacher managed to pull off – and settled in the run-down manor house, Bunce Court, in Kent.

The persecutions imposed on German Jews over five years were introduced in Austria almost overnight in March 1938. Jewish children and adults were forced to scrub the streets.

On the night of 9–10 November 1938 hundreds of synagogues were razed to the ground in a wave of violence that took place throughout Germany. An estimated one thousand Jews were murdered and 30,000 were sent to concentration camps.

A mother and child pass the remains of a Jewish-owned shop on the morning of 10 November 1938. The events of the previous night became known as Kristallnacht, The Night of the Broken Glass.

Most countries had strict immigration quotas and Jews in Greater Germany became trapped. After Kristallnacht, Britain agreed to take in an unlimited number of Jewish children.

Jewish refugee children from Germany and Austria wait to be collected by their relatives or sponsors at Liverpool Street Station.

Almost 10,000 Jewish children came to Britain on Kindertransport. Most never saw their parents again.

Thirteen-year-old Leslie Baruch Brent looks anxious photographed on his arrival at the Dutch border. Leslie was on the very first Kindertransport from Berlin, which departed on 1 December 1938.

Leslie Brent's passport photo, 1938.

ARRIVAL IN LONDON - Golders Green, March 1939

Ruth Boronow in London shortly before arriving at Bunce Court. Ruth had grown up with escalating Nazi persecution and felt hounded from her home country.

Mia Schaff, in the middle, with her older brother, John, and sister, Alice, in Berlin before the war. Mia and Alice fled on one of the later Kindertransports from Berlin, but Mia was soon separated from her sister.

Tante Anna placed equal emphasis on practical and intellectual learning.
Safe and secure, enveloped in the loving environment of Anna's
'home-school', the children thrived.

On 1 September 1939, German forces bombard Poland on land and from the air. Here a little boy sits amid the ruins of his home in the neighborhood of Praga in Warsaw.

During the siege of Warsaw, the city sustained heavy damage from artillery shelling and air attacks.

Kazia Mika mourns the death of her older sister, Andzia, who was killed during the Blitzkrieg. 'The child had never before seen death and couldn't understand why her sister would not speak to her', wrote the photographer later.

The Piotrkow Ghetto was created on 8 October 1939, shortly after the Blitzkrieg in Poland. It was the first Nazi ghetto in occupied Europe.

Menacing signs marked the perimeter of Piotrkow Ghetto. 'I don't think there was a fence. It was just, no one was allowed to leave', wrote Sidney Finkel, whose family were among the first to be ordered into the ghetto.

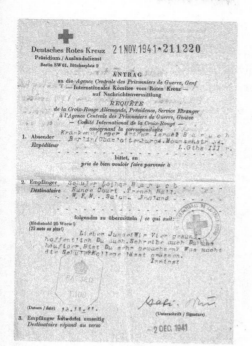

The children of Bunce Court were cut off from their parents in a wholly unpredictable way. For Leslie Brent, like many children, the Red Cross messages he received from his parents gave the first clues that something was horribly wrong.

The cook, Gretel Heidt.

With the Nazis just across the channel in June 1940, Tante Anna and her team faced a second exodus. The school resettled in Trench Hall in Shropshire.

Orphaned Sidney Finkel was traumatised for years by the fate of the women of his family. His older sister, Ronia (left), had been like a second mother. When he heard what happened to her 'I crawled under the bed and cried for hours. That's the most I ever cried' he says. Also pictured are Sidney's aunt Rachel (middle) and his sister, Frania, who sacrificed her own chances out of her love of their mother.

Jewish women and children arrive at Auschwitz-Birkenau.

Children from across Europe were sent to concentration camps where their chances of survival were slim. Here they pull up their sleeves to reveal number tattoos.

Transport to Auschwitz concentration camp.

Orphaned children inside a concentration camp in German-occupied Russia. The sign warns that anyone approaching the barbed wire to talk to prisoners would be shot.

Emaciated children who survived the Ravensbrück concentration camp in Germany.

Child survivors of Auschwitz dressed in clothing from adult prisoners.

Sidney Finkel endured slave labour camps and concentration camps before arriving in England after the war. Here he is pictured handing a baby to his older brother, Isaac.

Anna Rose and her older brother, Arthur, on their way to Bunce Court after surviving the war in hiding. Their parents are believed to have died trapped alive in a hole in a wall in an apartment in Lvov that was sealed by the gestapo.

Sam Oliner at Bunce Court. He escaped
the liquidation of Bobowa ghetto and hid
in plain sight in disguise as a Polish boy.
Jews were hunted down by both Nazis
and Poles and after many close shaves
Sam describes himself as little more than
'an animal' stripped of all humanity by
the time he reached Bunce Court.

Sidney Finkel as a young man
after leaving Bunce Court.

Frank Auerbach, pictured here at Bunce
Court, would go on to become one of
Britain's foremost modernist painters.
Many of Bunce Court's alumni went
on to have distinguished careers.

12

'What kind of animal had I become?'

13-year-old Sidney Finkel, Buchenwald, 1944

For twelve-year-old Sam Oliner in occupied Poland, school had become a distant dream, something that happened to other children. His life was boundaried by the neat wooden fence and swept yard of the Padworskis' farm, an order that belied the unspeakable fears that had taken over Sam's life. Jews like himself were being hunted down like animals. His survival in plain sight rested on the Padworskis continuing to believe the story that he was a Polish boy. Following the advice of the peasant woman, Balwina, he had searched for someone in need of a *pastuch*, a stable boy, eventually reaching the village of Biesnik, where he was directed to this farm. Bravely, Sam had told Mr Padworski that his father was dead and his mother couldn't manage and had sent him out to find work. He was amazed when Mr Padworski took him at his word.[1] But it wasn't long before Sam's lies were in danger of catching him out.

Mr Padworski wanted to meet his mother so they could agree Sam's terms of employment. It was a reasonable request that had Sam utterly at a loss. How could he produce a mother? He had had two, and neither of them were alive. He tried to sound calm as he mumbled that he would fetch her in a few weeks. Mr Padworski kept returning to the matter, as though he had suspicions. On his very first day in the fields, Sam returned to see a smart black car in the yard. Had Mr Padworski summoned the Gestapo? Struggling to marshal the details of his story, Sam waited until the Gestapo left before he ventured into the house. The Padworskis seemed to be behaving differently towards him, as though they knew something. Sam did not dare ask about the car until the next day. The Gestapo was searching for Jews from the ghetto, explained Mr Padworski. They hunt Jews 'like they hunt rabbits and foxes . . .'[2]

He was convinced the Padworskis suspected he was a Jew; the impulse to run was overwhelming. But that would confirm his guilt. He must stay. Sam struggled to fight the surges of panic that rose up inside him and made it impossible to think clearly. Terror lay in a harsh word or a cold look from his new employer. 'I was living constantly on the alert, constantly observing the mood, observing who was coming to the village . . .'[3]

Even if he could steady his own nerves, Sam soon found his cover could also be blown by the dozen or so Jews who had escaped the mass murder at Bobowa ghetto. Unbearable hunger was driving them to take risks in the open and this started to put Sam in danger, too. One day he was working in the fields with a Polish boy from the village when he saw someone he recognised from Bobowa ghetto scurrying towards them. It was his former Jewish landlord, Simcha. He could blow Sam's fake identity in an instant. Sure enough, as Simcha drew nearer, he began to call Sam's real name. Sam hurried over and begged him to leave at once. In return, he promised to bring Simcha food in the woods that night. It was a precarious solution that appeared to unravel almost immediately.

The village boy working with Sam was deeply suspicious that he had been talking to a Jew. Why did the stranger appear to recognise Sam, he asked. He questioned Sam persistently, anxious not to lose any possible bounty. Sam worried that the boy would start village talk. Then there was the nightmarish prospect of having to steal food from the Padworskis. He had longed to earn their trust. Now he was forced to steal from them like a common thief.

It was dark when Sam crept out of his straw bed in the barn and set off across the fields, with his precious cargo of stolen potatoes and bread. He found Simcha at the agreed spot in the woods. To Sam, Simcha seemed thin and dishevelled, a shadow of himself. It was as though 'he was only half there'. Even the whites of his eyes flashed in the darkness as though he were a ghost.[4] What he had to tell Sam was ghoulish, too.

Like Sam, Simcha had found a way to escape the liquidation of Bobowa ghetto. But while in hiding in the countryside he had come across another Jew who had been loaded on to one of the Nazi trucks in the main square and had seen what happened next. This man was so tormented by what he had witnessed that he appeared to have lost all reason. Fear had turned him into something unrecognisable. For Simcha, the man's eyes had seemed wild, his beard matted, his clothes filthy. With mangled sentences and half words, crying out in terror at what he had seen, he had tried to relay to Simcha just what the Nazis had done.

From the main square of Bobowa, the Nazis drove the trucks filled with Jews to the woods at Garbacz nearby. Hounded by vicious dogs and guns, the man had found himself standing with other Jews in a line at the edge of a very large pit. The pit was half filled with a tangled mass of bodies; some were writhing, still alive. It was impossible to tell where one person began and another ended. He could hear their sobs, their final death throes. He knew without turning round that the Nazis behind him were preparing to fire. Then he heard the order. He fell onto the mound of flesh and blood. Somehow, he had fallen somewhere near the top. It took time to realise that he was not dead. He lay stock-still. The Nazis did not bother to bury them. He felt a burning sensation as a chemical was poured over the bodies. Slowly the cries around him fell silent. At nightfall he managed to escape. But according to Simcha, 'in that hole filled with bleeding bodies he left his sanity . . .'[5] Simcha thought that terror had taken such a grip of the man's mind, he was incapable of survival. He stood no chance of evading capture.

Sam had already been told what had happened to his father and stepmother. But listening to Simcha in the dark woods that night, their final moments became real for him. 'The dead are watching us,' said Simcha solemnly. They must be avenged. He wanted Sam to live and make sure the world knew. Simcha himself no longer cared whether he lived or died. He would make his way to the Jewish underground and start the fight for vengeance and freedom.[6]

When Sam finally returned to the farm, he was alarmed to see a light coming from the barn. His absence had evidently been discovered. Mr Padworski turned on him angrily, demanding to know where he had gone. A cow was calving. He could not understand why Sam had disappeared from his bed in the stable in the middle of the night. Sam was at a loss to account for his odd disappearance. He felt certain that Mr Padworski had guessed the truth.

On Sundays Sam went to the local Catholic church in an effort to authenticate his story with the villagers. There were so many gestures to master convincingly. Even making the sign of the cross was fraught with pitfalls. Should he start at the head, or go from side to side? Nor did he know about confession. Standing in line he heard the person ahead of him start with, 'Father, I have sinned . . .' Sam followed suit.[7] Many times over the coming weeks he felt perilously close to giving himself away. Despite all his efforts to endorse his story with his employer, he kept stumbling up against the fact that he could not produce a Polish 'mother'. Sam had said she lived not far away in Luzna, but Mr Padworski could not understand why she never appeared. Then there was the heart-stopping day when the farm horse kicked Sam in the groin. Full of concern, the farmer's wife took charge, pinning him against the barn wall to try to inspect his injury. Sam clung helplessly on to his trousers. His being circumcised would give him away. Mrs Padworski insisted she see, but he gripped the top of his trousers as though his life depended on it, frantic to make her believe he was just shy.

Rumours continued to spread that Jews were still at large in the district. The exacting manhunt seemed never-ending. There had been sightings of two brothers, the sons of Mr Schiff, by chance the very Jew who had once owned the Padworskis' farm before it had been stolen by the Nazis, who had rented it to the Padworskis. Everything was leading the manhunt to the very place where Sam was hiding. The Gestapo ordered Poles to cooperate in the search to hunt down the two Schiff sons. Every household in the local area had to send a volunteer. Mr Padworski asked Sam, who found himself in the perilous position of being Jewish and having to pose as a Jew-hunter. Sam kept up a steady stream of antisemitic banter with the village search party, repeating everything he had learned from Mr Padworski about 'devil

Jews' and the favour the Nazis had done the Poles by 'cleaning Poland' of Jews.[8] It was late in the day before he returned to the farm.

As Sam walked through the kitchen door someone grabbed him from behind. He saw the terrified looks on the Padworskis' faces. They were backed into a corner. Sam was pushed roughly towards them. He turned and saw the very Jews they had been searching for. The Schiff sons were right there in the kitchen, holding his employers hostage. One of the two brothers instantly recognised Sam.

'Isn't this Aron's son?' he said in Yiddish.

Sam's heart was pounding so loudly he thought everyone could hear it.

They were about to expose his cover.

But the brothers knew better. They spoke to the Padworskis in Polish. 'We are going outside to look for our guns we buried. We are taking the boy with us. If you move we will kill him.'[9] They gave the impression there were five more of them outside.

Outside in the yard they soon extracted Sam's story, but there was a price for keeping his secret. He had to help them. Sam assiduously went with them round the farm, helping them to find their buried money. Back in the kitchen the Schiff brothers kept up the pretence. They hustled Sam roughly through the door as though they had given him a hard time. In the kitchen they recovered their guns, hidden in the ceiling, and made Sam fetch food from the larder. As a final parting shot, they told the Padworskis they wanted their farm back when the war was over.

But even the clever Schiff brothers did not manage to outwit the Nazis for long. As Christmas approached, Mr Padworski demanded to meet Sam's mother once more. 'This is long enough,' he insisted. 'Go home for Christmas and bring your mother back with you.'[10] Sam solemnly promised to return with his mother. He made his way across hills and vales, choosing the most desolate routes, to seek the help of the kindly peasant woman, Balwina, who had set up his disguise. She was pleased to see him, but very anxious. There was terrible news of the Schiff brothers. The brutal Jew-hunter, Krupa, who lived near Balwina, was boasting that he had claimed the reward for them. Krupa had captured one of them and tortured him so badly before handing him on to the Gestapo that he had apparently betrayed his own brother. The second Schiff son was hiding with his Polish lover when the Gestapo arrived. They shot the second brother and ordered the peasant girl to dig his grave in the dirt floor before she, too, was killed.[11]

Sam was appalled to hear of their deaths. The Schiff brothers' murders felt close to home; he was staying on their farm. The witch-hunt for Jews was driving him to the edge of reason. Once again, kindly Balwina came to his aid, permitting her own son, Staszek, to pose as Sam's younger brother and back up his cover story. They carefully rehearsed details of Sam's fake identity as a poor Polish boy, Jusek, whose mother could not afford to keep him. Staszek, 'the younger brother', returned briefly with Sam. Mr Padworski seemed duly taken in, but Sam was beginning to feel paranoid. Maintaining the lie forced him into a heightened state of alertness. One slip could cost him his life. Everything carried the death penalty.[12] Terror invaded his dreams. At night, he dreamed of his own mother, and she had a stark warning: his life was in danger from the one person in whom he had placed his total trust – Balwina.

Balwina knew everything. What would it take for her to

betray him? Krupa might threaten her. The Nazis might take her last food. All she had to do was tell the Gestapo and she could get three thousand zlotys. That bedrock of unquestioning trust that he had had for his parents had gone. Anyone could potentially be a traitor. He had to suspect everyone, ponder their motives. His life depended on Balwina's loyalty. But could he really trust her? Sam could see himself digging that ditch at gunpoint, taste the mud in his mouth, hear the gunshot, feel his life ebbing away . . . Every bone in his body told him he must run away. The world of his childhood had been wiped away. In this new, Nazi-run Poland, trust didn't exist.

*

While Sam Oliner was trying to survive in Poland by living in plain sight, six-year-old Anna Rose was embarking on a life in hiding. In a sack on a Nazi truck, she knew she was outside the ghetto somewhere in Lemberg in former eastern Poland. She heard the sound of the vehicle slowing. Peering momentarily out from her sack, she saw her older brother, Arthur. The truck was coming to a halt in an area of Lemberg popular with the Germans. This was extremely dangerous; for Jews to be caught here was certain death. 'I was really, really scared,' she remembers. The vehicle pulled up at a street corner. The German stranger 'opened the door and told us to get out'. Her fear was so intense, she has no recollection of what happened next.[13]

Nine-year-old Arthur knew where to go. Anna's next memory is of being inside a strange apartment with an elderly Polish couple who were friends of her father: Mr and Mrs Krzysztalowski. Mrs Krzysztalowski, whose thin, unsmiling face gave her a slightly forbidding air, showed them to a room. It was large enough to contain a bed, a wardrobe and a table and had an adjoining bathroom. They must not leave the room at any cost, she explained. The German Officer's Club was next door. The Ukrainian care-taker of their own apartment house was a pro-Nazi who would inform on them without hesitation. Anna and Arthur were to keep the curtains closed, talk in whispers and tread very lightly on the wooden floor. Any mistake, any unusual sound, might arouse the suspicion of a neighbour or the Ukrainian caretaker and they would all die. As Mrs Krzysztalowski shut the door behind her, their small world closed in on them. This was it. They were out of the ghetto, safe for the time being, but imprisoned.

Days turned to weeks and then months, confined within the same four walls. Mrs Krzysztalowski took little interest in them beyond delivering food and coaching them in a cover story. If anything should go wrong, they were Polish orphans visiting friends of their parents. Arthur was ingen-ious in trying to entertain his little sister. She loved her book of fairy stories, especially Hansel and Gretel, the brother and sister abandoned without their parents. Mrs Krzysztalowski had no ration books for them. Their father had given her money to buy food on the black market, but there was never enough and the children became thinner and thinner. Arthur tried to coax his sister to eat the lumpy gruel and watery soup with floating potato peels, encour-aging her to imagine her favourite dishes from their old life in Krakow so that she could be persuaded to swallow. He even created a little doll's house for her out of card-board, newspapers and wool. For weeks on end, she played imaginary games under the table, hidden by the long tablecloth, bestowing on her paper dolls the fine life with loving parents and edible food that she craved.[14]

They lived in terror of the house-to-house searches. On one occasion, a German was shot in the district and the Gestapo combed the neighbourhood with forensic vigilance. Mrs Krzysztalowski hurried into their room, stricken with fear. There were two sets of stairs in the apartment house and she ushered them down the back stairs into the neighbour's flat below just as the unmistakable sound of soldiers' heavy boots could be heard entering their own flat. Timing was everything. Anna was so unused to moving, so short of exercise, that her wasted limbs struggled to obey. Mrs Krzysztalowski told her neighbour that Anna and Arthur were visiting from another city without permission.

On another occasion the Gestapo came with so little warning that there was no chance to escape down the back stairs. Anna distinctly heard Nazi soldiers entering their apartment. 'I sensed we were going to die,' she says. Almost unbelievably, at this critical moment she began to giggle hysterically. She was out of control. 'I was so scared it was all I could do to stop myself.' Quick-thinking Arthur piled bedding on top of his sister. 'People did not sleep under blankets, they slept under feather quilts,' she remembers. Arthur pulled three or four of these feather quilts over her. 'It was incredibly hot.'[15]

Petrified, Anna tried to control her breathing. The door opened. There were German voices in the room, their sound distorted through the heavy layers. The toy house Arthur had made, her book of fairy stories: had he had time to hide them? She lay rigid. It seemed an eternity. Even when she heard the sound of the door shutting and footsteps receding, still she could not move, half expecting the bedding to be torn away and to find herself face to face with Nazi soldiers. But it was Mrs Krzysztalowski who appeared, thanking Arthur with great relief. 'I've often wondered to myself, did the soldiers see anything?' Anna recalls. 'Were they so tired of hauling people out, they just decided to leave? I'll never know.'[16]

'Arthur became my substitute father,' she says. 'I thought he was a god. He was only three years older.' Their parents, Jan and Irena, were still trapped in Lemberg ghetto. The days wore on, their cloistered, prison-like existence filled with immediate terrors and boundaried by any scraps of news that reached Mr Krzysztalowski. Around them it was as if the whole world was set alight in an ever-expanding conflagration. The Axis armies seemed invincible. Then in February 1943, Mr Krzysztalowski explained to Arthur that at last, Hitler's armies had surrendered to the Soviets at Stalingrad. But as the weeks passed, the fate of the Jews seemed to be inextricably tied to the reversal of fortune of the Nazi armies. The brutal murders of the Jews escalated.[17]

Mr Krzysztalowski knew that the Lemberg ghetto had become increasingly dangerous for Anna and Arthur's parents. He was careful in what he revealed to Arthur although he knew that Jews had been sent from Lemberg to their deaths in their tens of thousands. Records show that in the 'Great Aktion' of August 1942, over forty thousand Jews were deported from Lemberg to the extermination camp at Belzec. The following month, many members of the *Judenrat* were hung from impromptu gallows in the street. In January 1943 a further 15,000 Jews were shot. That spring rumours were rife that the Nazis were preparing to 'liquidate' those who remained. Meanwhile news spread of a Jewish uprising that was brutally crushed in Warsaw ghetto, the largest in Poland.[18]

One day Mrs Krzysztalowski came into Anna and Arthur's room with extraordinary news. Their parents had escaped the ghetto. Soon they learned further details. It was not safe for them to be reunited. Jan and Irena had a separate hiding place in the apartment of another Polish woman. This woman had a small cupboard-like space concealed behind a false wall. There was an opening at the bottom, which in turn was hidden behind a wooden chest. 'That's where they hid,' Anna recalled years later, 'in a literal hole in the wall.'[19]

Months elapsed before Mrs Krzysztalowski had more news of their parents. Her serious face looked even more solemn than usual. Jan and Irena had been discovered. The person who was hiding them was a drinker and very indiscreet. One day in a bar she had said enough to alert a local informer. Her flat was searched. Mrs Krzysztalowski explained that her parents had been discovered. 'Everyone was shot.'

Years later, Anna learned that Mr Krzysztalowski had told Arthur a different story that day – almost certainly the correct version of the heartbreaking tragedy. The Nazis had arrested the drunk and simply sealed her apartment. Her parents had been effectively entombed alive in their hiding place. For Anna, the idea of 'our parents being trapped in their hole in the wall – this was even more nightmarish than imagining them being shot.'[20]

*

While children like Sam Oliner and Anna Rose were struggling in different ways to hide in Nazi-occupied Poland, twelve-year-old Sidney Finkel was caught within the eye of the storm, clinging to an existence within the concentration camp system. Crammed into a cattle truck that was moving slowly somewhere in central Poland, Sidney knew only that for the first time in his life, he was separated from his father, Laib, and his brother, Isaac. Somewhere behind him was the known world of Piotrkow ghetto. Ahead was an unknown. 'I was totally withdrawn, tired, with no hope. None whatsoever,' he says. 'From that time, I was just on automatic reflexes.'[21]

He lay on the floor of the cattle truck, straining to interpret the sounds. Their train appeared to be snaking south but it was not possible to be sure. He had no idea where they were being taken. Thirst, hunger and revulsion at the horrific conditions in the cattle truck blotted out any other thoughts, but whenever the train stopped, his senses were suddenly razor sharp, straining to make sense of his world. There were shouted commands and the barking of dogs. At one point there was a clanging and jolting as some of the wagons were uncoupled. What did this mean? Those around him thought the cars carrying the women were being separated and they were being directed to a different destination. This, too, was hard to interpret.

Finally, the train came to a halt. The heavy wagon doors opened and Sidney was knocked back by a blast of icy air. Armed Nazi guards were forcing everyone out onto the platform. It was hard to tell where they were. His eyes scanned through the crowd. To his utter astonishment and relief, he saw Laib and Isaac. He ran over and hugged his father and brother, overwhelmed to see them again. They were taken to a large shed. The conditions were filthy and there were no beds. They were left to sleep on the dirt. The next day all the men were taken to work, leaving Sidney and a few other children to stay hidden.

Sidney disobeyed. Pressing himself against the sides of buildings, he crept out to see more. It was a large, old industrial complex. The noise from the machinery and lorries was deafening. The smell of chemicals was noxious. With a sense of shock, he caught sight of prisoners. They looked strange. Not just wasting; there was something else. He drew closer. 'Their faces were yellow,' he says. Yellow and dry like parchment. What kind of hellhole was this?[22]

When Isaac and Laib returned, he learned they were in a camp called Czestochowa in southern Poland where Jewish slave labour was used to make munitions. The prisoners were being slowly poisoned by the chemicals. Everything about this place made him think of hell. Apart from the overpowering, all-consuming hunger, lice were so prolific it was possible to scoop them off his skin by the handful. There was no way to be rid of them. Even the toilet shed filled him with revulsion. Inside, the nauseating stench made him retch. As his eyes adjusted to the darkness, he saw 'it was covered literally with shit. The walls. The floors. Everything was covered. You couldn't clean [yourself].' There was nothing resembling a toilet or running water. No means of keeping even a shred of human dignity.[23]

Sidney lost track of time and any sense of who he was. To a small boy, the evil seemed all-pervasive. Even the Jewish inmates here seemed different. 'Nobody cared for anybody else . . . People were not human.'[24] The days turned to weeks and he has no recollection of seeing his father or brother. Sidney felt utterly alone in the dark underworld of Czestochowa, knowing he had to rely on his wits to survive.

But his mind played cruel tricks. Ground down by the endless hunger and cruel treatment, it was no longer reliable. Sidney had always been able to trust his sharp thinking; his ability to hide or to have a ready answer if caught. But now he was changed. It was hard to make sense of what was going on. He knew that at one stage the commandant wanted all the children dead and that, somehow, he had escaped this fate. 'I can only surmise that the situations were so horrible that my memory shut down,' he wrote later.[25]

After two months in this industrial wasteland, Sidney learned that he was being moved to another camp. He and the other prisoners were led under heavy guard through the smoke and grime of the munitions works to the railway. Once again, he was locked into the dreaded cattle cars. This time they went west towards Germany. They were going right into the jaws of the enemy. Could that be worse? For three unendurable days they travelled with no food or water. Just the constant companions of the lice and fleas.

It was hard not to feel anxious as the changing sounds told him they were reaching their destination. Sidney heard the screech of the brakes and the soldiers banging on the wagons to hustle everyone out. The doors flew open. Outside, there was scarcely time to register that the cold was perishing. Snarling dogs and guards with guns hounded them out of the railway and into the camp. Heavy iron gates bearing the motto '*Jedem das Seine*' – 'To each what he deserves' – swung shut behind them.

They were kept waiting outdoors for hours. Numb with cold, he had a chance to take stock of his new surroundings. Even in the dark, he could tell this camp was vast and heavily guarded. The beam from the restless searchlights illuminated the perimeter, giving glimpses of an electrified barbed wire fence. It was very high and curved inwards at the top, with watchtowers along its length. The guards had machine guns. Whatever went on inside this place, there would be no escape.[26]

As they waited in the large parade area, they were ordered to leave behind their meagre possessions. Sidney had no idea what had happened to his father or his brother and now he had to abandon his one last reminder of his father, a blanket. Laib had always tried to make sure he was warm. Despite his hunger and fear, when it was finally his turn in the processing room Sidney knew enough to remember to be vague about his age. The official advised him to be sixteen. If he felt any pity or compassion for Sidney he did not show it, but his advice was life-saving; children were of little use in this place. Sidney was allocated a number: 25381. He was no longer a young boy, but a number. He had arrived at Buchenwald concentration camp.

It was hard to imagine that he would come out alive. Death was such a constant companion it was meaningless. When Sidney was forced into a large shower room, some people around began shouting in terror. Sidney could not see the danger. He was transfixed with fear when they said poisonous gas would come out of the shower. They had heard rumours of people being murdered this way in other camps. But no gas came. They were spared. Then they were marched through endless barracks. The place sprawled like a vast city. In their block the wooden shelves that served as bunks were stacked in tiers so tightly that it was hard to sleep. There was no straw or covering of any kind. Something was dripping onto him and he realised it could have been urine from the bunk above. In the morning he discovered the first job was to clear out the dead bodies. There was no dignity, no pause to remember a name or even a number. As he left the barracks for roll call, he saw there was a heap of dead bodies from the night, piled up like so much rubbish.

Even the roll call became a reminder of the closeness of death. Waiting for interminable hours in the yard, Sidney noticed a chimney with fire coming from the stack. Someone told him this was the crematorium and 'the only way out'.[27] All the dead ended up at the crematorium. Disease, malnutrition and exhaustion were killers, as well as the sadistic guards with their random beatings and executions. No wonder that some committed suicide by running into the fence.

Sidney was determined not to die. He felt a burning anger, which fuelled his desire to survive. One day in this hellish wilderness, he came across a boy he knew from Piotrkow: Harry. Harry and Sidney had both been in the ghetto and Bugaj labour camp. Now both were assigned to bricklaying. They began to look out for each other and soon became close friends, smuggling food and navigating the many dangers together.

Of all his appalling memories from this time, there is one that stands out and that, over the years, has given Sidney no peace. One day, Sidney was astonished to come across his father. Laib was skeletal, virtually unrecognisable as the forceful, independent-minded man he was once. But when he saw his son, Laib's dulled, sunken eyes seemed to shine more brightly. Tears glistened on his hollowed-out cheeks and then flowed freely over the parchment-yellow skin of his face. Even in this hellish wasteland, for Laib it was a moment of pure joy to have a chance to see his son again. He stretched out his wasted arms and drew Sidney into a tight embrace. Then he reached in his bag for a small piece of bread, the only thing he possessed that he could give his son. Later Sidney realised that this was all his father had for his journey out of Buchenwald.

Sidney felt painfully awkward. He loved his father, more than anyone in the world. But he felt nothing. He could not respond. He seemed incapable of demonstrating any affection at all. He could no longer behave like a son. The playful, loving child he had once been no longer existed. That boy was lost somewhere along the line between the camps and the cattle wagons. This new son 'was now more like an animal, with instincts only for survival,' Sidney wrote later. 'I turned my back on my own father,' and silently walked away.

As he returned to his block, Sidney found himself reasoning like the SS guards. 'Old people have no right to live,' he thought. They were taking precious food from the young.

'Who was I? What kind of animal had I become in the camps?' he wrote years later, astonished at his twelve-year-old self. At the time he felt no guilt at his lack of feeling. He was just a young boy who had unknowingly absorbed the Nazi perspective to survive. He never saw Laib again. It was only later that the full emotional impact of this final meeting with his father descended on him with punishing force.[28]

✳

Sam Oliner's years of living in plain sight as a Jew in Nazi-occupied southern Poland drove him to the point where he could not trust even the person to whom he owed his life: the peasant woman Balwina. She had helped create his false identity as the stable boy 'Jusek', and had put her own son, Staszek, at risk as an alibi. Now she got word to him through Staszek, urging Sam not to run away. He must stay in disguise at the Padworskis' farm.

Sam struggled to fathom her motive. Kindness, decency, love: these things no longer existed for him. Balwina's actions made no sense. Why was she helping him? People's decisions rested on cold-blooded calculation and she had far more to gain by giving him away. Sam was convinced his life hung by a thread. Every instinct told him to flee – but then new terrors took hold. If he left the farm, he would be even more exposed. Anxiously, Sam followed Balwina's advice.[29]

It was too dangerous to be caught with a radio and the newspapers were filled with Nazi propaganda. Even so, Mr Padworski knew enough to tell Sam the Soviet army was advancing across Soviet Russia, hounding the Nazi army back. Occasionally, Polish partisans brought welcome news to the village. In July 1944, the Soviets reached the pre-war Polish border. In August, the Red Army halted outside Warsaw, waiting as the Polish resistance led an uprising in the city, which was brutally crushed by the Germans. By the autumn, there were days when Sam could hear the Soviet guns pounding at a distance. He was beginning to feel his struggle to live was not in vain. The Nazi enemy surely must flee? But as the Soviets drew closer, the Nazis issued an order that for Sam was a death sentence. Every Polish household was to provide a pair of hands to help shore up defences for the buckling Nazi front line. Mr Padworski asked Sam.[30]

Sam joined the rest of the men from the village, who were ordered to march to the front. It was hard not to be terrified. Just as the end was in sight, he was as good as giving himself up to the Nazis. Living at close quarters with other Polish men and boys, under the close scrutiny of SS guards, Sam's terror of exposure as a Jew began to surpass even his fear of the Russian bombing.

In the evening, all the Polish boys in his barracks said their prayers kneeling down. Sam soon found the way he prayed aroused the suspicions of his neighbour.

'I've found a Jew boy,' the boy yelled out. The outcry that followed caught the attention of the guard. '*Jude, Jude,*' cried the Polish boy, pointing at Sam. The same evil taunt that had plagued Sam for years. This devilish, unthinking boy might just as well have cried, 'Kill, *kill* . . .'[31]

Sam felt certain when the guard said he would deal with the matter the next day that he knew the truth and was deliberately prolonging Sam's agony. He was cornered. All the guard had to do was lower Sam's trousers. The terrible struggle he had endured since the liquidation of the ghetto counted for nothing. Sam almost wished he had died with his family instead of torturing himself with foolish dreams of winning through. All those daydreams of England and America, a future life, a school . . .

The next day they were marched off early to help dig the anti-tank trenches. The scale of the task before them was gargantuan. To trap the advancing Soviet tanks, the Nazis wanted wide trenches stretching for some fifty miles. Hundreds of thousands of Polish men and boys were forced to help build these defences but Soviet bombing, wet weather and the lack of time worked against them. The Nazi guards were vigilant, beating anyone who was slow. Sam felt certain the guard who suspected he was a Jew was watching him more closely than the rest. By evening they were back in the barracks. The moment of inspection was almost at hand. That was when the bombs started falling.

In the days that followed, Russian bombing was so heavy that the struggle to survive overwhelmed everything else. Sam did not dare make a run for it. A couple of villagers who did flee were mown down by the Nazi guards.

The Russian planes flew so low Sam thought he could feel the wind on his face as they passed. He cowered with the Polish boys in the trenches that they had dug. He could hear cries of pain from those who were hit. Every moment seemed as if it might be his last. Again and again he wondered why he wasn't dead. After each raid, he checked to see if he could still feel his hands, his arms, his legs . . . In a daze he lifted himself up. Around him German soldiers lay dying. Sam could hear their cries of pain. He could not help feeling that this was justice. At last Nazi fortunes were being reversed.

In driving rain during a particularly heavy raid, Sam seized his moment. He crawled through the undergrowth, away from the front. The bombs illuminated the scene in flashes. There were moments when he knew he must be visible, his frame starkly lit in the wintry landscape. He cowered low. In the heat of battle it was impossible to tell if the Nazis were shooting at him. As the sounds retreated, he dared to go faster. It was the start of a long journey back to the Padworskis' farm. Sam was now doubly marked: a Jew and a rough-looking deserter from a Nazi labour camp.[32]

Several weeks elapsed until, by March 1945, the Russian army were approaching their area of southern Poland. The sound of bombs was deafening. The Padworskis took cover under the kitchen table. One night in the midst of a particularly heavy raid, a neighbour warned them that the Germans were leaving with the horses. Mr Padworski ordered Sam to hide their horse in the woods. Sam led it from the barn into what seemed like a thunderous battlefield. The night sky was lit up with explosions. The horse tried to bolt. Somehow, Sam regained control and rode it into the woods, only to fall when he was caught by a branch. Injured, he lay awake all night, watching the stupendous battle, drawing primeval comfort from the animal; horse and boy as one living creature against the mighty weaponry unleashed in this quiet corner of Poland. Finally, by daylight he saw what liberation looked like. Soldiers were walking across Mr Padworski's land in their winter snow uniforms. The Soviet army. In his excitement, he no longer felt pain. Freedom at last.

But Russian liberation did not bring the new life that he hoped. The Soviet soldiers were accustomed to dealing with such violence that they dispensed it equally unthinkingly, propped up by the vodka in their water bottles. They set up a command post in Mr Padworski's house. Soon they, too, were looking for Polish men and boys to shore up their front line. Mr Padworski's horse and cart were requisitioned. Sam, the Jew who had escaped the ghetto and forced labour on the Nazi front line, now had to drive Russian soldiers in the wagon and work on the treacherous Russian front.[33] Soviet soldiers piled onto the straw in the cart. Along the way to the front, Sam witnessed the vengeance of the Soviet army. German soldiers had been mutilated, their bodies hanging up in some kind of macabre ritual. The Soviet soldiers, armed with machine guns, expected the Poles to pay for liberation by providing women and food. Every now and then he was ordered to pull in at a farm and the pillage would begin. The women would be taken into the barn. Sam heard their cries. In the lawlessness of the no man's land near the front lines there seemed no limit to human depravity.

Against all this, an even darker evil was beginning to take shape. Scraps of information kept giving him a glimpse of something so wicked, so depraved, that it was almost inconceivable. Sam heard of places in Poland where the Nazis had gassed the Jews. He could barely imagine what this could even be, but he grasped that it was not just his family and the Jews in surrounding villages who had died. The Nazis had set up purpose-built factories of death. Gas chambers. Millions had been slaughtered. It scarcely seemed believable.

Sam began to wonder if his entire people had been wiped out. Was he the only Jew left in Poland?

In the baffling lawlessness of this treacherous new world, Sam was too frightened to reveal his identity. The war continued. There was still no real freedom. Was this what liberation would be like? The prospect of a new life free from fear receded ever further away.[34]

✳

By early April 1945 in Buchenwald concentration camp in central Germany, Sidney Finkel could hear the heavy guns of the American army drawing nearer. The deafening sound filled him with hope. An army of liberators was close at hand, although, listening to the pounding guns, it was hard to judge their distance. Some prisoners thought liberation was just days away. Freedom, now tantalisingly close, seemed ever more precious. Nothing must go wrong.

Despite the proximity of the Allied army, there was no let-up in the Nazis' murderous policy towards the Jews. One day the prisoners were herded to the assembly area. Camp leaders were ordered to mark out the Jews in their section. Sidney's leader, Gustav, evidently had had some idea of what lay in store. He had advised all Jews in his block to remove the 'J' sewn onto their prison uniforms. When the guards ordered the Jews in Sidney's barracks to take a pace forward, no one stirred.

This enraged one particularly brutal SS officer. He walked over to Sidney's line. Everyone was commanded to take down their trousers. They stood half naked in the square at Buchenwald, as the SS officer slowly inspected the line. He knew how to identify circumcision. Even as Sidney heard the

American guns promising a new life, he and his friend, Harry, were singled out as Jews. They were led at gunpoint into a crammed warehouse where hundreds of other Jews were already waiting.

They were under no illusion about what was next. The Nazis rounded up fifty men and drove them out of the warehouse. Inside, everyone fell silent. The machine-gun fire was close at hand. So this was what the end would look like. Standing before a blood-spattered wall in some godforsaken corner of some godforsaken camp. The Americans were too late. The SS intended to shoot them all. They were trapped.

Sidney railed against his plight. He longed to live. To die like an animal at a slaughterhouse when the end was almost in sight was unendurable. There had to be a way out. Posing as workers with a heavy load, he and Harry bravely gave the guards the slip. As they approached the SS guards at the entrance to the compound, at first it looked as though they would be waved on, but then one guard ordered them to stop. Sidney and Harry did not wait. They abandoned their container and made a run for it. The gunfire crackled around them but they were not hit. To Sidney, it seemed a miracle. Later he learned that everyone in the warehouse was murdered that day. He was burning up with anger. How could the Nazis continue to murder when the war was all but done?[35]

Sidney's trial was not over. With the Americans very close, the Nazis continued to destroy the evidence of their genocide. On 10 April, Sidney found himself in a crowd of three thousand, forming an orderly queue at the entrance to Buchenwald. Unbelievably, the gates swung open. Outside it was a beautiful spring day, the country vibrant with different shades of green. But there was no chance to look as they were marched swiftly on under heavy guard to Weimar station. Sidney was stunned after his years of deprivation to see German civilians at the station looking clean and tidy, behaving as though nothing was amiss. No one seemed to see them, this vast throng of emaciated prisoners. No one came over and offered them food or expressed kindness. It was as if they were not people at all as they were crammed into open wagons like so much freight. In his mind, Sidney raged against God.

Over the next few weeks the wagons wound across Germany, dodging the Allied planes, on a journey to nowhere. Sidney was astonished at the scale of the devastation. In every city, every town, there were piles of rubble, the bombed-out buildings stark shapes against the sky. At one stage they reached a city as bombs were raining down. Their train meandered through the fire and devastation as if it were a peaceful day.

For Sidney those weeks 'were without a doubt the most hellish in my life'. The prisoners were rarely let out of the wagons. There was no food for them. Nor was there water. Hunger and thirst soon pushed out any other thought. Whenever the train stopped, the guards trained their machine guns on the prisoners to prevent them escaping, but Sidney scavenged when he could. Occasionally he and Harry found a beetroot or potato in a field. 'We ate grass. We boiled it. It was green water,' he remembers. 'We were starving. Totally starving.' There was no chance to wash or use a toilet. Lice were spread thickly over their skin but such was his hunger, Sidney barely noticed. Corpses began to pile up in the wagons. The stench of death was overwhelming. He watched in revulsion as one of the Russian prisoners of war ate raw flesh from the body of a corpse. To the guards they were beasts in the field, inhuman, mere target practice.[36]

One day the hunger was so terrible that Sidney and some other boys leapt off the freight car and ran across to the Nazi soldiers, who were enjoying lunch. The guards turned their machine guns on them. A couple of the children got hit, but Sidney could not help himself. Even under fire he was not going to move. The young boy who had absorbed the Nazi point of view had reached a new phase of desperation. He felt barely human, just a creature needing food even if he died for it.[37]

13

'This was something the children should not see'

Tante Anna, 1945

In the closing weeks of the war at Trench Hall in Shropshire, Tante Anna found the years of struggle were taking their toll. She was losing her sight. Her thoughts kept returning to Bunce Court. She longed to go back. She was driven by the feeling that she had not done enough for the children.[1] Bunce Court would have room for them all, including old pupils who still returned many weekends, such as Leslie Brent, who was now a young officer in the Royal Warwickshire Regiment and was one of several former pupils serving in the British Army. Quite apart from his feelings of gratitude to Britain for his refuge, 'I saw this as the best possible way of helping my family in Germany,' Leslie explains.[2] Tante Anna knew everyone's thoughts were turning to life after the war. The children were excited that they would soon see their parents. Would their lives pick up where they had left off?

One day in late April 1945, Leslie was on leave in London when he went to the cinema. Before the main feature, a Pathé newsreel played. British troops were in northern Germany approaching Bergen-Belsen concentration camp, dark shapes on a wintry horizon, the tanks beside them throwing up palls of dust as they crossed a field. The film flickered and suddenly the images were from inside the camp. Soldiers were mingling with prisoners who seemed too weak to stand, skeletons in pyjamas, wide eyes in shrunken faces; the living dead. The camera panned to the left. It was hard at first for Leslie to make out what he was seeing. Then he realised there were piles of bodies, heaped up like the carcases of animals. As the camera drew closer, he could see the bodies were emaciated. These people had been starving before they died, their bones jutting out from wasted flesh, faces no longer recognisable as human. Leslie sat paralysed in the flickering light. He was in shock, unable to move and unable to look. The scene before him was beyond human imagining. What sort of hell was this?

Leslie realised he was about to vomit. He had to get out of the cinema. Could this have been the fate of his parents and his sister? He could conjure up their last meeting powerfully in his mind. The impoverished setting could not diminish them. They had seemed so full of life. Arthur and Charlotte had been certain their parting was only temporary, so full of words of reassurance for their departing son. Surely they were not now among all the shrivelled bodies discarded like rubbish?[3]

The shocking newsreels of the concentration camps were playing in cinemas across the country. Towards the end of the war, Tante Anna had made a block booking for many of her pupils to go to see Laurence Olivier's *Henry V* at the local cinema in Wem. The film was said to be a real morale-booster, as well as relevant to the school exams. Out of the blue, she received a call from the local cinema manager advising her to cancel the school's reservation. The cinema was also showing the Pathé newsreel of Bergen-Belsen concentration camp. It took a moment for her to grasp that the cinema manager's concern was not for her children. The Pathé footage was stirring local opinion, he explained, and there could be trouble if there were Germans in the audience. 'Tante Anna told me the locals could have attacked us,' Harold Jackson learned years later, such was the anger. There were still those who made little distinction between the Nazis and Jewish refugees.[4]

Tante Anna had some idea what to expect. On 19 April, the BBC had broadcast the first radio report from Bergen-Belsen. 'There was a whirling cloud of dust, the dust of thousands of slowly moving people laden with the deadly typhus germ,' reported the acclaimed war correspondent, Richard Dimbleby, as he passed through the barbed wire fence into the inner compound. The smell was 'sickly and thick, the smell of death and decay, corruption and filth'. On the heaps of naked bodies strewn along the side of the road, 'yellow skin glistened like stretched rubber on their bones'. To Dimbleby, they looked 'unreal, like polished skeletons'. Beside the road were young children sharing a morsel of food 'not six feet from a pile of decomposing bodies'. Inside the 'dreadful interior' of one of the barracks, Dimbleby singled out a girl. 'She was a living skeleton, impossible to gauge her age for she had practically no hair left and her head and her face was only a yellow parchment sheet with two holes for eyes.' She was stretching out her 'stick of an arm, crying, "English, English, medicine, medicine," and trying to cry but had not enough strength.' Further along, he passed an enclosure where five hundred children had been kept before reaching the crematorium, 'where the Germans had burned alive thousands of men and women'. A Polish prisoner informed him the SS guards had 'hit them on the back of the neck to stun them and then they were fed straight into the fire, three at a time . . . They burned ten thousand people in this fire in reprisal for the murder of two SS guards . . .'

The impact of Dimbleby's report is revealed by the fact that initially the BBC did not broadcast it. Although foreign secretary Anthony Eden had condemned the Nazis' mass extermination of the Jews in 1942 and since then many atrocities about concentration camps had been reported, nothing could quite prepare the public for something like this. Richard Dimbleby was the BBC's star reporter, but disbelieving senior executives would not air his report until he threatened to resign.[5]

Tante Anna's correspondence reveals that those around her sometimes observed her in tears at this time. This was out of character. Tante Anna was invariably the strong one, the one who knew what to do. Possibly it was the years of being there for others that had exacted a toll, or the tense, momentous events leading up to the defeat of the Nazis. More likely it was the full revelation of the evil and depravity of Nazism. She knew there had been children in the camps, but later she would learn that one and a half million children had been murdered and see photographs of the great pile of children's shoes outside the crematorium at Auschwitz. Her struggles to create something good seemed meaningless against such evil. Even knowing about the concentration camps, she had never conjured up such scenes in her mind. It was beyond all comprehension. She knew the children at Trench Hall were anxiously waiting for news, hoping their parents had survived the camps. She did not want them to picture their parents suffering and dying in such a barbaric way. Her first step was to ban them from the local cinema. This was something they should not see.[6]

At Trench Hall everyone was getting ready to celebrate. The kitchen hummed with activity amidst a general feeling of optimism. The end of the war was in sight. Historic events happened in quick succession. By mid-April, the Soviet Red Army began their final assault on Berlin; on 25 April, Soviet and American forces met at Torgau on the River Elbe in Germany and shook hands; a few days later the Italian fascist dictator, Benito Mussolini, was murdered. On 1 May came another stunning watershed. 'This is London calling. Here is a newsflash,' announced the BBC World Service. 'The German radio has just announced that Hitler is dead. I'll repeat that. The German radio has just announced that Hitler is dead . . .'[7] Children crammed into Tante Anna's office for the next bulletin. This really was the end. Ahead lay a new dawn. The German surrender must happen any day. VE Day – Victory in Europe Day – was fast approaching; the longed-for moment marking the end of the war in Europe and the prospect that life would go back to normal.

To mark the momentous occasion, on 8 May, Tante Anna led a festival in the morning. 'T.A. spoke, (in tears as usual) but short,' observed Hannah Meyer. This was followed by poems and music and after lunch, each class met with their form teacher for games. There was a treasure hunt, charades and a play reading. Everyone was eagerly waiting for the main event in the evening, 'a gigantic bonfire,' continues Hannah, which her husband was piling high with help from the older boys. 'It was lit by Tante Anna and Hans had built it up so beautifully that with one touch of the long spill, it flamed up about sixty feet into the night sky.'[8]

For a moment there was stunned silence. Having lived through six years of blackout darkness, 'many children had never seen friendly fire in their lives,' wrote Hannah. 'After a few seconds' silence they broke into such a loud cheer and applause such as I have never heard.' The children sang and danced around the fire until late: 'even the tinies were allowed to stay up,' said Tante Anna. For her the flames seemed to leap 'straight up to heaven'.⁹ No one wanted to go to bed. Even when the fire had died down to glowing embers, many children were still there, 'jumping over it, singly and in twos and threes. None of us will ever forget this night,' concluded Hannah.

British pupil Harold Jackson remembers how many of his European classmates thought, 'Oh we're going to see our parents now . . .' and that life would go back to the way it was before. 'We had no idea about the Holocaust,' he says.¹⁰ Behind the scenes, Tante Anna was working through the relief committees and the Red Cross to try to get answers for children and staff. Already she had found some parents had survived incredible odds. News had spread like wildfire around the school after the liberation of Belgium in September 1944, when one pupil, Ernst Weinberg, learned his parents were still alive. 'They had been in hiding for so long I had given them up,' Tante Anna confided to a friend, 'especially when I heard that most of the emigrant Jews in Belgium had been deported.' But she had been contacted by a British officer in Belgium with the good news. The Weinbergs' survival in hiding in Brussels gave hope to the others.¹¹

Letters began to arrive for the children from distant relatives; the Red Cross or sometimes unexpected visitors turned up with information. As they began to piece together the fate of the children's families a sense of apprehension gripped Trench Hall. No matter where parents had fled, they had struggled to escape the long reach of the Third Reich.

Helen Urbach had reason to hope her father, Otto, had survived. After all, he had escaped from Vienna to France with his mother before the war. But gradually it became clear that during 1942 the Nazis had deported tens of thousands of Jews in France to death camps with the collaboration of the Vichy government. 'My father was sent to Auschwitz and that was it . . .' says Helen. Helen had a distant relative who did survive Auschwitz, where she had been forced to keep the books. 'She saw my father's name. That he had been sent to the—' Helen stops. Even after the distance of a lifetime, she cannot bring herself to say that her father was sent to the gas chamber on arrival. 'I sorely miss him . . .' she says.[12] Years passed before her mother gave Helen his letters. Otto had appealed to friends in England after the fall of France in 1940. 'My dears, I am alive. I beg for help to bring us together with my wife and Helen . . .' His last letter to his daughter conveys the strength of his feelings for her. 'Don't forget me as there is no one, and will be no one, who loves you more than your Papa.'[13]

Eric Bourne also had a parent in France. He had heard nothing from his father, Robert, the campaigning left-wing journalist, during the war. Now he learned that Robert had managed to escape the round-ups in France. Via a tortuous route he had reached Morocco, a protectorate controlled by Vichy France, and then transferred to Martinique in the Caribbean. But the immense pressures of the previous few years had finally caught up with him and Robert became seriously ill and died. To the very end, the journalist with such fighting spirit was preoccupied with the tragedy that had befallen his beloved homeland. 'I am a German,' Robert wrote with passion, 'but by the end of this war, I want to see Germany on her knees . . .' Eric felt deeply the loss of his childhood inspiration and lamented that his father could no longer be part of creating a new Germany.[14]

Wherever they had fled in Europe, parents had struggled to escape the Nazi deportations. Jewish men, women and children had been deported from Austria, Czechoslovakia, Poland, the Netherlands, Belgium, Norway, France, Germany, Russia, Italy . . . As late as the summer of 1944, the Nazis deported almost half a million Jews from Hungary alone. At the school, everyone was waiting for news. Joseph Meyer, the young son of Hans and Hannah who felt privileged to have both his parents at the school, noticed how intently many of his classmates felt 'complete rootlessness' over their loss of family. 'There was a sense of – where do I belong?'[15]

Tante Anna pursued every avenue to help them. 'As there have been some miraculous survivals in all camps we are most anxious to find out if there any lists, perhaps in possession of the Russian embassy,' she wrote to Lord Samuel on 30 May 1945. 'Any certainty, no matter how hard, is easier to bear than this constant uncertainty . . .'[16] There seemed no geographical limits to the catastrophe. From Soviet Russia in the east to the Channel Islands to the west, from Norway in the north to the Greek islands in the south: nowhere had been safe.

Old pupil Heinz Redwood, now a postgraduate chemistry student at the University of Birmingham, knew his parents had escaped to the Far East, but with no news for years, he, too, thought he must be an orphan. 'One just didn't know. It was total ignorance. No news of any kind either good or bad.' Living with uncertainty, 'I felt very insecure,' he says. One day a stranger who had been trying to trace him came to his lodgings. He was a Jesuit priest returning to Ireland from Bangkok in Thailand. It proved to be an emotional meeting. 'Absolutely amazing,' recalls Heinz. 'He told me my parents were still alive.'

Through correspondence with his parents in Bangkok, Heinz began to piece together what had happened to his remaining family in Germany. He had lost a great many cousins, aunts and uncles. 'It was very emotionally troubling at the time,' he says, although perhaps most haunting of all was to learn the fate of his much-loved grandfather, Maximilian. Before the war, his grandfather had encouraged Heinz to study chemistry. 'Do something useful,' Maximilian had urged. Now Heinz was completing his PhD and had much to tell him. But it was too late. In 1942, when Maximilian had received his deportation order, he had decided not to obey it. Nothing would persuade this distinguished elderly gentleman, an assimilated Jew who regarded himself as German, to submit to a Nazi order. He knew what he must do.

Maximilian had invited a few of his non-Jewish friends for dinner and told them of his intention, asking his guests to trace his family after the war and tell them what happened that night. 'He was very dignified,' Heinz learned. After the meal, 'he went upstairs and took sleeping tablets and never woke up . . .' None of the guests could stop him. His mind was made up. 'They realised this was probably the most dignified way of dealing with the situation.' By that time, 'although they didn't know all the grisly details', they knew that there was little hope once Jews were deported. The only consolation for Heinz was that his grandfather was right to spare himself the cruelties of the extermination camps.[17]

For the few who found they did have a parent alive, reunions did not always go smoothly. Mia Schaff had lived through the war thinking she was an orphan. She had last seen her father, Oscar, at Easter before the war when he had returned briefly from Poland. Later she had learned through the Red Cross that he died in Auschwitz. There had been no word from her mother, Ida, for years. Mia had last seen her in July 1939 on that fateful day she left on Kindertransport from Berlin. Since 1941 there had been nothing to confirm that Ida was alive and well. After the war it came as a great shock when she received a letter from Berlin out of the blue. It was from her mother.

Ida Schaff had gone into hiding in Berlin in October 1941 when the Jewish deportations from the German capital began. Miraculously, she had survived for four years in the very eye of the storm, living off her wits with frequent changes of addresses. Different friends and contacts had sheltered her, sometimes just for a few days, to protect her from new check-points, lightning round-ups and successive deportations. Berlin, once home to a third of Germany's Jewish population, by the end of the war hid in its ruins an unknown number of 'underground' survivors like Ida, perhaps just fifteen hundred. But far from feeling happy to get her mother's letter, Mia felt confused. As she read and reread the letter her own feelings baffled her. Everyone around her was learning of the death of their parents and suffering. 'I should have been absolutely overjoyed, shouldn't I?' she says, seventy-five years later. 'But I was apprehensive . . . I felt apprehensive as soon as I got the letter.'

The nervous strain for Ida had been unrelentingly intense. After the war, she was very ill. She lived for the day when she might see her children, Mia, John and Alice, but had no idea where they were. Ida did not even have the means to get to England. One day she collapsed under the strain, in a Berlin street. The British soldier who came to her aid was a German-speaker. As she lay on the pavement, all Ida could say, over and over again, was that she must see her children. In hospital she had a nervous break-down. Her recovery was assisted by an English translator who helped her trace Mia and her brother and sister. But when Ida finally came to England, the longed-for reunion did not go as she hoped.

Mia was stunned to meet her mother, who after years of separation was like a stranger. 'She didn't look at all like herself. Through the war she had dyed her hair so she wouldn't be recognised and it had not grown out – she had been blondish and now she was reddish and darker. Obviously, she had aged considerably. I felt so awkward with her. I couldn't relate to her at all and she was so overjoyed. All she wanted to do was hug me and kiss me and I just felt . . . I just didn't want it. And she was so upset.' Mia's mother wanted her to go back with her to Berlin. Mia refused. 'I just wanted life to go on as it had been. I still don't like change . . . I didn't feel I was that close to her.' The school had become her family and her mother felt like a stranger. 'Obviously I got to love her more,' says Mia, 'but I didn't see much of her.' Years later she was consumed with guilt. 'I think how dreadful. How weird. I am still consumed with guilt . . .'[18]

Mostly the British children did not fully grasp the scale of the tragedy that had engulfed their classmates, but Harold Jackson did get an unexpected insight. One morning after breakfast Tante Anna asked him to come and see her. Harold couldn't imagine what she wanted to discuss. As he sat on the sofa in her office, he realised she was trying to reassure him. Something was amiss. Tante Anna was holding a letter. Suddenly he understood that she was hesitating to hand it to him. It was from his stepmother, she explained. Gently she revealed that his own mother had died of cancer. 'She did it beautifully,' says Harold, as, decades later, he recalls the emotional scene in Anna's room. It was not just the loss of his mother that distressed Harold, but the coldness of his own family. No one had come to break the sad news to him in person, not even his own father. They had left that to Tante Anna. 'It was extraordinary. I got the impression that Tante Anna thought it was a bit weird as well,' he says.[19] Harold, the self-contained loner, the boy who never showed his emotions and was invariably ready with an acerbic or witty retort, found tears rolling down his face. Tante Anna put her arms round him and did her best to comfort him.

It took time before the full implications for the school began to emerge. Tante Anna and the staff carefully managed how they broke any news of parents. 'It was gradually leaked to me that they were killed,' Frank Auerbach recalls. Like so many others, he came to understand that his parents had died in 1943 at Auschwitz. If Tante Anna was worried that the sensitive Frank did not appear anguished at the news, years later he would write an explanation. 'I did this thing which psychiatrists frown on – I am in total denial.'[20]

The staff tried to create opportunities that might encourage the children to express their feelings and build their self-confidence. William Marckwald, the school stoker and former director of the Deutsches Theater, remembered directing Frank Auerbach around this time in a production of *Everyman,* a morality play written in Tudor times. Marckwald knew that Frank was interested in becoming an actor and for years 'had been hankering after a part', he observed. Usually, the main parts were given to older boys and Marckwald would assign younger enthusiasts, such as Frank, a role such as assistant producer. Despite the complexity of the play's exploration of good and evil, Marckwald decided this was the right time to give Frank the lead role. Marckwald understood that Frank's parents had been swallowed up somewhere in the vast concentration camp system. He knew Frank wouldn't talk about it, but sensed that he 'must have felt terribly lonely all the time, although he never complained'.

Marckwald himself was reeling from the loss of his parents. His father had died within days of being transported to Theresienstadt in Czechoslovakia after being denied the use of his wheelchair even though he could not walk. 'He had had to die worse than an animal,' wrote Marckwald in his memoirs 'and what for?' He hated the thought of his mother 'completely alone in the horribly unpleasant surroundings of the concentration camp'. At one stage, Tante Anna managed to get news of prisoners released from Theresienstadt. Marckwald remembers scanning 'anxiously and eagerly' down the list, 'but Mother's name was not on it.' Like Frank's parents, she vanished somewhere, another nameless person missing somewhere in Nazi-occupied Europe. 'All this was spread over years and oppressed us unspeakably. Yet we went on living, working and hoping . . .'

Marckwald understood what boys like Frank Auerbach might be going through as he himself struggled to make sense of it. 'I have tried in vain to reconcile these events with the divine,' he wrote in his memoirs. 'How is it possible to accept that God could have permitted all this to happen . . . it is quite impossible to understand how and why human beings could ever inflict these unspeakable horrors on other human beings!' The torment of Thomas Paine in Georg Büchner's play *Danton's Death* ran through his mind again and again. 'Why do I suffer? This is the rock of Atheism. The slightest notion of pain, even if it stirs in only an atom, causes a tear in Creation from top to bottom.' What possible reason could there be for God to create suffering on such a global scale?[21]

No doubt Marckwald's agony of mind had some bearing on his production of *Everyman*. He describes working with Frank Auerbach as 'one of the most extraordinary experiences I have had'. There were rehearsals every afternoon for weeks. They focused on the emotional troubles of the characters in the play, rather than talking directly about what had happened to their families. Frank thrived on the 'guidance and comfort' of his teacher, according to his biography. Later he came to see Marckwald's exacting methods as a blueprint for creativity: 'for creating something unforeseen that is rigorously true: the repeated study of the script, the striving to get things right and then the moment of abandon,' Frank thought.[22] There came 'a heady moment' of the day of the first performance where Frank had to deliver a key speech as his character finally realises 'how wrong his life had been'. This particular speech had not been rehearsed but the weeks of work on the character had an effect. The audience was electrified by the way Frank delivered the words. Marckwald was astonished. 'It was like working with a grown-up mature man and not with a boy of barely fifteen. In the end he gave a most sincere and moving performance.'[23]

*

A couple of months after VE Day, Tante Anna made her first visit back to Bunce Court. For her it was a return to a special sanctuary, a place of joy and hope where she had first put down her roots in Britain, a place perhaps where grief might be laid aside. She knew it had been occupied by Royal Tank Regiments and the Grenadier Guards Armoured Corps, and had no idea what to expect. The army had moved out at the time of D-Day and since then the place had been unoccupied.

As they opened the front gate, they were struck by the changes. '"DANGER KEEP OFF HIGH EXPLOSIVE" was written on a hut that had not been there before,' recorded one dismayed pupil, Alexander Urbach. 'What a mess everything was in!' The once-gracious house looked forlorn. Tante Anna pushed open the front door. There was a musty, unoccupied smell. 'Was ever a sight more desolate than the wooden props holding up the ceiling?' continued Alexander. 'And what a state the stairs were in!' Upstairs on the girls' floor 'we found pin-ups wherever we went.' On the next floor there were diagrams of various shells and ARP notices pasted up all over the place. Electric sockets and even the taps had been 'liberated', observed Hanna Bergas. Coming down again, they heard a noise from the kitchen. Tante Anna discovered a tramp had settled in the manor house. She let him stay. There would be much work to do before they could call this place home.

They all felt 'down in spirits,' wrote Alexander as they explored the grounds. Large areas of lawn had been cemented over and Nissen huts erected. They walked past buildings marked as quartermaster stores, ammo stores and similar; barbed wire had taken the place of familiar garden features. The ornamental pond had taken a direct hit. The roses had disappeared from the rose garden. The remaining lawn was scarred with tank marks and 'had been trodden down by hundreds of heavy boots,' wrote Hanna. Although efforts had been made to remove the concrete, much remained and there were brambles sprouting through the cracks and invading the outdoor classrooms. Even the children's amphitheatre was very overgrown. 'A heartbreaking sight,' continued Alexander. All their efforts to transform the place had come to this. The unloved house seemed

diminished, shorn of its beauty. How could it ever be transformed back into that unique place, 'the keeper of their
dreams'?[24] As they looked further into the sheds outside,
Tante Anna was amazed to come across the children's
Würstchen car. It still had its tyres! These were now more
valuable than the car itself. Anna saw a ray of light. Here
was the start of their repair fund. They would find a way
to make this work.

Tante Anna was keen to involve the children. Once
repaired, Bunce Court would become their home, too. Susie
Davids recalls being part of another advance party sent on
to help prepare the school. Susie loved spending time with
Tante Anna and her sisters, Paula and Bertha. They made
her feel special. 'We were treated so nicely . . . we were treated
like adults,' she recalls. 'I helped polish the floors and getting
the whole school cleaned and ready for term. We cleaned up
everything. I loved working in the kitchen . . .' Susie felt
excited about the planned move back to Bunce Court.[25] Some
of Tante Anna's former pupils could not wait either. Her
niece, Dorle, got married that summer, to a British research
chemist called Alan Potten, and they chose the deserted manor
house for their honeymoon.

Tante Anna became an anchor, a central point of reference
for her pupils and former pupils, many now serving in the
armed forces across the world. Eric Bourne and several old
pupils were in the Far East in India or Burma. Others were
in Europe with British and American forces; some in Germany
itself. Tante Anna's correspondence shows she was in frequent
contact, passing on news of anyone's new postings and
promotions, or, most important of all, reunions with parents
and ways in which they could help each other. 'Leslie has
been here for five weeks' embarkation leave,' she wrote in

one circular. He was returning to Germany, 'where he will try to make enquiries about his and other people's parents.' Peter Stoll – 'Sparks' – was returning from Singapore and hoped to get compassionate leave to visit his parents in Holland, while another former pupil, Joyce Wormleighton, working with the military government in Frankfurt, had made frequent visits to see Heidtsche's mother and sister, 'which of course, makes Gretel very happy . . .'[26] Post was not yet reliable to relatives abroad and so these personal contacts proved vital. Through Tante Anna as the central hub of information, ex-pupils in Europe were well placed to help each other to trace missing parents or to visit those newly found.[27] For the pupils there was a network they could trust, like extended family, to help piece together the patchwork of their former lives.

Through her correspondence with pupils overseas, Tante Anna built up a vivid picture of what had happened to the country of her childhood. 'Cleves, Emmerich, Bucholt, everywhere complete destruction,' wrote one pupil travelling along the Rhine with the Allies in western Germany. 'Drive through Münster. A heap of rubble . . . The steel works in Kassel are well hit. Town again in ruins.' He joined the famous autobahn at Eisenach. 'It's like an Exodus. There are just millions on the roads . . .'[28, 29] Everywhere, it was the same story of devastation. 'We passed through Cologne in moonlight, where the magnificent cathedral towered majestically over the vast sea of ruins,' wrote another former pupil, Walter Bloch. How could this have happened? Why had the German people continued to support Hitler? Did they even know about the atrocities in the concentration camps? When Walter tried to seek answers he drew a blank. No one wanted to talk about politics. 'The Nazis never existed because, as everyone will tell you, he personally was against the regime,' Walter wrote. 'I can only suggest that Hitler must have survived by a miracle as apparently, he had eighty million opponents and no supporters.'[30]

One of Tante Anna's former pupils found himself at the centre of the Allied search for answers at Nuremberg. Twenty-two-year-old Richard Sonnenfeldt was a private in the American army, serving in Austria. By chance one day, General William Donovan, chief of the US Office for Strategic Services, a predecessor to the CIA, needed a German interpreter. Richard was bilingual and he soon found himself on a plane to Nuremberg on a special mission: to assist with the war crimes trials of captured Nazi leaders. This was the very place that gave its name to the 'infamous' Nuremberg laws, Richard wrote in his memoirs, where the vast and deserted square once pulsed to 'Nazi mass hysteria and venomous xenophobia'. Looking down from the plane, Richard saw 'a city utterly destroyed' save for the Palace of Justice. As a former Jewish refugee, it was hard not to feel a sense of grim satisfaction.

It was barely eight years since Richard's brave mother, in her desperation, had suggested a family suicide after Kristallnacht. Since then, Richard had been educated at Bunce Court, deported on a prison ship, crossed the world from Australia in wartime and acquired American citizenship. 'Except for the resourcefulness of my mother and the generosity of an English school principal, I would assuredly be dead . . .' he wrote.[31] Yet unbelievably, here he was, with a 'once-in-a-lifetime assignment' to help gather the evidence against 'those Nazi monsters that had terrorised the civilised world'. Despite his youth, on account of his linguistic skills Richard was appointed chief interpreter for the American prosecution, with a ringside seat at the Nuremberg trials.

In the interrogation rooms on the second floor in the Palace of Justice, Richard came face to face with leading perpetrators of Nazi evil. One by one they shuffled in, those men who had determined the fate of millions and once straddled the German government like little emperors, directing armies, the secret police and the entire machinery of state. Stripped of their great offices, now they stood accused of war crimes, crimes against humanity and genocide. Richard was appalled to find himself face to face with 'mediocrity, lack of distinction of intellect, knowledge or insight'. Was this the face of evil? How was it possible that a man like Joachim von Ribbentrop, this 'ashen faced, worried looking, hand wringing, wreck of a man' could ever have risen to become foreign minister of Germany? Then there was Rudolf Hess, 'that loony Nazi Party deputy', who at Nuremberg 'claimed to be an amnesiac'. Hans Frank, 'a Hitler yes-man', had run occupied Poland and, before that, served as chief legal officer in Nazi Germany. For Frank, German law had been reduced to a matter of implementing Hitler's wishes. Hermann Göring, the highest-ranking captured Nazi, managed to convey an air of authority despite his addiction to drugs. Richard saw him as a 'caged and clever rogue trying to confound his captors'.[32]

As he carried out his interpretations and translated captured German documents, Richard was stunned by the lack of substance of Nazism. 'Not one of the prisoners offered a defence or even an intelligent explanation of the so-called doctrine of National Socialism,' he wrote. It was nothing more than an empty 'bag of hate'.[33] It was as though 'Goethe, Beethoven, Brahms, Schiller, Luther and the great German philosophers never existed . . .' There was no humanity in Nazism, he thought, 'no defence of the rights of man, no definition of nobility or honour, only blind obedience.' As he flew around Europe assisting in the forensic gathering of evidence, he saw where that obedience had led as 'the enormity of the carefully organised Nazi killing machine . . . began to dawn on me.' This 'organised hatred . . . on a scale never before known to man' had made it possible to keep the cattle trucks rolling across Europe, carry out selections and oversee the entire apparatus of death.[34]

Who was responsible? Many of those whose names arose in the interviews were conveniently dead, including Hitler himself. In May 1945, Heinrich Himmler, chief of the Gestapo and the SS, had committed suicide with a cyanide pill when arrested by the British. Himmler's notorious deputy, Reinhard Heydrich, had also died, assassinated in 1942 in Prague. Others, such as Adolf Eichmann, slipped the net, using false papers to evade capture in Argentina until 1960. Nonetheless, the defendants at Nuremberg included key political and military leaders of the Nazi regime. As the interviews progressed, Richard recognised the scale of the task before them. This was 'a never-to-recur opportunity to write the history of Nazi Germany by extracting it under oath from those who made it the crime of the century,' he wrote.[35] But they had to assume all defendants innocent until proven guilty. They needed to gather the evidence for their crimes and set a new international standard for judging war crimes and crimes against humanity.

It took time even to assess the exact toll. Sixty million people had died in the Second World War. Seventeen million had been systematically murdered by the Nazis, including Slavs, Soviet prisoners of war, the Romanies and other minorities such as people with disabilities, those with mental health problems and those who were homosexual, as well as the Nazis' political opponents, and especially the Jews. Jewish men, women and children had died in pogroms, mass shootings, during deportations, in labour camps, concentration camps, extermination camps and on death marches. By the end of the war the Nazis had murdered around six million Jews, a staggering two-thirds of the Jewish population of Europe. In Jewish circles, people began to use the Biblical word Shoah or 'calamity'. Tante Anna noticed that some newspapers coined a new term to try to convey the enormity of what had happened to the Jews: a Holocaust.[36]

The war may have been over but the suffering was not. Tante Anna read in the press of the 'Displaced Persons camps' set up by the Allies, which helped to house former prisoners of war and concentration camp survivors, many of them Jews. Ever practical, her thoughts turned to her original school at Herrlingen as she wondered if its buildings could also be used by survivors. Gradually, she pieced together the school's shocking wartime history. Tante Anna's own Uncle Jacob had been forcibly detained there, along with other elderly Jews. 'Their wailing and lamentations chilled me to the bone,' recalled one witness to when the elderly residents had been deported in the summer of 1942. The records revealed that on arrival at Theresienstadt, Jacob and his companions were subjected to such inhumane treatment that a third of them died within weeks; by December Uncle Jacob, too, lost his fragile hold on life.

But Tante Anna's former school at Herrlingen was still standing, along with Ulm Minster with its improbable towering spire, despite the obliteration of much of the old town below. Ulm was now in the American zone. 'I am very anxious to have Herrlingen used for Displaced Jews,' Tante Anna wrote to the authorities, 'so they have a roof over their heads this winter if possible.' Determined to help Jewish survivors in whatever way she could, she wrote to the Displaced Persons Executive in Frankfurt, the High Commissioner of Refugees, the Jewish Chaplain under General Eisenhower. When she heard nothing, she wrote to former pupils serving in Germany to see if they could speed up the process of turning her former school into a home for displaced persons. 'I hope things can be done quicker if someone is on the spot, so will you help?' she asked.[37]

The letter she received from Major Rev. Judah Naditch, special adviser to Eisenhower on Jewish problems, contained more unexpected news. He confirmed her former school was in 'excellent condition' and was arranging to help displaced Jews in accordance with her wishes. 'You will be interested to know that one of the houses was used by Field Marshal Rommel,' added Naditch.[38] After the elderly Jews had been deported, the legendary 'Desert Fox' and his family had been given use of the spacious Haus Friedenthal, in recognition of his achievements. The junior pupils' house had been renamed 'Rommel Villa', but the German general had not been able to enjoy it for long. After an unsuccessful attempt on Hitler's life in July 1944, Rommel had fallen into disgrace, although his exact link to the conspiracy remains unclear. During the night of 13 October 1944, a detachment of the SS had silently cordoned off the former school at Herrlingen. The next morning, two generals had knocked on the door of Rommel's villa. The Desert Fox was given a fatal choice: a public trial and imprisonment of his family or suicide with a cyanide capsule. Rommel said goodbye to his wife, Lucie, and stepped into the waiting car with the two generals. Fifteen minutes later he was dead.[39]

By 20 September 1945, Tante Anna wrote to her former pupils serving in Germany. Her former school at Herrlingen was transformed yet again. No longer 'Rommel Villa', it was now a convalescent home for Displaced Persons, 'chiefly Jews liberated from concentration camps'. She urged anyone in the region to visit and see 'what people are there. I should love to know . . .' She wondered if children were among them. It was hard to conceive how they would put their lives back together but Tante Anna knew her school must help.[40]

*

For three weeks before the end of the war, the open freight train with prisoners from Buchenwald was zigzagging around Germany, apparently on a route to nowhere. Thirteen-year-old Sidney Finkel's luck had run out. Within twenty-four hours of being marched through the gates of Buchenwald, the American army had liberated the camp. He had missed freedom and survival by less than a day. His freight train was under heavy guard and more than half the prisoners died. For days, the rear wagon was piled high with corpses. He and his friend Harry clung to life, although Sidney was beginning to lose hope. He felt feverish. He could no longer think clearly. There seemed no end to his suffering in sight.

One day in early May 1945, the train arrived at Theresienstadt in Czechoslovakia. As their open wagons pulled into the station, Sidney was astonished to see Czech people on the platform welcoming them and offering food. The sight was so alien it was hard to register what was happening. Suddenly the situation became dangerous. The guards threatened to shoot the prisoners. They had not abandoned their posts in spite of the reported death of Hitler and they, too, appeared confused by the unexpected circumstances. When the civilians turned on the guards, they ran off. Everything happened so fast, Sidney barely had time to see his tormenters melting into the crowd.

The children on the train were taken to a centre in Theresienstadt concentration camp, where they were cleaned and shaved to remove the lice. Sidney learned that the SS guards had fled the camp and they were free. This was the moment he had dreamed of, prayed for, yearned for, in spite of not quite believing it could ever happen. Now it was here and it was meaningless. The shabby room, the heat, the devouring pain: that was real. He was diagnosed with typhus. An epidemic was sweeping through the concentration camps. Thousands who had survived the Nazis and witnessed liberation succumbed to the disease in their weakened state.

In a makeshift Russian hospital, Sidney drifted in and out of oblivion. 'I think I was unconscious for days and days and days. I think I was dying . . . it was just a matter of one way or another, going over that edge.'[41] He seemed to be hearing voices from his early childhood. Sometimes he was back in a safe, secure world with his mother and father. He distinctly heard his parents urging him never to give up. One day as he was coming round, he heard his name being called again. He was no longer delirious. He realised he was in a different place; he had been moved from the hospital. The voice was not in his head. It was coming from the street below. It was a voice he recognised.

He looked from the window. There was his brother, Isaac, calling his name. He was thin and worn, noticeably older, but still his brother.

'Issie, *Issie* . . .' Sidney called out.

They hugged and embraced and cried. It was hard to believe that this was real, that he was holding his very own brother. Isaac explained that he had just arrived and had heard that a contingent of children had been brought here from Buchenwald. 'Hoping you were among them, I was walking the streets, shouting your name . . .'[42] Somehow in this wasteland of devastation, in spite of everything that had happened, Sidney still had his beloved big brother.

Their joy in finding each other was soon overshadowed. Sidney found Isaac unrecognisable as the confident teenager who had tried to help his father take care of the family at the beginning of the war. Now they were both broken as they tried to piece together what had happened to their family. The unbearable confirmation that their mother and youngest sister, Frania, had both died in Treblinka hit Sidney like a tidal wave. He felt overwhelmed, raging in his grief at their loss. He raged, too, at the news of their Aunt Rachel, who had managed to survive the concentration camps and return to Piotrkow only to be robbed and murdered shortly after she negotiated the sale of her old house. Then came word of their father, Laib. His name was on a list somewhere. Another godforsaken slave labour camp in central Germany called Mittelbau Boelcke-Kaserne. This was a subcamp in the Mittelbau-Dora complex where many slave labourers were worked to death making V_1 and V_2 rockets in hellish conditions in a vast underground tunnel complex in the Harz mountains. Laib had died just over two months before the end of the war. His death certificate stated that he died of a heart attack, but Boelcke-Kaserne was the dreaded place where those no longer able to work were sent to die. Conditions were so foul in this cramped, hellish underworld that prisoners called it 'the living crematorium'.[43]

Isaac wanted to know about Sidney's last meeting with their father in Buchenwald. Sidney found he could not bring himself to reveal exactly what had happened. The more Isaac pressed him, the more uncomfortable Sidney felt. It struck Sidney suddenly that he had failed his father, just when he needed him most. He had been unable to respond to Laib, to show the love he actually felt and ease Laib's peace of mind before his journey out of Buchenwald. Guilt settled over Sidney like an oppressive force. There was so much more he longed to say to his father. The unbearable pain of this last meeting 'stayed with me for the rest of my life'.[44]

*

The end of the war brought little relief for fifteen-year-old Sam Oliner in southern Poland. He managed to escape working for the Red Army on the Soviet front line. Streetwise Sam waited until the guards had fallen into a particularly drunken sleep one night before he bravely unhooked his horse and quietly sneaked past. It took him a week to reach the Padworskis' farm.[45] Even though the war was over he kept his false identity until late May, when he received a message to visit Balwina. She told him it was safe for him to leave the farm. Some Jews had come out of hiding and established a small Jewish community in the nearby village of Gorlice.

Sam joined the Jewish survivors but struggled to settle. In the seething cauldron of revenge and chaos of post-war Poland, he felt deep, conflicting emotions. He heard that Jewish-sympathising Russian officers were dispensing almost medieval justice to Poles who had turned Jews over to the

Nazis. They tracked down the notorious Polish bounty hunter, Krupa, who had betrayed many Jews to the Nazis including the Schiff brothers. Word spread that Krupa was beaten until he was virtually blind and crippled before a final blow put an end to his misery. At the other extreme, there were stories of Jews emerging from their hiding places, only to be killed by Polish citizens. Sam felt there was no peace. Sometimes he was overwhelmed by feelings of shame, sorrow or pity. At other times he felt intense loathing for those who had created all the terror.

Sam tried to trace what had happened to his family. Knowing of the mass shooting on the day of the liquidation of Bobowa ghetto, he went out to the little wood at Garbacz in search of the mass grave. The horror of what had happened here felt vivid. It could never be obliterated from his mind. Now there was little to see. Grass and scrub had taken over. A profound silence protected this place where so many people had been executed. He knew that people had been buried where they fell, heaped one on top of the other. How would he ever retrieve the bodies of his father, his stepmother and his little stepbrother and stepsister? Could he ever bury his family properly? 'I cried out loud. I yelled to heaven . . .' he wrote later. He looked up through the trees, almost expecting to see some sign of their presence. Were his family there? Had not his father said, 'death is just for a little while'? Did he mean life after death? An unrecognisable sound seemed to come from his lips; a cry from the core of his being. But no soul responded to his lament; no kind embrace; no comfort. No familiar face except in his memory. Just deep silence. A slight breeze in the trees. It was incomprehensible. Why was he alive at all?[46]

After this, Sam could not bring himself to trace the fate of his beloved sister, Feigele, his brother, Moishe, and maternal grandmother, Reisel. He knew that they had been shot near the ghetto in Dukla. If he understood exactly what happened, saw the very spot, would he be able to bear it, he wondered? Or would it live on in his mind for ever, giving him no peace? It was all beyond endurance. 'I did not want to know the facts . . .' he wrote later. He felt angry and unsettled. He was utterly alone. Poland was 'nothing but a graveyard'. Whenever he thought of his situation, 'a sense of desperation gripped my mind'.[47]

Sam refused to give up on himself. He wanted to be made whole again. He must leave Poland. He befriended three older boys who also wanted to leave. At the Czech border the guard turned them back; they were just more displaced youths with nowhere to go. Sam and his travelling companions found a way to cross the border in the dead of night. Setting out across Europe, they hitched lifts across Czechoslovakia. Sam was not sure what he was seeking, what hope there might be. At least if he could reach the western side, he could continue his search for relatives. His father had talked of a distant cousin in America. 'Maybe I could get an education,' he thought.

The older boys left Sam at a Displaced Persons camp at Föhrenwald near Munich in the American sector of Germany. He was all alone again. It hit him in sickening, deadening waves. The camp was impersonal, an ex-Nazi barracks. The officers' quarters were comfortable enough and there was food, newspapers, even some classes. Sam put himself forward for any job needed. All the time, he felt utterly adrift and groundless. 'I'm relatively certain if somebody wanted me to kill somebody I would have done it. Some German or Nazi . . .' he recalls.[48]

Then he heard the British government had agreed to take

several hundred refugee orphans from the German Displaced Persons camps. Sam thought he had nothing to lose and went to register.

'Would you like to go to England and be educated?' asked the camp official.

Sam hesitated. This was the dream that had held his life together during the nightmare years. Could he believe it? Trying very hard not to give away the depth of his emotion, the words came quietly.

'Yes, sir,' he said.

14

'The school turned me back into a human being'

Fourteen-year-old Sidney Finkel, 1945

S am Oliner nearly missed his first ever flight. When the RAF came to Munich to pick up child survivors from the Displaced Persons camp, Sam was with friends in a distant camp. Luckily, fog delayed the departure. Knowing how desperately Sam wanted to be on this flight, an official intervened, tracked Sam down and arranged transport to get him to the airport with just moments to spare.

When he stepped off the plane in England, he was greeted by the flashing cameras of the newsreels and kindly Jewish officials from the Central British Fund who had obtained permission from the British government to bring up to one thousand orphaned child survivors to Britain. Sam and the other children were whisked off to a hostel for medical care and good food. After a few months, some of the children were deemed ready to restart their schooling. Tante Anna was among those approached. In the spring of 1946, she had moved her school back to Bunce Court and settled in. Could she help? Tante Anna did not hesitate.

Fifteen-year-old Sam was almost illiterate when he arrived at Bunce Court; and broken in spirit, witness to repeated acts of such horror that all his faith in human behaviour had gone. He had survived for six years by lies and deception, by toughness and self-reliance. Accustomed as he was to endless brutality, it was difficult to conceive of other ways of living. Bunce Court was completely outside his experience. He found it hard to trust, to place any kind of confidence in the seemingly well-intentioned strangers around him. Could he really believe in this apparently warm-hearted new setting or would it all be whisked away from him by some unforeseen sleight of hand? Decades later Sam could still remember his raging, turbulent feelings. 'I did not feel at peace at all,' he recalls.[1]

Tante Anna tried to find words of reassurance for each new pupil. 'I had a strong feeling that she had a keen interest in helping us,' Sam recalls. 'She would invite me to her office to talk about how I was feeling, how is school, how was I getting along . . .' He realised her eyes were giving her difficulty. Sometimes he had to stand close for her to see him since 'she couldn't see too well'.[2] Before returning to Bunce Court, Tante Anna had, in fact, suffered what she referred to as 'a very nasty accident'. Her train carriage had stopped short of the platform at Wem station and she had fallen onto the tracks, no doubt on account of her failing eyes. At the time, she felt 'lucky to be alive,' she wrote to friends.[3] Despite this, she was determined to make a difference to her new pupils' lives.

Tante Anna understood it was best for the 'concentration camp boys', as they became known, not to dwell on the past but to focus on the present and their future. In the 1940s, it was widely believed that this was the best way of dealing with extreme trauma. The case notes of each child Holocaust survivor set out the stark details of their suffering. There was no need to put them through trying to explain. 'We were basically told to forget all that bad stuff that had happened to us,' recalled one. 'This was a new day and life would begin all over again . . . and since we had been spared, we had to live a life that would make our parents proud of us.'[4]

Sam accepted this approach. He felt an immediate bond with the other new pupils who had survived the Holocaust. Along with Sam in the first group of about eight 'concentration camp boys' to arrive at Bunce Court were Erwin Buncel from Czechoslovakia, two Hungarian brothers, William and Leopold Frischmann, and a Russian camp survivor called Shaya Kushnirovski. By some unspoken code the boys recognised that they were set apart by their extreme suffering. Photographs of Sam at Bunce Court in the early months show him frequently with another boy from his own neighbourhood in Poland: Zisha Schwimmer. Zisha came from a village near Gorlice and had endured brutal labour and concentration camps during the war. Now here they were, standing by a neatly trimmed hedge in an English garden, neither Sam nor Zisha's youthful faces betraying any trace of the terrible turmoil they had lived through. Zisha has his arm around his friend, a gesture of warmth and solidarity. Nothing need be said. They shared a common background. 'I think I felt more comfortable not exposing, not telling what happened,' Sam Oliner recalls. 'It was just too painful; like living it all over again.'[5]

British pupil Anna John remembers vividly these new arrivals after the war. Sam Oliner, or 'Sammy' as she called him, was 'suddenly in our midst,' she recalls. 'He appeared with several lads from the camps and they just joined in as though they had come from across the street.' She found him 'a rather withdrawn boy, a bit overweight, believe it or not.' The teachers had tried to prepare pupils like Anna John for what to expect. The child survivors 'might be quarrelsome', Hanna Bergas had warned, because they had never been cared for, or 'they might be greedy', because they had been under-nourished for years.[6] 'We were very accepting,' recalls Anna. 'Sam did not seem to express anything of what he had been through so we English kids really had not a clue about these things . . . It was only little by little that they would say something . . .' As Anna John tried to reach out to Sam she began to sense that he 'was still raw in his mind. Every now again he would talk a little about it. We didn't know the magnitude of it.'[7]

To help them integrate, Tante Anna arranged for certain pupils to form small teams to 'adopt' one of the concentration camp boys. Language was an immediate barrier. British pupil Harold Jackson remembers making 'a terrible blunder' right away. The Holocaust survivors all spoke different languages. Apart from Sam, one of the few who spoke both Polish and German, there were children from Hungary, Czechoslovakia, Russia and Poland. 'The first question was, what language shall we teach them?' recalls Harold. 'And I said, "we all speak German, why don't we teach them German?" Well of course that went down like a lead balloon.'[8] Such was their revulsion at anything to do with the Nazis that even the few survivors who knew German were unwilling to speak it.

Initially much communication was non-verbal. Harold Jackson was part of the small team who 'adopted' the Russian survivor, Shaya Kushnirovski. 'We took him down for break-fast on the first day and Shaya looked at his bowl of cornflakes and had absolutely no idea what they were. He just sat and stared at them . . .' Harold demonstrated how to eat corn-flakes. When the time came for the boys to take a shower, there was another shock. Shaya had an enormous scar on his buttocks. The injury was so deep Harold realised it 'obviously had been a gaping wound'.[9] Shaya would not reveal what happened to him, although Harold worked out it was an injury from a bayonet.

Anna John noticed that several of the newcomers had numbers on their forearms. She had not seen the Pathé newsreels about the concentration camps. 'We did not know anything about it. It did not cross my mind that such dreadful things had happened.' Sam did not have a tattoo on his arm, but many of the others did. Anna John did not know this marked them out as former prisoners at Auschwitz.[10] Still trying to find a way to cross some invisible barrier between them, Harold Jackson felt he blundered once again when he offered to help remove Leopold Frischmann's tattoo. Leopold swore at him. It was a scar that gave meaning to his suffering and pain; a scar that marked the place where he had lost his parents; a scar for life that could never be erased. Gradually Harold came to realise that the 'sort of trauma they had been through could not be spoken about'.

As the new arrivals began to learn English, the other pupils caught unexpected glimpses of their lives under Nazi occupation. One day as the pupils were forming a line for breakfast, fifteen-year-old Erwin Buncel suddenly came out with something truly shocking, although he said it in passing, observed Anna John, as though it were entirely normal. 'He was in a row of people and every tenth person was shot – he was eight or nine – it stuck in my mind.' The few words he spoke conjured up a scene so far removed from her own experience it was hard to imagine. Anna felt instinctively: 'I'll hug you for that. I wanted to give him something . . . That was the response I always had for them.'[11]

Returning whenever he could from the army for weekends, former pupil Leslie Brent followed the progress of the concentration camp boys. He knew 'they were thought to be quite a difficult group because they were too traumatised'. The staff found that despite their best efforts, at first, the survivors 'tended to keep themselves to themselves and didn't easily make friends with the other children'. Leslie wondered if 'they were afraid of rejection possibly – that's guesswork on my part. Or they were distrustful.' In the concentration camps it could be dangerous to make friends. Leslie tried to befriend Sam and the others. He remembers trying to find ways of drawing them in, discussing light-hearted matters such as sport and the comings and goings of the school. 'Bunce Court was an extraordinary environment for them to come into from their past environment. There were no rules; no disciplinary processes. No one was forced to do anything. There was a curious kind of self-discipline that worked very well.' But that in itself could make it difficult. Like prisoners coming out of prison, he knew, there were times when they could be utterly lost.[12]

*

While there were new beginnings at Bunce Court for the child survivors, there were also some painful goodbyes. Released from the terms of their internment, much-loved refugee teachers, such as William Marckwald, were ready to restart their careers or left in search of better-paid jobs. Hanna Bergas, Hans and Hannah Meyer and Heidtsche were among those who chose to remain, determined to stand by Tante Anna. There was no further funding from the relief agencies, who prioritised urgent help to those in Displaced Persons camps on the continent. However, around sixty English boys and girls were admitted in addition to the children who had moved from Trench Hall. To help with the occasional staff shortages, Tante Anna was able to enlist some of her former pupils. Both Leslie and Eric returned when they had leave, Eric teaching maths and Leslie introducing science subjects.[13]

One day Leslie found some old chemistry equipment that had found its way to the school and never been used. As he cleaned off the dust and polished the glass, he could see it was distillation apparatus. Leslie hit upon the idea of giving the concentration camp boys a chemistry lesson – the first ever in the school. He wanted to create a little bit of magic. He would show them how to make salt crystals. Sure enough, it worked. The liquid was heated in a flask and duly changed state to a vapour, curling through the long glass tubes, before eventually it cooled, mysteriously newly born as solid pure crystals on the other side. 'They were fascinated by it,' he remembers. 'That was probably the only science lesson they ever had.'[14]

Tante Anna also recruited a specialist to help mentor the traumatised new arrivals, Dr Fridolin Friedmann, or 'Ginger', as he was known on account of his red hair. Dr Friedmann had taught at progressive schools in Germany, becoming headmaster of the school at Caputh near Potsdam, and Tante Anna was considering him to take over from herself. 'Even when he was just sitting in an armchair reading a paper, he could make a room feel homely,' according to one former colleague.[15]

After the war, Dr Friedmann had worked with traumatised child survivors while running Wintershill Hall, a reception centre near Southampton. He was familiar with the kind of difficulties that could arise. He knew children who had lived through the Holocaust could be 'terribly restless'; they were so accustomed to a life of violent change. They had survived by looking out for themselves and often showed little sense of the 'sharing or communal spirit' that was integral to Bunce Court. Trust was invariably an issue; the world had let them down too many times. Depression, too, was commonplace. 'Suddenly it will come over a child: I have no father or mother. I am alone. I do not know what will happen to me . . .' he observed. Sam found he could be suddenly overcome by the thought that he was an orphan, with no idea if he had relations anywhere in the world. Dr Friedmann also found that child survivors could have unpredictable responses. They might perhaps be 'highly critical' of any help offered. Give them a coat and they will 'object to the cut or the quality of the cloth', he explained. 'It is not lack of gratitude, it is that they worry about their futures.'[16]

Finding the right balance between acceding to the concentration camp boys' demands and reproving them if they stepped too far out of line was not easy, especially when it came to displays of aggression. All the survivors had witnessed extremes of violence, although Dr Friedmann noted, 'their terrible sufferings have not made them vicious'. Sam had struggled with feelings of aggression in the Displaced Persons camp in Munich, but not in the benign environment at Bunce Court. For others, feelings of anger were never too far from the surface. British pupil Harold Jackson remembers that two brothers who had survived the concentration camps often fought each other ferociously. One day at a football match, they started 'really seriously fighting,' Harold recalls. This time it fell to the English teacher, Mr Davis, who was referee, to decide the best course of action. He wanted to let them off but several of the pupils objected. 'I thought they should be told that's not the thing to do in English surroundings,' recalls Harold, 'lashing out at one another in the middle of a game. Mine was a very English attitude. You just didn't behave like that.' The brothers were let off, but the discussion on the pitch was enough to show them they had overstepped some crucial mark.[17]

Sometimes the staff found it justified to permit the concentration camp boys things that were counter to the general rules. 'We let them go to the town to the pictures or shopping – or at least window shopping – during work time once in a while when their craving for "freedom" became particularly strong,' remembers Hanna Bergas. They had been so restricted and locked up for years 'that they thought they would burst if denied free movement at this moment.' They angered the other children 'when they "pulled" – a Bunce Court term for choosing a generally favoured kind of sandwich from the bottom layer of a platter'; the rule was that everybody must take a piece from the top. A soothing word from a grown-up would conciliate bad feelings.[18]

Coming from a Polish village and accustomed to farming, Sam responded to the strong emphasis on the outdoor life at Bunce Court. He enjoyed the practical tasks, especially gardening. His confidence was low, but growing vegetables for the kitchen was something he could do. Tante Anna noticed his interest. She talked to him about his gardening and made sure he had a plot of his own, where he decided to grow carrots. Sam noticed that the teachers took a keen interest and were always ready to answer any questions. He responded to other acts of kind-heartedness. Miss Ney of the Jewish Refugees Committee 'made sure I got clothes, clothing that was useful for the weekend, several sets of clothing . . .' Sam knew it was all donated, but her concern about working out what would fit each boy seemed to him 'a tremendous act of kindness'. Sam also appreciated the music at Bunce Court. He found 'it calmed me down'.[19]

As Sam responded to the efforts of those around him, he became convinced there must be a more compassionate side to life. He had once felt loved. He didn't have his mother's photograph, but he could remember that feeling. Balwina, the kindly country woman, had also not let him down. Sam had promised to write to her and he was as good as his word. As Sam got to know Tante Anna, 'I had the feeling she was very genuine,' he says. He was beginning to feel here was someone he could trust. 'I didn't feel threatened,' he says. 'I felt absolutely comfortable with her right away. I felt she was motherly.' Sam had already lost two mothers, but here was someone apparently looking out for him just like a mother would.[20]

*

The numbers of Holocaust survivors at the school increased steadily, including the only girl, twelve-year-old Anna Rose from Poland. It had proved much harder for girls to survive the Holocaust than boys since they were more likely to be killed on arrival at the concentration camps. Anna never forgot the day in late summer, after three years in hiding with her older brother in Lemberg in one small room, when she arrived at Bunce Court. She and Arthur stood outside for a moment, taking in the handsome, wisteria-clad manor house and the large grounds. 'Is it possible,' she wondered, 'that we could be accepted at such a beautiful school?'[21]

After the shocking news of the death of their parents,

the Polish couple who looked after Anna and Arthur, the Krzysztalowskis, had become obsessively protective. When the war ended, their guardians had turned into their torment-ors, prolonging their captivity in the one room. Arthur had bravely devised their escape from the Krzysztalowskis and made contact with the Jewish Rescue Committee in Lemberg They had reunited Anna and Arthur with a surviving cousin who arranged their next escape, to England. Now Anna found herself standing in front of their improbable new home in the English countryside. Momentarily she felt like the heroine in one of her fairy stories. 'The change in environment was so beautiful, so total.'[22]

At first, for Anna life at Bunce Court was no fairy tale. She did not speak a word of English and her isolation was emphasised in that 'she was the only girl in the group of Holocaust survivors,' observed Harold Jackson. He was keen to help but Anna was desperately shy. As the only Pole in a dormitory full of lively English-speaking girls, inevitably she struggled. 'It was a difficult situation because they couldn't talk to me,' Anna recalls. 'Some of them spoke German, which terrified me.' She was even more puzzled to find that Tante Anna, Paula and Bertha were German. Unlike her brother, Arthur, who was soon firm friends with Sam Oliner and the other Polish concentration camp boys, sensitive Anna felt her early weeks at Bunce Court 'were filled with silence and loneliness'. She did all she could not to be noticed but soon found even that was denied her.

Not long after her arrival, Anna felt her head itching. She faced the awful realisation that she had head lice. She was too embarrassed to tell anyone and desperately tried to comb the lice out in front of the bathroom mirror, even though she was annoying everyone by always being in the bathroom. It was no use. It wasn't long before all the girls in her dormitory were scratching their heads. Anna's misery and mortification were complete.[23]

Her housemistress soon got to the bottom of the problem and every girl in Anna's dormitory had to have their head shaved, the only treatment for lice at the time. For Anna it was torture, her deep feelings of shame mingling with the painful memories of having her head shaved in the ghetto. 'It didn't help with my lack of ability to relate to them as they saw me as the one who had done this terrible thing to them,' Anna recalls. Fortunately the cook knew the answer for young ladies with hair problems. Hearing of the girls weeping at losing their hair, Heidtsche appeared with a plateful of hot jelly doughnuts, for Anna an unheard-of treat.[24]

Bertha soon understood that the new Polish girl loved stories. 'She took me to the library. That was a godsend. There were Polish books,' says Anna. She could immerse herself in a world she understood. She also has a vivid memory of the old Bunce Courtians. 'Leslie came so often, and so many of the other alums popped in and out, there was a continuity, as though they were uncles,' she says. They took a keen interest in the troubled new arrivals. 'Leslie was such a nice guy. Everybody liked him.' Gerard Hoffnung, who returned as part of a musical group, also spotted the new loner and found a unique way to help. Anna had the typical rounded stomach of a child who has suffered prolonged hunger. 'I thought I was a freak,' she says. 'Most English girls had very tight tummies. Mine was very round because of malnutrition.' She couldn't help noticing that Gerard also had a large stomach, 'though not through hunger. I think he was quite a gourmet.' Gerard sat down with her to draw her a cartoon. As it took shape, she recognised 'a little caricature of himself with his tummy in a wheelbarrow'. Anna loved it. 'Gerard was making fun of his tummy. It just spoke to me in a way that I don't think anything else could have. He was very, very funny.'[25]

Perhaps unsurprisingly, Anna loved working in the kitchen. She joined the younger children in a room off the kitchen. Before her was the astonishing sight of a huge pile of potatoes, while the homely scent of cooking wafted in from next door. 'I really looked forward to the potato peeling,' she says. It was all such a long way from the meagre gruel that Mrs Krzysztalowski had given her to eat. Pupil Helen Urbach remembers trying to make the newcomers feel at home. 'We used to sit in a circle when we were peeling the potatoes and tell stories or jokes. We would try to get them to join us, singing or talking . . .' Helen found it was hard. 'They were very quiet.'[26]

But their efforts did not go unnoticed. 'I thought Heidtsche was wonderful,' recalls Anna. 'Somehow, she made us feel part of something larger. That cooking was a very important part of life . . .' Heidtsche made her feel secure. 'We knew she would do everything to keep us as healthy and well fed as she possibly could with the scant supplies she had.' In retrospect, Anna feels the practical tasks helped with her trauma. 'The fact that we felt we were running the school, we felt useful, important and a sense that we were learning how to be grown up . . . We were made to appreciate the simple life. There was a horror of ostentation of any kind. All of this stuck with me.'[27]

But during the winter of 1947, Bunce Court was snowed in and food deliveries could no longer reach the school. Looking out across the blanket of white snow that blotted out the landscape, Anna suddenly realised the men digging them out were speaking German. They were German prisoners of war! 'I had these incredible emotions,' she remembers. Her 'feelings of hatred' towards the Germans mingled with the knowledge that these men were now their rescuers. Her greatest fear was that the food would run out, and that is exactly what happened. With supplies dwindling rapidly, even talented Heidtsche's creativity hit rock bottom. Anna recalls that in desperation the cook came up with a milk broth with Bovril. The greyish-looking soup that tasted of nothing was returned to the scullery. The temperamental cook announced she would leave. Anna spent many hours at her window, her intense fear of food running out fighting traumatic memories of the Germans. She watched and waited as the road slowly reappeared beneath the snow, food was delivered again, the cook did not resign and the Germans left: all the time she was in turmoil about her conflicting feelings.[28]

Such struggles were commonplace among the survivors. As teacher of European history, 'Ginger' Friedmann tried to ease feelings of fear and anger through classroom discussions. Any chance remark might be a pretext to open up the conversation. On one occasion, one of the Frischmann brothers happened to remark, 'If I met a German in the desert, I would not offer him a glass of water.' Such was his loathing for the Nazis that he could not act with compassion. Should the Germans be punished, Dr Friedmann asked? The older children were following the Nuremberg trials closely and he used this to explore the concept of justice. When some of the concentration camp children argued that all Nazis should be killed, he pointed out that if 'the English kill them without trial . . . then the English are no better than the Nazis themselves.'[29] They learned about this at first hand when former pupil Richard Sonnenfeldt returned to the school from Nuremberg while he was on leave.

Anna found the passing of time helped to ease her turbulent feelings. Looking back, she feels that Tante Anna's advice to focus on the future and not dwell on the past was right for the times. 'Less was known about trauma then,' she reasons. 'There were not many professional therapists and at the time, therapists really did not know how to deal with trauma and even now, it's a very, very difficult area. And let's face it, Britain had suffered terribly during the war and the only way people got through was this famous stiff upper lip and I think that Tante Anna and her sister had decided that, to get through, we needed to become as British as we could and that was the best that they could have done for us.' Even though the trauma was not discussed, she did feel 'the people understood the trauma we kids had been through and really tried to deal with it'.[30]

Anna remembers watching the British girls closely. 'I always watched Anna John and her sister, Natalie, to see how English girls behaved.' She also became firm friends with the girls in her dormitory, prompted by the discovery that one of her room-mates, dreaming of becoming a ballerina, was in possession of a pink tutu, pointe shoes, dance music and a gramophone. Anna was an excellent dancer. No English was needed. She knew many of the steps. They played the Viennese waltz records 'over and over,' she remembers, 'and we spun more or less gracefully.'[31] Anna continued to refuse to speak any German but once she had mastered English, Harold Jackson observed that she 'had a wonderful sense of humour and would turn things into a joke'. In spite of all her bad experiences, he was beginning to glimpse another side to Anna. She had a sense of fun.[32]

Anna never forgot her first spring at Bunce Court. 'I saw snow melting and crocuses and snowdrops and thought it was so beautiful I was mesmerised.' Then came primroses, daffodils, baby lambs and cherry blossom so thick it was like a pink canopy against the blue sky. 'I took my first walk alone in the nearby woods, the beauty of the delicate buds beckoned me in.' No one threw stones or called her names. 'I no longer had to fear ambush or murder. To venture out into the woods by myself, now I think what an incredible leap.' Safe and secure, 'enveloped in this totally engaging, affectionate environment,' Anna was beginning to feel 'this is what home is like'. She thought it was a 'wonderful' school.[33] Years later she realised that gradually the brave-spirited little four-year-old that she had once been was being created anew.

By the arrival of spring Sam Oliner, too, was gaining confidence with each step. His intuitive skill with animals had been spotted at Bunce Court and soon he had his own pet rabbits. 'I was one of the bigger boys and it was fun to show off these pets to the younger boys and girls.' He built his own hutches for his pets, and came alive when working in the garden, too. 'When you see the vegetables grow – and then it comes to picking them and delivering them to the kitchen.' He felt proud to take in his first crop to Heidtsche to cook. He knew this was a healing process for him, and such a striking contrast to Poland, where anyone might come along and destroy everything. He was invited to join the Bunce Court football team as right back. It was the first time Sam had ever played school games. He soon found he excelled, winning certificates for weight throwing and distance running on sports day. 'Achievement did help a little bit . . . passing a grade or getting good comments on my paper . . . also conversation, the feeling that I am somebody,' he says.[34]

Classes were not so easy at first. 'It felt hard because I compared myself to the other students and sometimes felt inferior,' says Sam. 'I didn't feel that I knew as much as they . . . I felt really so very ignorant.' He credits the Bunce Court culture for making all the difference. 'These were refugee professors. Higher educational background, multi-lingual – I felt loved because they really paid attention to us.' In addition to the kindly Dr Friedmann, 'the teacher I would go to quite a bit was HB.' Listening to her talking about the scriptures, Sam felt 'it was the first time I understood the interpretation of the Bible'. He also remembers the 'very approachable' maths teacher, Schneidy, who showed 'endless patience' demonstrating certain concepts on the blackboard.[35] Mr Archenholt, whose hobby was astronomy, 'led us in the evening to views the stars,' adds Erwin Buncel. They seemed so far away; nothing to do with humanity, remote and beautiful.[36] Although Sam remembers not all the teachers went the extra mile for the concentration camp boys. 'Heidtsche tried to teach us how to do dishes. But she was a tough lady. She would yell at you as soon as she found something wrong.'

As time passed Sam found he was changing, too. A photograph of an older Sam at Bunce Court shows him in a jaunty white jacket, his mop of light-coloured hair brushed forward in a different style. Another shows a picnic, blankets spread on the long grass; some of the girls and teachers sit on stools. Sam felt he could join in with the other children. He was no longer the outsider. He even joined in their teenage antics. The girls slept on the second floor of the main brick building, well away from the boys whose headquarters were the barracks left behind by the army. 'We agreed that one girl would tie a sheet to the bed leg and hang it out of the window,' he remembered with amusement some seventy-five years later. 'We boys sneaked up to the window and pulled on the sheet and that was the signal for the girls to get going, to sneak out of the door.' Once united, the big adventure for the boys and girls was merely to go for a walk or a long bicycle ride. On one occasion they got as far as Whitstable. 'It was really innocent,' Sam continues. Nothing more than holding hands, 'though the ending was unpleasant': the teachers were waiting on the doorstep when they returned.[37] The punishment was extra duties all round.

'Totally uneducated and forlorn' when he arrived, Sam gradually learned 'not only reading and writing but also how to cooperate, how to be kind'. Everything was done 'that enabled us to recuperate emotionally from our wartime experiences . . . The people of Bunce Court showed us love.'

The dreams that had sustained him had, at last, come true. He felt reborn. He found Tante Anna 'a farsighted and truly altruistic human being'. England was 'like reaching paradise,' he wrote years later, and at Bunce Court he had 'some of the most memorable and happy years of my entire life'.[38]

✳

Fourteen-year-old Sidney Finkel took the bus from London to Kent; it let him off in the middle of nowhere four miles from the school. His bag held a few donated clothes but little else; no memento of his early family life. He had refused to be accompanied by an adult and was feeling anxious. It was six years since he had been at school. Sidney could barely read or write in English; nor was he familiar with using a knife and fork.[39]

He walked across gentle hills and meadows, impressed by the peaceful, settled landscape, so far removed from Poland at war. Suddenly there it was: a large manor house screened by a high hedge, with a rose garden at the front. This was the place he had been told about. He was taken to see 'Miss

Anna' and was immediately taken aback. 'It's just that she was German . . .' he remembers. It was confusing. Could he trust this woman? She had an air of authority but the warmth of her greeting reassured him. 'She was really very kind,' he remembers. 'She was a very warm person.'[40] After a while, Tante Anna asked Sam Oliner to join them. She had been impressed with Sam's progress and had asked him to mentor Sidney. Sam spoke in Polish to put Sidney at ease as he showed him around the school and introduced him to others who had come from concentration camps.

Even with Sam's help, Sidney struggled to fit in. 'I felt a terrible loss – I thought I just wouldn't ever fit into society. I felt odd, a misfit,' he recalls. Feelings of aggression could flash to the surface from nowhere and Sidney was soon involved in fights. There was one German Jewish pupil who, to Sidney's astonishment, was pro-Nazi. 'He said he loved Hitler,' recalls Sidney, 'so I hit him.' There was uproar and the pupil was soon bleeding. Sam rushed over to push them apart. 'No! You can't do that,' Sam said. You have to get along with people.' Sidney was astonished. Like so many others, he had been brutalised by the Nazis and thought that surely he had done the right thing? 'Sam said "no" and that made a big impression on me.' Sidney didn't want to lose his new friend but struggled to adapt. It seemed illogical to accept someone with Nazi sympathies.[41] Sam found Sidney unbalanced and unpredictable. He was 'unstable emotionally – though we became friends,' he adds.[42]

Tante Anna sat next to Sidney at mealtimes to guide him. Accustomed as he was to wolfing down his food, he needed to understand that it was better to slow down. She showed him how to use his knife and fork, 'and made me eat the vegetables too,' he remembers. He would not touch anything green, such as salad. It took him straight back to eating grass. Not long after arriving at Bunce Court, boils erupted on his body. Tante Anna made arrangements for the doctor to come and tried to reassure Sidney about the treatment, explaining that the boils would be burst. Sidney was full of protest. 'I didn't want to go to the medical room. I didn't know what the doctor would do.' He had only had experience of people doing harm to his body; it was hard to grasp the concept of medical care. When the doctor arrived, Tante Anna made it clear he had no choice in the matter. 'She took me and stayed during the procedure. She was there too . . .' says Sidney. 'She gave me confidence. It amazed me someone would care so much. It felt good . . . By her actions, she showed she really cared.'[43]

In addition to Sam, Tante Anna enlisted Helen Urbach to help guide Sidney. Helen was the same age as Sidney and very taken with him. 'I remember him more than the others,' she said years later. 'He wouldn't really say much at first.'[44] Helen hoped that the beauty and peace of the garden and the strolls through the countryside would restore him, but Sidney pushed her away. 'Helen loved nature,' he recalls. 'For me nature had no meaning. It was all about survival. If you can't wear it or eat it what good is it?' The more Helen put herself out to help him the more he rejected her. After all, he had survived concentration camp so why did he need her help? The fact that Helen herself was reeling from the loss of her father in Auschwitz was lost on him. 'She was very nice but I didn't know how to handle things,' he recalls.

Sidney also found lessons a struggle. The other students seemed so self-assured. 'I was terrible . . . really, really, *really* behind.' First there was the question of mastering a new language. His teacher, Helga, tried to put him at his ease, her ready smile intending to reassure, without success. Sidney inevitably compared himself to the other Holocaust boys. Next to the Hungarian survivors he felt at a disadvantage, possibly even a bit jealous. 'They went to school until 1944 and had a normal life, while our life was cut off in 1939,' he says. He was beginning to wonder if he would ever fit in.[45]

But Sidney found he could respond to music. If Tante Anna could not get through to them with words, she could with music. Music was part of daily life, with Friday concerts for the whole school, impromptu recitals, Mozart, Beethoven and Brahms resounding through the rooms. 'I liked it very much,' he remembers. He loved to listen to the talented pianists such as Abe Herman, another survivor like himself. As the weeks passed, Sidney started to play the piano. He learned to read music and practised every day. As he mastered his first pieces it felt 'incredible', he remembers. One Friday in the end of his second year, Sidney was able to take centre stage and play a short piece by Mozart in front of a gathering of all the others. Tante Anna, sitting nearby, was in tears. The savage part of Sidney was slowly becoming civilised.

Sidney began to take more interest in those around him. As well as Sam, he befriended Erwin Buncel and Abe Herman. 'Abe was withdrawn, a bit of a loner, and that's what attracted me because I was too,' he continues. They never discussed their past. 'It just wasn't done. You didn't talk about it. You forget it and go on,' Sidney recalls. 'Bunce Court gave us a common thing.' Sam's patient intervention was slowly finding its mark. 'Sam was my best friend. He was a real nice loving caring guy,' Sidney recalls. 'He mentored me to get along with others and not to fight.'[46] Among Sam's collection of photographs is one of him and Sidney at Bunce Court. Sidney had given it to him years later, writing proudly on the back: 'To Sam, my friend'.

Gradually Sidney began to appreciate Bunce Court. His brother, Isaac, who was working in London, gave him ten shillings and he bought a bicycle to explore the countryside. He loved to read stories and began to ask questions in class. English grammar was still baffling but he was making progress and he reached the point where his homework was printed in the school magazine. It was a thoughtful essay expressing his fears of another war in a nuclear age.[47] He began to look beyond the Holocaust survivors' circle for friends and was enchanted by one pretty girl, Martha. 'She wasn't Jewish,' he recalls. 'She had her dark hair in pigtails . . . We liked each other.'[48]

On another occasion when he ventured out on his bicycle, he found an orchard and started eating the cherries. The orchard owner approached. Far from the ticking-off that Sidney expected, the man asked him to pick the rest of them and said he would pay him. Sidney was delighted. He picked the cherries and then raced back to the school to tell everybody. He had made some money. But Tante Anna objected. 'She had visions of me falling off a ladder,' he recalls. It was soon clear that other children wanted to join Sidney and Tante Anna relented. 'I began to belong in Bunce Court. It was a wonderful thing,' he says.

Sidney was changing. He had confidence in Tante Anna, too. 'I knew she was good. I knew she was on my side. I knew she had authority that was used in a loving way. I was sure about that.' He felt her to be 'very loving and very just'. Although Sidney didn't have the confidence to take part in the school plays, nothing would keep him away from the amphitheatre to watch. Before the school open day, an important event, he saw how hard everyone was working to make it a success. It was clear the teachers were proud of the children and wanted the day to go well. There was a feeling of solidarity, of everyone pulling together . . . and he could join in, too. The play was *My Heart's in the Highlands* by William Saroyan, and it became Sidney's favourite. He loved feeling part of the big day. 'Everyone joined in,' he remembers. 'I began to feel I loved the school . . . The school saved me.'[49]

As he became more outgoing, Sidney had the idea of holding a big school dance. There could be music and dancing and everyone having fun . . . But Tante Anna held out against the idea. Influenced perhaps by the more formal behaviours of her youth, to her such an event seemed improper. Over her years as head teacher, Tante Anna had held concerts, recitals, plays, even operas. But might Form IV's plan for a 'Grand Ball' led by Sidney be a little forward for her boys and girls? Possibly she felt awkward for herself.[50]

But Sidney was turning into quite a gentleman. Everyone supported him. The older girls enthusiastically taught him how to dance and helped him with his social skills. Others too blossomed, such as Anna Rose. 'I loved to dance,' she recalls. 'My cousin had taught me some steps in Poland.' She started showing the others. The girl who had survived the Holocaust and initially seemed such a misfit suddenly found herself at the centre of it all with all the moves.[51] The sewing room was busy, Hanna Bergas observed, as girls eagerly converted anything they could into 'lovely evening dresses'. The hall was festooned with coloured chains. Sidney set about finding dance music. Staff brought in gramophone records. Harold found the perfect role as a learner broadcaster. Too shy to dance, he planned on being in the upstairs room in charge of putting on the records, introducing each one with some witticism. He went through them all with the English teacher, Mr Davis, and prepared what he could say.

As the excitement grew, in the end, Tante Anna found she was able to overcome her objections. After one particularly rowdy, impromptu Boys' House party, which elicited 'cautioning as to "decorous" behaviour,' recalled one pupil, Robert Simpson, Tante Anna had a change of heart and 'reluctantly' agreed. It was 'a bloodless revolution,' he says. 'Ballroom dancing was officially sanctioned.'[52]

On the big night of the 'Grand Ball', Sam remembers dressing as smartly as he could. 'It was stylish,' he remembers. 'You were supposed to wear your best shirt.' On the dance floor, budding relationships hitherto discreetly hidden from Tante Anna began to emerge into the limelight. Both Eric and Leslie had fallen in love. 'It all happened in a trice,' recalls Leslie fondly. 'I was in uniform and came down the staircase as the school was assembled at dinner time.' There she was at Tante Anna's table, 'wearing for some reason, a traditional Dutch costume and cap which was extremely fetching . . . it was love at first sight.' Her name was Karin Jonker, and she was a young Dutch woman who had just joined the school as a housemother.[53]

Eric was in love with another new housemother called Catriona. Younger children watched how the older students behaved as they asked their girlfriends to dance. Mia Schaff, still suffering teenage crushes, was now 'totally in love with Eric,' who she considered very dashing.[54] But Mia had admirers of her own, including a British pupil, John Lewis, whom she would later marry.

For Sam, it was all a world away from his wartime childhood in Poland. Here he was with his future before him, for the first time in his life about to ask a girl for a dance. Anna Rose has a vivid impression of Sam that evening. She watched, almost disbelieving, as he walked across the ballroom floor to ask *her*. She was convinced he was 'taking pity on his best friend's sister'. It made no difference. She was delighted. He led her onto the floor. 'I don't remember the conversation,' she says. 'Teenage boys didn't have much to do with the younger girls but we looked up to Sam.'[55] Sidney watched as the older boys found partners and then braced himself to copy the others. He plucked up the courage to seek out Martha. 'Would you like to dance?' he asked. He was thrilled when Martha accepted.[56]

And as Tante Anna heard the excitement all around her at the ballroom dance that she had not quite approved of, she could see little but a vague blur of colour and movement, music weaving through the gaiety and sounds of delight. She understood that it really was a joyous event. Her children were growing up. It seemed to encapsulate what her life stood for. She knew they were not all fully recovered, but they were making new beginnings. These were her children and their heroism stood as a flag for all humanity.

Epilogue

Some of Tante Anna's pupils believe that the very characteristics that led her to create and lead her school with
such drive and certainty may also have contained her key
weakness. It was hard for her to conceive of Bunce Court
being run any other way. Dr Friedmann was considered as a
potential successor, but 'Tante Anna could not accept a
person with new ideas,' Leslie thought, 'and so it never
worked out'.[1] Other pupils are convinced a suitable candidate
never came forward. In some indefinable way, Anna was
irreplaceable. Others still believe that the school was of its
time, saving hundreds of children from the continent, but
could not continue in the same way after the war. Whatever
the case, to the disappointment of many, in July 1948 the
doors to Bunce Court finally closed.

In a solemn ceremony, pupils and teachers gathered to mark
the event. Tante Anna thanked the staff who had generously
supported her 'and caught the spirit that she was trying to
instil'. There was a vote of thanks for those who had been at
the school the longest: Hanna Bergas, Paula, Bertha, Heidtsche,
and Hans and Hannah Meyer, 'whose spirit blended with
Tante Anna's own vitality and wisdom,' said former student
Wolfgang Hermann. In sombre mood, pupils rose one by one
to express their appreciation for Tante Anna's lifetime's work,
an achievement 'of almost heroic proportions,' said one.[2] For
many the school was the only home they had ever had. There
was a feeling that something irreplaceable was being lost.

Eric and Leslie were feeling desolate. For months they had fought hard to keep the school open, even contemplating taking it over themselves. But both had embarked on university degrees after leaving the army and, after much soul-searching, had concluded that they were not in a position to take it on. The school was 'not just a home,' said Eric. 'There must have been something more than this which made it intolerable for us to imagine that one day there would be no more Bunce Court, and that all that it stood for should pass away.' He tried to define the Bunce Court spirit, that 'invisible force that tied together groups of children coming from totally different surroundings', and resolved that 'someday, somehow, somewhere, we shall build up a new Bunce Court, a school which shall embody as many of the qualities and characteristics of Bunce Court as possible . . .'[3] Then Hans lit a fire on the sports grounds and everyone gathered round for the last time.

Tante Anna retired to the isolation hut and was cared for by her sister, Paula, and former pupils, who visited frequently. Freed from the responsibility of the day-to-day running of the school, she seemed more relaxed, and friendships deepened as she guided her children in their next steps in the outside world. She would go to great lengths, making contacts, finding suitable openings and writing letters of recommendation. Nothing was too much trouble. Leslie has a vivid recollection of her comfortable sitting room, filled with plants, Anna herself ensconced in an armchair, her knitting at her side. Devoted to the woman who had become family to him, he used to go whenever he could and read to her, 'because by that time she was virtually blind,' he recalls.[4]

Tante Anna lived long enough to help launch the children's careers but died in 1960, before many of them had achieved their greatest successes. From modest beginnings as a lab technician in Birmingham, Leslie Brent went on to study under the leading immunologist Peter Medawar, who won the 1960 Nobel Prize for advances in understanding immune tolerance. 'It was his (Leslie's) PhD thesis, not mine, that won the prize,' Peter Medawar acknowledged.[5] Sam Oliner became a professor at Humboldt State University in California, where he founded the Altruistic Behaviour Institute, specialising in the study of tolerance and altruism. He has taught about the Holocaust and international race relations for over thirty years, inspiring a new generation with a more compassionate perspective. Anna Rose also settled in California, where she was eventually elected city auditor in Berkeley. Sidney Finkel became a successful Chicago businessman and, in recent years, has given many moving talks on his experiences of the Holocaust and the importance of confronting one's fears.

Among those Bunce Courtians who escaped from Europe before the war, after the Nuremberg trials Richard Sonnenfeldt went on to have a scientific career, culminating in responsibility for the computers used in NASA's lunar landings. When Frank Auerbach left Bunce Court he continued with acting for a while before enrolling at St Martin's School of Art. He never looked back and is now recognised as one of Britain's foremost contemporary painters. Others who rose to acclaim from Bunce Court's unusual educational regime include the playwright Frank Marcus, the film-maker Michael Roemer, and the impresario and raconteur Gerard Hoffnung, whose amusing performance at the Oxford Union in 1958 on a bricklayer's misfortunes is cited even today as a witty satire on the British stiff upper lip. Mia Schaff and Susie Shipman both settled in Britain and married and have families of their own. Among the British pupils, Harold Jackson started his career as a messenger boy at the *Guardian*. His flair for languages was soon spotted by the foreign editor who happened to find him reading the European papers. This led to him being given a break as a reporter and he rose to become an acclaimed foreign correspondent.

*

Despite their outward successes, for most of the pupils there was a long, painful journey to come to terms with the past. Leslie Brent was one of many who had lost all their family. He retraced their last steps, longing to know what happened to his parents and sister. While serving in the British army in Germany after the war, he tracked down Arthur and Charlotte's last address from their Red Cross messages. 'We drove through Berlin on these very bad roads, full of holes,' he remembers. 'Berlin was in indescribable ruins.' It was a surprise to find the shabby apartment block near the railway still standing in all the post-war desolation of bombed-out Berlin. Anxiously, he made his way to the third floor and knocked on the door. The woman who answered was unwelcoming. She knew nothing, she said curtly, and shut the door.

Leslie made his way to Berlin's makeshift town hall. In all this chaos, there was a department dealing with records. A clerk went to search through the archives. The Nazis had kept forms; so many people whose lives were reduced to just a name or a number on a list in a file somewhere. It took time before the clerk returned. There was news. He had found their names: Arthur, Charlotte and his sister, Eva, listed merely as 'sent east'. What did that mean? The clerk could not say. The best guess was that they died in a concentration camp somewhere, probably Auschwitz. The absence of exact information, the element of uncertainty, made it hard for Leslie to come to terms with their deaths. Whenever footage was shown of concentration camps, he still found himself searching among the ruined faces. Could his family be among them? Would they find a way to get in touch with him through Bunce Court?

It was not until 1976 that he finally visited Auschwitz. Still there was no proof, no name, no certainty. But with the passage of time, he had come to terms with their fates. He stood in front of the huge memorial and, for the first time, suddenly found himself weeping, a lament that seemed to contain years of pain discreetly hidden behind the charm and politeness that he presented to society and his brilliant scientific career. 'It was quite a shattering moment when I broke down,' he recalls. 'I didn't have a grave for Mum and Dad, and I didn't know where they died. I thought at last I've found their place of death.' He placed his white roses and tried to piece himself together before rejoining his friend.[6]

It was only when the Berlin Wall fell in 1989 that he finally uncovered the truth. The Berlin Archives Office had access to many more documents. His family did not die at Auschwitz. In October 1942, Arthur, Charlotte and Eva were on Transport 44 with 897 other Jewish people. They left Berlin in crammed wagons from Güterbahnhof goods station for the three-day journey to Riga in Latvia. The records show everyone was shot in the woods on arrival. 'They probably had to dig their own graves first,' says Leslie. The Nazi form for his sister, Eva, still survives. She was required to list details of her possessions. Leslie was shocked to see Eva had nothing but the clothes she stood up in. It was painful to grasp the extent of his family's degradation before they left Berlin and how much they concealed from him in their last short Red Cross message to Bunce Court. They must have had a pretty good idea of what lay ahead, he says, and 'the letter shows such restraint'. They could not even write 'goodbye'.

Later Leslie learned that it was possible that Eva, as a trained paediatric nurse, did not have to accompany their parents on their last trip. It was her heroic choice to accompany her parents to the end. 'It is one of my greatest horrors that she did not survive,' he recalls.[7] He tried to find out more. He wrote to the hospital in a Berlin suburb where she worked. There were no records; nothing, as though her very existence had been wiped out.

Leslie no longer feels anger about what happened. 'It's grief more than anger,' he says, but a grief that in his ninetieth decade still held sway. In 2019, even when he was close to death himself and travel was impossible, he struggled with the hope that he could make one last pilgrimage to his family's resting place in the Latvian woods. One last chance to say goodbye.[8]

*

For other pupils such as Sam Oliner and Sidney Finkel, who had suffered extreme trauma during the war, their time at Tante Anna's school was just the starting point of their journey of recovery. For Sidney, this path did not run smoothly. He emigrated to America, where outwardly he appeared to have all the trappings of success, but there were setbacks. His first marriage ended in divorce and he suffered from bouts of heavy drinking, 'though he's been sober now for forty years,' explains his daughter, Ruth Wade.[9] Ruth believes his problems were due to his Holocaust childhood. For many years Sidney was burdened by gruesome childhood memories, an essential part of who he was, but so painful he could not speak a word to a soul, even his own wife. There was no release, no way of blotting out the smouldering hurt, barely hidden in some subterranean part of his mind. Sidney utterly rejected anything to do with his wartime childhood; nor would he speak of it to his children, fearing to inflict his pain on them. He married for a second time and his family continued to grow, with five children. It was not until his daughter, Ruth, was grown-up and about to have a child of her own that it became clear to him from her insistent questioning that she had a keen desire to understand what had happened. What was this burden that had invaded her father's very soul? 'We didn't know anything,' says Ruth.[10]

Fifty years after his childhood experiences of the Holocaust, he drove to Champaign, Illinois and spoke to his pregnant daughter. A lifetime's pain was unleashed. Ruth felt grateful. She felt she loved her father even more. His family was a gift. 'I had a grandmother named Faiga, a grandfather named Laib, and two new aunts, Ronia and Frania,' she said.[11] She tried to picture them. Ronia, the brilliant young woman who was murdered for having her baby outside the ghetto. Frania, the loving teenager who could not bear her adored mother to face transportation alone. Now Ruth embraced their short lives and longed to know more. Their bravery and heroism in face of the Nazi slaughtering machine was of immense significance. She felt strongly that their suffering must not be in vain.

In 1994 the whole family went together to the new Holocaust Museum in Washington. Conjured up before them were fragments of their father's past made real, but still unimaginable, the visitors around them stunned into silence as they saw the exhibits. Suddenly Sidney glimpsed a railroad cattle car ahead. For him, this was the moment when past terrors flooded back with such volcanic force he could have been that boy in the cattle cars with the SS guards. Tears were streaming down his face. Everything he had suppressed was real again. The whole family hugged him. Visitors waited in respectful silence, as though they understood. Later, in the Hall of Remembrance, they lit memorial candles. Sidney felt that after all these years he had, with his family's help, at last found a place of peace in his mind for his mother, father and sisters, Ronia and Frania.[12]

When he had found the courage to confront his fears and tell his family, it became important for Sidney to tell others, to make sure the next generation understood what is meant by the Holocaust; that humanity never forgets what it is to endure such hatred and evil. Released from half a century of silence, he wanted to share his experiences and gave talks to many schools. But the trauma of his last encounter with his father, Laib, could still catch him unawares, overwhelming him with unassuageable feelings. 'I felt very, very, very guilty,' he says. In spite of years of therapy, he couldn't get past the horror of their last encounter.[13]

On the 66th anniversary of the liberation of Buchenwald, Sidney went back with his wife, son and daughter. They entered the gates of the camp, past the loathsome Nazi sign, '*Jedem das Seine*', or 'To each what he deserves'. It was a grey day. Much of the complex had been levelled, the ground on which rows and rows of barracks once stood now blanketed in gravel. Sidney asked them to follow as he found the very place in this vast compound where he had last seen his father. The family had travelled a long way to stand on the exact spot, and now there was nothing to see. They formed a circle, arms on each other's shoulders, 'and we spoke to my dad,' says Sidney. All around was a numbing silence, in his mind the horror of the past alive. There was his father, starving, indescribably altered, lavishing his last piece of bread on his son . . . But now he was bringing something back. 'I know that you can feel,' he heard himself say, 'so here I am with your grandchildren. I can see you smiling and embracing and how happy you are that I survived, that you have these wonderful grandchildren, that you live with my spirit and that I loved you . . .'[14]

For Sidney, the experience brought acknowledgement of everything that had happened. It helped to validate everything he and his father had been through. 'I know my father absolutely adored me,' he says. For years the good memories had been blotted out by the bad. Now it was possible to get back to the years before the war and see his father taking him as a young boy on business trips, coming from the factory specially to pick him up in the car, which was an exciting novelty. He could remember the camaraderie of father and son, the happy-go-lucky spirit of the times, that feeling of certainty that came from being loved. Above all, he wanted his father to know that he loved him. He felt he had his father's forgiveness for their last encounter in Buchenwald. As for the question of whether he is healed, 'I am not sure I ever truly changed,' he admits. 'I'm just more tolerant of things.'[15]

*

When Sam Oliner left Bunce Court in 1948 and embarked on working life as an apprentice in London, once again, he became filled with an overpowering sense of loneliness. His mission to find out about surviving relatives, however distant, assumed some urgency. To his delight, his father's distant cousin, Saul Oliner, answered his advertisement and urged him to come to America. Sam worked for Saul before he was drafted and sent to serve in the Korean War. It was only when he returned that he could begin afresh. After Bunce Court, he saw acquiring knowledge as 'my key', he says. 'I knew I wanted to advance my learning as soon as I possibly could.'[16] Taking advantage of the GI Bill, he began with a BA and then progressed to a PhD at the University of California before finally taking a teaching position at Humboldt State University, where he is still, at ninety, an emeritus professor.

Along the way, Sam endeavoured to reconcile with his past. On a trip back to Poland in the 1980s, he longed to see his rescuer, Balwina. She had saved him and here he was, a grown man with a loving wife, Pearl, a young family and successful career. He wanted to tell Balwina what she meant to him, to thank her and embrace her; but she had already died. Sam searched out her son, Staszek, who had been crucial to his cover when he posed as Sam's 'brother'. It was an emotional reunion. Gradually Staszek helped Sam piece together information about his family. As a child after the war, Sam had felt unable to retrace his footsteps to his maternal grandmother's farm in Zyndranowa, high in the Carpathian Mountains. Almost fifty years elapsed before he could bring himself to go back. His maternal grandparents, Reisel and Isak, his brother, Moishe, and his sister, Feigele, were among seven hundred Jews slaughtered on 13 August 1942 in a pit in the local forest. Beautiful, gentle Feigele, who in all innocence as a child he had escorted to the local Gestapo headquarters. What life had she had? As they approached the spot in the forest where the pit had been dug, Sam asked

Pearl and their Polish escort to wait. There were no words for the intense pain he felt. His lament was visceral. 'I broke out into loud screaming,' he wrote in his memoirs.[17]

Sam's great-uncle's house was all that remained of his family in Zyndranowa. It was a broken-down shack, little more than a ruin. With local support, Sam made arrangements to turn it into a museum. There had been Jews in Poland for a thousand years but now little remained. Sam wanted to acknowledge the lives that had been cut short and honour them. After his speech on the day of the museum opening, he was approached by someone who had known him growing up. Sam was astonished to learn someone in the village had photographs. As a child, Sam had risked his life going back into the liquidated ghetto at Bobowa to search for the precious photograph of his mother. Now his research brought him a picture of his grandfather, Isak, with his chestnut-coloured horse. Sam never found a picture of his mother but he did meet a distant cousin, Joe, who could bring some reality to the lost childhood locked in his memory. Joe described Sam's father as 'happy-go-lucky' and his mother as 'beautiful and very gentle'.[18] Piece by piece, fragment by fragment, Sam put their lives back together in his mind.

Even after years of searching and all the visits back to Poland, Sam still felt 'that I am not ok. There's something not ok about me, some sort of guilt about me,' he said in 1994 to his Shoah interviewer.[19] His years of study of the Holocaust at Humboldt State University in California led him to focus not on the evil, but on the good: the heroism of rescuers who selflessly saved others, often at risk of death. His American friends accused him of being a workaholic. For Sam it was urgent to understand 'altruism, compassion and infusing caring into society'. At his institute, his team interviewed thousands to understand the motivation of altruistic individuals. He disagrees with those who claim that altruism does not exist, that it is merely some form of self-interest in disguise. Sam feels he owes his life to the altruism of others. For him, altruism is a powerful characteristic, an aspect of humanity that he sees as 'essential for the survival of the planet'. Selflessness, compassion and empathy can be taught and nurtured, he argues, in schools, alongside academic subjects. He has a firm conviction that the world can be a better place. For him selflessness is deeply human; at its best, a transformational act of love.[20]

Studying 'goodness' was also self-healing. Sam has been repeatedly asked in lectures whether he still hates the Germans. 'Hate is self-destructive,' he replies. 'It does not help heal the pain . . . healing and forgiveness are possible.'[21] But after a lifetime of researching altruism he still feels something is missing. Has he completely forgiven the Nazis who destroyed his family and took away his childhood? 'Not really,' he replies with brutal honesty. 'When you forgive you also forgive yourself . . . you relieve your pain.' There are moments when Sam in his heart still feels the pain.

*

Tante Anna had long since passed away when in 1987 Julia Miller and her family bought part of the old house of Bunce Court in Kent. Julia had no idea it had once been a school, although she sensed a special feeling there, as though, she says, a benign spirit somehow pervaded its very fabric. Even though the handsome old manor was in decline once again and had been split into four dwellings, inexplicably Julia

sensed something wonderfully good about the place, something blessed and happy. The Millers bought the central
section of the old house, once the school's dining room and
hallway.

As she and her family settled in, they were surprised by
the number of visitors. Sometimes Julia would come across
people at the front gate, discreetly looking over the high
hedge, even bringing their families. She invited them in and
showed them round, gradually piecing together the story of
Tante Anna's school. Here was a hidden history, almost lost,
existing only in the minds of grateful former pupils who
came from all over the world. Julia was amazed at their
reverence for Bunce Court. 'It was like entering hallowed
ground,' said former pupil Martin Lubowski as he walked
the path to the front door.

Deeply touched by the story, Julia opened her doors for
Bunce Court reunions as former pupils sought to honour
Tante Anna. They brought back the old school bell, resur-
rected with due ceremony to its original position and rung
with some delight by Hans Meyer. Much thought also went
into a plaque for Tante Anna. Leslie was among those who
oversaw every detail; he had long championed her cause and
wanted every detail to be just right. For the unveiling ceremony many former pupils gathered from across the world
with their families. Leslie gave a moving speech and then the
plaque was unveiled for Tante Anna, 'who gave a home and
a sound education to hundreds of refugee children . . . remembered with affection by so many for her great foresight,
progressive educational endeavour, wisdom and compassion'.
Julia understood that this was a way of bringing back all
that had been lost; of thanking Tante Anna for all that she
had given them. For her, there is a feeling of peace that

pervades Bunce Court. 'Long after all of us have gone, I utterly believe that all of that feeling will remain (in the walls),' she says. 'I like to think that it is due to the spirit of Tante Anna and the school. I utterly believe it. All of that resolve, all of that trauma, all the good – it's such a good feeling, we have always felt that.'[22]

Many of the survivors acknowledge how they felt sustained by the frequent Bunce Court reunions. Although dispersed, they met often, becoming the supportive family that so many of them no longer had. 'We were like brothers and sisters,' says Helen Urbach. 'I used to go to England almost every year to see everyone . . . We had lived together for all those years and had so much in common. I just loved everyone,' she says. As for Tante Anna, 'what she did was wonderful and saved lots of lives.'[23] Harold Jackson marvels that so many of her nine hundred former pupils became leading figures in their professions. 'An amazing track record for an institution that seldom had two pennies to rub together.'

One of those who spoke at the plaque-unveiling ceremony in 2007 was Hansjörg Greimel, a former teacher from Ulm who has led the recognition for Tante Anna in her home country. As Germany comes to terms with its past, there is growing recognition of Anna Essinger and two Schools have now been named after her. Ironically, for years the museum at Herrlingen commemorated Field Marshal Rommel. People came to see his country retreat at the former Herrlingen School, from where the famous German general drove to his enforced suicide. 'But we wanted to give equal weight to one of Nazi Germany's foremost educational pioneers,' explains Hansjörg, the museum's curator. In November 2019 the museum at Herrlingen created a permanent exhibition in belated recognition of Anna Essinger. 'Tante Anna's school is the most famous German school in exile suppressed by the Nazis,' he says. It provided a unique experience in progressive education, where with minimal resources, children who had experienced the very worst of humanity were given a profound appreciation of the beauty and magnitude of human achievements.[24]

Tante Anna's efforts hold up a mirror to a different world. 'We weren't coddled', observes Anna Rose. 'We lived a very simple life but we were never without the things that were necessary for us.' Tante Anna created a 'can do' culture, where with minimal resources, children took responsibility for their school while teachers reached for the stars to make a world worth fighting for feel real for them. Today's children sometimes report increasing mental health problems, but Tante's Anna's school appeared to help build strong mental and emotional foundations against impossible odds. Her success raises questions about whether her pioneering educational methods still have something to offer for children today. 'I can never understand why more schools are not run on a similar basis', muses Anna Rose.[25]

Tante Anna did not attach any names to what she did or the standards she lived by. Nor did she write any grand theories setting out her ideas on education. Her story could easily be lost to us, existing as it does principally in the minds of her elderly former students. She has been overlooked by a history frequently beguiled by male-dominated narratives of power and decision-makers. But Anna's story arguably stands for the efforts of generations of women in history. She is a symbol of caring and loving; qualities that are just as important in shaping human history though much more easily overlooked. As women increasingly ask, 'where is our place in history?' – perhaps the time has come where narratives such as Anna's can be celebrated in their own right.

Anna herself may have been short-sighted to the point of blindness, but she had a far-sighted vision, and nothing, not even Hitler, was going to get in her way. As she grappled with the destructive forces of a cataclysmic epoch and her school became a mirror of European catastrophes, she herself had to find reserves of strength beyond the ordinary. Not seeking anything for herself, she tried to show her pupils a path that would lead them away from pain and hatred towards healing and love. Without subscribing to the Jewish faith, she fulfilled in her own unique way the old Hebrew saying, *'Tikkun Haolam'* – 'mend the world'.

Notes

Prologue

1 Oliner, Samuel, *Narrow Escapes: A Boy's Holocaust Memories and their Legacy,* Paragon House, Minnesota, US, 1979, p. 6
2 Dr Samuel P. Oliner, interview 14 January 1994, United States Holocaust Memorial Museum Collection
3 Oliner, Samuel, *Narrow Escapes,* p. 8
4 Dr Samuel P. Oliner, interview 14 January 1994, United States Holocaust Memorial Museum Collection
5 Ibid
6 Oliner, Samuel, *Narrow Escapes,* p. 162 & p. 167
7 Dr Samuel P. Oliner, interview 14 January 1994, United States Holocaust Memorial Museum Collection & Oliner, Samuel, *Narrow Escapes,* p. 14

Introduction

1 Essinger, Paula, *Die Geschichte des Landschulheims Herrlingen/Bunce Court*, memoirs recorded 1968, Wiener Holocaust library, Bunce Court Collection, Box 11
2 Bourne, Eric, *A European Life*, Bank House Books, New Romney, UK, 2012, p. 11
3 Author interviews with Leslie Brent
4 Author interview with Ruth Danson, 24 January 2019, p. 5

5 Author interview with Sam Oliner, 30 September 2019, p. 4

6 Oliner, Samuel, *Narrow Escapes,* p.167

7 Finkel, Sidney, *Sevek and the Holocaust: The Boy who Refused to Die,* self-published, printed by Thomson-Shore, Illinois, 2006, pp. 85–86 & 91–92

8 Ibid p. 92

9 Author interview, Anna Rabkin, 9 September 2020, p. 11

Chapter 1

1 Max Kantorovitz to his parents, 5 November 1932, Wiener Library, 2018/9 Box 17, translated by Quirin Luebke

2 Fast, Vera K. *Children's Exodus: A History of the Kindertransport*, I.B. Tauris, London, 2011, p. 4–5

3 Max Kantorovitz to his parents (undated), Wiener Library, 2018/9 Box 17

4 Author interview, Hansjörg Greimel

5 Anna Essinger, *Bunce Court School, 1933–1943*, p. 1 & Anna Essinger exhibition, Herrlingen Museum

6 Wiener Library, 2018/9, Box 11, Paula, *Memoirs*

7 Schachne, Lucie, *Education towards Spiritual Resistance: The Jewish Landschulheim Herrlingen* 1933–1939, Verlag, Frankfurt, 1988, pp. 33–34

8 Author interview, Hansjörg Greimel

9 *Oberer Kuhberg, Human Dignity is Inviolable,* p. 6, Herrlingen Museum

10 Louise Avery, archivist, Gordonstoun

11 Bailey, Brenda, *A Quaker Couple in Nazi Germany*, Sessions, York, 1994, p. 38

12 Potten, Dorle, *Des Kindes Chronik*, privately published, pp. 19–21

13 Ibid pages 8 & 150

14 Smith, Lyn, *Heroes of the Holocaust: Ordinary Britons who Risked their Lives to Make a Difference*, Random House, London, 2013, p. 32

15 Wiener Library, 2018/9, Box 11, Paula Essinger, *Memoirs*, p. 1

16 Bailey, Brenda, *A Quaker Couple in Nazi Germany*, Sessions, York, 1994, p. 7

17 *Education Under Hitler, The New Statesman and Nation*, 3 June 1933, pp. 725–6

18 Neill, A.S. *Summerhill*, Victor Gollancz, London, 1962, pp. 23–4

19 Wiener Library, 2018/9, Box 11, Paula, *Memoirs*, p. 2

20 Translation of Anna Essinger Exhibition, Herrlingen Museum, courtesy Hansjörg Greimel

21 *Anna's Children*, produced by Angelika Schubert, Peter Schubert & Gabrielle Krober, 1994

22 Potten, Dorle, *Des Kindes Chronik*, privately published, p. 151

23 *Anna's Children*, 1994

24 Bergas, Hanna, *Fifteen Years lived among, with and for Refugee children*, 1979, Palo Alto, California, unpublished memoir, pp. 1–2

25 Friedlander, Saul, *Nazi Germany and the Jews: The Years of Persecution, 1933–39*, Weidenfeld and Nicolson, London, 1997, pp. 28–30

26 Bergas, Hanna, *Fifteen Years lived among, with and for Refugee children*, 1979, Palo Alto, California, unpublished memoir, pp. 1–2

27 Major, Alan, *Bunce Court, Anna Essinger and her New Herrlingen School, Bygone Kent*, vol. 10, no. 8, p. 550 & Rabkin, Anna, *From Krakow to Berkeley: Coming out of Hiding*, p. 60

28 New Herrlingen School Guide

29 *Einstein and Ulm*, p. 22, Herrlingen Museum

30 Author interview, Hansjörg Greimel

31 Schachne, Lucie, *Education towards Spiritual Resistance: The Jewish Landschulheim Herrlingen 1933–1939*, Verlag, Frankfurt, 1988, pp. 32–33 & 37–9

32 Kubler, pp. 87–97, Herrlingen Museum

33 Wiener Library, 2018/9, Box 11, Paula Essinger, *Memoirs* p. 4 & interview 5, Hansjörg Greimel

34 Bergas, Hanna, *Fifteen Years lived among, with and for Refugee children*, 1979, Palo Alto, California, unpublished memoir, p. 4

35 Ibid

36 Anna Essinger, *Bunce Court School, 1933–1943*, p. 2

37 Bergas, Hanna, *Fifteen Years lived among, with and for Refugee children*, 1979, Palo Alto, California, unpublished memoir, p. 6

Chapter 2

1 Wiener Library, 2018/9, Box 14 Reflections on Bunce Court, Hanna Bergas & Maria Dehn

2 New Herrlingen School Guide

3 NA/Ed 35/4723, Anna Essinger, 29 January 1933

4 Wiener Library, 2018/9, Box 14 First impressions of Bunce Court, Eric Bourne

5 Bourne, Eric, *A European Life*, pages 1, 7 & 15

6 *Reflections, Bunce Court*, Hadlum printers, 2004, p. 96

7 Anna Essinger, *Bunce Court School, 1933–1943*, p. 10

8 Bergas, Hanna, *Fifteen Years lived among, with and for Refugee children*, 1979, Palo Alto, California, unpublished memoir, p. 9

9 Wiener Library, 2018/9, Box 11, Paula Essinger, *Memoirs*, p. 3

10 Major, Alan, *Bunce Court, Anna Essinger and her New Herrlingen School, Bygone Kent*, vol. 10, no. 8 pages 551 & 553

11 Wiener Library, 2018/9, Box 11, Paula Essinger, *Memoirs*, p. 5

12 Major, Alan, *Bunce Court, Anna Essinger and her New Herrlingen School, Bygone Kent*, vol. 10, no. 8, p. 551

13 Anna Essinger, *Bunce Court School, 1933–1943*, p. 2

14 NA/Ed 109/2514 Report of Education of New Herrlingen School, Otterden, Kent, 1937, Board of Education, pages 2, 4, 11

15 Wiener Library, 2018/9, Box 9, Stoatley Rough School, Anniversary Reunion, (2004) pages 8 & 11

16 Louise Avery, archivist, Gordonstoun

17 Wiener Library, 2018/9, Box 2, Hanna Bergas speech (1948)

18 Brent, Leslie Baruch, *Sunday's Child? A Memoir*, p. 49 & author interview, Joseph Meyer

19 Potten, Dorle, *Des Kindes Chronik*, privately published, p. 160

20 *Reflections, Bunce Court*, Hadlum printers, 2004, Lucas Mellinger, p. 80

21 Wiener Library, 2018/9, Box 11, Paula Essinger, *Memoirs*, p. 9

22 Major, Alan, *Bunce Court, Anna Essinger and her New Herrlingen School, Bygone Kent*, vol. 10, no. 9, p. 627

23 NA/Ed 35/ 4723; AE to Board of Education, 12.10.34; Memorandum, Mr Hankin, 17 December 1934 & 20 February 1935; Letter Mr Rokeling to AE, 14 March 1935

24 Gilbert, Martin, *Kristallnacht: Prelude to Destruction*, Harper Collins, London, 2006, pages. 120 & 123

25 Schachne, Lucie, *Education towards Spiritual Resistance: The Jewish Landschulheim Herrlingen 1933–1939*, Verlag, Frankfurt, 1988, pp. 47–48 & 53–57
26 Ibid p. 58
27 Ibid pages 115 & 197–200

Chapter 3

1 Author interview 1, 20 December 2018, Leslie Brent, pp. 1–2
2 Ibid & Brent, Leslie Baruch, *Sunday's Child? A Memoir*, pages 16 & 19
3 Author interview 4, 12 November 2019, Leslie Brent, pp. 1–3
4 Author interview 4, pp. 4–5 & interview 2, 4 February 2019, Leslie Brent, p. 8
5 Brent, Leslie Baruch, *Sunday's Child? A Memoir*, p. 18
6 Potten, Dorle, *Des Kindes Chronik*, privately published, pp. 36–7
7 Wiener Library, 2018/9, Box 9, Stoatley Rough School, Anniversary Reunion, (2004) p. 15
8 Evans, Richard J. *The Third Reich in Power, 1933–1939*, Penguin, 2005, pages 263 & 265
9 *Education Under Hitler, The New Statesman and Nation*, 3 June 1933, pp. 725–6 & 10 June 1933, pp. 758–9 & 787
10 Schachne, Lucie, *Education towards Spiritual Resistance: The Jewish Landschulheim Herrlingen 1933–1939*, Verlag, Frankfurt, 1988, pages 59 & 128
11 Potten, Dorle, *Des Kindes Chronik*, privately published, p. 84
12 Friedlander, Saul, *Nazi Germany and the Jews: The Years of Persecution, 1933–39*, Weidenfeld and Nicolson, London, 1997, pages 122 & 161

13 Potten, Dorle, *Des Kindes Chronik*, privately published, p. 84

14 Ibid p. 86

15 Brent, Leslie Baruch, *Sunday's Child? A Memoir*, p. 21

16 Author interview 1, 20 December 2018, Leslie Brent, pp. 1–2 & interview 4, p. 5

17 Author interview 1, 20 December 2018, Leslie Brent, p. 3

18 Turner, Barry, *And the Policeman Smiled: 10,000 Children Escape from Nazi Europe,* Bloomsbury, London, 1990, p. 12

19 Author interview 1, 20 December 2018, Leslie Brent, p. 3 & interview 2, 4 February 2019, p. 8

20 *Manchester Guardian*, 20 September 1935

21 Evans, Richard J. *The Third Reich in Power, 1933–1939*, Penguin, 2005, p. 87

22 Schmitt, Hans A. *Quakers and Nazis: Inner Light in Outer Darkness*, Univ. of Missouri, Columbia, 1997, pp. 70–1

23 Bailey, Brenda, *A Quaker Couple in Nazi Germany*, Sessions, York, 1994, pages 47 & 61

24 Schmitt, Hans A. *Quakers and Nazis: Inner Light in Outer Darkness*, Univ. of Missouri, Columbia, 1997, p. 70 & Smith, Lyn, *Heroes of the Holocaust: Ordinary Britons who Risked their Lives to Make a Difference,* Random House, London, 2013, p. 37

25 Potten, Dorle, *Des Kindes Chronik*, privately published, p. 84

Chapter 4

1 Sonnenfeldt, Richard W. *Witness to Nuremberg*, p. 111

2 Bourne, Eric, *A European Life*, Bank House Books, New Romney, 2012, p. 9

3 Wiener Library, 2018/9, Box 2, *Peregrinations*, Peter Stoll

4 Bourne, Eric, *A European Life*, Bank House Books, New Romney, 2012, p. 14

5 Wiener Library, 2018/9, Box 9, Stoatley Rough School, Anniversary Reunion, (2004) p. 16

6 Anna Essinger, *Bunce Court School, 1933–1943*, p. 6

7 NA/Ed 35/4724; AE to Board of Education, 5 February 1937 & NA/Ed 35/4724; Memorandum, Hankin to Duckworth, 31 May 1937

8 Trede, Michael, *Der Ruckkehrer: Skizzenbuch. Eines Chirurgen. Reihe*: Ecomed biographien, (2003) Chapt. 3

9 Author interview, 23 May 2020, Joseph Meyer, p. 3

10 Anna Essinger, *Bunce Court School, 1933–1943*, p. 1

11 Wiener Library, 2018/9, Box 11, Paula Essinger, *Memoirs*, p. 6

12 Bergas, Hanna, *Fifteen Years lived among, with and for Refugee children*, 1979, Palo Alto, California, unpublished memoir, p. 18

13 Author interview 4, 6 June 2020, Hansjörg Greimel, p. 4

14 Anna Essinger, *Bunce Court School, 1933–1943*, p. 9

15 NA/Ed 35/ 4724; Board of Education Minutes, C.I.M. Duckworth, 31 May 1937 & NA/Ed 109/2514 Report of Education of New Herrlingen School, Otterden, Kent, 1937, Board of Education, pp. 6–10

16 Anna Essinger, *Bunce Court School, 1933–1943*, p. 1

17 NA/Ed 109/2514 Report of Education of New Herrlingen School, Otterden, Kent, 1937, Board of Education, p. 11

18 NA/ED 109/2514, *New Herrlingen School*: For the Use of the Office of the Inspectorate Only, Oct. 1937, pp. 2–3

19 Author interview, 21 January 2019, Karl Grossfield, pp. 1–4

20 'Austria: "Spring Cleaning"', *Time* Magazine, 28 March 1938, Vol XXXI, No 14

21 Cesarani, David, *Eichmann: His Life and Crimes,* Vintage, London, 2004, pp. 60–62, 67 & 73 & Whiteman, Dorit Bader, *The Uprooted: A Hitler Legacy*, Perseus, UK, 1993, pages 14, 19

22 Author interview, 21 January 2019, Karl Grossfield, pp. 3–6

23 Leverton, Bertha & Lowensohn, Shmuel (eds), *I Came Alone: The Stories of the Kindertransports,* The Book Guild, Sussex, UK, 1990, p. 381

24 Turner, Barry, *And the Policeman Smiled: 10,000 Children Escape from Nazi Europe,* Bloomsbury, London, 1990, p. 20

25 Bentwich, Norman, *My Seventy-Seven Years,* The Jewish Publication Society of America, Philadelphia, 1961, pp. 144–6

26 Schachne, Lucie, *Education towards Spiritual Resistance: The Jewish Landschulheim Herrlingen* 1933–1939, Verlag, Frankfurt, 1988, pp. 88–9

27 Bergas, Hanna, *Fifteen Years lived among, with and for Refugee children*, 1979, Palo Alto, California, unpublished memoir, pages 30, 35–6

28 Litvinoff, Barnet (ed), *The Letters and Papers of Chaim Weizmann,* Series B, Dec 31–Apr 52, Transaction Publishers,(1984) p. 102

29 Bentwich, Norman, *My Seventy-Seven Years,* The Jewish Publication Society of America, Philadelphia, 1961, pp. 147–8

30 Friedlander, Saul, *Nazi Germany and the Jews: The Years of Persecution, 1933–39,* Weidenfeld and Nicolson, London, 1997, pp. 248–9

31 Potten, Dorle, *Des Kindes Chronik*, privately published, pages 134 & 164

32 Sonnenfeldt, Richard W. *Witness to Nuremberg*, p. 121

33 Brent, Leslie Baruch, *Sunday's Child? A Memoir*, p. 27

34 Friedlander, Saul, *Nazi Germany and the Jews: The Years of Persecution, 1933–39*, Weidenfeld and Nicolson, London, 1997, p. 249

35 Author interview 1, 20 December 2018, Leslie Brent, p. 3

Chapter 5

1 Author interview 2, 4 December 2019, Mia Lewis, pp. 1–3

2 Gilbert, Martin, *Kristallnacht: Prelude to Destruction*, Harper Collins, London, 2006, pp. 23–4

3 Evans, Richard J. *The Third Reich in Power, 1933–1939*, Penguin, 2005, p. 580

4 Author interview, 1 February 2021, Dr Christoph Kreutzmuller, Jewish Museum in Berlin & Gottlieb, Amy Zahl, *Men of Vision: Anglo-Jewry's Aid to Victims of the Nazi Regime 1933–1945*, Weidenfeld and Nicolson, London, 1998, p. 112

5 Gilbert, Martin, *Kristallnacht: Prelude to Destruction*, Harper Collins, London, 2006, pages 13 & 50–51

6 Evans, Richard J. *The Third Reich in Power, 1933–1939*, Penguin, 2005, pp. 580–3

7 Author interview 4, 12 November 2019, Leslie Brent, p. 7

8 Author interview, 29 November 2019, Mia Lewis, p.1 & interview 2, p. 4

9 Author interview, 24 January 2019, Ruth Danson, pp. 1–3

10 Author interview, 2 December 2019, Susie Shipman, pp.2–3

11 Author interview, 9 December 2019, Heinz Redwood, pp. 3–4. & Gilbert, Martin, *Kristallnacht: Prelude to Destruction*, Harper Collins, London, 2006, pp. 70–2

12 Author interview, 6 September 2019, Helen Kotler, pp. 6–7

13 Friedlander, Saul, *Nazi Germany and the Jews: The Years of Persecution, 1933–39,* Weidenfeld and Nicolson, London, 1997, p. 275 & Turner, Barry, *And the Policeman Smiled: 10,000 Children Escape from Nazi Europe,* Bloomsbury, London, 1990, p. 28

14 Harris, Mark Jonathan, & Oppenheimer, Deborah, *Into the Arms of Strangers*, Bloomsbury, London, 2000, pages 58 & 74

15 Hansard, 21 November 1938, vol. 341, Mr Noel-Baker, 1430

16 Gilbert, Martin, *Kristallnacht: Prelude to Destruction*, Harper Collins, London, 2006, p. 30

17 Author interview, 1 February 2021, Dr Christoph Kreutzmuller, Jewish Museum in Berlin & Evans, Richard J. *The Third Reich in Power, 1933–1939*, Penguin, 2005, p. 590

18 *Manchester Guardian*, 18 November 1938, diplomatic correspondent

19 Author interview 3, Hansjörg Greimel, p. 7

20 Meth-Cohn, Otto, *The Nearly Man*, printed in the UK, 2015, p. 18

21 Hansard, 21 November 1938, vol. 341, Mr Noel-Baker, 1430

22 Schachne, Lucie, *Education towards Spiritual Resistance: The Jewish Landschulheim Herrlingen 1933–1939*, Verlag, Frankfurt, 1988, p. 201

23 Author interview 1, Hansjörg Greimel, pp. 3–4

24 Friedlander, Saul, *Nazi Germany and the Jews: The Years of Persecution, 1933–39,* Weidenfeld and Nicolson, London, 1997, p. 272

25 Sonnenfeldt, Richard W. *Witness to Nuremberg*, p. 122

26 Joseph, Zoe, *Survivors: Jewish Refugees in Birmingham, 1933–1945*, Meridian, UK, 1988, p. 138

27 Turner, Barry, *Marks of Distinction: The Memoirs of Elaine Blond*, Vallentine Mitchell, London, 1988, p. 72

28 Anna Essinger, *Bunce Court School, 1933–1943*, p. 6

29 Shepherd, Naomi, *Wilfrid Israel: German Jewry's Secret Ambassador*, Weidenfeld and Nicolson, London, 1984, pp. 146–7

30 Amy Zahl, *Men of Vision: Anglo-Jewry's Aid to Victims of the Nazi Regime 1933–1945*, Weidenfeld and Nicolson, London, 1998, p. 105

31 NA/CAB 23/96/7 The Jewish Problem

32 Schmitt, Hans A. *Quakers and Nazis: Inner Light in Outer Darkness*, Univ. of Missouri, Columbia, 1997, p. 104

33 Shepherd, Naomi, *Wilfrid Israel: German Jewry's Secret Ambassador*, Weidenfeld and Nicolson, London, 1984, p. 147

34 Hansard, 21 November 1938, vol 341, Samuel Hoare, 1475

35 Smith, Lyn, *Heroes of the Holocaust: Ordinary Britons who Risked their Lives to Make a Difference*, Random House, London, 2013, pages 38 & 40

36 Fast, Vera K. *Children's Exodus: A History of the Kindertransport*, I.B. Tauris, London, 2011, pp. 14–15

37 Bentwich, Norman, *They Found Refuge: An Account of British Jewry's Work for Victims of Nazi Oppression*, The Cresset Press, London, 1956, p. 66

38 Anna Essinger, *Bunce Court School, 1933–1943*, p. 6.

39 Turner, Barry, *Marks of Distinction: The Memoirs of Elaine Blond*, Vallentine Mitchell, London, 1988, p. 72

40 Bergas, Hanna, *Fifteen Years lived among, with and for Refugee children*, 1979, Palo Alto, California, unpublished memoir, p. 39

Chapter 6

1 Gilbert, Martin, *Kristallnacht: Prelude to Destruction*, Harper Collins, London, 2006, p. 184

2 Brent, Leslie Baruch, *Sunday's Child? A Memoir*, pp. 29–30

3 Author interview 1, 20 December 2018, Leslie Brent, p. 7

4 Gilbert, Martin, *Kristallnacht: Prelude to Destruction*, Harper Collins, London, 2006, p. 196

5 Author interview 1, 20 December 2018, Leslie Brent, p. 7 & interview 4, p. 7 & author interview 1, 20 December 2018, Leslie Brent, p. 5

6 Turner, Barry, *And the Policeman Smiled: 10,000 Children Escape from Nazi Europe,* Bloomsbury, London, 1990, pp. 51–2

7 Bergas, Hanna, *Fifteen Years lived among, with and for Refugee children*, 1979, Palo Alto, California, unpublished memoir, p. 39

8 Turner, Barry, *Marks of Distinction: The Memoirs of Elaine Blond*, Vallentine Mitchell, London, 1988, p. 72

9 Author interview 2, 4 February 2019, Leslie Brent, p. 7 & interview 3, p. 10

10 Potten, Dorle, *Des Kindes Chronik*, privately published, p. 197

11 Brent, Leslie Baruch, *Sunday's Child? A Memoir*, p. 39 & author interview 1, 20 December 2018, Leslie Brent, p. 7

12 Bergas, Hanna, *Fifteen Years lived among, with and for Refugee children*, 1979, Palo Alto, California, unpublished memoir, p. 42

13 Turner, Barry, *Marks of Distinction: The Memoirs of Elaine Blond*, Vallentine Mitchell, London, 1988, p. 73

14 Author interview 3, 20 December 2018, Leslie Brent, pages 10 & 20

15 Gottlieb, Amy Zahl, *Men of Vision: Anglo-Jewry's Aid to Victims of the Nazi Regime 1933–1945,* Weidenfeld and Nicolson, London, 1998, p. 114 & Turner, Barry, *And the Policeman Smiled...* pp. 41–2

16 Author interview 1, 21 January 2019, Karl Grossfield, pp. 6–8

17 Anna Essinger, *Bunce Court School, 1933–1943,* p. 6

18 Turner, Barry, *And the Policeman Smiled*: *10,000 Children Escape from Nazi Europe,* Bloomsbury, London, 1990, pp. 64–66 & author interview 6, 15 July 2020, Hansjörg Greimel, p. 6

19 Bergas, Hanna, *Fifteen Years lived among, with and for Refugee children*, 1979, Palo Alto, California, unpublished memoir, p. 41

20 NA MH 55/689/14 Minute Sheet to C.F. Roundell, 14 December 1938 & NA MH 55/689/21, *Report of Jewish Refugees Camp, Dovercourt*, by C.F. Roundell, 21 December 1938 & further reports, 16 January 1939 & 1 February 1939

21 Author interview 2, 4 February 2019, Leslie Brent, p. 2

22 Brent, Leslie Baruch, *Sunday's Child? A Memoir*, pp. 40–1

Chapter 7

1 Author interview 4, 12 November 2019, Leslie Brent, p. 10 & Brent, Leslie Baruch, *Sunday's Child? A Memoir*, p. 42

2 *Reflections, Bunce Court*, Hadlum printers, 2004, Walter Block, p. 22

3 Author interview 3, 3 September 2019, Leslie Brent, pages 10 & 20

4 Wiener Library, 2018/9, Box 3, *Bunce Court Memories*, Eric Bourne

5 Brent, Leslie Baruch, *Sunday's Child? A Memoir*, pages 43 & 47 & author interview 1, 20 December 2018, Leslie Brent, p. 10 & author interview 3, p. 4 & interview 2, p. 3

6 Turner, Barry, *And the Policeman Smiled: 10,000 Children Escape from Nazi Europe*, Bloomsbury, London, 1990, p. 47

7 Gilbert, Martin, *Kristallnacht: Prelude to Destruction*, Harper Collins, London, 2006, p. 212

8 Author interview 1, 29 November 2019, Mia Lewis, p. 1 & interview 2, p. 3

9 Author interview 1, Helen Kotler, 16 September 2019, pages 1 & 7

10 Evans, Richard J. *The Third Reich in Power, 1933–1939*, Penguin, 2005, p. 683

11 Bentwich, Norman, *My Seventy-Seven Years*, The Jewish Publication Society of America, Philadelphia, 1961, p. 159

12 London Metropolitan Archives, ACC/2793/01/06/11 *Memorandum of the Proposed Purchase of the New Herrlingen School* (undated)

13 Wiener Library, 2018/9, Box 11, Paula, *Memoirs*, pages 6 & 11

14 *Reflections, Bunce Court*, Hadlum printers, 2004, Eric Bourne, p. 8

15 Author interview with Ruth Danson, 24 January 2019, pp. 3–7

16 Author interview 2, 4 February 2019, Leslie Brent, p. 1 & Interview 4, p. 9

17 Brent, Leslie Baruch, *Sunday's Child? A Memoir*, p. 69

18 *Reflections, Bunce Court*, Hadlum printers, 2004, Douglas Boyd p. 31 & Eric Bourne, p. 12

19 Author interview 2, 18 January 2021, Michael Roemer, p. 5

20 Trede, Michael, *Der Ruckkehrer: Skizzenbuch. Eines Chirurgen. Reihe*: Ecomed biographien, (2003) Chapt 3

21 Author interview 1, 11 December 2019, Hanni Howard, p. 3

22 Hoffnung, Annetta, *Gerard Hoffnung: His Biography*, Aurum Press, London, 1988, pages 25 & 32

23 Author interview 1, 20 December 2018, Leslie Brent, p. 13

24 Author interview 8, 10 May 2021, Hansjörg Greimel, p. 1 & Schachne, Lucie, *Education towards Spiritual Resistance*, p. 211

25 Herrlingen Museum, Anna Essinger Exhibition texts (English trans), pages 45 & 47–9

26 Author interview 3, 3 September 2019, Leslie Brent, p. 7

27 Wiener Library, 2018/9, Box 11, Paula, *Memoirs*, p. 6

28 Catherine Lampert, *Frank Auerbach: Speaking and Painting*, pp. 15–16

29 Author interview 3, 3 September 2019, Leslie Brent, pages 5 & 9, 11, & interview 2, pages 4 & 8

30 Author interview 1, 9 December 19, Heinz Redwood pp. 6–7

31 *Reflections, Bunce Court*, Hadlum printers, 2004, Judith Adler, p. 15, Walter Block, p. 22, & Maria Peters, p. 42

32 Wiener Library, 2018/9, Box 3, *Bunce Court Memories*, Eric Bourne

33 Wiener Library, 2018/9, Box 3, II, *Open Day, The Messenger* School Magazine & Alan Major, *Bunce Court, Part Three, Bygone Kent*, vol. 10, no. 10, pp. 653–4

34 Author interview 1, Mia Lewis, 29 November 2019, pages 2 & 10

35 *Manchester Guardian*, 25 and 30 August 1939

36 Author interview 2, Karl Grossfield, p. 3

37 Gottlieb, Amy Zahl, *Men of Vision: Anglo-Jewry's Aid to Victims of the Nazi Regime 1933–1945*, p. 125 & Emanuel, Muriel, & Gissing, Vera, *Nicholas Winton and the Rescued Generation*, p. 125

38 Brent, Leslie Baruch, *Sunday's Child? A Memoir*, p. 55 & author interview 2, Leslie Brent, p. 4

39 Sonnenfeldt, Richard W. *Witness to Nuremberg*, pp. 134–135 & Alan Major, *Bunce Court, Part Three, Bygone Kent*, vol. 10, no. 10, p. 644

40 Author interview 2, 4 February 2019, Leslie Brent, p. 4 & Brent, Leslie Baruch, *Sunday's Child? A Memoir*, pp. 55–6

Chapter 8

1 Finkel, Sidney, *Sevek and the Holocaust: The Boy who Refused to Die*, self-published, printed by Thomson-Shore, Illinois, 2006, p. 21

2 Ibid p. 22

3 Sidney Finkel, USC Shoah interview, 7 April 1995, Tape 2, 13.55

4 Ibid 14.54

5 Finkel, Sidney, *Sevek and the Holocaust*, pp. 22–3

6 Sidney Finkel, USC Shoah interview, 7 April 1995, Tape 2, 16.00

7 Finkel, Sidney, *Sevek and the Holocaust*, p. 23

8 Sidney Finkel, USC Shoah interview, 7 April 1995, Tape 2, 19.40

9 Ibid 19.50

10 Finkel, Isaac, unpublished memoirs, p. 9

11 Giladi, Ben (ed), *A Tale of One City: Piotrkow Trybunalski*, Shengold, New York, 1991, p. 164

12 Oliner, Samuel, *Narrow Escapes*, p. 43

13 Dr Samuel P. Oliner, interview 14 January 1994, United States Holocaust Memorial Museum Collection

14 Oliner, Samuel, *Narrow Escapes*, p. 43

15 Dr Samuel P. Oliner, interview 14 January 1994, United States Holocaust Memorial Museum Collection

16 Oliner, Samuel, *Narrow Escapes*, p. 47

17 Dr Samuel P. Oliner, interview 14 January 1994, United States Holocaust Memorial Museum Collection

18 Ibid

19 Oliner, Samuel, *Narrow Escapes*, p. 50

20 Ibid

21 Dr Samuel P. Oliner, interview 14 January 1994, United States Holocaust Memorial Museum Collection

22 Oliner, Samuel, *Narrow Escapes*, p. 56

23 Ibid p. 57

24 Dr Samuel P. Oliner, interview 14 January 1994, United States Holocaust Memorial Museum Collection

25 Author interview, Anna Rabkin, 9 September 2020, p. 1

26 Rabkin, Anna, *From Krakow to Berkeley: Coming out of Hiding*, Vallentine Mitchell, London, 2018, p. 4

27 Author interview, 9 September 2020, p. 1

28 Ibid p. 2

29 Rabkin, Anna, *From Krakow to Berkeley: Coming out of Hiding*, pp. 17–18

30 Gilbert, Martin, *The Boys: The Story of 732 Young Concentration Camp Survivors*, Henry Holt, New York, 1996, p. 71

31 Finkel, Sidney, *Sevek and the Holocaust*, p. 31

32 Author interview 4, Sidney Finkel, 15 March 2020, p. 3

33 Finkel, Sidney, *Sevek and the Holocaust*, pp. 31–2

34 Finkel, Isaac, unpublished memoirs, p. 27

35 Author interview 4, Sidney Finkel, 15 March 2020, p. 3

36 Finkel, Isaac, unpublished memoirs, p. 28

37 Finkel, Sidney, *Sevek and the Holocaust*, p. 30

38 Ibid

39 Author interview 4, Sidney Finkel, 15 March 2020, p. 3
40 Finkel, Sidney, *Sevek and the Holocaust*, p. 30

Chapter 9

1 *The Times*, 4 September 1939
2 Bergas, Hanna, *Fifteen Years lived among, with and for Refugee children*, 1979, Palo Alto, California, unpublished memoir, p. 67
3 Wiener Library, 2018/9 Box 3, Bunce Court Memories, Eric Bourne
4 Brent, Leslie Baruch, *Sunday's Child? A Memoir*, pp. 72–3
5 Author interview 4, 12 November 2019, Leslie Brent, p. 2
6 Author interview 4, 12 November 2019, Leslie Brent, p. 3
7 Rees, Laurence, *Auschwitz, The Nazis & The 'Final Solution'*, pages 228 & 195 & Cesarani, David, *Eichmann: His Life and Crimes*, p. 107
8 Author interview 4, 12 November 2019, Leslie Brent, p. 2
9 Wiener Library, 2018/9 Box 3, Bunce Court, England, 1939, by Walter Kaufmann
10 Bergas, Hanna, *Fifteen Years lived among, with and for Refugee children*, 1979, Palo Alto, California, unpublished memoir, p. 45
11 *Reflections, Bunce Court*, Hadlum printers, 2004, p. 15
12 Bergas, Hanna, *Fifteen Years lived among, with and for Refugee children*, p. 47
13 Wiener Library, 2018/9 Box 14, *Kennaways*, by Ernst Weinberg
14 Hoffnung, Annetta, *Gerard Hoffnung: His Biography*, p. 32
15 Author interview 2, Leslie Brent, 4 February 2019, p. 2 & interview 1, p. 9

16 Author interview 3, 3 September 2019, Leslie Brent, p. 12

17 Author interview 2, Leslie Brent, 4 February 2019, p. 5

18 Author interview 4, 12 November 2019, Leslie Brent, p. 13 & interview 3, p. 2

19 Martin Lubowski in *Anna's Kinder*, documentary, 1994

20 *Reflections, Bunce Court*, Hadlum printers, 2004, p. 42

21 Author interview 3, 3 September 2019, Leslie Brent, pages 10 & 13

22 Ibid p. 7

23 Author interview 1, Leslie Brent, 20 December 2018, pages 9 & 11

24 Author interview 2, Karl Grossfield, p. 4

25 Wiener Library, 2018/9 Box 3, *Bunce Court Newsletter*, July 1947, Hanna Bergas

26 Author interview 1, Leslie Brent, 20 December 2018, p.12

27 Anna Essinger, *Bunce Court School, 1933–1943*, pp. 6–7

28 Sonnenfeldt, Richard W. *Witness to Nuremberg*, p. 137

29 BBC news, 10 May 1940

30 Sonnenfeldt, Richard W. *Witness to Nuremberg*, p. 138

31 Ibid p. 139

32 *Reflections, Bunce Court*, Hadlum printers, 2004, p. 9

33 Anna Essinger, *Bunce Court School, 1933–1943*, p. 7

34 Bergas, Hanna, *Fifteen Years lived among, with and for Refugee children*, 1979, Palo Alto, California, unpublished memoir, p.50

35 Turner, Barry, *And the Policeman Smiled*, pp. 144–6

36 https://blog.nationalarchives.gov.uk/collar-lot-brit-ains-policy-internment-second-world-war

37 Sonnenfeldt, Richard W. *Witness to Nuremberg*, p. 139

38 London Metropolitan Archives, ACC/2793/01/06/011, Anna Essinger to Central Council for German Jewry, 18 May 1940 & 23 May 1940

39 London Metropolitan Archives, ACC/2793/01/06/011, Central Council to Anna Essinger, 28 May 1940

40 *Manchester Guardian*, 31 May 1940

41 Author interview 1, Heinz Redwood, 9 December 2019, p. 8

42 Author interview 3, Harold Jackson, 5 November 2019, p. 20

43 Author interview 1, Heinz Redwood, 9 December 2019, pp. 8–9

44 Anna Essinger, *Bunce Court School, 1933–1943*, p. 7

45 Bergas, Hanna, *Fifteen Years lived among, with and for Refugee children*, 1979, Palo Alto, California, unpublished memoir, pp.51-52

46 Anna Essinger, *Bunce Court School, 1933–1943*, p. 7

47 Author interview 1, Heinz Redwood, 9 December 2019, p. 9

48 Anna Essinger, *Bunce Court School, 1933–1943*, p. 7

49 Author interview 4, 12 November 2019, Leslie Brent, p. 5

50 Wiener Library, 2018/9 Box 11, Bunce Court School, Trench Hall, Wem, circular letter no. 4, August 1940

51 Ibid

52 Brent, Leslie Baruch, *Sunday's Child? A Memoir*, p. 73

Chapter 10

1 Evans, Richard J. *The Third Reich at War: How the Nazis led Germany from Conquest to Disaster,* p. 264

2 Cesarani, David, *Eichmann: His Life and Crimes,* Vintage, London, 2004, pp. 111–114

3 Oliner, Samuel, *Narrow Escapes,* pp. 77–8

4 Dr Samuel P. Oliner, interview 10 May 1999, by Joseph Belanoff, USC Shoah Foundation Institute, Tape 1, 47.30

5 Oliner, Samuel, *Narrow Escapes*, pp. 81–2

6 Dr Samuel P. Oliner, interview 14 January 1994, United States Holocaust Memorial Museum Collection 54.00 *on*

7 Oliner, Samuel, *Narrow Escapes*, pages 83, 85–6

8 Ibid

9 Dr Samuel P. Oliner, interview 14 January 1994, United States Holocaust Memorial Museum Collection, 1.05 *on*

10 Oliner, Samuel, *Narrow Escapes*, p. 95

11 Rabkin, Anna, *From Krakow to Berkeley: Coming out of Hiding*, Vallentine Mitchell, London, 2018, pp. 18–19

12 Rees, Laurence, *Auschwitz, The Nazis & The 'Final Solution'*, p. 70

13 Author interview with Anna Rabkin, 9 September 2020, p. 2

14 Ibid p. 3

15 Ibid

16 Rees, Laurence, *Auschwitz, The Nazis & The 'Final Solution'*, p. 86

17 Evans, Richard J. *The Third Reich at War: How the Nazis led Germany from Conquest to Disaster*, pp. 257–8

18 Rees, Laurence, *Auschwitz, The Nazis & The 'Final Solution'*, pp. 87–90

19 Author interview with Anna Rabkin, 9 September 2020, p. 3

20 Rabkin, Anna, *From Krakow to Berkeley: Coming out of Hiding*, p. 24

21 Author interview with Anna Rabkin, 9 September 2020, p. 4

22 Finkel, Sidney, *Sevek and the Holocaust: The Boy who Refused to Die*, self-published, printed by Thomson-Shore, Illinois, 2006, pp. 36–7

23 Rees, Laurence, *Auschwitz, The Nazis & The 'Final Solution'*, p. 201

24 Sidney Finkel, USC Shoah interview, 7 April 1995, Tape 3, 11.00 *on*

25 Finkel, Sidney, *Sevek and the Holocaust: The Boy who Refused to Die,* p. 39

26 Gilbert, Martin, *The Boys: The Story of 732 Young Concentration Camp Survivors,* pp. 116–7

27 Finkel, Isaac, unpublished memoirs, p. 30

28 Finkel, Sidney, *Sevek and the Holocaust: The Boy who Refused to Die,* p. 41

29 Ibid p. 40

30 Dr Samuel P. Oliner, interview 14 January 1994, United States Holocaust Memorial Museum Collection, 1.09 *on*

31 Oliner, Samuel, *Narrow Escapes,* p. 88

32 Dr Samuel P. Oliner, interview 14 January 1994, United States Holocaust Memorial Museum Collection, 1.00 *on*

33 Oliner, Samuel, *Narrow Escapes,* p. 92

34 Ibid

35 Dr Samuel P. Oliner, interview 14 January 1994, United States Holocaust Memorial Museum Collection, 1.05

36 Sidney Finkel, USC Shoah interview, 7 April 1995, Tape 3, 12.29

37 Finkel, Isaac, unpublished memoirs, p. 29

38 Gilbert, Martin, *The Boys: The Story of 732 Young Concentration Camp Survivors,* p. 127

39 Finkel, Sidney, *Sevek and the Holocaust: The Boy who Refused to Die,* p. 49

40 Ibid p. 51

Chapter 11

1 Wiener Library, 2018/9, Box 11, Anna Essinger, Circular letter no. 42, August 1940

2 Author interview, Michael Roemer, p. 2

3 Wiener Library, 2018/9, Box 11, News Bulletin, 1 July 1940

4 Wiener Library, 2018/9, Box 11, Paula Essinger, *Memoirs,* p.7

5 Ibid

6 Marckwald, William, Unpublished memoirs, p. 410

7 Wiener Library, 2018/9, Box 11, Paula, *Memoirs,* p. 7

8 Wiener Library, 2018/9, Box 14, *House Cleaning of our Cosy Saddler's Shop,* Werner Krebs

9 Wiener Library, 2018/9, Box 14, *What Passes by the Musical Room Window,* Ursula Solmitz

10 Wiener Library, 2018/9, Box 14, *Sparks,* Peter Stoll

11 Wiener Library, 2018/9, Box 14, *Stoking,* Leo Dreiling

12 Wiener Library, 2018/9, Box 14, *People We Have Worked For,* Hermann Essinger

13 Author interview 1, Leslie Brent, 20 December 2018, p. 6

14 TNA Ed/35/4724 Anna Essinger to Midlands Education Board 28 September 1940, & Robling to Marshall, 27 November 1940

15 Whiteman, Dorit Bader, *The Uprooted: A Hitler Legacy,* p. 319

16 Sonnenfeldt, Richard W. *Witness to Nuremberg,* pp. 143–6 & 148

17 Bourne, Eric, *A European Life,* pp. 23–4

18 Author interview 1, Heinz Redwood, 9 December 2019, p. 9 & interview 2, p. 3

19 Author interview 2, Michael Roemer, 18 January 2021, p. 2

20 Author interview 2, Heinz Redwood, pp. 5–7

21 Author interview 2, Leslie Brent, p. 6

22 TNA Ed/35/4724 Anna Essinger to Under Secretary, DoH, 7 January 1942

23 TNA Ed/35/4724 Mr A.R. Marshall to Board of Education on 1 October 1940 & 26 November 1941

24 TNA Ed/35/4724 Internal memo, Midlands Education Board, 26 November 1941

25 Author interview 3, 3 September 2019, Leslie Brent, p. 14

26 Brent, Leslie Baruch, *Sunday's Child? A Memoir*, p. 73

27 *Manchester Guardian*, 29 September 1942

28 Anna Essinger Museum, Ulm, Exhibits, English translation, p. 51

29 *New York Times*, 25 November 1942, 'Details Reaching Palestine'

30 *Manchester Guardian*, 15 December 1942, 'Rescuing Jews from Poland. Suggested approach to Neutrals'

31 Hansard, vol. 385, cc 2082–7, Secretary of State for Foreign Affairs, (Anthony Eden)

32 BBC *On this Day*, 17 December 1942

33 *Manchester Guardian*, 31 December 1942, p. 6

34 Hans Meyer in *Anna's Kinder,* documentary, 1994

35 Author interview 4, 12 November 2019, Leslie Brent, p. 11

36 Wiener Library, 2018/9 Box 14, *Islands* by Leslie Brent

37 Anna Essinger, *Bunce Court School, 1933–1943*, p. 6

38 Author interview 1, Mia Lewis, 29 November 2019, pp. 5–7 & 9 & interview 2, p. 5

39 Author interview 1, Susie Shipman, 2 December 2019, pages 3, 5, 6–7

40 Author interview 2, Harold Jackson, 19 October 2019, p. 4

41 Ibid p. 1

42 Author interview 2, Harold Jackson, 19 October 2019, p. 10 & interview 3, pp. 10–11

43 Author interview 1, Anna John, 18 January 2019, pages 1, 3, 6–7, 10. Interview 2, pp. 1–3, 5–6, & 7

44 Author interview 1, Helen Urbach, 17 September 2019, pp. 2–6

45 Author interview 1, Mia Lewis, 29 November. 2019, pages 5 & 8

46 Author interview 3, Harold Jackson, 5 November 2019, p. 17

47 Marckwald, William, unpublished memoirs, p. 412

48 Author interview 1, Susie Shipman, 2 December 2019, p. 5

49 Author interview 1, Nuri Wyeth, p. 4

50 Marckwald, William, unpublished memoirs, pp. 416–18

51 Author interview 3, Harold Jackson, 5 November 2019, pp. 14–15

52 Wiener Library, 2018/9, Box 14

53 Wiener Library, 2018/9, Box 11, Anna Essinger, round robin no. 58, January 1944

54 *Reflections, Bunce Court*, Hadlum printers, 2004, p. 34

55 Author interview 3, Harold Jackson, 5 November 2019, p. 13 & interview 2, p. 7

56 Author interview 1, Susie Shipman, 2 December 2019, pages 4 & 7

57 Author interview 1, Anna John, 18 January 2019, p. 3

58 Author interview 2, Harold Jackson, 19 October 2019, p. 12

Chapter 12

1 Dr Samuel P. Oliner, interview 10 May 1999, by Joseph Belanoff, USC Shoah Foundation Institute, Tape 1, 1.09

2 Oliner, Samuel, *Narrow Escapes,* p. 103

3 Dr Samuel P. Oliner, interview 14 January 1994, United States Holocaust Memorial Museum Collection, 1.23

4 Ibid 1.26

5 Oliner, Samuel, *Narrow Escapes,* p. 109

6 Ibid

7 Dr Samuel P. Oliner, interview 14 January 1994, United States Holocaust Memorial Museum Collection, 1.23

8 Ibid 1.22

9 Oliner, Samuel, *Narrow Escapes,* pp. 118–9

10 Dr Samuel P. Oliner, interview 14 January 1994, United States Holocaust Memorial Museum Collection, 1.21 & 1.37

11 Oliner, Samuel, *Narrow Escapes,* p. 125

12 Dr Samuel P. Oliner, interview 14 January 1994, United States Holocaust Memorial Museum Collection, 1.35

13 Author interview with Anna Rabkin, 9 September 2020, p. 4

14 Rabkin, Anna, *From Krakow to Berkeley: Coming out of Hiding,* Vallentine Mitchell, London, 2018, pp. 26–8

15 Author interview with Anna Rabkin, 9 September 2020, p. 5

16 Ibid

17 Rabkin, Anna, *From Krakow to Berkeley: Coming out of Hiding,* Vallentine Mitchell, London, 2018, p. 29

18 Friedman, Philip, *The Destruction of the Jews of Lwow 1941–1944* in *Roads to Extinction* (eds) Ada June Friedman, New York, 1980

19 Rabkin, Anna, *From Krakow to Berkeley: Coming out of Hiding,* Vallentine Mitchell, London, 2018, p. 29

20 Ibid p. 31

21 Sidney Finkel, USC Shoah interview, 7 April 1995, Tape 4, 20.00 & 24.30

22 Ibid 26.15

23 Ibid 25.30

24 Finkel, Sidney, *Sevek and the Holocaust: The Boy who Refused to Die,* pp. 53–4

25 Ibid p. 55

26 Gilbert, Martin, *The Boys: The Story of 732 Young Concentration Camp Survivors*, pp. 189–193

27 Finkel, Sidney, *Sevek and the Holocaust: The Boy who Refused to Die*, p. 59

28 Ibid p. 64

29 Oliner, Samuel, *Narrow Escapes* pp. 127–8

30 Dr Samuel P. Oliner, interview 14 January 1994, United States Holocaust Memorial Museum Collection, 1.45

31 Ibid Tape 2, 2.02

32 Oliner, Samuel, *Narrow Escapes* pp. 139–40

33 Dr Samuel P. Oliner, interview 10 May 1999, by Joseph Belanoff, USC Shoah Foundation Institute, Tape 1, 1.17

34 Oliner, Samuel, *Narrow Escapes*, p. 150

35 Finkel, Sidney, *Sevek and the Holocaust: The Boy who Refused to Die*, pp. 67–9

36 Sidney Finkel, USC Shoah interview, 7 April 1995, Tape 5, 10.00 *on*

37 Finkel, Sidney, *Sevek and the Holocaust: The Boy who Refused to Die*, p. 76

Chapter 13

1 Bergas, Hanna, *Fifteen Years lived among, with and for Refugee children*, 1979, Palo Alto, California, unpublished memoir, p. 67

2 Brent, Leslie Baruch, *Sunday's Child? A Memoir*, Bank House Books, New Romney, 2009, p. 77

3 Author interview 1, Leslie Brent, 20 December 2018

4 Author interview 2, Harold Jackson, 19 October 2019, p. 3

5 BBC archives, *On This Day*, 19 April 1945

6 Author interview 2, Harold Jackson, 19 October 2019, p. 3

7 BBC World Service, 1 May 1945

8 Wiener Library, 2018/9 Box 10, Hannah Meyer to Ursula Solmitz, 21 May 1945

9 Wiener Library, 2018/9 Box 11, Anna Essinger to Walter Seymour, 15 May 1945

10 Author interview 2, Harold Jackson, 19 October 2019, p. 3

11 Wiener Library, 2018/9 Box 11, Anna Essinger to Ursula Solmitz, 20 October 1944

12 Author interview 1, Helen Kotler, 17 September 2019, pp. 2 & 6

13 Undated letter, Otto Urbach to Helen Urbach

14 Bourne, Eric, *A European Life*, p. 10

15 Author interview 1, Joseph Meyer, 2 May 2020, p. 5

16 LMA, ACC 2793/01/06/011 Anna Essinger to Lord Samuel, 30 May 1945

17 Author interview 1, Heinz Redwood, 9 December 1919, pages 6 & 9–10

18 Author interview 2, Mia Lewis, 4 December 2019, p. 9

19 Author interview 2, Harold Jackson, 19 October 2019, pp. 10–11

20 Auerbach, Frank, *Speaking and Painting*, pages 19 & 20

21 Marckwald, William, unpublished memoirs, pp. 420–4

22 Auerbach, Frank, *Speaking and Painting*, pages 20 & 21

23 Marckwald, William, unpublished memoirs, p. 420

24 Bergas, Hanna, *Fifteen Years lived among, with and for Refugee children*, 1979, Palo Alto, California, unpublished memoir, p. 65

25 Wiener Library, 2018/9 Box 4, *Bunce Court Revisited,* Alexander Urbach

26 Author interview, Susie Shipman, 2 December 2019, pages 10 & 6–7

27 Wiener Library, 2018/9 Box 4, Anna Essinger round robin, March 1946

28 Wiener Library, 2018/9 Box 4, Anna Essinger to Walter Seymour, 18 October 1944

29 Wiener Library, 2018/9 Box 14, unnamed pupil to Anna Essinger

30 Wiener Library, 2018/9 Box 14, Walter Bloch, *Germany Revisited* in *The Diagonal*

31 Sonnenfeldt, Richard W. *Witness to Nuremberg*, p. 194

32 Ibid pages 16, 20, 25–26, 34–36

33 Ibid pp. 25–6

34 Ibid pages 48 & 56

35 Ibid pages 20 & 22

36 Early contemporary reports referring to a 'Holocaust' include *News Chronicle*, 5 December 1942

37 Wiener Library, 2018/9 Box 11, Anna Essinger correspondence, 27 August 1945

38 LMA, ACC 2793/01/06/011 Naditch to Essinger, 18 September 1945

39 Evans, Richard J. *The Third Reich at War, How the Nazis led Germany from Conquest to Disaster*, pp. 642–3

40 Wiener Library, 2018/9 Box 3, Anna Essinger to old Bunce Courtians, 20 September 1945

41 Sidney Finkel, USC Shoah interview, 7 April 1995, Tape 5, 19.04

42 Finkel, Isaac, unpublished memoirs, p. 45

43 Wagner, Jens-Christian, *Produktion des Todes*, Gottingen, 2001, p. 495

44 Finkel, Sidney, *Sevek and the Holocaust: The Boy who Refused to Die*, p. 64 & pp. 78–9

45 Dr Samuel P. Oliner, interview 14 January 1994, United States Holocaust Memorial Museum Collection, Tape 2, 12.00

46 Oliner, Samuel, *Narrow Escapes,* pages 156 & 159
47 Oliner, Samuel, *Narrow Escapes,* p. 160
48 Dr Samuel P. Oliner, interview 14 January 1994, United States Holocaust Memorial Museum Collection, Tape 2, 30.00

Chapter 14

1 Author interview 1, Sam Oliner, 30 September 2019, p. 1
2 Ibid p. 2
3 Wiener Library 2018/9
4 United States Holocaust Museum Collection, interview Anna Rabkin, Tape 2, 11.30
5 Author interview 1, Sam Oliner, 30 September 2019, pp. 3–4
6 Bergas, Hanna, *Fifteen Years lived among, with and for Refugee children*, 1979, Palo Alto, California, unpublished memoir, p. 68
7 Author interview 1, Anna John, 10 January 2019, pages 4 & 9
8 Author interview 2, Harold Jackson, 19 October 2019, p. 5
9 Ibid pp. 2–3
10 Author interview 1, Anna John, 10 January 2019, p. 4
11 Ibid p. 9
12 Author interview 3, 3 September 2019, Leslie Brent, pages 2 & 4–5
13 Potten, Dorle, *Des Kindes Chronik*, privately published, p. 166
14 Author interview 3, 3 September 2019, Leslie Brent, pp. 3–4

15 Sophie Friedlander, in Anna Essinger Museum, Ulm, Exhibits, English translation

16 Gilbert, Martin, *The Boys: The Story of 732 Young Concentration Camp Survivors*, Henry Holt, New York, 1996, pp. 317–9

17 Author interview 3, Harold Jackson, 5 November 2019, pp. 5–6

18 Bergas, Hanna, *Fifteen Years lived among, with and for Refugee children*, 1979, Palo Alto, California, unpublished memoir, p. 69

19 Author interview 2, Sam Oliner, 11 October 2019, p. 5

20 Author interview 1, Sam Oliner, 30 September 2019, pp. 2–3

21 Rabkin, Anna, *From Krakow to Berkeley: Coming out of Hiding*, p. 61

22 Author interview with Anna Rabkin, 9 September 2020, p. 6

23 Rabkin, Anna, *From Krakow to Berkeley: Coming out of Hiding*, p. 63

24 United States Holocaust Museum, oral history, Anna Rabkin, Tape 2, 15.00

25 Author interview with Anna Rabkin, 9 September 2020, pp. 6–7

26 Author interview 1, Helen Kotler, 16 September 2019, p. 3

27 Author interview with Anna Rabkin, 9 September 2020, p. 10

28 Rabkin, Anna, *From Krakow to Berkeley: Coming out of Hiding*, p. 67

29 Gilbert, Martin, *The Boys: The Story of 732 Young Concentration Camp Survivors*, p. 321

30 Author interview with Anna Rabkin, 9 September 2020, p. 9

31 Rabkin, Anna, *From Krakow to Berkeley: Coming out of Hiding,* p. 64

32 Author interview 3, Harold Jackson, 5 November 2019, p. 2

33 Author interview with Anna Rabkin, 9 September 2020, pp. 7 & 10

34 Author interview 2, Sam Oliner, 11 October 2019, pp. 2–3 & interview 1, pp. 5–6

35 Ibid pages 1 & 4

36 *Reflections, Bunce Court,* Hadlum printers, 2004, p. 34

37 Author interview 2, Sam Oliner, 11 October 2019, pp. 4–5

38 Oliner, Samuel, *Narrow Escapes,* pages 162 & 168

39 Finkel, Sidney, *Sevek and the Holocaust: The Boy who Refused to Die,* pages 87, 89 & 91

40 Author interview 3, Sidney Finkel, 5 May 2020, p. 4

41 Author interview 1, Sidney Finkel, 19 September 2019, p. 2

42 Author interview 1, Sam Oliner, 30 September 2019, p. 2

43 Author interview 3, Sidney Finkel, 5 May 2020, pages 1 & 5

44 Author interview 1, Helen Kotler, 16 September 2019, p. 3

45 Author interview 1, Sidney Finkel, 19 September 2019, pages 1 & 2 & interview 3 p. 3

46 Author interview 1, Sidney Finkel, 19 September 2019, pp. 1–2 & 4

47 Wiener Library, 2018/9 Box 15, *Another War?* by Sevek Finkelstein

48 Finkel, Sidney, *Sevek and the Holocaust: The Boy who Refused to Die,* p. 94

49 Author interview 3, Sidney Finkel, 5 May 2020, pages 3, 4 & 5, & interview 3, p. 3

50 Finkel, Sidney, *Sevek and the Holocaust: The Boy who Refused to Die,* p. 94

51 United States Holocaust Museum, oral history, Anna Rabkin, Tape 2, 16.00

52 Wiener Library, 2018/9 Box 14, *A Bunce Court Affair, Diagonal*, Nov 49 & Box 5, *Bunce Court Review* by Hanna Bergas (undated)

53 Author interview 3, 3 September 2019, Leslie Brent, p. 15

54 Author interview 2, Mia Lewis, 4 December 2019, p. 6

55 Author interview with Anna Rabkin, 9 September 2020, p. 8

56 Author interview 3, Sidney Finkel, 5 March 2020 p. 3

Epilogue

1 Author interview 1, Leslie Brent, 20 December 2018, p. 15

2 Wiener Library, 2018/9 Box 5, Minutes of OBCA, 17 May 1948

3 Wiener Library, 2018/9 Box 4, Eric Bourne, July 1942

4 Author interview 3, 3 September 2019, Leslie Brent, p. 8

5 Brent, Leslie Baruch, *Sunday's Child? A Memoir*, p. 122

6 Author interview 2, 4 February 2019, Leslie Brent, pp. 9–10

7 Author interview 1, Leslie Brent, 20 December 2018, p. 16

8 Author interview 4, 12 November 2019, Leslie Brent, p. 4 & interview 2, p. 10

9 Author interview 1, Ruth Wade, 24 September 2019, p. 2

10 Ibid p. 1

11 Finkel, Sidney, *Sevek and the Holocaust: The Boy who Refused to Die,* p. 4

12 Ibid p. 3

13 Author interview 3, Sidney Finkel, 5 March 2020, p. 4

14 Sidney Finkel at Buchenwald, video

15 Author interview 1, Sidney Finkel, 19 September 2019, p. 1

16 Author interview 2, Sam Oliner, 11 October 2019, p. 5
17 Oliner, Samuel, *Narrow Escapes,* pp. 187–8
18 Ibid p. 211
19 Dr Samuel P. Oliner, interview 14 January 1994, United States Holocaust Memorial Museum Collection
20 'Ordinary Heroes' in *Yes Magazine*, Sam Oliner, Winter 2002
21 Oliner, Samuel, *Narrow Escapes,* pp. 164–5
22 Author interview, Julia Miller, 23 February 2020, p. 1
23 Author interview 2, Helen Kotler, p. 7
24 Author interviews, Hansjörg Greimel, Ulm historian and creator of Anna Essinger Museum
25 Author interview 2, Anna Rabkin, 9 September 2020, p. 10

Further Notes

The Wiener Holocaust Library

The Wiener Holocaust Library in London holds twenty-four uncatalogued boxes on Bunce Court School, gathered and donated by former pupil, Martin Lubowski. Records used from this archive are shown by Box Number.

Oral histories

Many former pupils, teachers or their relatives gave interviews, listed below in alphabetical order. For simplicity, where possible the anglicised versions of names have been used in the book.

Leslie Brent (Lothar Baruch)
Ruth Danson (Ruth Boronow)
Karl Grossfield (Karl Grossfeld)
Hanni Howard
Helen Kotler (Helen Urbach)
Mia Lewis (Mia Schaff)
Martin Lubowski
Joseph Meyer
Heinz Redwood (Rothholz)
Michael Roemer
Susie Shipman (Susie Davids)

Pupils arriving post-war
Sidney Finkel (Sevek Finkelstein)
Sam Oliner (Shmulek Oliner)
Anna Rabkin (Anna Rose)
Arthur Rose (Artek Rose)

British pupils
Anna John
Harold Jackson

Additional contributors
Marion Gaze (great-niece of Anna Essinger)
Hansjörg Greimel (director of the Anna Essinger exhibition
    at the Herrlingen Museum)
Julia Miller (current owner of the central section of Bunce
    Court)
Nuri Wyeth (daughter of teacher, William Marckwald)
Ruth Wade (daughter of Sidney Finkel)

Select Bibliography

Auerbach, Frank, *Speaking and Painting*, Thames and
    Hudson, London, 1981
Bailey, Brenda, *A Quaker Couple in Nazi Germany*, Sessions,
    York, 1994
Baumel-Schwartz, Judith, *Never Look Back, The Jewish
    Refugee Children in Great Britain 1938–45*, 2012
Beevor, Anthony, *The Second World War*, Weidenfeld and
    Nicolson, London, 2012
Bentwich, Norman, *My Seventy-Seven Years*, The Jewish
    Publication Society of America, Philadelphia, 1961

They Found Refuge: An Account of British Jewry's Work for Victims of Nazi Oppression, The Cresset Press, London, 1956

Beorn, Waitman Wade, *The Holocaust in Eastern Europe: At the Epicentre of the Final Solution,* Bloomsbury Academic, London, 2018

Brent, Leslie Baruch, *Sunday's Child? A Memoir,* Bank House Books, New Romney, 2009

Brown, Becky, (eds) *Blitz Spirit 1939–1945, Mass Observation Archive,* Hodder and Stoughton, London, 2020

Bourne, Eric, *A European Life,* Bank House Books, New Romney, 2012

Bullock, Alan, *Hitler, A Study in Tyranny,* Konecky & Konecky, New York, 1962

Cesarani, David, *Eichmann: His Life and Crimes,* Vintage, London, 2004

Drucker, Olga Levy, *Kindertransport,* Henry Holt, New York, 1992

Elon, Amos, *The Pity of it All: A Portrait of Jews in Germany 1743–1933,* Penguin, London, 2004

Emanuel, Muriel & Gissing, Vera, *Nicholas Winton and the Rescued Generation,* Vallentine Mitchell, London, 2002

Evans, Richard J. *The Coming of the Third Reich,* Penguin, 2003

The Third Reich in Power, 1933–1939, Penguin, 2005

The Third Reich at War: How the Nazis led Germany from Conquest to Disaster, Penguin, London 2008

Fast, Vera K. *Children's Exodus: A History of the Kindertransport,* I.B. Tauris, London, 2011

Fairweather, Jack, *The Volunteer: The True Story of the Resistance Hero who Infiltrated Auschwitz,* Penguin, London, 2019

Finkel, Sidney, *Sevek and the Holocaust: The Boy who Refused to Die,* self-published, printed by Thomson-Shore, Illinois, 2006

Friedlander, Saul, *Nazi Germany and the Jews: The Years of Persecution, 1933–39,* Weidenfeld and Nicolson, London, 1997

Giladi, Ben, (ed) *A Tale of One City, Piotrkow Trybunalski,* Shengold, New York, 1991

Gilbert, Martin, *Kristallnacht: Prelude to Destruction,* Harper Collins, London, 2006

The Boys: The Story of 732 Young Concentration Camp Survivors, Henry Holt, New York, 1996

Gottlieb, Amy Zahl, *Men of Vision: Anglo-Jewry's Aid to Victims of the Nazi Regime 1933–1945* Weidenfeld and Nicolson, London, 1998

Grenville, Anthony, *Jewish Refugees from Germany and Australia in Britain 1933–1970,* Vallentine Mitchell, London, 2010

Harris, Mark Jonathan & Oppenheimer, Deborah, *Into the Arms of Strangers,* Bloomsbury, London, 2000

Herman, David, *David's Story,* Herman Press, 2016

Hoffnung, Annetta, *Gerard Hoffnung, his biography,* Aurum Press, London, 1988

Joseph, Zoe, *Survivors: Jewish Refugees in Birmingham, 1933–1945,* Meridian, UK, 1988

Kershaw, Ian, *Hitler 1889–1936: Hubris,* Penguin, London, 1998

Leverton, Bertha & Lowensohn, Shmuel, (eds) *I Came Alone: The Stories of the Kindertransports,* The Book Guild, Sussex, UK, 1990

Meth-Cohn, Otto, *The Nearly Man,* printed in the UK, 2015

Naomi Shepherd, *Wilfrid Israel: German Jewry's Secret*

Ambassador, Weidenfeld and Nicolson, London, 1984

Neill, A.S. *Summerhill,* Victor Gollancz, London, 1962

Oliner, Samuel, *Narrow Escapes: A Boy's Holocaust Memories and their Legacy,* Paragon House, Minnesota, 1999

Pavlovich, Henry, *Worlds Apart,* Lulu, London, 2006

Potten, Dorle, *Des Kinder Chronik: A Chronicle of Childhood,* self-published, 2002

Rabkin, Anna, *From Krakow to Berkeley: Coming out of Hiding,* Vallentine Mitchell, London, 2018

Rees, Laurence, *Auschwitz, The Nazis & The 'Final Solution',* BBC Books, London, 2005

Segal, Lore, *Other People's Houses,* Victor Gollancz, UK, 1965

Shepherd, Naomi, *Wilfrid Israel: German Jewry's Secret Ambassador,* Weidenfeld and Nicolson, London, 1984

Sonnenfeldt, Richard W. *Witness to Nuremberg,* Arcade, New York, 2002

Schachne, Lucie, *Education towards Spiritual Resistance: The Jewish Landschulheim Herrlingen 1933–1939,* Verlag, Frankfurt, 1988

Schmitt, Hans A. *Quakers and Nazis: Inner Light in Outer Darkness,* Univ. of Missouri, Columbia, 1997

Smith, Lyn, *Heroes of the Holocaust: Ordinary Britons who Risked their Lives to Make a Difference,* Random House, London, 2013

Turner, Barry, *And the Policeman Smiled: 10,000 Children Escape from Nazi Europe,* Bloomsbury, London, 1990

Marks of Distinction: The Memoirs of Elaine Blond, Vallentine Mitchell, London, 1988

Whiteman, Dorit Bader, *The Uprooted: A Hitler Legacy,* Perseus, UK, 1993

Ziegler, Philip, *London at War, 1939–1945,* Mandarin, 1986

Unpublished Memoirs

Bergas, Hanna, *Fifteen Years lived among, with and for Refugee children*, 1979, Palo Alto, California

Meyer, Hans and Susanne, (eds) *Reflections Bunce Court*, Privately published, 2004

Marckwald, William, *Memoirs*

Acknowledgements

I would like to thank most warmly the many Bunce Court alumni who brought the story of the school to life. I am particularly indebted to Leslie Brent who inspired me to take on this project and, over several interviews, conveyed his harrowing childhood experiences of Nazi Germany and why Bunce Court School meant so much to him. Sadly, he is not with us to see the book to publication but I am grateful to his wife, Carol, for her continued support.

This book would never have reached completion without the help of three remarkable former Bunce Courtians who survived the holocaust in Nazi-occupied Poland: Dr Sam Oliner, Sidney Finkel and Anna Rabkin. I would like to express my thanks for their unforgettable interviews and for permission to quote from their memoirs: *Narrow Escapes, A Boy's Holocaust Memories and their Legacy,* by Samuel Oliner, Paragon House, Minnesota, US, 1999; *Sevek and the Holocaust, The Boy who Refused to Die,* by Sidney Finkel, self-published, printed by Thomson-Shore, Illinois, 2006; and *From Krakow to Berkeley, Coming out of Hiding,* by Anna Rabkin, Vallentine Mitchell, London, 2018. Their families, too, provided generous assistance including Sam's son, David Oliner, and Sidney's daughter, Ruth Wade. In piecing together this hidden history I am also indebted to the following former pupils who generously shared their childhood experiences: Karl Grossfield, Helen Kotler, Mia Lewis, Martin Lubowski, Joseph Meyer, Heinz Redwood, Michael Roemer, Hanni

Howard, Ruth Danson with her daughter, Jacqueline Boronow Danson, and Susie Shipman and her daughter, Elaine Freedman, and former British pupils, Anna John and Harold Jackson.

While writing this book there are many who helped me along the way and I would particularly like to thank historical consultants, Dr Helen Roche, Associate Professor in Modern European Cultural History, Durham University, and Dr Anthony Grenville, chair of the Research Centre for German and Austrian Exile Studies, University of London, for reading and advising on the manuscript and for their many insights into life in the Third Reich. Thank you also to Dr Richard Williams, one of the first readers, for his insights on the text and Dr Christoph Kreutzmuller, chairman of the Active Museum, Fascism and Resistance in Berlin, who provided invaluable guidance on the events of Kristallnacht. I can hardly overstate my debt to the Ulm local historian, Hansjörg Greimel, who has been an inspiration on Anna's story. Hansjörg prepared the Anna Essinger exhibition at the Herrlingen Museum at Linderhof 2, 9134, at Blaustein and has championed her cause in her home country. There are now two schools named in her honour in Ulm: the Anna Essinger Gymnasium and Anna Essinger Realschule and most recently of all, even a tramcar. I am also grateful to Dr Manfred Kindl, archivist and curator of the Herrlingen Museum, Dr. Kelly Del Tredici-Braak, the translator of the exhibition texts, and the late Heinz Krus, who started the first working group in memory of Tante Anna in Ulm in the 1980s.

At the Wiener Holocaust Library in London, former director, Ben Barkow, the current director, Dr Toby Simpson, and senior archivist, Howard Falksohn, gave invaluable support. There are twenty-four uncatalogued boxes on Bunce Court School in the Wiener archives, gathered over many years by former pupil, Martin Lubowski. I was delighted to be the first historian to have access to these records and am most grateful to Quirin Luebke, postgraduate at University College London, for his outstanding research and translations. Quirin's searching enquiries in the London Metropolitan Archives and The National Archives provided many wonderful insights and much new material. Every effort has been made to contact all contributors quoted from these archives or their descendants and all copyright holders. If any have been inadvertently missed, I will endeavour to correct this in later editions.

Tante Anna's niece, Dorle, never forgot her best friend, Marianne Weil, in Germany and named her youngest daughter 'Marion' in her memory. With the help of her other daughter, Jill Wisternoff, Dorle compiled a family chronicle, *Des Kindes Chronik*, by Dorle Potten, privately published (2002). Thanks are due to Marion Gaze for permission to quote from this memoir and to Nuri Wyeth, daughter of former teacher, William Marckwald, for permission to quote from Marckwald's unpublished memoir and Anita Gritz, daughter of Isaac Finkel, for permission to cite from Isaac Finkel's unpublished memoir.

The following publishers kindly gave permission to quote from biographies of former Bunce Courtians: Dave Randle, Publishing Director, Bank House Books, for *Sunday's Child? A Memoir* by Leslie Baruch Brent, Bank House Books, New Romney, Kent, UK (2009) and *A European Life* by Eric Bourne, Bank House Books, New Romney, Kent, UK (2012); Thames and Hudson, London, for permission to reprint from *Frank Auerbach: Speaking and Painting*, London, text © 2015 Catherine Lampert; Skyhorse Publishing for permission to quote from Richard Sonnenfeldt's *Witness to Nuremberg*,

Acknowledgements

Arcade, New York (2002); Vallentine Mitchell, London, for Anna Rabkin's *From Krakow to Berkeley, Coming out of Hiding* (2018); and Paragon House, Minnesota, US, for Sam Oliner's *Narrow Escapes, A Boy's Holocaust Memories and their Legacy* (1999).

At Two Roads in London it has been a great pleasure to work with publisher, Lisa Highton, who saw the potential of the project and my editor, Kate Craigie, for her expert guidance and wonderful support throughout. Thank you also to Jacqui Lewis for her thoughtful copy-edit and editorial assistant, Charlotte Robathan. At Public Affairs, Hachette Book Group in New York I was delighted to have the opportunity to work again with publisher, Clive Priddle, and his team including managing editor, Melissa Raymond. This project would never have happened without Gordon Wise at Curtis Brown who encouraged me from the outset, helped to shape the idea and provided excellent oversight through the many months of writing.

Lastly, heartfelt thanks to friends and family who have lived with this book for several years. To Pete and Jo and most of all to Julia Lilley for the wonderful discussions and insights that sustained me through the years of writing.

Picture Acknowledgements

Every reasonable effort has been made to trace the copyright holders of photos reproduced in this book. Any copyright holders not credited are invited to be in touch with the publishers.

Section 1: Nazi forces parade in front of Hitler, 1933: © Roger Viollet via Getty Images; Hitler Youth marches through Neue Gasse: © Picture Alliance/DPA / Bridgeman Images; Celebrating Nazi success, 1933: © FPG/Hulton Archive/Getty Images; Students singing Nazi Party anthem: © SZ Photo / Bridgeman Images; Illustration from *Trust No Fox*: © Granger/Shutterstock; Demonstrating 'race science': © SZ Photo / Scherl / Bridgeman Images; 'The Jew is our greatest enemy': © TopFoto;; New Herrlingen School: courtesy of Carol Brent, personal collection; Scrubbing the streets, 1938: © World History Archive / Alamy Stock Photo; *Kristallnacht* © Pictorial Press Ltd / Alamy Stock Photo; Mother and child outside Jewish-owned shop: © Pictures from History / Bridgeman Images; Child refugees: © Stephenson/Topical Press Agency/Getty Images; Liverpool St Station: © IWM HU 88872; Kinderstransport: © Imagno/Getty Images; Photographs of Leslie Brent: courtesy of Carol Brent; Ruth Boronow: courtesy of Jacqueline Boronow Danson; Mia Schaff: courtesy of Mia Lewis; Photographs of pupils at Bunce Court: courtesy of Carol Brent. Section 2: Ruins of Praga, 1939: © Universal History Archive/UIG / Bridgeman Images; Siege of Warsaw: © Sueddeutsche Zeitung Photo /

Alamy Stock Photo; Kazia Mika ©INTERFOTO / TopFoto; Piotrkow Ghetto: © picture alliance / TopFoto; 'Ghetto' skull: © picture alliance / TopFoto; Red Cross messages: courtesy of Carol Brent; Trench Hall: Shropshire Archives MI7628/1; Gretel Hiedt: Shropshire Archives MI7628/8; Sidney Finkel's female relatives: courtesy of Ruth Wade; Auschwitz-Birkenau: © Shawshots / Alamy Stock Photo; Children showing tattoos: © REUTERS/HO-AUSCHWITZ MUSEUM KS/DL; Transport to Auschwitz: © ullsteinbild / TopFoto; Carriage 15: © IMAGNO / TopFoto; Prisoners will be shot: © Galina Sanko/Sovfoto/Universal Images Group via Getty Images; Emaciated children: ©Alinari / TopFoto; Child survivors: ©Bridgeman Images; Sidney Finkel arriving in England: courtesy of Ruth Wade; Anna and Arthur Rose: from family collection; Sam Oliner: from family collection; Sidney Finkel as a young man: courtesy of Ruth Wade; Frank Auerback: courtesy of Mia Lewis

Index

Index

Deborah Cadbury is the author of eight acclaimed books, including *Chocolate Wars*, *The Dinosaur Hunters*, *The Lost King of France*, *Princes at War*, and *Seven Wonders of the Industrial World*, for which her accompanying BBC series received a BAFTA nomination. As a BBC TV producer and executive producer, she has won numerous international awards, including an Emmy. She lives in London.

PublicAffairs is a publishing house founded in 1997. It is a tribute to the standards, values, and flair of three persons who have served as mentors to countless reporters, writers, editors, and book people of all kinds, including me.

I. F. STONE, proprietor of *I. F. Stone's Weekly*, combined a commitment to the First Amendment with entrepreneurial zeal and reporting skill and became one of the great independent journalists in American history. At the age of eighty, Izzy published *The Trial of Socrates*, which was a national bestseller. He wrote the book after he taught himself ancient Greek.

BENJAMIN C. BRADLEE was for nearly thirty years the charismatic editorial leader of *The Washington Post*. It was Ben who gave the *Post* the range and courage to pursue such historic issues as Watergate. He supported his reporters with a tenacity that made them fearless and it is no accident that so many became authors of influential, best-selling books.

ROBERT L. BERNSTEIN, the chief executive of Random House for more than a quarter century, guided one of the nation's premier publishing houses. Bob was personally responsible for many books of political dissent and argument that challenged tyranny around the globe. He is also the founder and longtime chair of Human Rights Watch, one of the most respected human rights organizations in the world.

．　　　．　　　．

For fifty years, the banner of Public Affairs Press was carried by its owner Morris B. Schnapper, who published Gandhi, Nasser, Toynbee, Truman, and about 1,500 other authors. In 1983, Schnapper was described by *The Washington Post* as "a redoubtable gadfly." His legacy will endure in the books to come.

Peter Osnos, *Founder*